DE GAULLE

A POLITICAL BIOGRAPHY

ALEXANDER WERTH

Simon and Schuster
New York

CONTENTS

INTRODUCTION

TODAY, at the age of 75, de Gaulle has become the most controversial figure of the international scene. Perhaps his Stendhalian *qualité suprême* has been his tendency always to *rebel* against something. As a young officer, he already rebelled against the French military Establishment which, between the two Wars, was living in a world of dreamy and dreary routine, wholly unaware of what was coming in 1940. When the blow fell, he rebelled against that Armistice which the runaway generals of 1940 were now seeking. He rebelled against their comfortable view that, in 1940, it was 'simply the Germans' turn to win'; during the war, he was rebellious in his attitude to both Churchill and Roosevelt; after the Liberation of France, he rebelled against that very Resistance to which he himself owed so much. In 1946 he rebelled against the Fourth Republic, and twelve years later he helped to overthrow it. But soon afterwards, as head of the central government, he began his long struggle against those very generals and those Algerian *colons* who had brought him back to power. Internationally, he rebelled against the Atlantic Order, as it had existed under the Fourth Republic. He fought against the 'satellization' of France; he declared the world based on the 'two rival superhegemonies, the U.S.A. and the U.S.S.R.', to be a thing of the past. He rebelled against the American concept of ideological war, and regarded the nation and national consciousness, even in Russia, China, or Vietnam, as something deeper and more lasting than any ideology. Had not Communist Russia's *national* war against Hitler in 1941–5 amply proved it?

In his view, America's war against Vietnam, which was Vietnamese first and Communist only second, was therefore profoundly wrong. And although he himself had been one of the Guilty Men of the equally 'dirty' French war against Vietnam between 1945 and 1954, he liked nothing better, now in 1965, than his new role of the World's Number One Decolonizer – the man who had 'liberated' Africa, had ended the war in Algeria and was the best-liked (or, at any rate, least disliked) of all European statesmen among the backward and underdeveloped countries of the globe.

And Europe? Here his policy was perhaps the most puzzling of all. Without repudiating America's 'friendship', he wanted Europe as independent of America as possible, now that the security of Europe would not necessarily be America's prime concern 'in certain conditions'. He excluded Britain from the Common Market as 'America's Trojan Horse'; while wholly conscious that France was not a major world power, he tried, for a time, to give her a leading position in the Little Europe of the Six with the help of Adenauer. It did not work, especially after Adenauer had gone. Western Germany under Erhard, much more than Britain, proved to be the 'Trojan Horse'. He then turned to Russia. Had he not in his blood still something of the old *alliance franco-russe* of his childhood, that old alliance of which he had spoken to Stalin, without much effect, back in 1944? It now seemed to de Gaulle that France and Russia had much in common; they were, apart from Germany, *the* two great continental powers of Europe; they both had strong 'neutralist' tendencies, they agreed in the main on Vietnam, and both, at heart, desired to maintain in Europe the *status quo* for as long as possible. He now dreamed of a Europe 'from the Atlantic to the Urals' in which, without American interference, everything – above all, the German problem – could be gradually settled among the 'Europeans' themselves. He firmly belived that, quite regardless of any ideologies, it would, sooner or later, be in Russia's interests to join up with 'Europe' against 'Asia'. But to settle the problem of a Greater Europe, time and infinite patience were needed. But 'patience' was the operative word, and it was no use trying forcibly to 'put an end to the shame of Eastern Germany', as the Americans were now saying.

Stalin said of de Gaulle at Yalta: 'He is not a complicated man.' In reality, he is much more complicated than he appears at first sight. He has been colonialist and anti-colonialist; he has been a passionate believer in the American alliance, and an equally passionate opponent of American influence in Europe; he was violently anti-Russian in 1947 and distinctly pro-Russian in 1965; his hostility to a 'supra-national' Europe has zig-zagged from very mild to frantic; his attitude to Germany has varied from a Bainvillian *delenda est* in 1945 to the sunny 'Charlemagne' partnership of 1962 and the frost of 1965; while the 'wretched yellow multitudes of China' of 1960 became, in 1964, 'China's great and ancient civilization'. The would-be Fascist dictator of the R.P.F. days in 1948 became the relatively liberal and benevolent 'King' of the Fifth Republic – the man who, during his years in the wilderness, in 1953–8, had pondered deeply on the question of the kind of authoritarian ruler the French people were most likely to welcome or, at any rate, accept.

This book is no more than what it claims to be. It is a political biography of de Gaulle, one of the key figures of our time – a man who has been immensely admired (though never really worshipped in any hysterical way, as certain vulgar dictators have been), a man who has been loved by a small minority and bitterly loathed – but also by only a small minority, above all by the traditional French *extrême droite*; a man who was 'accepted' by the great majority of the French people in 1958, less because he represented drastic change than because he meant to them an *escape* from such drastic change, and also because he flattered them and very largely cured them of that inferiority complex from which they had suffered ever since 1940. At the same time, the French have poked fun at de Gaulle, just as de Gaulle has poked fun at them; but neither side minds that. *Le Canard Enchaîné*, with all those outrageous jokes and cartoons about *Mongénéral*, is, next to *Le Monde*, the General's favourite reading. For seven years de Gaulle has (above all with the help of television) 'imposed himself' on France. There has been much opposition to him, but seldom very violent or very active opposition.

But he is growing old; and although nobody is irreplaceable, the question of replacement is more difficult in the case of de Gaulle than in any other; for he is a combination of an exceptional mind and character, an exceptional 'legend' and exceptional historical circumstances. Something will no doubt be left of Gaullism even after de Gaulle – but what and how much?

The scope of this book is limited. It deals, above all, with the man and his ideas. There was no room here for anything so long and intricate as a discussion of the Constitution of the Fifth Republic and the controversies it aroused, or of the de Gaulle régime's inner workings, the technicalities of the Common Market or the economic problems of France over the past years. Most of these questions are touched upon only incidentally. De Gaulle himself has been interested above all in military and foreign policy, leaving social and economic questions – *l'intendance* (the commissariat), as he disdainfully calls them – mostly to his ministers and top civil servants. France under the Fifth Republic is a reasonably flourishing economic concern, but not so very much better than she was during the last few years of the Fourth.

De Gaulle is interesting, first as an extraordinary human being, and, second, as an international phenomenon of these 1960s, with his sharp reaction against what, for the sake of simplicity, he calls 'the Yalta Order'; with his insistence on the immense importance of *the nation*, and the ever-waning importance of *ideologies*. Thus, he thinks the American notion of a monolithic 'Free World' just as false and primitive as the 'Socialism' of the increasingly incoherent 'bloc' on the other side. As he recently remarked, there are, and have been, so many different kinds of 'communism' that the word no longer means much, least of all in international terms. And what has 'Free World' ideology got to do with the massacres of Santo Domingo?

If these Gaullist reflections annoy many Britons and, especially, Americans, is it not because, at heart, they suspect that he may have got something there?

THE PRESENT American edition is an enlarged and updated version of the book that originally appeared in England in October 1965. The whole final chapter has been specially rewritten so as to include the crucial story of the French presidential election of December 1965. De Gaulle won in the end with fifty-five per cent of the people voting for him, but in the first round he had failed to secure an absolute majority – a clear indication of a certain erosion of the seven-year-old régime. The final chapter also deals with the Ben Barka Affair, the big political scandal which shook France only a few days after de Gaulle had officially entered his second term as President.

The Ben Barka Affair showed that behind the majestic façade of Gaullist France many dirty and disturbing things could go on, just as they did under the Third and Fourth Republics. And some of the dirt – particularly the 'parallel' police – was, somehow, inherent in the Gaullist régime itself. Scandals big and small happen in all countries, but the Ben Barka Affair, coming on top of de Gaulle's mediocre election victory, rudely shook – at least for a time – what faith was still left in the longevity of the Fifth Republic.

Scandals, however, are often easily forgotten, and in this case the big villains were Moroccans and not Frenchmen. The future course of France will largely be determined by what happens between now and the 1967 election. By then we shall know whether the General and the Gaullists can, in the interval, restore faith in the régime after the shaking it got in the bitter winter of 1965–6.

CHAPTER 1

THE GREAT MAN'S RETURN

ONE wonders how many people in the world today – or even in France – remember the word Sakhiet. Yet it was in the Tunisian village of that name, a few miles from the Algerian border, that something happened on 8 February 1958 which was to lead, within less than four months, to the final disintegration of the French Fourth Republic and the return to power of General de Gaulle.

The Algerian war had gone on since the end of 1954, and certain French Army commanders – as well as the whole European population of Algeria – were growing increasingly exasperated by the relative impunity with which Algerian 'rebel' forces were able to maintain bases in Tunisian territory and operate from these against the French. There had already been a number of frontier incidents, the most serious of which occurred on 15 January, when a number of Algerian 'rebels' allegedly penetrated into Algerian territory from their hide-outs near Sakhiet, captured four French soldiers and killed several others. There followed, on 20 January, an angry debate in the French National Assembly, during which the 38-year-old Radical premier M. Félix Gaillard,[1] was sharply attacked for not breaking off diplomatic relations with Tunisia, and one of the few remaining 'Gaullist' deputies, M. Dronne, declared that *General de Gaulle alone had sufficient prestige and authority both to end the war in Algeria and to normalize relations with Tunisia and Morocco.* This was almost the first time that a 'de Gaulle solution' was mentioned – at least in Parliament. In the same

1. He has been in office since November 1957.

debate, Jacques Soustelle, the most influential of the 'Gaullist' deputies,[1] alleged that the Gaillard government was under the thumb of the United States, which was a 'protector' of Tunisia and was 'willing to sacrifice its European allies in its ridiculous search for Arab friends, lest they fell under Communist influence'. He also alleged that the French Foreign Office was 'disloyal', 'pro-American' and 'defeatist in its whole attitude to the Algerian war' – a charge which was to be taken up, soon afterwards, by M. Lacoste, the Socialist Minister representing France in Algiers, who had become the best friend of the colonialist diehards.

On the following day M. Christian Pineau, the Socialist Foreign Minister in the Gaillard government, faced by all this strident criticism from the Right, also sharply criticized the Tunisian government, and declared that if there were any more incursions into Algeria from Tunisian territory, France would have to react 'in a legitimate state of self-defence'.

In itself, this was not very explicit; but the military in Algeria knew that they were unlikely to be disavowed by the government, still less punished, if they took the law into their own hands. . . .

And that was what they did on the morning of Saturday, 8 February. In the village of Sakhiet there were two Tunisian anti-aircraft batteries and, at some short distance from the town, reputedly two 'fellagha (i.e. rebel) hide-outs'. The raid on the town by twenty-five French (American-made) bombers on that Saturday morning – which also happened to be market-day – was of no military value but seventy-five people were killed, including some thirty children in the local school; apart from the dead, there were over a hundred wounded, many of them children. General Salan, the French Commander-in-Chief who had ordered the raid, promptly reported that only military objectives had been hit, and that

1. For the composition of the Assembly, see p. 19.

the dead were nearly all Algerian fellaghas; but both the diplomats and journalists who were rushed to Sakhiet from Tunis told a very different story – a familiar story of wartime 'frightfulness'.

The bombing of Sakhiet had immediate political repercussions. President Bourguiba of Tunisia (whom the United States considered the world's most 'liberal' and pro-western Arab, a strong bulwark against communism) now demanded the 'immediate evacuation' of the 20,000 French troops still stationed in Tunisia, and even the surrender of the French naval base at Bizerta. He also decided to lodge a complaint against France before the U.N. Security Council. The U.S. government, anxious to avoid having to choose between France and Tunisia, began to consider the possibility of sending a 'good offices' mission to put an end to the conflict. Meantime, Bourguiba was getting tough; French troops in Tunisia were confined to barracks, and the Tunisians, feeling confident of American support, declared that no French ships would be allowed to dock in Bizerta. M. Masmoudi, the Tunisian Ambassador in Paris, was recalled. But before leaving, he visited General de Gaulle, and after the visit a special communiqué was issued by the General's secretariat saying that de Gaulle had received M. Masmoudi at his own request; that he had listened to what the Ambassador had to say on the recent frontier incidents; and that

the General replied that he wished the Tunisian government would not allow the present difficulties to ruin the future chances of a Franco-Tunisian association. In the General's view, such an association is more desirable than ever both for the West and for the world at large.

It was a very strange move for the Tunisian Ambassador to make, since the General seemed to have retired for good from French public life three years before; yet there was already something in the air that had made him think de Gaulle might, before long, be called upon to 'arbitrate' in the North-African conflict. Mendès-France, who had been in close contact with Masmoudi, had already been privately saying for some time that de Gaulle might perhaps be 'the only solution' – a striking attitude when one considers that the same Mendès-France sharply turned against de Gaulle after the General was 'imposed' on France by the Algiers Rebellion three months later.

The Gaillard government was at sixes and sevens over the Sakhiet raid. Foreign Minister Pineau, in an interview with Joseph Alsop, declared the bombing of Sakhiet to have been 'a deplorable mistake', and roundly condemned the military in Algeria for having exceeded their authority; but this produced such an uproar from the 'Algerian' diehards in the government – notably Lacoste and the 'Gaullist' Minister of Defence, Chaban-Delmas – that Pineau, without much conviction, it is true, denied having given such an interview to the *New York Herald Tribune*. Gaillard himself, frightened of both the Army and the 'Algerians' inside his government, finally justified the Army's action at the end of the National Assembly debate on 11 February. In the lobbies it was openly said that he had been given a clear warning: had he disavowed the Army, the effect in Algeria would have been 'incalculable'. He was given a substantial – though very half-hearted – vote of confidence; but a few of the more eminent leaders – Robert Schuman, Edgar Faure and Paul Reynaud – abstained in order to show their disapproval of the Prime Minister's timidity. Part of the press – notably *Le Monde* – commenting on Gaillard's failure to disavow the Sakhiet raid, found it only too clear that there was, in fact, *an occult government that was running Paris from Algiers* – a government backed by the Army and the colonialist interests.

One of the immediate results of the Sakhiet Raid was the constitution of an Anglo-American 'good offices' mission to bring Paris and Tunis together. Why was this accepted? The United States government had impressed on both parties how undesirable it would be if the dispute were debated before the U.N. On this point both governments were, broadly, in agreement: neither Tunisia (in view of the frontier violations) nor France (in view of Sakhiet) had a foolproof case to take before the U.N.

The 'good offices' were conducted by Mr Robert Murphy accompanied, chiefly as a matter of form, by a British Foreign Office official, Mr Harold Beeley. It was Murphy who did most of the talking, and Murphy was not a name popular in France, least of all with the Gaullists. It was he who, in 1942, as American Consul-General in Algiers, had negotiated with the Vichyites, with Darlan and with Giraud, and had done his utmost to keep de Gaulle and the Free French out of North Africa. In his talks with him, Bourguiba did not hesitate to tell Murphy that, in his view, the French ought to get out of Tunisia altogether, and that Bizerta had better be handed over to N.A.T.O., i.e., in effect to the United States, and that the whole of Algeria should be put under international control. All these stories got back to Paris and Algiers, and there were loud protests that the United States was trying to 'grab North Africa'; the nightmare of American oil tycoons outwitting the French with the help of Bourguiba and turning North Africa into an 'American sphere' was terrifying enough to prompt even the Soviet Ambassador, Mr S. Vinogradov, to call on the French Foreign Office and declare that the Soviet Union would much rather see the French stay at Bizerta than see it handed over to N.A.T.O. and the U.S.A.! Significantly, Vinogradov also called personally on General de Gaulle, during one of the latter's weekly visits to Paris – where he had an office in the rue Solférino – to intimate his worries to him.[1]

1. Vinogradov was one of the few diplomats who arduously continued to maintain contact with de Gaulle – even when the latter was generally believed to have 'finally' retired.

Nearly everybody in France was opposed to Mr Murphy:
the Communists, because he represented 'American imperialism'; the Right, because he was obviously against
'French Algeria'; the Gaullists and, indeed, many liberals,
too, because they remembered his persistent hobnobbing
with Darlan and the Vichyites back in 1942–3. Of all the
public figures in America, Robert Murphy was the man most
likely to alarm, irritate and annoy French opinion and his
appointment as mediator between France and Tunisia was
one of the biggest psychological mistakes ever made by the
State Department. Between February and May 1958 anti-
American feeling was growing more and more violent in
France, and it played a very important part in bringing about
the Algiers explosion of 13 May, which, in turn, led to the
'De Gaulle Revolution' in France itself.

It was also the Murphy Mission which brought about the
downfall of the Gaillard government, the last government of
the Fourth Republic to be normally overthrown by the
National Assembly. The proposals that Murphy and Beeley
produced after their endless negotiations with Bourguiba
were no more than a few minor concessions concerning the
'gradual' evacuation of French troops from Tunisia, with
the neutral control of four (but only four) airfields in the
country; the reopening of certain French consulates which
had been closed after Sakhiet; negotiations over a new
statute for Bizerta and the readmission to Tunisia of certain
French citizens who had been expelled. But on the crucial
question of an international control of the Tunisian-
Algerian border Bourguiba would not yield. To add to
Gaillard's troubles, the news leaked out that Eisenhower had
written to him, urging him to accept the Murphy proposals,
and leaving the question of frontier control for later discussion. M. Monnet, who had only recently negotiated a
large loan in the U.S.A. and thought that France would soon
need more money from America, favoured the acceptance

of the Murphy proposals. Gaillard, suddenly imagining himself the blue-eyed boy of Washington, thought that the U.S.A. might gradually help to normalize relations with Tunisia and Morocco and even use its influence to bring about a settlement in Algeria favourable to France; he was therefore inclined to respond favourably to Eisenhower's appeal. But that was to underrate the violence of the anti-American mood in the country. In the Assembly he was attacked by the Communists whose spokesman, Jacques Duclos, proclaimed that Jean Monnet 'who had negotiated those loans, had now also brought the British and Americans into North Africa'; he was attacked by an *ultra* like Le Pen, who declared, much to the delight of the Communists, that 'the American menace to France was far greater now than the Soviet menace', while Soustelle, for the Gaullists, referring to the Eisenhower letter, accused Gaillard of surrendering to American pressure. On the same day, in the Senate, Michel Debré, de Gaulle's future Prime Minister, declared:

'There is now a clear danger that the British and Americans will dominate the Atlantic Alliance, and that Germany will dominate Europe. The government of M. Gaillard is unworthy of representing France.'

Both Gaillard and Foreign Minister Pineau were very much on the defensive and merely argued that the acceptance of the Murphy proposals as a 'basis of discussion' – which might lead to some more positive results in future – was a lesser evil; a greater evil would be an occupation of Tunisia, which might lead to endless international complications.

Despite Gaillard's warning that there would be an 'inextricable situation in parliament' and great financial difficulties if his government were overthrown, it was defeated by 321 votes to 255. The Socialists and M.R.P. supported it but not without a touch of reluctance.

There were a number of reasons for the collapse of Gaillard, in addition to the Eisenhower letter. The Gaillard government generally, with Chaban-Delmas as its Minister of Defence and Robert Lacoste as its Minister for Algeria, was an incoherent mixture of 'Paris' and 'Algiers'. It had also, over the months, greatly succeeded in antagonizing liberal opinion, by creating a sort of McCarthyite atmosphere in Paris, with the confiscation of newspapers and the seizure of books like Henri Alleg's *La Question* on torture in Algeria, and by proving its utter lack of authority when a thousand Paris policemen took on 13 March the unprecedented step – under the influence of Dides, Tixier-Vignancour, Le Pen, and other *ultras* – of holding a noisy anti-parliamentary demonstration outside the National Assembly. It was a sign of the times: under Gaillard, a Radical premier, not only the communists, but even the moderate leftists were persecuted, while the Algiers-inspired *ultras* could do what they liked, since the government was too frightened of offending Algiers or the Army. Jean-Paul Sartre described it: '*For thirteen years the French Republic was dominated by its War Lords*'. The War Lords and colonialist interests, with their parliamentary lobbies, had, indeed, exercised a powerful influence on French politics. They had made their influence felt during the war in Indo-China, then again during all the trouble in Tunisia and Morocco; but never had the pressure of the War Lords and of the colonialists been so strong as since the beginning of the Algerian war in November 1954.

Paradoxically, this very sick political situation went together with an almost robust economic progress. As distinct from the last ten years of the Third Republic, the Fourth Republic had, especially since 1952 (a year marked by a relative stabilization of prices) been expanding economically at a highly satisfying rate. The real trouble came from Algiers. In Algiers, especially since Sakhiet, a revolutionary situation was developing at great speed. In France, on the contrary, after a peculiar spell of anti-Arab nationalism which reached its height in 1956 at the time of Suez, opinion was becoming increasingly tired of the war in Algeria. It was the realization of this growing desire in France to wind up the Algerian war, to which should be added all the acute suspicions aroused by the Murphy Mission, which prepared the ground for the Algiers *putsch* of 13 May.

*

To make it clear why the parliamentary system was declared by the Gaullists – and, before long, by de Gaulle himself – to have finally broken down with the overthrow of the Gaillard government, one should recall here the composition of the National Assembly elected on 2 January 1956.

Extreme Left	Communists: 142 (Thorez, Duclos, etc.)
	Progressistes: 6 (Cot, etc.)
Left	Socialists: 97 (Mollet, Deixonne, Pineau, Lacoste, etc.)
Left Centre	U.D.S.R. (Union démocratique et socialiste de la Résistance): 20 (Mitterrand, Pleven, etc.)
	Radicals: 42 (Mendès-France, Bourgès-Maunoury, etc.)
Centre	R.G.R. (Rassemblement des Gauches Républicaines) (Faure, etc.)
	M.R.P. (Mouvement Républicain Populaire – the Christian Democrats): 75 (Bidault, Pflimlin, Teitgen, Schuman, etc.)
	Gauche démocratique: 13 (Badie)
	Regroupement africain: 16 (Senghor, etc.)
Right	Républicains Sociaux (Gaullists): 20 (Soustelle, Chaban-Delmas, Triboulet, Dronne, etc.)
	Indépendants, (the 'classical Right'): 89 (Pinay, Pierre André, Isorni, etc.)
	Paysans: 11
Extreme Right	Union de Fraternité Française (Poujadists): 30

Others (Fascists, ex-Poujadists etc.): 8 (Dides,
Le Pen, Tixier-Vignancour, etc.)

This meant that, with the Communists in systematic opposition (where they had been ever since their breach with
Mollet's socialists – on the Algerian issue – soon after the
1956 election), any government coalition based on the
Socialists, the Left Centre, the Centre, and the Right
enjoyed only a very precarious majority. Although there
were divisions inside every party (there were 'Algerian'
diehards both inside the Socialist Party and the M.R.P.),
the fundamental weakness of any such coalition was its
dependence on the support of the Right. It was the Right
(both the 'Independents' and the 'Gaullists') who imposed
on all the governments a diehard Algerian policy; as soon as
any government showed the slightest sign of weakness, it was
overthrown. The minor concessions which the short-lived
Bourgès-Maunoury government (the predecessor of the
equally short-lived Gaillard government) had proposed to
make to the Algerians, had been overthrown on the Algerian
issue; and it was this issue, too (with the Americans
'meddling in North-African affairs'), that led to the downfall
of Gaillard.

The London *Economist* now correctly remarked that, in
the circumstances, the French parliament could have a solid
working majority on one condition only – that the Communists should support the government or, at any rate,
abstain. And that is precisely what was going to happen
after the Algiers *putsch* of 13 May when, to 'defend the
Republic', the Communists came to the rescue of the hard-
pressed Pflimlin government, the last of the Fourth Republic. But this no longer suited the Right and the Gaullists; and
it was the outside pressure of Algiers, and of its accomplices
in France, which, quite regardless of 'democratic legality'
and parliamentary arithmetic, imposed de Gaulle on France
by threatening her with civil war. In purely parliamentary

terms, there could have been a solid communist-supported (or at least communist-tolerated) government in France which might well have negotiated a peace settlement in Algeria; but the Gaullists and the Right dreaded this most of all, and, to save 'French Algeria', they brought de Gaulle back to power.

De Gaulle, it is true, insisted on maintaining a semblance of 'republican legality', and the National Assembly, thoroughly frightened of civil war in France, gave him plenary powers at the beginning of June – 'committing hara-kiri', as one paper put it, 'with a smile on its lips'. In the end, de Gaulle did nothing to save 'French Algeria', and, at heart, never had any intention of doing so, but 'French Algeria' was the springboard from which he leaped back into power. At the time of Gaillard's fall, there would scarcely have been a hundred parliamentary votes in favour of bringing de Gaulle back. For, at that time, even the 'classical' Right, with their strong 'Vichyite' traditions, were not entirely favourable to de Gaulle. To them, his past 'liberalism' in colonial matters was suspect, while he had said many offensive things about Marshal Pétain and had even – both before and for two years after the Liberation – 'collaborated' with the Communists. Certainly the *colons* in Algeria were very far from being 'Gaullists'. They remembered how, fifteen years before, he had outwitted the Vichyites and their General Giraud, to become, by the end of 1943, the sole master of what he then used to call a French 'revolutionary' government. It was, in fact, the temporary reconciliation between the Gaullists and the Algerian *colons* – symbolized, as it were, by the agreement between Soustelle and Alain de Sérigny, the influential 'Vichyite' editor of the *Echo d'Alger* – which helped to prepare the ground for the Algiers *putsch*. The Army leaders, some of them 'Gaullist', others pro-*colon* (but now also temporarily 'Gaullist') supported the rebellion.

After the fall of the Gaillard government, President Coty was faced by his third cabinet crisis within a year. This in itself was bad enough; public opinion had, in the last few months, become increasingly conscious of the double *impasse* – that of the Algerian problem, and that of the parliamentary majority. The acceptance of the Murphy–Beeley Mission was like a confession of parliamentary helplessness. Although, in ordinary parliamentary terms, a return to power of de Gaulle seemed entirely out of the question, his name began to be mentioned more and more frequently after Sakhiet. On 8 March, Maurice Duverger in *Le Monde* said: 'The return of de Gaulle is no longer a question of *whether*, but of *when*'. This, in itself, meant that some 'extraordinary procedure' was already on the cards. The fact that the cabinet crisis following the fall of the Gaillard government should have lasted *for nearly a month* added to the great feeling of uneasiness and uncertainty in the country, even though the local elections in April had pointed to a remarkable political stability, to a sharp decline in *poujadisme*, and a striking unawareness of any 'Fascist menace'.[1] Since Soustelle had been the principal 'chucker-out' of the Gaillard government, Coty should, normally, have asked him to form the next cabinet. But Soustelle had not the slightest chance of accomplishing a majority. Moreover, Coty was reluctant that Soustelle should, as premier-designate, have radio and television time placed at his disposal. Instead, he called on Bidault (one of the three M.R.P. members who voted against Gaillard) to form the next government. His chances were no better than Soustelle's, but although he was just as much an Algerian *ultra* as Soustelle, he lacked the latter's rabble-rousing vigour. The Bidault attempt at cabinet-making, however, came to

1. The Poujade poll had dropped from some ten per cent in 1956 to two per cent in 1958. The Gaullist vote in these local elections was only 3.5 per cent of the total.

nothing since, under the influence of M. Pflimlin, the governing body of the M.R.P. decided to refuse him their support. They objected to the inclusion of Soustelle in the Bidault government, for, as Pflimlin said, Soustelle was quite capable of starting a war against Tunisia – a course favoured by some of the military in Algeria. Bidault, while agreeing that he had failed in forming the government because there was no 'French Algeria' majority in parliament, added ominously: 'But such a majority exists in any case in the nation and amongst our soldiers'.

President Coty then thought of calling on M. Mitterrand, whom he considered 'one of the most intelligent people in parliament'; but, in the end, he decided against so notorious a 'liberal' in respect of Algeria, 'owing to the threats that had come from Algiers'.

He then called on the colourless M. René Pleven, who had been a close associate of de Gaulle's in London, had then been his Minister of Finance, and had supported a diehard policy in Indo-China. But Pleven had parted company from de Gaulle long ago, and was now thought to be reasonably 'liberal' in his attitude to Algeria. Unfortunately, in order to get a parliamentary majority, he thought that he would have to be all things to all men. By 7 May, after endless negotiations, he succeeded in getting a government together – but only for a few hours; three of the Radical ministers quit after learning that, under the pressure of the Algiers generals, Pleven had included at the last moment as Minister of Defence none other than M. André Morice, an *ultra* closely associated with Bidault and Soustelle, and, as Minister of State for Sahara affairs, Senator Duchet, another diehard. The Army and the *colons* were again blackmailing the Fourth Republic.

It should be recalled here that, for the first time in years, the Socialists decided against joining a government. A sharp crisis had, indeed, been brewing inside the Socialist Party

for some time. Guy Mollet himself had been supporting a
diehard Algerian policy, above all by appointing as Resident-
Minister in Algiers his fellow-'Socialist' Robert Lacoste,
who had condoned, if not personally encouraged, the use of
torture against Algerian 'rebel' prisoners and 'suspects' like
Audin and Alleg.[1] Not joining the Pleven government was a
convenient way for Mollet of withdrawing Lacoste from
Algiers. Early in May there had been an outcry at a meeting
of the Socialist International in London against Lacoste,
and inside the Socialist Party there was now an increasingly
strong movement, led by Gazier, Defferre and Savary, in
favour of a negotiated peace in Algeria.

A parallel development was taking place inside the
M.R.P., its 'liberal' wing being led by Pierre Pflimlin, the
deputy for Strasbourg, who had held government posts for
many years, either as Minister of Agriculture or as Minister
of Finance. Algiers was, of course, fully aware that opinion
in France was becoming increasingly tired of the Algerian
war, with its tiredness reflected in the evolution that had
been taking place for some time in the two principal government parties, the Socialists and the M.R.P. The signal
for the Algiers *putsch* was Pflimlin's successful attempt
to form a government – a government which came before
the National Assembly on the afternoon of 13 May, a few
hours before the Algiers explosion.

*

1. The disclosures made in February 1958 about Marcel Audin, a
lecturer in mathematics at Algiers University who had been tortured
to death by General Massu's paratroopers in the summer of 1957 and
M. Lacoste's attempts to hush up the matter were to cause great
indignation on the French left, particularly among intellectuals, and
also inside the Socialist Party. Henri Alleg, editor of a near-communist
paper in Algiers, described in his book, *La Question*, also published in
February 1958, but later confiscated by the police, how he had been
tortured by the same paratroopers who had murdered Audin.

In *The de Gaulle Revolution*[1] I described in great detail the dual conspiracy – one 'Gaullist', the other *ultra* – mounted in both Paris and Algiers during the months preceding the Algiers *putsch*, and particularly since the French air-raid on Sakhiet and the subsequent constitution of Murphy's 'good offices' mission. Significantly enough almost as soon as this last had been formed, M. Soustelle, the leading Gaullist in parliament, published on 27 February an angry article denouncing Murphy in Alain de Sérigny's *Echo d'Alger*. This marked, as it were, the *prise de contact* between the Paris Gaullists and the *ultras* in Algiers. Lacoste, for his part, made a violent anti-Murphy speech at Philippeville the same day, declaring that Murphy was preparing to 'internationalize' the Algerian war. Only a few days later, stories began to circulate that the Murphy Mission would soon be replaced by a Hammarskjöld Mission. Thereupon, on 15 March, a meeting was arranged at Nice between Sérigny and Soustelle, whom Sérigny himself described in a book, published a few months later, as 'the man who had been the real spearhead in France of the Battle for French Algeria'. Roger Frey, Triboulet, Michelet and Michel Debré were also present at the meeting – all of them future Ministers of de Gaulle. Soustelle had, some time before, set up a 'French Algeria' organization called U.S.R.A.F., and it was agreed that the U.S.R.A.F. would establish a network in Algeria. But what troubled Sérigny, an old Vichyite, was de Gaulle's own attitude to Algeria, as distinct from that of Gaullists like Soustelle.

'Is de Gaulle,' Sérigny asked Soustelle, 'in favour of integration? [i.e. the kind of "integrated" French Algeria, as the *ultras* now understood it]. No doubt there is every reason to suppose that de Gaulle approves of your attitude, your speeches in the National Assembly, your articles, etc. But here's the point: you realize that (*European*) *Algerian opinion is very badly prepared for*

1. London, Robert Hale, 1960.

a return of de Gaulle. However, within the means at my disposal, I am prepared to modify this.'

Sérigny then asked Soustelle to find out from de Gaulle how he envisaged his return to power, and what his attitude to 'integration' was. On 28 March Sérigny received a somewhat disappointing answer from Soustelle saying that de Gaulle did not think there was much he could do for the present, and that he was therefore unwilling to talk. The political parties, he had told Soustelle, had placed insuperable obstacles in the way of his return to power. He had no illusions. He thought the political parties would, in the end, yield to foreign pressure and accept the internationalization of the Algerian problem. This was not to say that de Gaulle was satisfied with so dismal a prospect, and he was certainly interested in the battle waged against Algerian secession. But he felt uncertain that integration was favoured by Moslem opinion. Instead, he thought pacification should be pursued with renewed energy, provided that it was accompanied by a large-scale psychological, economic, social, political, and educational effort.

There is no evidence that Soustelle's message to Sérigny was actually based on any conversation with de Gaulle. In any case, Sérigny was not impressed and hesitated to come out openly for de Gaulle in his paper – a paper read as gospel truth by the French-Algerians. It was not indeed till 11 May, i.e. two days before the *putsch*, that the *Echo d'Alger* appeared with a sensational article addressed to de Gaulle: 'Speak up, General, speak up quickly; your words are worth actions'.

It is now clear that both Sérigny and Soustelle were *using* de Gaulle for their own ends. De Gaulle was to become, for a time, the rallying point for all those anxious (like Sérigny) to save their colonialist privileges in Algeria; for those anxious to overthrow the Republic in France: for those (like Soustelle) thinking in terms of an authoritarian régime in

France which would 'save' Algeria; even for those who were planning a military-fascist dictatorship in France. Finally, by the end of May, he was to receive the full support of the greater part of French opinion which was *not* interested in Algeria, but which saw in de Gaulle a bulwark against a military-fascist dictatorship.

The Gaullists set up, during March and April, a substantial 'network' of their own in Algeria, or at any rate, at Algiers, and its main ringleader was a North-of-France industrialist, Léon Delbecque, who happened to be a member of the secretariat of M. Chaban-Delmas, the Minister of Defence in the Gaillard government! Chaban-Delmas had, in March, 'lent' Delbecque to Soustelle's U.S.R.A.F. network in Algiers, and it was one of Delbecque's jobs to 'canalize' the greater part of the Army leaders into Gaullist allegiance. Thus there were, at the time of the Algiers *putsch*, two seemingly allied, but, in fact, rival organizations in Algiers – the Gaullist organization, led by Delbecque, and the *ultra* organization, largely composed of the local teddy-boys and led by Lagaillarde.

Already, on 26 April, there had been some violent demonstrations in Algiers, organized by Delbecque, and carried out with the tacit consent of Lacoste, who was now raging about the 'diplomatic Dien-Bien-Phu'[1] that France would soon suffer in Algeria, thanks to Murphy and the other American plotters.

During the next fortnight tension in Algiers rapidly grew, and as the *Canard Enchaîné* wrote just before the 13 May *putsch*:

> The Republic has suddenly begun to feel terribly wobbly.
> Because of Algiers, where the Street is on the move.
> With the silent blessing of Comrade Lacoste.

1. Dien-Bien-Phu was the place in Western Vietnam where the French suffered a military defeat in 1954 which soon led to the end of the war in Vietnam.

And because, in the background, the Army is also very much on the move ...

And, the other day, General Salan, the C. in C. in Algeria, sent a report to General Ely, the Chief of Staff in Paris, on the state of mind existing amongst the officers about Little Plum (i.e. Pflimlin).[1]

They were in a state of frenzy, and he (Salan) wouldn't answer for anything. Ely hastened to take the message along to President Coty, who nearly fell off his chair.

Also, Salan and other high officers sent a circular to the various Army headquarters saying that, until further notice, they, and only they, were in command, and that no notice whatsoever need be taken of any cease-fire talk emanating from Little Plum.

In short, the Army is, as ever, in the service of the Republic. To defend it. Or, if necessary, to strangle it.

Around 6 p.m. on 13 May the Algiers *putsch* accordingly took place. It started with the *ultra* teddy-boys, led by a bearded young thug, Pierre Lagaillarde, who wore paratroop uniform, storming the gates of the *Gouvernement-Général* building and then breaking into it. The *ultras* had forestalled the 'Gaullists'; but these soon appeared on the scene, together with Delbecque and General Massu, the famous paratroop general who, by murder and torture, had won the 'Battle of Algiers' against terrorism. Massu ordered his paratroopers to throw the teddy-boys out, and occupy the building themselves, The C.R.S. – the armed police, ostensibly loyal to Paris – had discreetly withdrawn without offering any resistance to Lagaillarde's young men. At 7.35 General Salan made a brief appearance at the G.G., but was shouted down by the crowds outside, who did not quite know what his policy would be. It was during the next two and a half hours that momentous decisions were taken inside the building, and at 9.10 p.m. General Massu appeared on the balcony to announce that a telegram had been sent to

1. Pflimlin meaning 'Little Plum' in Alsatian dialect.

President Coty informing him that a civil and military Committee of Public Safety had been formed under his (General Massu's) présidency.

This has been formed in view of the absolute necessity to maintain order and avoid bloodshed. We demand the creation in Paris of a Government of National Safety, alone capable of keeping Algeria as an integral part of Metropolitan France.[1]

As a result of months of anti-American propaganda over the Murphy Mission, *the first victim of the Algiers rioters that day was, characteristically enough, the American Information Centre*, where windows and doors were broken, the streets were littered with American books and magazines, and the sign with the American eagle was smashed to pieces.

With the Committee of Public Safety formed, European Algiers was in a jubilant state. At midnight, Massu's paratroopers occupied Radio-Algiers, and an 'observer', representing the Committee, was appointed to censor all broadcasts. Salan (without mentioning the instructions he had just received from Gaillard) broadcast that he was 'temporarily taking over the destinies of French Algeria' and (an hour later) that 'he was acting in full agreement with the Committee of Public Safety'.

Then, at 3 a.m., the news reached Algiers that the Pflimlin government had been invested by the National Assembly. It caused wild consternation among members of the Committee, and Massu at first believed that he had made a hopelessly bad mistake, for he exclaimed: '*Maintenant nous somme foutus!*'

It was then that Delbecque and others apparently

1. A comic aspect of that crazy evening was that teddy-boys tried at first to set up the Committee *without* the Gaullists; but when Delbecque heard what was going on at the G.G., he and three others rushed there and declared themselves 'the representatives of Jacques Soustelle'; as such, they had to be admitted to the Committee.

persuaded him that no retreat was possible now, for at 5 a.m. (there were still many people milling about in the Forum, the square outside the G.G. building), Massu again appeared on the balcony, called on the people of Algiers 'to fight till final victory', and 'implored General de Gaulle to break his silence'. These people now realized that *de Gaulle alone could enable them to save their own skins.*

'Pending the arrival of M. Soustelle' [Massu then said], 'the bureau of the Committee of Public Safety is composed as follows: General Massu, M. Delbecque, representing Soustelle; M. Madhani; and M. Lagaillarde.'

Madhani was a Moslem who seemed to have appeared from nowhere in the last few hours. The Moslems had, in reality, been conspicuous by their absence during the 13 May events; the inclusion of a Moslem in the Committee marked the beginning of that 'Operation Fraternization' (another of Delbecque's fertile ideas) of which so much was to be heard for the next few weeks and which, for a time, suited de Gaulle's designs perfectly.[1]

Although there had been various dark rumours in Paris for several days past, and some street demonstrations by *Algérie française* supporters, the news of the Algiers *putsch* still came to the capital as a violent shock. The new government under Pierre Pflimlin had appeared before the National Assembly on the afternoon of 13 May. Not to annoy the

1. Thousands of more-or-less terrorized Moslems were, during the following days, brought to the European part of Algiers in army lorries, to take part in 'fraternization' demonstrations, shouting '*Algérie Française*' slogans and the like. Most of the Moslem women who, as a particular sign of friendship, took off their veils during these rejoicings, turned out to be professional prostitutes. De Gaulle was, during the early stages of his premiership, in June 1958, to make much of this 'fraternization', while his Minister of Information, André Malraux, rapturously exclaimed on one occasion: 'This is something unique! Who ever heard of any Pakistani shouting: "*Pakistan anglais!*"?' (*The de Gaulle Revolution*, p. 199.)

Right and the Army, the prospective new premier, in his ministerial declaration, went back on his earlier 'negotiated-peace' speeches, and now suggested that no peace in Algeria would be possible without a French military victory over the rebels. It was not till after the dinner recess that the news reached the National Assembly of the Algiers *putsch*. But while the routine debate continued in the Assembly, there was much coming and going amongst the political leaders, many of them now intriguing against Pflimlin, and the question even arose of forming a 'National Government' under the Socialist leader Guy Mollet. The Socialist deputies themselves, however, stirred by the news of a 'Fascist plot against the Republic', decided to support the new government. Some of its members sounded full of fight. The Minister of Defence, M. de Chevigné, declared:

'Just give me a few hours. I don't think this nonsense can last very long. This Army rebellion in the midst of a war situation is something I am not going to tolerate.'

Pflimlin, in winding up the debate in the early hours of 14 May, also sounded energetic. He squarely condemned 'the insurrectionist attitude of certain army leaders' and said that if the unity between France and Algeria was not restored, the country would be faced with a civil war situation.

Despite the attacks Pflimlin had made on them, the Communists decided to abstain in the name of 'republican defence', and the Pflimlin government was invested by 274 votes to 129. The question that now arose was whether the new administration would get tough with the Algiers revolt, as General Massu feared it would when he heard of the large confidence vote.

Paris was shaken by the news of the Algiers *putsch*. On the morning of 14 May, newspaper kiosks were stormed, and during the day the sales of *France-Soir* alone shot up from a

million to three million copies. Its first edition, which came
out at 11 a.m., carried a huge headline:

COTY: I ORDER THE ARMY IN ALGERIA TO OBEY

In this message – as head of the armed forces, in virtue of
Article 33 of the Constitution – the President of the Republic
appealed to the patriotism and common sense of officers
and soldiers serving in Algeria. 'Any breach of discipline',
he said, 'can only benefit those whom we are fighting. . . . I
order you to follow the path of duty under the authority of
the government of the French Republic.' Most striking,
however, was that this order did not contain even an implicit
threat of reprisals should it be disobeyed.

That day of 14 May was crucial. In Paris, the Pflimlin
government made a show of energy by virtually placing
Jacques Soustelle under house arrest (from which, it is true,
he was to escape to Algiers a few days later) and by arresting
some 150 members of four small extremist right-wing organizations. But its attitude to Algiers remained highly ambiguous. Pflimlin could think of nothing better than to
entrust General Salan with the task of maintaining order in
Algiers and to do nothing at all about General Massu. The
Pflimlin government, instead of taking action of any kind
against Algiers, or even threatening it with financial and
economic reprisals, still hoped that Salan, Massu, and the
other generals would somehow manage to 'restore legality'
and call the *coup d'état* elements to order, including the
ultra paratroop colonels like Thomazo and Trinquier. It
was this total incoherence that played into the hands of de
Gaulle. 14 May being a Wednesday, de Gaulle came, as
usual, to Paris from his country house at Colombey-les-
deux-Eglises, but he was said to have stayed all the time at
his office in the rue Solférino and not to have seen anybody
but a representative of Plon, his publisher!

He still said nothing. But some influential papers, such as

Le Monde, were already beginning to speak of de Gaulle as providing the only solution. Beuve-Méry, the editor of *Le Monde*, noted that, thanks to the Communists, the Pflimlin government had a more solid majority in parliament than any government had had for a long time, and he called on it therefore to enforce 'republican legality' *everywhere and by every means*, but he made clear his doubt that it would in fact do so. If it did not, then there was only de Gaulle. The big question, however, was whether de Gaulle approved, or not, of the Algiers *putsch*. Another writer in the same paper, M. Duverger, argued, on the contrary, in favour of organizing 'republican defence' and risking a civil war, rather than submit to Algiers. The three main trade union organizations declared themselves that day in a 'state of alert', but waited to see what would happen next. That night, the Socialists entered the Pflimlin government, and the energetic Jules Moch – who had been tough with both Gaullists and Communists back in 1947–8 – was appointed Minister of the Interior.

And then, on the 15th, came two bombshells. At Algiers, General Salan, the Commander-in-Chief 'representing' the Paris government, addressed that morning a crowd of 15,000 people and concluded by crying: '*Vive la France! Vive l'Algérie Française! Vive de Gaulle!*'[1]

In the early afternoon de Gaulle at last broke his silence. In a written statement issued to the press he said:

The degradation of the State inevitably leads to the alienation of the peoples associated with France, to confusion in the fighting forces, to national dislocation and to the loss of independence. Faced with problems too hard for the régime of parties to tackle, France has, for the last twelve years, followed a disastrous road.

In the past, the country from its very depths, entrusted me with the task of leading it to salvation. Today, with new ordeals facing

1. It was soon learned that Delbecque, standing behind him, had prompted him at the last moment to add the '*Vive de Gaulle!*'.

it, let the country know that I am ready to assume the powers of the Republic.

Clearly, de Gaulle did not take Pflimlin's greatly strengthened parliamentary position seriously and considered that the time was ripe to wreck the 'régime of parties'. His statement did not imply any condemnation of the Algiers rebellion. Apart from some Fascist extremists who did not care for de Gaulle's reference to 'the Republic', Algiers now felt that it had the full backing of de Gaulle. As Eugène Mannoni cabled to *Le Monde* from Algiers:

De Gaulle's message has greatly consolidated the unity of the Committee of Public Safety – a unity which seemed very uncertain yesterday. It amply makes up for the disappointment caused by the investiture of the Pflimlin government.

In Paris that day there was a general feeling that a major showdown was now imminent. There was a slump in French shares at the Bourse, and a sharp rise in gold and foreign currency. Amongst housewives, there was a run on grocery shops; this had already begun on the 14th, but now it assumed alarming proportions. Everybody was buying up coffee, oil, sugar, macaroni and tinned milk. In one shop I saw a woman carrying off 100 kilos of sugar in a taxi. Soon grocers were obliged to start 'rationing' purchases. Some had run completely out of certain durable foodstuffs.

Pflimlin meanwhile went through his usual strong-man motions. The *Jeune Nation* and three other minor Fascist movements (with only a few hundred members in all) were dissolved, but though he spoke severely of certain things that General Salan had done in Algeria (such as arbitrarily dismissing republican officials), he still took no action against him or any of the generals. In response to the de Gaulle statement, he merely declared his refusal to believe that de Gaulle could think of violating republican legality; but he would like the General to throw some light on this point.

On the night of 16 May Pflimlin was given extensive emergency powers by the National Assembly, the Communists this time actually voting for him 'as a challenge to de Gaulle'.

Already, by the 16th, rumours were current in Paris of possible paratroop landings from Algeria in Paris and other parts of Metropolitan France; and already it was becoming clear that there were serious doubts about the 'republican loyalty' of the Army in France itself, especially of the 'regulars' and the officers. Military aircraft flying over Colombey had, in the last couple of days, made a point of dipping their wings to salute de Gaulle. M. Moch, the Minister of the Interior, was also rumoured to have grave doubts about the police and even the Prefects. These rumours were to be confirmed by him later, when it was all over.

On 16 May in Algiers there took place the first great 'fraternization' rally, at which Europeans and Moslems walked through the streets shouting '*Intégration!*' '*Algérie Française!*' and '*Vive de Gaulle!*' This highly artificial stunt, thought up by Delbecque (and probably Massu) was intended to suggest that the war would now simply peter out, since the 'Algerian people' were, in fact, repudiating the 'rebels' and wanted nothing as much as to be 'Frenchmen'.

On 17 May, the sensational news reached Paris that Jacques Soustelle, after escaping to Switzerland from his police 'protectors' in the boot of a friend's car, had flown from there in a privately-chartered plane to Algiers, where he was being acclaimed, amidst great rejoicings, as 'de Gaulle's representative'. Salan hastened to appoint Soustelle his 'political adviser' – an act which meant, in effect, the Commander-in-Chief's final breach with Paris. Even so, Pflimlin tried, for a few days longer, to sustain the myth that Salan was acting under the orders of the Paris government. It was not till the Corsican *putsch* a week later that Pflimlin realized how lost was his hope of still controlling Salan.   *

In the midst of all these dramatic happenings, de Gaulle decided to hold a press conference at the Hotel du Palais d'Orsay on Monday afternoon, 19 May, so giving his famous statement of 15 May four days to mature before making another public move. Already, in that statement, he had informed France that he was now 'available', and questions were being asked everywhere of how he envisaged his return to power. Guy Mollet, the Socialist leader, and now Pflimlin's vice-premier, had already asked three questions: whether de Gaulle recognized the Pflimlin government as the only legal government of France: whether he disavowed the promoters of the Algiers *putsch*; and whether he was prepared, if called upon to form a government, to appear before the National Assembly with a programme and withdraw if he were defeated. It was quite clear that, even at this early stage of the crisis, the Socialist leader was considering de Gaulle's return to power as probable, if not inevitable, and that he was hoping to save parliamentary appearances. He had, in fact, already decided, if the choice lay between de Gaulle and a Popular Front – a course for which the Communists were clamouring – that de Gaulle was, for him, by far the lesser evil.

At heart, de Gaulle despised the politicians and despised parliament, with its 'party' system, but he was willing to use them as a stepping-stone for returning to power, and the implicit overtures Mollet had made to him suited him perfectly. He knew that if he were to return to power by a 'legal' (even if 'exceptional') procedure, he needed the parliamentary support of at least part of Mollet's S.F.I.O. – in addition to that of the Right and Centre parties, on which he could count now that Algiers was threatening France with civil war.

Thousands of journalists and others crowded the vast banqueting hall of the Palais d'Orsay long before 3 p.m., when de Gaulle was to make his first public appearance in three years. He looked distinctly older and his voice had a tired and somewhat mellowed tone at first; but he soon recovered his old self-assurance, his irony and quiet arrogance.

He recalled that, three years before, he had decided to remain silent until such time as he could again serve the country. Things had, since then, gone from bad to worse, and what was happening now might well lead to 'a great national crisis'. But, he added, all this 'might also mark the beginning of some kind of resurrection' – a clear suggestion that the Algiers *putsch* was perhaps a blessing in disguise.

And now he thought he could again be 'useful to France', for three reasons. First, under his rule in 1944–6, many important things had been achieved, and his own 'moral capital' might still count – in France, in the overseas territories and abroad.

Secondly, because the exclusive régime of parties will never solve the enormous problems facing us, particularly that of our association with the peoples of Africa and the different communities in Algeria.

This régime, for all its good intentions, could settle nothing and, in the end (clearly an allusion to Murphy!), the outside world might inflict a solution on France – and this would be the worst of all solutions.

Finally, he (de Gaulle) could be useful because he belonged to no party.

'I am a man who belongs to nobody, and who belongs to everybody.' In concluding this introductory part of his conference, he said that he could be useful by placing himself at the head of the French Republic, 'if the people wished it'.

Answering questions, de Gaulle had another dig at Murphy. After years of bloodshed, he said, the 'system' had lately resorted to the 'good offices' of the outside world. After paying a compliment to Lacoste, who had so clearly seen the danger of the Murphy Mission, de Gaulle then said that he was scarcely surprised that Algiers had rebelled, for how could it have gone on expecting salvation from 'just some new parliamentary combination'? Suddenly there came the real touch of Gaullist arrogance:

'Now the Algerians shout "*Vive de Gaulle*", just as the French also do in moments of acute anguish, and are yet carried on the wings of hope.'

And now, he said, a wonderful thing had happened: that great movement of fraternization between the two communities in Algeria 'which proves a basis for agreements and arrangements which are vastly better than battles and ambushes'. This phoney 'fraternization' had, clearly, played into de Gaulle's hands.

But more important still was the full approval he gave to the Army's attitude; for the Army, he declared, was simply sharing the Algerian population's desire to see Paris 'capable of assuming its responsibilities'. He wanted, however, the Army to remain 'coherent and united' – at a time when there was no other coherent and united force in the country. 'The Army,' he said, 'is the instrument of the State; but what we need *is* a State. And there is no time to lose.'

In passing, he significantly warned the government against taking a strong line over Algiers – for instance, by cutting communications between France and Algeria, a step some members of the Pflimlin government had obviously considered in their braver moments.

And then came de Gaulle's surprising – or not so surprising – compliments to Mollet, a fine man but one who, obviously, did not get much of a chance in a régime like the present one. All he had to say in reply to Mollet's questions was this:

'If de Gaulle is given exceptional powers, for an exceptional task, at an exceptional moment, then, surely, de Gaulle will also have to be given these powers by an exceptional procedure ... an investiture by the National Assembly, for instance.'

Clearly, de Gaulle's acceptance by the National Assembly through an 'exceptional procedure', depended on the Socialists; and de Gaulle knew what he was doing in paying these compliments to Mollet. Having got over these pleasant overtures, de Gaulle became ironical and, indeed, satirical, in making hay of the hopelessly false position in which the Pflimlin government had placed itself with regard to the generals in Algiers:

'There are some who treat as rebels the Army leaders who have not been punished by the government and who, indeed, have been delegated governmental authority in Algeria! Now, I am *not* the government: so why should anybody expect *me* to treat these Army leaders as rebels?' (*Loud laughter*.)

Asked whether he would respect public freedoms, de Gaulle replied with an air of superb disdain: 'It was I who re-established these public freedoms. Do you believe that, at sixty-seven, I shall start a dictator's career?' There were some who murmured: 'What about Pétain, who started at eighty-four?' In conclusion, he spoke of France's high birth-rate and her great economic possibilities; but to make the best of these, a strong government would be required. 'If called to power, I shall need the help of the men and women of France ... I have said what I had to say. Now I shall return to my village and remain there at the country's disposal.'

*

I talked to several people after the meeting. Philippe Barrès, the ex-Gaullist deputy, declared: 'It's in the bag now, don't you think?' I said I thought it looked rather like it. Communist Pierre Courtade of *L'Humanité* shrugged his shoulders and said: 'It'll be difficult to keep him out, especially if the Socialists – or most of them – eat out of his hand; and it's beginning to look like it. They've got cold feet.' 'And the working-class?' I asked. 'The anti-Fascist feeling amongst them is strong enough. But let's face it; the Communists are feeling very isolated; a lot of the rank-and-file are terribly a-political; and the idea that de Gaulle is a 'lesser evil' is already making headway. He's playing a devilishly clever game. . . .'

It *was* devilishly clever and, with every day that passed, the de Gaulle solution began to look more and more inevitable.

It is sufficient here to enumerate only briefly the progress of events during the fantastic twelve days that followed de Gaulle's press conference.

20 May. Having already, on the previous Saturday, taken the incongruous step of enforcing exit visas on all French citizens leaving France, the Pflimlin government now placed insuperable exchange restrictions on almost anybody leaving the country.

The Socialist governing body and parliamentary group held a joint meeting declaring that de Gaulle had 'turned his back on the Constitution' and was demanding an 'exceptional procedure the rules of which he himself intended to lay down'.

In various parts of the country 'Defence of the Republic' committees were being set up, some of them including Communists. For all that, the Socialist leaders were very uncertain about what to do, and Mollet continued to be particularly hostile to any revival of a Popular Front.

At the meeting of the National Assembly that day, Pflimlin said the importance of 'fraternization' should not be exaggerated, since the actual fighting between French troops and the F.L.N. was as violent as ever. He then declared that proposals would, in the next few days, be submitted to the Assembly for a reform of the Constitution, a reform which would give the government greater stability.

Mendès-France sharply criticized de Gaulle for undermining the Republic in its hour of deadly danger.

The Assembly renewed Pflimlin's emergency powers for Algeria by a large majority, though this was as good as meaningless.

22 May. The right-wing ex-premier Antoine Pinay went to see de Gaulle at Colombey. De Gaulle treated him to a cup of tea and was 'most affable and amiable'. During the one hour and forty minutes he spent with de Gaulle, Pinay succeeded in paving the way for an early meeting between de Gaulle and Pflimlin – and possibly Mollet. He also discussed with the General the 'exceptional procedure' whereby he could be 'legally' invested as Premier.

The Pflimlin government met to consider a draft of the Constitutional Reform, aimed at setting up a 'Gaullist régime without de Gaulle'.

23 May. The draft met with opposition from President Coty, and further discussion was adjourned till the following week. Mendès-France acidly commented on Pflimlin's desire to rush a far-reaching constitutional reform through parliament 'in five or six days' as a 'sheer piece of Kerenskyism'.

In Algiers, demonstrators now began to shout a new slogan: '*Les paras à Paris!*' foreshadowing the following week's nightmare of an airborne invasion of France by paratroopers. Numerous French military planes from Algeria began to fly over Tunisia, and the Tunisian Government, fearing a French-Algerian invasion, sent a complaint to the U.N.

Colonel Lacheroy, Salan's official spokesman, declared that France might need the direct help of Algiers to enforce the de Gaulle solution.

24 May. The 'conquest of France' by Algiers began with a successful 'Gaullist' *putsch* in Corsica. Following the directives of M. Arrighi the Corsican deputy, who flew there from Algiers, the local paratroopers – some 250 men – 'occupied' Ajaccio, where a Committee of Public Safety was set up along Algiers lines. There was practically no resistance anywhere on the island, and when a company of C.R.S. guards were flown to Ajaccio from the mainland, on instructions from M. Moch, they were promptly disarmed by the paratroopers who had already occupied the airfield.

Meantime, Algiers had started a 'war of nerves' against France on the radio, calling on various cities, towns and even villages to set up their own Committees of Public Safety in anticipation of further *putsches* on Corsican lines. Also mysterious code messages – which might mean anything or nothing – were broadcast. The chief organizer of this radio war was M. Roger Frey, de Gaulle's future Minister of the Interior.

25 May. This was Whit-Sunday, and 800,000 Parisians had left the capital for the week-end, apparently not greatly worried about Corsica, and somehow assuming that a de Gaulle government would be formed in the next few days.

Pflimlin, however, was very upset by the Corsica *putsch* and, in his broadcast made an absurd distinction between the Algiers *putsch*, which was 'understandable', and the Corsica *putsch*, which was 'intolerable'. He declared that 'legal action' would be taken against all who had taken part in the latter. There were rumours all day that the government had decided to send a battleship to Corsica to land 'loyal' troops there; later it was learned that Moch had proposed this, but that Pflimlin had turned down the idea as 'appallingly dangerous'. A press censorship was established.

26 May. At the meeting of the National Assembly, Pflimlin helplessly declared that it had not yet been decided whether to send any troops to Corsica to restore law and order. He said that France was now in danger and that 'the whole nation' must help to avert this danger. But what this meant in practice was not clear. Instead, Pflimlin persisted with his Constitutional Reform Bill, which, he said, must be urgently passed. He also proposed that the Assembly raise the parliamentary immunity of Pascal Arrighi, one of the leaders of the Corsican *putsch.*

Duclos, for the Communists, asked why such reprisals should be taken against Arrighi, and not against Soustelle and other Algiers plotters. The Corsican *putsch* was only the second act of the Algiers operation. And there was real danger of more trouble: there were paratroop concentrations in various parts of France, especially in the south; in the army the officers were mostly Gaullist, and so was the police. He called for a *levée en masse* of the working class, and regretted that the Socialist leaders were already flirting with de Gaulle. In the end, Arrighi's parliamentary immunity was raised, but that was all.

That night Pflimlin had a secret meeting with de Gaulle. But press censorship did not allow the news to be published in next morning's papers.

27 May. Ever since M. Pinay's visit to de Gaulle on 22 May, there had been secret contacts between the latter and certain republican leaders, notably an important exchange of letters between him and Guy Mollet, the Socialist leader; the tone of de Gaulle's letter (not to be published until much later) was almost overwhelmingly cordial. But even before any reliable news could be obtained about de Gaulle's mysterious meeting with Pflimlin on the night of 26–27 May, de Gaulle suddenly produced a bombshell of a new order. At 12.30 p.m. de Gaulle's secretariat issued this extraordinary statement:

I yesterday embarked on the regular process necessary for establishing a republican government which would be capable of maintaining the unity and independence of our country.

I trust this process will continue and that the country will show that it wishes this process to succeed.

In these conditions any action, wherever it may come from, which would disturb public order, risks producing the gravest consequences. While making allowances for circumstances, I cannot approve of any such action.

I expect the land, sea and air forces to maintain the strictest discipline under the command of their chiefs, General Salan, Admiral Auboyneau and General Jouhaud. I express confidence in these chiefs and intend shortly to establish contact with them.

What was behind all this? Pflimlin had not resigned; President Coty had not called on de Gaulle to form the next government; so what did it mean? There were many who, especially after Duclos' disclosures the day before, guessed what it meant; but it was not till later that M. Jules Moch, the Minister of the Interior, told the full story. The gist was simply that de Gaulle had learned *from his own sources* that a military *putsch* was being prepared for the following night (27–8 May) by paratroop units at Toulouse and other places, and that a paratroop landing in Paris was planned; at the same time, the police and army in France were wholly unreliable as supports for the government. De Gaulle (anxious to take over by 'legal' methods, and not as a result of such a *putsch*) knew that he alone could stop such action with a categorical statement that he was already 'taking over'.[1]

This, as it turned out, was to prove perhaps the greatest piece of statesmanship in the whole of de Gaulle's career; while now making his return to power practically certain, it at the same time averted the establishment of a military dictatorship in France or, more likely still, the outbreak of a civil war.

1. On 6 July 1958 M. Moch was to give a Socialist conference a detailed account of what was being prepared for the night of 27–8 May by at least four military regional commands in France; after the 'conquest' of Corsica, they were going to 'conquer' Paris and other French cities. The ordinary conscripts had little say in the matter; while the police, according to Moch, not least in Paris, were wholly unreliable. Nor, as the experience of Corsica had shown, could the prefectoral corps be counted upon. (*The de Gaulle Revolution*, pp. 176–80.)

The whole significance of de Gaulle's statement was, clearly, not understood when the National Assembly met that afternoon to discuss Pflimlin's constitutional reform, and, among the Socialists, feeling was running high against de Gaulle, despite Mollet's attempt to argue in favour of the general. Pflimlin maintained an ambiguous attitude, though he thanked de Gaulle for his statement calling to order those 'who were perhaps tempted to start an insurrection against the republican order'. Later in the evening Pflimlin disclosed, much to the Socialists' consternation, that Mollet had written to de Gaulle a few days before urging him to use his moral authority with the potential trouble-makers.

Pflimlin was anxious, by this time, to make room for de Gaulle. He even thought up a scheme for claiming that he had been defeated at the National Assembly on his Constitutional Reform proposals, since his huge majority of 408 included some 130 communists, who could not be counted as a 'national party'; without their votes, he had not received a 'constitutional majority' of 296![1]

On the following morning he offered President Coty his resignation, but Coty prevailed on him not to make this official until a new government had been formed.

28 May was the day marked by the great 'anti-Fascist March' of some 300,000 people in Paris. Composed of Socialists, Communists and other left-wingers, the procession carried banners, proclaiming *Vive la République, Non à de Gaulle* and 'Down with Fascism!' The whole affair was extraordinarily morose and half-hearted, for all these people knew that while they were 'demonstrating' against de Gaulle, the Socialist leader was negotiating de Gaulle's return to power! It was nothing like the dynamic mass demonstrations of the Left in the mid-1930s. At most, the

1. He was following in this an absurd precedent first created by Mendès-France in 1954.

huge march showed that the working-class would not remain indifferent if there were a military *putsch*. But, as one talked to these people, one felt that they had no strong feelings against de Gaulle personally, and would do nothing if some form of 'legal investiture' could be devised for him. And there was certainly not much Republican *mystique* among them after all that had happened. How could there be? Nobody was going to die for Pflimlin.

All the same, this demonstration was sufficient to scare a number of papers and politicians into talking about a revival of the Popular Front. President Coty was particularly frightened, or claimed to be. Perhaps, in reality, he was more frightened of those paratroop landings in Paris and elsewhere, which de Gaulle's statement of the previous day had possibly only 'postponed'. What worried him also was the 'obstructive' attitude of the Socialist deputies who, regardless of Mollet's pleading for de Gaulle, had been 'galvanized' (as one paper put it) by the Nation-République demonstration. So, on the afternoon of 29 May, he sent a Message to parliament saying that he intended to turn to 'the most illustrious Frenchman' and ask him to set up a government 'within the framework of republican legality', and then to bring about 'a fundamental reform of our institutions'. If the Assembly did not accept this, he would resign. No vote was taken, but the Socialists were, it was clear, badly shaken. Soon afterwards they were shown the letters exchanged a few days before between ex-President Vincent Auriol and de Gaulle; de Gaulle himself sounded remarkably conciliatory, and even claimed that all the 'Gaullist' agitation that had been going on in Algiers had taken place 'without his ever having been involved in the developments there in any way'.

That night de Gaulle conferred with President Coty at the Elysée Palace, while thousands of cars outside hooted their ... – – signal, meaning '*Algérie française*', and the

-- ... signal, meaning '*de Gaulle au pouvoir*'. There were also great 'Gaullist' demonstrations in Algiers.

De Gaulle accepted Coty's offer, but left Coty to start the initial conversations with the parliamentary groups. And he added: 'You had better also see the Communists; after all, they *are* Frenchmen. . . .'[1]

On the following day, making his headquarters a hotel near the Etoile, he conversed with the various politicians (some of them, like Mitterrand, very hostile at first), and argued with them in an easygoing, even jocular vein; many of them left, feeling both puzzled and charmed by the man. In particular, he assured Mitterrand that, just as in 1944, so now, he was opposed to any autonomous powers which would conflict in any way with the central government; just as in 1944 he had not tolerated the Liberation Committees set up by the Resistance, so he would not allow the Algiers Committees of Public Safety to interfere with the central authority in Paris. He even spoke of Algeria as a Federation, forming part of a Confederation which would comprise both France and the various overseas territories – a proposal very unlike the 'integrationism' of Algiers – and said that he would rapidly revoke Pflimlin's emergency powers, with its censorship and other restrictions.

Among the Socialists there was still much opposition to de Gaulle; but, by the end of that day, Mollet had won over nearly half the deputies.

By the end of that day, too, de Gaulle was already forming his government. This indeed was to prove a very mixed crew – and not at all to the liking of the Algiers extremists. For one thing, it included four Ministers of State, among them Mollet and Pflimlin, and several other deputies and senators; the Minister of Finance was M. Pinay. Some key posts had been given to non-parliamentarians; a Prefect,

1. The Communist (as well as the C.G.T., the Communist Trade Union Federation) refused to see either Coty or de Gaulle.

M. Pelletier was Minister of the Interior; M. Couve de Murville, a career diplomat, Foreign Minister; and M. Guillaumat, a high official, Minister of the Armies. But *ultras* like Bidault and Soustelle (the latter still in Algiers) were not included. The Minister of Information was André Malraux, that intellectual ornament of the R.P.F., and the Gaullist senator, Michel Debré, was appointed Minister of Justice. He was to play a leading role in the subsequent drafting of the new Constitution.

De Gaulle despised parliament, and wanted at first simply to send a Message to the National Assembly, but Mollet thought this would be taken badly and would cost him many votes, and persuaded him to appear at the Palais-Bourbon in person.

*

This he did on Sunday, 1 June. Thousands of police had roped off the whole area round the National Assembly that afternoon, before de Gaulle's arrival. The Assembly was packed, when de Gaulle, looking a little nervous and uneasy, took his seat on the government bench. He had not been in this building, which he had never liked, since that day in January 1946 when he had thrown up the sponge.

Then, in complete silence, he walked up the steps of the tribune and proceeded to read out his seven-minute Message. Again he spoke about the 'degradation of the State', of the fact that the Army had been 'scandalized' by the previous governments' lack of authority, and of the danger of civil war. But now that, in response to President Coty's appeal, he had agreed 'to lead the country, the State and the Republic along the road of salvation once again', he was asking parliament for six months' plenary powers, and the necessary legal machinery for drawing up a new constitution which would be submitted to a referendum. He then gave a few details of what he had in mind. The same constitutional reform, he said, would provide the 'solemn occasion' for 'organizing the relations between France and the people with whom she is associated'. He asked that the relevant Bills be voted with the greatest possible speed. The cheers were slow in coming. When the Right and Centre finally applauded, somewhat half-heartedly, one had the impression that many of them were disappointed by the vagueness of de Gaulle's references to Algeria, and – in the case of the Right and Extreme Right – by the moderation of his statement.

After throwing a quick glance round the Assembly, de Gaulle then left, and the strange 'investiture debate' began in his absence. Those 'for' de Gaulle, such as M. P. H. Teitgen, the M.R.P. leader, argued that he had not been brought into power by Algiers; that he had observed republican legality throughout; that Algiers and Corsica would be now called to order; and (apparently on the strength of what de Gaulle had told him himself) that 'personal rights, trade-union and all other freedoms' would be respected under the plenary powers.

Some of those 'against' him argued, on the contrary, that a de Gaulle régime might well pave the way for a totalitarian system and for persecution. Mitterrand and Mendès-France both held that the Algiers rebellion had imposed de Gaulle on parliament, and that the 'civil war blackmail' was continuing; they both hoped that de Gaulle would not allow himself to be dominated by the people who had brought him to power, but meanwhile they could not vote for him.

In the end, de Gaulle's investiture was approved (still in his absence) by 329 votes to 224, with the Radical and Socialist votes being almost equally divided between Ayes and Noes.

Three Bills were to come before the Assembly the next day: the renewal of special powers for Algeria; the Plenary Powers Bill; the Bill modifying Article 90 of the Constitution, which was necessary if a new constitution was to be drafted within a short time. It looks as though de Gaulle was not quite sure that parliament would easily endorse all this.

So, on 2 June, the Assembly had the surprise of seeing appear before it a new and almost unsuspected kind of de Gaulle – not the stiff, haughty, 'Louis XIV' kind of de Gaulle of the day before, but one who was to carry out what a Communist deputy, Kriegel-Valrimont, was later to describe as 'Operation Seduction'.

No one had expected [wrote *Le Monde*] that he would exercise such skill, and show such gifts of diplomacy and psychological understanding. ... Sitting like a good boy on the government bench (with Guy Mollet beside him and looking like his secretary), de Gaulle patiently listened to the *rapporteur*. Only after that did he say in the mildest tone that either the Plenary Powers would be accepted, or he would go.

Throughout his several speeches de Gaulle used – seemingly with complete sincerity – phrases like 'the pleasure and honour of being in your midst'. It was, *Le Monde* put it, as though 'de Gaulle had made one step towards the System, while the System had made two or three steps towards him'.

And, during an interval, people could watch a sight worthy of Molière, La Bruyère, Saint-Simon and Marcel Proust rolled into one – countless deputies trying to get sufficiently close to the government bench to be able to shake the great man's hand. In particular, Georges Bonnet was seen manoevring his way to the place where de Gaulle sat and managing to extract from him a handshake; one observer said it was 'a very short and dry one', another that 'it looked as though de Gaulle had touched a slug, so quick was he in withdrawing his hand'.[1]

De Gaulle's good grace and humour were all the more surprising as the discussion on the plenary powers and on the 'principles' of the new constitution could not have been more confusing and irritating, amendment after amendment

1. *The de Gaulle Revolution*, p. 173.

was proposed, only to be swept aside, sometimes at once, sometimes after obscure and hair-splitting dispute.

For all that, the discussion ended almost in an atmosphere of mutual friendship and confidence between de Gaulle and the Assembly. De Gaulle assured the deputies that his great aim was to 'let the Republic continue'. It was then that Kriegel-Valrimont exclaimed: 'After "Operation Sedition" we are now being treated to "Operation Seduction"!', while Mendès-France remarked that such supreme politeness was, in reality, the height of insolence.

In any case, de Gaulle twisted the Assembly, with its detested 'Party System', round his little finger by turning on it his charm. The greater part of the deputies did not look too closely at the Bills they had voted, and seemed perfectly content with the assurances de Gaulle had given them, and with the supplementary assurances they received from Pflimlin or Mollet – even though it was not sure that these were binding on de Gaulle. Thus the Fourth Republic went into voluntary liquidation. 'Operation Seduction' had worked perfectly.

Never, except in 1940 – when, over the B.B.C., he proclaimed that France would continue to fight – did de Gaulle look as much as in May-June 1958 the Great Man, the Man of Destiny. But how much did de Gaulle have to do with 'Operation Sedition' – i.e. with that Algiers *putsch* twenty days earlier which had made his return to power inevitable?

In a sense, he was telling the truth when he said that he had not taken part in organizing the Algiers *putsch*; but he was extremely well-informed throughout of what was going on. He allowed those who claimed to be 'Gaullists' to play their part in bringing matters to a head in Algiers and in precipitating that 'degradation of the State' which he had been watching for several months past. He now had that 'insuperable urge to act' – of which he had already spoken in *Le fil de l'épée* back in 1932. But the question of timing was of the utmost importance. And the timing of his three great public appearances – his first statement of 15 May, his press conference of 19 May, and his 'I have embarked . . .' of 27 May – was a masterpiece of political precision-work. The first ruined Pflimlin's last chance of quelling the Algiers revolt; the second prepared his 'parliamentary' return to power; the third prevented a military *putsch* which would not have served de Gaulle's purpose. He wanted to create precisely those conditions in which he could now set up that very type of régime of which he had dreamed ever since 1946 – and perhaps long before that.

At heart, very few mourned the passing of the Fourth Republic. For one thing, it had sickened beyond remedy over the Algerian problem. De Gaulle was the only man with sufficient prestige, with a sufficiently great 'legend', to be able to treat that disease with a fair chance of success.

One of the paradoxical aspects of de Gaulle was that he was not 'popular' in the ordinary sense; he aroused no mass enthusiasm, still less mass hysteria, as Hitler, for instance, had done. And yet, in 1958, practically the whole of France accepted him as her Leader – or at least as the Lesser Evil. To those for whom de Gaulle was the Lesser Evil, his return to power meant *not so much change as an escape from drastic and violent change* – which the 'colonels' would have brought about.

Who then was this Man of Destiny?

CHAPTER 2

WHEN DE GAULLE WAS STILL UNKNOWN

1. That 'Certain Idea of France'

THERE were many *crises du régime* of one kind or another, before the great crisis of May 1958, when France sought salvation by calling some elder statesman to the rescue. Clemenceau, then nearly 80, was made head of the government during one of the worst moments of the First World War; Poincaré was brought back to power in 1926 to 'save the franc'; after the anti-parliamentary riots of 6 February 1934, ex-President Doumergue was called upon to form a national coalition government which would 'save the Republic' and 'save France from civil war'; similarly, in 1940, the 84-year-old Marshal Pétain was expected to rescue what could still be rescued after the fearful military defeat France had suffered.

Although Doumergue, a mediocre Third Republic politician in the past, and only a superficially popular President between 1924 and 1931, was the least impressive of France's 'saviours', the 1958 situation resembled the 1934 *crise du régime* more than any other – except that the challenge to the Republic came from inside France in 1934, and from Algeria and the Army in 1958. Doumergue made an abortive attempt to reform the Constitution, but was turned out of office eight months later, leaving the Third Republic to achieve apparent normality again and be swept away, five years later, by the débâcle of 1940. De Gaulle was, if one may say so, a much more successful M. Doumergue. Doumergue was a small man and a clumsy politician, and once he had served the immediate purpose of 'restoring order', he could be discarded. There was no Doumergue Legend as such.

But there certainly was a de Gaulle Legend, and even after he had 'finally' retired from public life in 1955, he knew that, some day, his 'Legend' could still serve a purpose. Pierre Mendès-France, perhaps the shrewdest of the Fourth Republic politicians – who was head of the government in 1954–5, and himself adopted a certain 'Gaullist' style of governing the country – believed, both then and later, that de Gaulle alone had the authority to put France's house in order. In a sense, Mendès-France had also, for a short time, played the role of 'saviour', when it became urgent to wind up the Indo-China war and settle the questions of Tunisia and German rearmament; but when he had done that, parliament turned him out. He was full of bitterness against the National Assembly; but he had neither the means nor the personal prestige to reform the system as de Gaulle was to do after returning to power in 1958.

*

The de Gaulle legend, though seemingly dormant in the Spring of 1958 was, nevertheless, a real source of strength. Since 1940, de Gaulle had been France's 'man of destiny'; and although, since then, he had had many ups and downs, had suffered a great reversal with his ill-considered R.P.F. movement of 1947–53, and had begun to be considered a back-number by 1955, he still remained a great man in popular imagination. His career was, indeed, an extraordinary one.

One of the strangest things about it was that a man of his exceptional ability, character and sense of purpose, with so enormous a faith in himself, should have remained unknown to the vast majority of his countrymen until he had reached the age of 49. No doubt his obscurity till so advanced an age could be explained by two things: by the French Army Establishment, such as it existed in the 1920s and 1930s, and by the very nature and 'bad habits' of the Third Republic.

Over many years de Gaulle was to store up a deep grievance against both the generals and the Republic; for it was they who had both led France along the path of disaster and had maintained him – Charles de Gaulle – in obscurity. Though, paradoxically, as President of the Republic after 1959 he liked to be referred to as *General* rather than as *President* de Gaulle, *all the bitterest quarrels in his life were with the Army*: in the '20s and '30s he helplessly battered his head against the stone wall of the General Staff's routine; in 1940, he rebelled against the Army leaders, and became a 'deserter' whom the Vichy military then sentenced to death; and if, in 1958, it was in effect the Army that brought him back to power, it was also certain elements in the Army which on two occasions, between 1959 and 1962, nearly overthrew him. Before the Fifth Republic could be considered safe, de Gaulle had to 'tame' the Army. Like the American generals in Vietnam in 1964–5, many of the French Generals and all the 'psychological warfare' colonels in Algeria persuaded themselves that they were fighting 'world Communism'; seeing much more clearly than they, de Gaulle knew from the outset that the Algerians were fighting primarily for their national independence. It took de Gaulle four years to 'break' the generals; and, towards the end of the Algerian war, he remarked, not without a touch of sarcastic bitterness: 'The Army – it was against Dreyfus; it was for Vichy; it was for Algerian integration.' And nothing was more typical of de Gaulle's stored-up resentment against the generals who had bungled everything between the two World Wars than his refusal in 1965 to allow a grand state funeral with full military honours, to be given at the Invalides to 98-year-old General Weygand, the runaway commander-in-chief of 1940 who had so placidly and cheerfully accepted France's defeat – and had continued to remain a revered member of the Establishment even after de Gaulle had put him in jail for a short time.

*

So de Gaulle is certainly not a 'typical' general. But is he a 'typical' Frenchman? The question has often been asked, and it is not an easy one to answer. For what *is* a 'typical Frenchman'? He himself has often said that he does not fit into any 'category'. It might, indeed, be argued that de Gaulle is without precedent. If one takes earlier 'saviours' of France – whether Clemenceau, Poincaré, Doumergue, or even Pétain – each, in his own way, was a 'typical' Frenchman: the ruthless, sarcastic 'Jacobin' Clemenceau; the humourless, hard-working, drearily legalistic Poincaré; Doumergue, the average politician with his false bonhomie; Pétain, the traditional general, suddenly called upon to play the Father Figure.

Through a long process of reasoning, and with evergrowing conviction, de Gaulle, by 1940, already identified himself with France. That year he had done the *one* right thing which nobody else had done; and he was deeply convinced that he was right. The *Je suis la France* of the war years (which exasperated Churchill and Roosevelt); the *J'étais la France* during the more melancholy middle 1950s are not phrases pointing, as has so often been suggested, to some morbid state of megalomania, but are simply the expression of a deep-seated conviction that de Gaulle knows what is 'good for France' better than anybody else. No doubt there is in this attitude a strong element of ambition and personal vanity; but stronger even is de Gaulle's belief that no man can *serve* France as well as he. *But by 'France' he means much less the French people and their day-to-day interests than France as a nation and a state, her place in the world and her 'historical destiny'.* Most readers may remember that famous opening passage in his *Mémoires*:

All my life I have kept alive in myself a certain idea of France
... I early came to believe that France, like the Princess in a fairy
tale or the Madonna of the Frescoes, had an eminent and exceptional destiny. ... But when mediocrity marks her acts or her
attitude, I have the feeling of an absurd anomaly, due to the
defects of the French, but not to the genius of the Nation. ...
I am convinced that France is really herself only when she is in
the front rank; only great enterprises can compensate for the
disrupting ferment that her people carry in themselves ... Our
country must, under pain of mortal danger, aim high and stand
upright. In short, France, as I see her, cannot be France without
greatness.

In a book published in 1956[1] I described de Gaulle as 'a
noble anachronism'; and, at that time, it seemed true. In a
sense, it is still true; for there is a genuine touch of melancholy in de Gaulle's recent remark: 'Ah, *cher ami*, if only
we were a nation of 180 million people!' But I am prepared
to eat my 1956 words. For, in the last few years, de Gaulle
has shown that even if he is 'a man of yesterday', he is also
'a man of tomorrow'; a man who likes to impersonate the
heir of the old Kings of France, but who, at the same time,
wants to be the ruler of a thoroughly modern and efficient
State and who is, above all, a man who has moved with the
times. He has done some hard thinking, and has, even in his
seventies, *learned* much – much more than the leaders of
certain other countries about the gradual erosion of the
Power Blocs that emerged from the Second World War. Not
only that: despite a certain air of 'liberalism' which he
assumed during and soon after the Second World War over
the French colonial territories, he was (as his whole immediate post-war attitude to Indo-China showed), a 'French
Empire' man; gradually, over the next fifteen or twenty
years, he became the most convinced decolonizer: and he has
succeeded, accordingly, in making France – still the most

1. *France 1940–1955*, Robert Hale.

diehard colonialist power as late as 1952 – the best-liked (or,
at any rate, the least disliked) of the Western Powers in the
'Third World' and even among the Communist countries.
In the eyes of Belgrade and Moscow, Algiers and Tunis,
Peking and Hanoi, Buenos Aires and Bogota, Delhi and
Mexico, France is today the most 'progressive' of the old
'imperialist' powers. Throughout Black Africa, de Gaulle
is a name to conjure with... When Americans destroy
thousands of Vietnamese with napalm like so much vermin,
de Gaulle thinks *them* anachronistic. This is the kind of
'radiance' that France has succeeded in achieving in the
last few years throughout the Third World. It is better than
the old-time imperialism in which de Gaulle still believed
twenty years ago. So de Gaulle has certainly been changing and evolving with time.

In recent years, he has been believing less and less in the
Power Blocs. The atomic balance of terror between the
Big Two has given France a certain freedom of movement
she did not have before. His main charge against the
Fourth Republic was that, under it, France was simply a
satellite of the United States. The French atom bomb may
ultimately be of questionable value; yet it gives not only de
Gaulle, but also a surprisingly high proportion of Frenchmen (even though they object to its cost) at least the
pleasant illusion of greater independence.

In this respect, at any rate, de Gaulle is 'typically French'.
France must have a 'special' place in the world; since she
is only a nation of less than fifty millions, she must do so by
being the 'leading' nation in Western Europe, if necessary
through close agreement with Western Germany; but she
must not be either an American or a Russian satellite. The
German factor, as we shall see, is, of course, the most doubtful of all; nevertheless, de Gaulle's desire to be as independent of the United States as possible (and, at the same
time, of America's satellite, Great Britain) reflects a state

of mind that is highly typical of France. It is not that de
Gaulle is, as has often been said, 'pathologically' anti-
British or anti-American; but, to him, Continental Europe
(Western Europe to begin with, and, eventually, a Europe
'from the Atlantic to the Urals') is in a respectable French,
partly Napoleonic, tradition, though the atomic balance of
power in the world today has created a number of new factors which never existed in the nineteenth century. When de
Gaulle speaks of an 'Atlantic-to-Urals Europe', he looks, of
course, very far ahead; at the back of his mind there is
China on the one hand, and the fundamental Europeanism
of Russia on the other. To de Gaulle, ideologies are the most
unstable elements in the world; the most stable of all are
Nations. In this respect he sees the future much more clearly
than the Pentagon does, with its primitive black-and-white
concept of Communism and anti-Communism.... To de
Gaulle, Ho Chi Minh is much more an anti-Chinese North
Vietnam nationalist than a representative of 'world Communism'; what the Pentagon was doing in 1964–5 was, in
his view, to throw North Vietnam into the arms of China....

*

De Gaulle, as he says, may all his life have had the same
'certain' idea of France. But he realizes fully that the France
of today cannot be the same as the France of Louis XIV
or of Napoleon, and that she must constantly adapt herself
to new conditions. Hence the new kind of 'eminence' she
has acquired in recent years. All the same, there is much in
Gaullism which can be traced back to his early upbringing,
and which also has certain ideological and philosophical
cousins both on the Right and the Left. Much has, of course,
been made of de Gaulle's *maurrassisme*; no doubt he was
familiar in his youth with the writings of Charles Maurras
and with the *Action Française* generally. He sympathized
with Maurras's anti-parliamentarianism; his advocacy of

the Strong State; his concept of Graeco-Latin civilization as the highest of all civilizations (there were echoes of this in de Gaulle's slightly incongruous speeches during his progress across Latin America in 1964); and though he cannot possibly have approved of Maurras's lunatic *la France seule* concept in its Vichy context, the phrase itself was not without charm for him. He has also tended, at various times, to share Maurras's deep-seated antipathy for the 'Anglo-Saxons' and, above all, to make much of his famous distinction between *le pays légal* and *le pays réel* – a concept of which there are echoes in countless de Gaulle speeches, like the first statement made after the Algiers *putsch*.

Similarly, Gaullism has some ideological cousins on the Left; the French anti-Atlantic 'neutralism' of 1949–50, as advocated by papers like *Le Monde*, *Combat*, and *Observateur*, and cherished by large groups of French intellectuals with their dislike of both America and Russia, is one of them.

Of course, it is no use over-simplifying. Thus, de Gaulle may be said to be 'anti-American'; but at the time of the Cuban Crisis in 1962, he made it quite clear to Kennedy that France was on the side of the United States, and he was wholehearted about it. In the same way, it is absurd to exaggerate de Gaulle's *maurrassisme*. Here there is an important *personal* element in de Gaulle which is very different from the approach of Maurras. Maurras radiated hatred. For fifty years his writings were just one continuous song of hate – hate for democracy, for the politicians, for Germany, for England, for Communism, for international finance, for Jews and Freemasons. De Gaulle, on the other hand, is rich in contempt, but very poor in hatred. Apart from monstrosities like Hitler, perhaps the only man in the world he really hated was Roosevelt. For, to him, Roosevelt was the man who persisted in humiliating France and humiliating de Gaulle.

And although de Gaulle has been called a 'dictator', he is one of the most un-bloodthirsty dictators the world has ever seen. There is no streak of cruelty in de Gaulle, and he certainly hates physical violence. His attitude to torture in Algeria, which made him wince, was much less cynical than Mollet's or Lacoste's. He hated to think of the French army engaged in such degrading practices.

Nor does he divide humanity into good and bad categories, as Maurras tended to do. The interests of France come first. If he thinks it in the interests of France to include Thorez and other Communists in his government, he does so, as in 1945-6. If he thinks it in her interests to make an alliance with Soviet Russia, he goes to see Stalin in Moscow. There is, furthermore, a complete lack of racialism in de Gaulle. Félix Eboué, the first French governor in Africa to go over to the Free French in 1940, was a negro; and de Gaulle has always treated negroes as equals. Nor has he ever shown the slightest sign of anti-Semitism, and what anti-Semitism there was among the Free French at London in 1940-1, he promptly stamped out. In his view, there are good Jews and bad Jews, just as there are good and bad Frenchmen; some of his worst enemies in London were Jews – the Gombaults and Louis Lévy, but so were also some of his most ardent supporters – René Cassin, Georges Boris, and many others.

*

It has also been said that de Gaulle is 'inhuman', his human feelings crushed by his all-embracing sense of mission. I think this is quite untrue. If there is any 'inhumanity' about de Gaulle, it is, as I once observed, a kind of warm inhumanity, like that of a prince of the Church. But even that is perhaps putting it too strongly. He can certainly be roused to deep emotion: in his *Mémoires* there is a notable passage where he describes how, on hearing of Bir Hakeim, the first real French victory on land, he locked himself up in a room and wept. It is also well known how he showered the most tender and pathetic affection on that idiot daughter of his, who finally died at the age of twenty in 1948.

There is somewhere, deep down in de Gaulle, a rich store of genuine Christian charity; it does not often openly manifest itself, but it is there, and it would be rash to attribute his attitude to Africans, for instance, to sheer hard-headed calculation; he seems genuinely conscious of the plight of the under-developed countries. . . .

It has also been said that de Gaulle is humourless. This again is untrue. His humour is very like Churchill's – mocking and ironical. Could anything, for instance, be more Churchillian than his comment on the P.S.U., the small 'independent socialist' party: 'Oh yes, that party with six members and seven tendencies!' Or the story of the English lady who, back from a visit to Australia, was raving to him at dinner about all the wonderful beasts and birds she had seen there. Finally, de Gaulle, very bored turned to her with: 'I'm told they've also got kangaroos'.

There are, indeed, no end of *mots*, true or apocryphal, attributed to de Gaulle. If he were completely humourless, it would have been impossible for the satirical journal, *Le Canard Enchaîné*, to run for years a brilliant weekly feature called *The Court*. In this superb imitation of the Saint-Simon *Memoirs* on the Court of Louis XIV, are related the weekly goings-on at the Elysée Palace; and many of the 'King's' stinging remarks are known to have been actually uttered by de Gaulle only a few days before. . . . Some of the *mots* are invented, but not all. His is not a gay, *méridional* kind of humour; it is Northern, and on the dry side, without the usual French *persiflage* and irresponsibility – two qualities among his countrymen he particularly dislikes.

Whether, ultimately, both his régime and his foreign policy will succeed or not, today de Gaulle is the last great figure of the Second World War, and one of the most important men on the international scene. It took him a long time to be taken very seriously; Churchill, Roosevelt, Stalin persistently refused to do so; and it was not perhaps till 1958, or even 1962–3, that de Gaulle, through sheer persistence, attained the world stature of a major statesman. It was a long and arduous climb. How did it all start?

2. The Family Background – Early Years

Charles-André-Joseph-Marie de Gaulle was born on 22 November 1890 at an old house belonging to his mother's family in the rue Princess in Lille, an unlovely smoky city of the North, lacking all the charm of southern or central France. De Gaulle is, indeed, a northerner, wholly devoid of the fantasy and gay irresponsibility one usually associates with the Midi. His father, Henri de Gaulle, had married in 1886 Jeanne Maillot-Delannoy. Both his father's and mother's family belonged to the conservative and Catholic bourgeoisie of the North. But, unlike his mother, whose family owned a tobacco factory at Dunkirk, his father could claim aristocratic descent. In de Gaulle's family tree there figures a Richard de Gaulle who, in 1210, was given the fief of Elbeuf by Philippe-Auguste. Two centuries later, 'the valiant knight, Messire Jehan de Gaulle' fought the English archers in 1415 at the Battle of Agincourt. In 1418, after a further defeat at the hands of the English, he refused to take service under Henry V and had his Norman domain confiscated.[1] Other de Gaulles are to be found in the history of France; and it appears to be established that de Gaulle's direct ancestors were particularly active in the eighteenth century as both soldiers and Crown lawyers, thus belonging to the so-called *noblesse de robe ou d'épée*. De Gaulle's great-grandfather, Jean-Baptiste-Philippe, was ruined by the Revolution and narrowly escaped the guillotine, but we find

1. Paul-Marie de La Gorce, *De Gaulle entre deux mondes*, Paris, 1964, p. 14.

him, under Napoleon, holding again a high government position as director of posts in the Grande Armée. The literary and scholarly tradition in the de Gaulle family can be traced back to his two paternal grandparents. His grandfather, Julien-Philippe de Gaulle, wrote a *History of Paris and its Surroundings*, with a preface by Charles Nodier, the famous Romantic writer, and edited a *History of St Louis* at the request of the Society for the History of France. It was also he who drew up the de Gaulle family tree. More remarkable was the literary career of his grandmother, Josephine-Anne-Marie Maillot, who wrote a successful novel and a travel book on the North of France, a biography of Chateaubriand – a writer whom she admired as much as her illustrious grandson was to do – and a *Life of O'Connell, Liberator of Ireland*. She also showed a certain socialist and revolutionary romanticism as editor of a journal in which she published some of the early works of Jules Vallès and commented favourably on the writings of Proudhon. One of de Gaulle's biographers traces back to her influence a certain 'liberal' streak in de Gaulle, and his 'feminism' as well. It was under de Gaulle in 1945 that women were at last given that vote which the Third Republic had persistently refused them.

Henri de Gaulle, Charles de Gaulle's father, the second of Julien-Philippe's three sons, who was born in 1848, seems to have inherited few of his mother's progressive and 'socialist' ideas. He married a cousin, Jeanne Maillot-Delannoy, a member of his mother's family. Her two sisters were nuns, and, in the words of de Gaulle himself, 'she had an intransigent passion for France, equal only to her religious piety'. Like his wife, Henri de Gaulle was intensely conservative and patriotic, and France's defeat in 1870–71 had left a deep mark on him. He himself had fought in that war, and had been wounded in an unsuccessful sortie during the siege of Paris. A war memorial was later erected near the spot where he had been wounded, and when Charles de Gaulle was still a child, his father would take him and the four other children on pilgrimages to it. This represented a broken sword, and bore this epitaph: 'The sword of France, broken while in their valiant hands, shall be forged anew by their descendants.'

Significantly, in his book, *La France et son Armée*, which de Gaulle published in 1938, the three chapters on the period covering his childhood and early youth were called '*Vers la revanche*'. The cult of the Army, with dreams of a *revanche* against Germany and of the recovery of Alsace-Lorraine, undoubtedly coloured de Gaulle's outlook on life during his childhood and adolescence. Both his father and mother were also fervent Catholics and, about the time of his birth, his father became lay headmaster of the Jesuit College of the Immaculate Conception in the rue Vaugirard in Paris. Later, in 1907, when the Jesuits were expelled from France, he liquidated the school, but founded a private school of his own, the Ecole Fontanes, in the rue du Bac. In all these schools Henri de Gaulle taught Latin, Greek, philosophy and literature. The more conservative part of the bourgeoisie liked to send their children to schools like these, and the future Marshals de Lattre de Tassigny and Leclerc de Hauteclocque, the future Cardinal Gerlier and the writer Georges Bernanos (highly conservative at first) were among Henri de Gaulle's pupils.

There can be little doubt that Henri de Gaulle was Royalist and anti-republican, and he is even said to have been a personal friend of Charles Maurras, the royalist leader, fire-eating anti-republican and anti-semitic thinker and pamphleteer, the most rabid supporter of the anti-Dreyfus cause.

De Gaulle's own books inevitably pose one central question. To what extent are these history, and to what extent are they merely an *apologia pro vita sua*? Does de Gaulle tell in his *Mémoires* or even in *La France et son Armée*, with its curiously autobiographical undertones, what he really felt as an adolescent, and what he was *really* told by his parents, particularly by his father? Or does he give an account of himself and of the pre-1914 period as he thinks, in retrospect, it should be given? It is curious, for instance, that there should be no mention of Maurras either as a personal acquaintance of the de Gaulle family, or even as a political influence on himself. It is, of course, inconceivable that de Gaulle should not, like all the conservative youth of his generation, have been a reader of *L'Action Française*. But, in retrospect, he obviously looked upon *maurrassisme* as a pernicious factor in the history of France – not only during the Second World War, when Maurras became Vichy's leading ideologist and even adapted himself to the German occupation in 1942, but also in the 1930s, when the *Action Française* acted as a major disruptive and defeatist influence in the French Army. So if young de Gaulle was *maurrassien*, he did not like to admit it in later years.

Of his father he merely says this:

My father, a man of thought, culture and tradition, was permeated by his feeling for the dignity of France. He discovered History for me. ... Nothing in Paris struck me more deeply than the symbols of our glory: night descending on the Notre-Dame, the majesty of the evening at Versailles, the sunlit Arc de Triomphe, the captured enemy banners under the porch of the Invalides.

He rejoiced when France was successful – when he saw the enthusiasm with which the French welcomed their ally, the Tsar; or the wonders of the 1900 Exhibition, or the first flights of French airmen.

But nothing saddened me more than our weaknesses and our errors which were revealed to me in my childhood by the faces around me, and the words I heard spoken: our withdrawal at Fashoda, the Dreyfus Affair, labour conflicts and religious discord. And nothing moved me so much as stories of our past misfortunes ... such as my mother's story of her own despair when, as a small girl, she saw both her parents in tears: 'Bazaine has capitulated!'[1]

Of the political words spoken in his family while he was a child, he says very little; but one can imagine how a family like de Gaulle's was affected by Fashoda, where the English had 'humiliated' France. Perhaps de Gaulle's partial antipathy for England in later years may be partly traced back to Fashoda. As for the Dreyfus Affair, in a memorable passage which de Gaulle wrote in 1938 he deplored the fearful strife inside France to which this was to give rise for years, with all the dirty intrigues and forgeries and mutual slander. Above all, what hurt him most was that, as a result of the Dreyfus Affair, a great part of the French people began to hate and despise the Army and the military hierarchy. Although there had, to all appearances, been a miscarriage of justice, the anti-Dreyfusards wanted to preserve the infallibility of a command devoted to the service of the country – and did so 'either in good faith, or for reasons of State'. On the strength of this passage written thirty-five years after the *Affaire*, one of de Gaulle's biographers concludes that de Gaulle's father, 'as distinct from the traditional environment to which he belonged, was personally convinced of Dreyfus's innocence'.[2] This seems a very rash conclusion. What is certain is that, in de Gaulle's view, the Dreyfus Affair had 'weakened' France. It gave rise to antimilitarism and pacifism; the Army Law of 1905 substantially reduced the size of the French Army:

As a result of pacifist illusions and a distrust of the military spirit, the Army was going to lose its former strength and cohesion.[3]

1. *Mémoires de guerre*, vol. 1, p. 2.
2. La Gorce, op.cit., p. 24.
3. *La France et son Armée*, p. 213. He also deplored the popularity of satirical books on army life, especially Courteline's.

Those years were also marked by a wave of militant anti-clericalism in France, with the separation of Church and State, which can only have distressed the de Gaulle family. There was also something else that seems to have worried young de Gaulle. From the Revolution up to the Paris Commune, the French working class had, he says, been nationalist and patriotic. Now many began to believe in internationalism – with no enemies, except the enemies of the proletariat.[1] The inclusion of the Commune among the respectable manifestations of the French spirit is typical of de Gaulle; it had, in his view, been largely prompted by national patriotic motives. Many years later he was, by the same token, to 'cooperate' with the Communists when these, at the time of the Liberation, were prepared to work for the victory and restoration of France.

De Gaulle received his secondary education at Jesuit colleges – first in his father's school and then, when this was closed in 1907, at a Jesuit college in Belgium. He then returned to Paris to prepare for the entrance examination at the famous military school of St Cyr. The education he had received was the typical classical training of his time, complete with a good grasp of mathematics but, above all, of Latin and Greek, and an asiduous study of the French classics, especially of the seventeenth century. De Gaulle's cultivation of a 'noble' style of writing, derived from the classics – Bossuet and Chateaubriand are his most obvious models[2] – finds its closest parallel perhaps in the writings and speeches of Winston Churchill, a man with whom, despite their love-hate relationship, he has so many other points in common. Little light is thrown, however, by his biographers or himself on the contemporary writers who influenced his way of thinking when he was a young man; but he had, obviously, read not only Maurras (whose *Kiel*

1. ibid, p. 212.
2. François Mauriac, *De Gaulle*, Paris, 1964, p. 126.

et Tanger – that 'clarion call to prepare for war' – had come out in 1910), but also Nietzsche, Bergson, Barrès, and Péguy – all these constituting a potent corrective to the hidebound monarchism of Maurras.[1] Curiously, de Gaulle's 'certain idea' of France is more reminiscent of Péguy than of any other writer. And Nietzsche? He speaks with some disdain of the 'Nietzschean' Germans of 1914 (*La France et son Armée*, p. 248); yet there are obvious, if unconscious, echoes of Nietzsche in *Le fil de l'épée* and so many other manifestations of de Gaulle's own 'personality cult'. Another writer who undoubtedly exercised a strong influence on de Gaulle was the *Action Française* historian, Jacques Bainville, with his central idea that German unity must again be smashed, since only a disunited Germany was 'safe'.

*

Young de Gaulle's determination to become a soldier was typical of his family milieu. Whatever his exact feelings about the Republic, the Army remained the quintessence of France, not only the noble national instrument of colonial expansion (on which much could be said one way or the other) but, above all, the weapon that would protect France against invasion, and even win back Alsace-Lorraine.

What little evidence there is of de Gaulle's political views in those years tends to show that he was neither monarchist (as

1. In Bergson de Gaulle saw 'a revival of French spirituality', as he himself later put it; and Barrès, while rejecting Maurras's monarchy as 'repellent' to the French, cultivated a kind of French version of *Blut und Boden* nationalism bordering on racialism, with a peculiar brand of 'socialism' thrown in since, in his view, capitalism tended to disunite the nation. In reality, this 'socialism' was not very different from Mussolini's future corporatism, itself a concept not very different from what de Gaulle himself was to favour during his 'silliest' R.P.F. period of 1947–52, when he liked to think in terms of his capital-labour 'association'.

his father apparently still continued to be 'in principle'),
nor enthusiastic about the Republic. But there were certain
republican leaders whom he genuinely admired: Clemenceau, who had waged for years a campaign against frittering
away France's strength on remote colonial expeditions,
instead of concentrating her attention on the Rhine;
Barthou, who got through Parliament the three-year service
law of 1913, which increased the standing army to 750,000
men; Poincaré, who was elected President of the Republic
that year, was a man of great caution, 'but who was seeing
the war coming not without something of a secret hope'.
(*La France et son Armée*, p. 273). There is little doubt that
such a 'secret hope' was shared by young men like de
Gaulle.

In August 1909 he passed the entrance examination to St
Cyr, but in accordance with a recent law, had first to spend a
year in the Army as an ordinary soldier. He was drafted into
the 33rd Infantry Regiment at Arras, and here, perhaps for
the first time in his life, mixed with 'ordinary' Frenchmen,
his fellow-conscripts, most of them, like himself, northerners
– peasants' and miners' sons. At St Cyr, where he then spent
two years, he was among the first ten of that year's *pro-
motion*, the top graduate being the future Marshal Alphonse
Juin. He returned, as a sub-lieutenant, to his old regiment,
whose colonel was none other than Philippe Pétain. But, as
La Gorce says, 'this coincidence was of no significance. The
commander of a regiment in those days was totally in-
accessible to an ordinary trooper, and very remote even to a
sub-lieutenant'. (op.cit., p. 39)

When the war broke out, Lieutenant de Gaulle was 23
years old.

3. *In the First World War*

There are not many pages in all de Gaulle's writings as
striking as those in *La France et son Armée* on the first stages

of the 1914 war. He notes the great enthusiasm with which the troops first went to the Front; he rejoices, even in retrospect, over that *union sacrée* which united the entire French nation in the supreme moment of danger.

Not a single group to protest against the mobilization. Not a single strike to interfere with it. Not a single vote in parliament to refuse the war credits. ... Even the suspects figuring in *Carnet B* now begged to be sent to the Front.

But the war was not what all these people had imagined it to be. The first clashes with the Germans turned out to be an 'immense surprise':

Tactically, the realization of the German fire power made nonsense of the current military doctrines. Morally, all the people's illusions, with which they had steeled themselves, went up in smoke. ... Between 20 and 23 August a perfect sense of security was turned into a frantic feeling of danger. (p. 238).

And there follows, in de Gaulle's story, an account of various engagements, in which the French were slaughtered by the hundreds in an unequal battle while the Germans suffered almost no casualties. 'Soon it became only too clear that all the bravery in the world could not cope with such fire-power'. Already, among the French troops, there were moments of panic and demoralization. This was, however, still unusual and, during the disastrous weeks before the Marne, the Germans took relatively few French prisoners. In short, there was nothing like what France was to see in 1917, let alone 1940.

And yet, those first unhappy battles were to be followed by a precipitate French retreat. Nearly the whole north of France was lost, with its economic and industrial wealth, and Paris seemed in imminent danger. The Russian offensive in East Russia had, no doubt, relieved the pressure on France; but had it not been for Joffre, the game would still have been lost. 'The German, incomparable when acting according to plan, loses his grip once the unforeseen happens.' Joffre's tactics and strategy on the Marne 'were what the Germans had least expected. Moreover, in September the French troops fought no longer the way they had fought in August.' And now 'the charm was broken. For the first time in over a century France had defeated Germany in a general battle.'

As early as 15 August Lieutenant de Gaulle was wounded for the first time while fighting on the Belgian frontier. Having returned to his regiment in January 1915, he was wounded a second time two months later. If de Gaulle speaks with enthusiasm of the Battle of the Marne, he speaks with nothing but horror and disgust of that trench warfare of 1915–16, with its blood and mud, its aimlessness and frustration, the fearful casualties suffered by the French compared with those inflicted on the Germans. During 1915 alone, in just France, the French suffered 1,350,000 casualties; and the Germans, 550,000. The French equipment was inadequate, and 'past errors had to be paid for in human lives, those human lives of which we were so short'. In the infantry alone, 'by the end of 1915, one career officer in two had been either killed or crippled'. The mutinies that finally spread through the French Army in 1917, de Gaulle regards as more than understandable; it is surprising, he says, that they did not break out long before. He then credits Pétain with having reduced the damage to a minimum by treating the mutineers with understanding and a relative humanity.

It is not quite clear when exactly de Gaulle came to the conclusion that Pétain was France's greatest general in the First World War; but this was the view he expressed repeatedly after the war, and one from which he did not depart even after 1940. In retrospect, indeed, de Gaulle considered Pétain one of the few French generals who long before 1914, had understood the real nature of the coming clash. His doctrine, summarized in the phrase, *le feu tue*, stressed the

utmost importance of heavy artillery, and the total in-
adequacy of the famous seventy-five mm. gun which was
then considered the backbone of the French army. The
pounding that the French received in 1914, the fearful
casualties they suffered in 1915 and 1916 from the superior
fire power of the Germans were what Pétain had foreseen;
no doubt his formula 'the gun conquers, infantry occupies'
was not impeccable, but it was typical of Pétain's aversion to
'fighting with men against equipment' and partly accounts
for his reluctance to embark on murderous offensives at any
price – an attitude which, in turn, made Poincaré and others
later charge him with gutlessness, pessimism and defeatism.
When, in 1917, at the height of the French army mutinies,
Pétain was able to calm and reassure the mutineers, it was
largely because these were aware of Pétain's unwillingness to
waste human lives indiscriminately. So, in de Gaulle's view,
it was Pétain who, at the height of the 1917 crisis, 'saved
France'.

Much later, he was also to compare himself with Pétain –
the 'unorthodox' Pétain who had foreseen before 1914 the
cardinal importance of heavy artillery, and the 'unorthodox'
de Gaulle who, defying the official General Staff doctrine,
had foreseen, long before 1940, the equally cardinal importance of tanks. If, in the 1930s, Pétain did not share de
Gaulle's views, it was because, by then, he was living in the
past and had gone hopelessly senile.

*

By the time of the 1917 mutinies de Gaulle was a prisoner in
Germany. At Verdun on 2 March 1916 he was wounded in a
bayonet charge and left unconscious on the battlefield, where
the Germans picked him up. He was 'posthumously'
awarded the Legion of Honour, and a warm tribute was
paid him by General Pétain in person.

He made five attempts to escape, but his unusual tallness

made camouflage difficult. In the end, he was imprisoned at
Ingolstadt, in Bavaria, a prison earmarked for officers who
had made several attempts to escape. Among his fellow-
prisoners were the future General Catroux, the only five-star
general to join the Free French in 1940, and a Russian
officer, the future Soviet Marshal Tukhachevsky.

4. Post-War Disillusionment – Pétain – De Gaulle, 'Man of Destiny' – His Prophetic Book

Soon after his return from captivity, de Gaulle, still only a
captain, joined a Polish infantry division formed in France
under the command of General Joseph Haller. After being
moved to Poland, this division fought the Russians, first in
Volhynia and then in the Battle of the Vistula where
Weygand acted as French military adviser to Pilsudski. The
Russian offensive against Warsaw failed and, when the war
was over, de Gaulle stayed for some time in Poland to teach
at a military college. What impressed him during the whole
campaign was not only that a Tsarist officer like Tukhachevsky should continue to serve Russia, regardless of her régime,
but that the poverty-stricken Polish peasantry should, like
one man, have fought for Poland, and should have remained
totally immune to Bolshevik propaganda. This, to de
Gaulle, was natural; it was only in France, in 1940, that,
much to his disgust, he was to find this 'natural' national
reflex sadly lacking, especially among a large part of the
French bourgeoisie.

On his return to France in 1921 he married Yvonne
Vendroux, the daughter of a Calais industrialist.[1]

*

1. The Vendroux were actually biscuit manufacturers. According to a
recent catty paragraph in Viansson-Ponté, de Gaulle did not like to be
reminded of this fact, and even took it badly when at a reception in a
French town the local mayor wanted to please him by displaying an
old publicity plate marked 'Biscuits Vendroux'!

For a time, after his marriage, he taught military history at St Cyr, and then spent two years as a student at the École Supérieure de la Guerre, the staff college for the officer *élite*.

Among his teachers and superiors he was noted for his brilliance, intelligence, high culture and phenomenal memory. He was also noted for his nonconformism, his 'self-sufficiency', his arrogance, and conduct 'like a king in exile'. The majority of the military teaching staff were antipathetic to him and he barely scraped through with a '*Bien*'. When informed of this, Marshal Pétain, by this time a personal friend and 'protector' of de Gaulle's, urged that de Gaulle be given a '*Très bien*', but in vain. De Gaulle was furious.

A very strange episode now occurred in the de Gaulle-Pétain relationship. Since 1920 or 1921 Pétain had taken a great liking to de Gaulle, and considered him one of the most brilliant officers of the younger generation. De Gaulle was a frequent guest at the Marshal's house, and in 1921 Pétain became the godfather of de Gaulle's son Philippe, named after the Marshal.[1] In 1925, when Pétain was vice-president of the Supreme War Council and so generalissimo-designate in case of war, he appointed Captain de Gaulle to his secretariat. In 1927 de Gaulle was promoted to the rank of major, and Pétain demanded that General Hering, the

---

Their family life appears to have been a happy and harmonious one apart from the tragedy of one daughter who was mentally defective and died in 1948.

There is an astonishing description in Tournoux's *Pétain et de Gaulle* of de Gaulle's tender and compassionate care for his idiot child – a 'mongol' with a big tongue hanging out. He would seat her on his knee, and he was the only person she never scratched. He appears, in fact, to be genuinely devoted to all the members of his family.

1. He was, in fact, his 'lay' godfather; his godparents in the eyes of the church were de Gaulle's father, Henri de Gaulle, and Mme Jacques Vendroux, the child's maternal grandmother. It would have offended the older de Gaulles if Pétain had been the child's godfather in the 'church' sense; he had married a divorced woman only a year before.

new head of the École Supérieure, let de Gaulle give a number of lectures at the school, adding that he, the Marshal, would introduce him and act as Chairman. It was an unprecedented request (or rather, order). Pétain said that the 'bien' awarded de Gaulle was scandalous and that it had prevented him from becoming a teacher at the Staff College; he (Pétain) accordingly wished its students to 'listen to de Gaulle all the same'. This request caused considerable commotion inside the school and, but for the high patronage of the Marshal, the very subject of the major's lectures would have been thought an intolerable piece of impertinence; they dealt with nothing less than Leadership, i.e. a subject that, on the face of it, directly concerned the High Command.[1] After delivering his lectures – which were later, in 1932, incorporated in de Gaulle's famous book, *Le fil de l'épée* – at the École Supérieure, de Gaulle repeated them, also at Pétain's suggestion, before a larger audience at the Sorbonne.

From 1927 to 1929 Major de Gaulle served with the Army of Occupation in the Rhineland, and then spent two years in the Middle East. On the Middle East itself he commented at the time with some bitterness, saying that no human contact at all had been established in ten years between the French authorities and the people of Syria and the Lebanon, then under French Mandate.

Finally, in 1932, on Pétain's initiative, he became secretary of the *Conseil Supérieur de Défense Nationale*, a permanent body at the disposal of the government to organize the nation for war. Here, for five years, he was to stay close to the levers of military and political power, and acquire a first-hand understanding of military affairs in France.

Not only in retrospect, but certainly also at the time, he

1. This extraordinary episode is described in great detail in J.-R. Tournoux, *Pétain et de Gaulle*, Paris, 1964, pp. 102 ff.

had grave misgivings about both the military policy of France in the 1920s and 1930s, and about the effectiveness of the Third Republic. His service on the *Conseil Supérieur* coincided with Hitler's rise to power and German rearmament, alongside years of intense restlessness in France itself, marked by the rise of various forms of Fascism – which first fully manifested themselves in the Paris riots of 6 February 1934 – and by that left-wing reaction to them which took the form of the Popular Front.

Despite Pétain's patronage, de Gaulle's army career was far from spectacular; for nine years he had remained a captain. He did not become a major until 1927, lieutenant-colonel until 1932, and colonel until 1938; by this time, Alphonse Juin, his fellow-graduate of St Cyr, was already a general. The various reminiscences about de Gaulle in the 1920s are not particularly illuminating, but they stress a certain physical awkwardness about the man – an excessive tallness, a small head perched on a long neck, unusually long arms; a man given to brooding, but also one of great intellectual alertness and curiosity. In fact, the most important insight into the Major de Gaulle of those years is provided by his own writings, and, above all, by his extraordinary little book *Le fil de l'épée*, published in 1932, but written in part, as we have seen, as early as 1927. 1927 was the heyday of Poincarism in France. After the various commotions of the immediate post-war years – the abortive Ruhr Occupation in 1923, followed by the 'Locarno' era in 1925, and the great financial crisis of 1926 – France at last seemed, under the wise leadership of Poincaré, to have settled down to a long period of stability and prosperity. The Army, still resting on its hard-won laurels of 1914–18, ranked as 'the greatest Army in Europe', though nobody could be sure that this military superiority would last forever. The great victory of 1918 had cost France one and a half million men, not counting the hundreds of thousands of war

invalids; her birthrate was low; and although she had built
up an elaborate system of alliances in Europe (Poland,
Czechoslovakia, Rumania, Yugoslavia), her chief concern
was security. Without going into all the details of French
military doctrine during those years, one may say that the
men in charge of the French Army – all of them veterans of
the 1914–18 war, and largely themselves reflecting the
pacifism and war-weariness of the French people – thought,
first and foremost, in terms of preventing another invasion
of France. In 1929 the government and parliament adopted
the costly programme for building the so-called Maginot
Line, first between the Moselle and the Rhine, and then
along the Rhine itself. These fortifications were not completed until 1934, and owing to the financial difficulties of the
early 1930s, the Line was never to be properly extended
along the Franco-Belgian border, despite the latter's fearful
vulnerability.

Even before the building of the Maginot Line (which he
was later to criticize) de Gaulle already felt in 1927 that there
was something seriously wrong with the French army
command, as well as with the complacent pacifism of the
French people. He wrote in 1927:

The times through which we are living are ill-suited to the
choice and formation of military leaders. The very intensity of
our recent ordeal has had the effect of letting the spring of
determination run down too quickly. There has been a lowering
of pressure where strong character is concerned, and we are now
in a period of moral lassitude which has brought the profession of
arms into disrepute. ... In these sceptical days, the chain of
French military strength must not be allowed to sag, nor the
ardour and high quality of those born to command, to weaken.[1]

Le fil de l'épée – composed partly of lectures delivered,
between 1927 and 1932, and partly of articles written during
the same period – is, indeed, an astonishing book in more

1. C. de Gaulle, The Edge of the Sword, New York, 1960, p. 34.

ways than one. Few Frenchmen in those years of pacifism would have been anything but shocked by de Gaulle's glorification of war:

Although Lucifer has used war for his purposes, so sometimes has also the Archangel. With what virtues has it not enriched the moral capital of mankind! Because of it, courage, devotion and nobility have scaled the peaks. ... War has been an instrument of the best and of the worst. It has brought to birth both infamy and greatness. ... And it is an illusion that the role of the warrior ... is now destined to disappear.[1]

But this is not so much a glorification of war as an expression of the certainty that war will come again, and perhaps soon.

Even more famous than these reflections on war is de Gaulle's characterization of the ideal leader of men (and the ideal military leader) as a man with three essential elements: *a doctrine, character, and prestige*. This little book of just over a hundred pages has sometimes been described as de Gaulle's *Mein Kampf*. In some ways it is even more uncannily prophetic, and the passages in which the 'future' de Gaulle is described have frequently been quoted. This, for instance:

The passion to act by one's self is accompanied by a certain roughness. The man of character embodies the harshness inherent in his effort. His subordinates feel it, and often suffer from it. Such a chief is distant, because authority does not go without prestige, and prestige does not go without distances being kept.

And then – this prophesy of 1940:

But when the danger becomes pressing ... a kind of tidal wave sweeps a man of character right to the forefront. ... Where, indeed, did one ever see a great human task being achieved without a man of character feeling this irresistible urge to act? ... Nothing would have been achieved if counsels of base caution

1. ibid., pp. 73–4.

had prevailed. ... More than that: those who do great things must often *ignore the conventions of a false discipline*. Thus in 1914 Lyautey kept Morocco despite orders from above; and after the Battle of Jutland Lord Fisher bitterly complained of Jellicoe's dispatches: 'He has all Nelson's qualities, except one: he has not learned to disobey.'[1]

But if the book clearly foreshadows the de Gaulle who, in 1940, ignored, like so many of his heroes, 'the counsels of faint-hearted prudence and modesty', it also throws some light on the obscure army officer of 1927 or 1932:

In his relations with his superiors he is generally at a disadvantage. He is too sure of himself, too conscious of his strength to let his conduct be influenced by a mere wish to please. ... The authorities dread any officer who has the gift of making decisions and cares nothing for routine and soothing words. 'Arrogant and undisciplined' is what the mediocrities say of him.[2]

5. *The Battle for the New Army*

In 1934 de Gaulle published *Vers l'armée de métier*. In later years, it was to be part of the Gaullist mythology to claim that if only France had listened to the advice it contained, the disaster of 1940 would have been avoided. This is, of course, an over-simplification.

De Gaulle's book should, first of all, be looked at in its original 1934 context. What he then said about the ineffectiveness of the Maginot Line and the fearful vulnerability of France along her Belgian border strikes one today as totally elementary. Anyone with a minimum of common sense should have seen it. But that was not the view held either by the French Army leaders, or by an inert and pacifist public opinion, which, somehow, assumed that there was nothing wrong with the French Army. As tactfully as possible, de Gaulle demonstrated that something, in fact, was very seriously wrong with this Army. It was, in the

1. ibid., p. 45.   2. ibid., p. 43.

main, composed of men with no proper experience of handling modern weapons of war. As a result he predicted, 'there will be a fearful waste of both men and equipment when it comes to the test'. In 1934, the military service for conscripts lasted only one year, and during that year they learned next to nothing. There was specialization in the navy and the airforce, but not on land, and what specialists there were, were lost in the crowd. De Gaulle himself, called for the constitution of six mechanized, motorized and largely armoured divisions, which would be a striking force immediately available in any emergency. Very rightly, he argued that the current French military system, based on the defence of France's frontiers, took, in fact, no account of France's allies in Eastern Europe.

Whether we like it or not, we are part of an established order in Europe, and we cannot confine ourselves to the defence of our frontiers. Think how much blood and how many tears we were to shed in 1870–71 for having given Prussia a free hand at Sadowa in 1866. If we do not want to be isolated and be left to the mercy of the enemy, we must be ready to act outside our frontiers at any moment and on every occasion.[1]

Here was a clear warning against letting Nazi Germany reoccupy the Rhineland, then Austria, then Czechoslovakia, until the day when France would, in fact, be virtually alone, and 'left to the enemy's mercy'. Quick action, de Gaulle argued, was not possible, if it depended on the slow job of mobilizing reserves. He had no great illusions about Britain's supplying sufficient help in time to save France from her 'isolation'. Belgium had fought gallantly in 1914; but there was no guarantee whatsoever that that country composed of two different races, a 'new, suspicious and touchy' country, would commit itself to the hilt. 'There may be no Albert I next time; let us not expect Belgium to sacrifice herself to protect us.' Sure enough, two years later, Belgium

1. *Vers l'armée de métier*, p. 87.

broke her alliance with France and Britain. In short, the
Maginot Line, though valuable up to a point, was not
necessarily invulnerable if attacked by heavy tanks, a modern
air force and gas; it lacked depth. And, worst of all, it could
be by-passed through Belgium.

The French concept of the Armed Nation was also in-
comparably more wasteful than a professional army – one of
100,000 men which should, de Gaulle argued, be the spearhead of conscript forces. Although, de Gaulle declared,
'nobody could seriously imagine that the next war would be
like the last one', contemporary French military doctrine
was, somehow, assuming that it would not be very different
from 1914–18 – except that, this time, the Germans would
scarcely be able to invade France. This, de Gaulle held, was
all wrong, and it was essential that France should have a
powerful striking force, which should be ready, if need be, to
invade Germany. He did not hesitate to call such a force
'preventive'.

There are, of course, weaknesses in de Gaulle's argument.
He did not foresee Hitler's boundless ambitions. He thought
'the era of great conquests closed'; doubted whether Hitler
would aim at much more than 'limited objectives', such as
Austria or the Saar, or whether Italy would want anything
more than 'the Dalmatian Coast'. Long after the event, his
critics, such as that old Vichyite, Alfred Favre-Luce, ridiculed
de Gaulle's 'prophetic book' for not having realized the full
importance that *planes*, as well as tanks, would play in
the future invasion of France, and for not having specifically endowed his own *armée de métier* with dive-bombers.

There is another weakness in de Gaulle's argument. His
blueprint for a professional army laid down *six years* as the
period necessary to constitute it, which suggests that he did
not foresee the spectacular speed of German rearmament.
Could this elite army of 100,000 men have saved France in
1940? One may doubt it; de Gaulle himself speaks of

Germany's immense superiority over France in human, industrial and economic resources. What is certain, however, is that *if at least part of such a striking force had been available in 1936, it could have prevented Hitler's re-occupation of the Rhineland, and so the war itself.* Without this re-occupation of the Rhineland, there is unlikely to have been the Anschluss, and certainly there would have been no Munich, with its dismemberment of Czechoslovakia.

*

De Gaulle's book made very little impact on the France of 1934; she was, as he put it, 'suffering from an anti-war psychosis which went to dangerous extremes', especially at a time when, in Germany, a 'war-like nationalism' was being excited. But there were other reasons for the failure of de Gaulle's proposals. The year 1934 saw the rise of various brands of Fascism in France, as exemplified by the Concorde riots of 6 February. When, some time after the publication of the book, the right-wing *Echo de Paris* published several articles drawing attention to de Gaulle's ideas, the Left, and particularly Léon Blum, the Socialist leader, were roused to righteous indignation, arguing that a professional army might well become the 'praetorian guard' of a Fascist régime in France, and was, anyway, contrary to the great democratic principle of Jaurès's *nation armée.*

The opposition came, furthermore, not only from the Left, obsessed, as it then was, by the 'Fascist danger', but also from the French generals. Paul Reynaud was, in fact, the only political leader to take up de Gaulle's proposals seriously in parliament, but with little or no effect. Reynaud's central argument was that there was a blatant contradiction between France's foreign policy, with its East European commitments, and her defensive military policy. General Maurin, who succeeded Pétain as Minister of War after the fall of the Doumergue government at the end of 1934, publicly declared in parliament: '*It would be pure folly to take the offensive. We have spent billions on the Maginot Line.*' As de Gaulle later remarked, it was easy for Hitler to draw appropriate conclusions from such remarks. Not that this defensive strategy had yet been finally adopted by 1935. Gamelin who had, that year, replaced Weygand as commander-in-chief, still thought the French could march into the Rhineland if Germany attempted to occupy Austria.[1]

In March 1935 Reynaud tabled in the Chamber of Deputies a Bill largely based on de Gaulle's book, providing for a striking force of six armoured divisions each with 500 heavy tanks, and proposing that the whole force be completed by April 1940. The Bill was rejected at the end of 1935. Three months later, Hitler occupied the Rhineland with impunity, and soon afterwards Belgium broke off her alliance with France. In pamphlets, articles and speeches Reynaud continued to agitate for an armoured force, but only to meet with either sharp opposition or indifference. The topbrass continued to think in terms of a 'static and continuous front'.[2]

French opinion was, in the main, wholly indifferent to this controversy. Since 1934, France had been in a state of ferment, and the May 1936 election resulted in a great victory of the Popular Front parties. What struck me most of all during the election campaign,[3] which began barely a month after Hitler's reoccupation of the Rhineland, was the almost unbelievable indifference to international affairs. De Gaulle, in his *Mémoires*, relates a very curious conversation he had some months later with Léon Blum, the head of the Popular Front government. Blum, who, two years later, was

1. Paul Reynaud, *La France a sauvé l'Europe*, Paris, 1947, vol. I, p. 321.

2. De Gaulle, *Mémoires de guerre*, Paris, 1954, vol. I, p. 5.

3. This is described in detail in my book, *The Destiny of France*, London, 1937.

to wring his hands over Munich, 'with a mixture of cowardly relief and shame', already then argued that France could do nothing to help Austria, Poland or Czechoslovakia, but consoled himself with the thought that they could only be 'temporarily submerged'; Hitler would accomplish nothing permanent, since France's defences made her invincible. De Gaulle wholly disagreed with this, but failed to convince Blum.

Throughout that period and right up to 1940, Daladier was Minister of War, and his dislike of de Gaulle was notorious. There is little doubt that Daladier had something to do with de Gaulle's removal from Paris in 1937, when he was promoted to the rank of colonel and placed in command of a tank regiment at Metz, to remain there for the next few years, far from the places where decisions were taken. In retrospect, he describes his deep pessimism in that immediate pre-war period. Already in May 1937 an entire new panzer division, with hundreds of planes flying overhead, paraded through the streets of Berlin. Ambassador François-Poncet was shaken; but still nothing was done in Paris. Then came the Anschluss, then Munich, and then the invasion of Poland and the war. As was to be expected, France was not going to help Poland, any more than she had helped Austria or Czechoslovakia. De Gaulle was not surprised or even out-raged by the Soviet-German Pact:

Poland was smashed in a fortnight by the panzer divisions and the Luftwaffe. No doubt the Polish rout was speeded up by Soviet intervention. But Stalin's decision to gang up with Hitler had clearly been dictated by his conviction that the French would not budge, that the Reich had a free hand in the East, and that it was preferable for Russia to share in the spoils than to become Hitler's victim herself. (*Mémoires*, vol. I, p. 22.)

One may well believe that the author of *Vers l'armée de métier* was deeply agitated during all those years between Hitler's reoccupation of the Rhineland in 1936 and the

outbreak of war in September 1939. In his *Mémoires* he
speaks harshly of the violent opposition which his ideas met
from the generals – Debeney, Weygand, Gamelin; and from
the War Ministers – General Maurin, M. Fabry and M.
Daladier. As for Pétain, de Gaulle scarcely made a secret of
his view at the time that the Marshal had gone gaga – and it
was, indeed, in 1938, that Pétain wrote a laudatory preface
to a preposterous book by General Chauvineau, *L'invasion
est-elle encore possible?*, in effect debunking de Gaulle's
theories on the cardinal role armour would play in the next
war, denouncing the *blitzkrieg* as moonshine, and defending
French defensive strategy, the 'continuous front', the
Maginot Line and the rest.

6. *Quarrel with Pétain*

It seems appropriate here to mention a seemingly insignificant episode, but one that has been held against de Gaulle
as an early example of his 'unscrupulousness', and which, in
retrospect, is also of some historical importance.

Those who knew of de Gaulle's strained relations with
Pétain must have rubbed their eyes as they read this dedication in a new book, *La France et son Armée*, that de Gaulle
published in 1938, about the time of Munich:

> To Marshal Pétain
> who wished this book to be written;
> who, with his counsels, helped in the writing of the first
> five chapters, and, thanks to whom, the last two are
> the story of our victory.

The story, an outraged Pétain tried to make out, was not as
complicated as it looked. Pétain had planned this book as
long ago as 1922, and de Gaulle was his ghost-writer. The
bulk of the book – an admirably-written popular history of
the Army throughout the history of France – had been
completed by 1928, but Pétain hesitated to publish it under

his name since, it seems, it was too obvious that he had not written it himself.[1] So the greater part of the book was to remain in Pétain's archives unpublished. De Gaulle, feeling that it would be a pity to waste so good a book which would, moreover, be 'good for morale', then decided to publish it under his own name, all the more so as he had written every word of it, and had also already used much of it for his lectures in the Rhineland and the Middle East.

Pétain was furious: first he demanded that the book should not be published at all; then, as 'a token of benevolence', he wrote both to de Gaulle and to Plon, the publisher, asking that a different dedication be published (he enclosed the text of this), and stressing that this piece of 'general staff work' could not be appropriated by de Gaulle, even though he admittedly *was* the author. When the book was nonetheless published with the original dedication, the Marshal charged de Gaulle with a gross 'breach of confidence'. De Gaulle shrugged the matter off by saying that the man was 82 and *gâteux*. The Marshal was to bear him a grudge for years afterwards, and often recalled the episode even after he had become head of the Vichy Government.

It is curious to think that this rather trivial episode should have marked, as it were, the beginning of the final breach between Pétain and de Gaulle.[2]

1. One story is that Lyautey had made some highly sarcastic remarks about Pétain's 'forthcoming' book and its alleged authorship.

2. The text of the Marshal's letters to both de Gaulle and Plon is reproduced in Tournoux op.cit. pp. 174–5. Tournoux adds that only a small number of copies of de Gaulle's book were sold, some of them already during the German occupation of France. It did not figure among the *verboten* books. My own copy, bought in 1938, is marked '7th thousand' – not much for a cheap paperback.

CHAPTER 3

THE 1940 DISASTER

THE grim story of the French débâcle in May–June 1940 has been told so often that it is necessary to do no more than summarize the main elements. Militarily, the war had begun in September 1939 under the worst possible conditions for France. Owing to the appeasement policy that the British and French governments had pursued for years – a policy encouraged (a) by British military weakness and pacifism; (b) by the French people's almost pathological horror of war after the fearful blood-letting of 1914–18; and (c) by the failure of the generals to build up an army that would correspond with France's foreign policy and treaty obligations – Britain and France found themselves, at the beginning of the war, in a state of virtual isolation, without any allies in the East – or in the West, for that matter. Munich had destroyed Czechoslovakia and, at the same time, discouraged Russia, a potentially-active anti-German Power. After the outbreak of war, Britain and France allowed Poland to be crushed within three weeks.

If, during the weeks before Munich, the fighting spirit among the French people was reasonably high (higher certainly than in 1936), it collapsed again after Munich, and was much worse in September 1939 than in September 1938. The Communists had been confused by the Soviet-German Pact, while the bourgeoisie, scared of the Popular Front, had in varying degrees developed strong fascist and/or defeatist leanings. Nor was there much enthusiasm for the war among the soldiers; still less, among the officers. Although active anti-war propaganda, either on the Right or the Left,[1] was prohibited by censorship, the main official propaganda lines during the 'phoney war' from September 1939 to May 1940 were that, thanks to the Maginot and other defence lines, France could not be invaded; and that, economically, France and Britain were much more powerful than Germany (*'nous vaincrons parce que nous sommes les plus forts'*). If anyone expressed any doubts about the Belgian border, officials, quoting M. Daladier, would say that a 'tremendous' system of field fortifications had been built there.

Throughout the bitterly cold winter of 1939–40, the French soldiers in the frontier areas were generally fed up and intensely bored. During the Soviet-Finnish war, a determined effort was made by right-wing propaganda to substitute Stalin for Hitler as Enemy Number One, and there was much disappointment on the Right when the Finns made peace. Then came Norway, and the dismal failure of the resistance there was only too obvious by the time that the Germans struck out in the West on 10 May.

The campaign went almost exactly as Reynaud and de Gaulle had foreseen it: an intensely mobile war, with no sign of any 'continuous front' developing anywhere. After their breakthrough at Sedan on 14 May, the German panzers swept all the way to the Channel with little or nothing to stop them. Large French and British forces were trapped in Belgium and Flanders; on 27 May the Belgian

1. In the right-wing press, e.g. the *Action Française*, widely read, particularly by reserve officers, the violent campaign against declaring war on Germany if she invaded Poland went on until the censorship clamped down a few days before war was declared. Although the Communists maintained at first an anti-Nazi line, even after the Soviet-German Pact, they started on their 'imperialist war' slogans, especially after the collapse of Poland; since the official Communist press was prohibited, this propaganda went on in the clandestine papers they published.

Army capitulated; and then came Dunkirk, where the evacuation was completed by 4 June. France was now in effect left entirely to her own devices. Most of her best troops had been lost in Belgium. And as was to be expected, the 'Weygand Line' along the Somme proved a myth. This was overrun by 6 June; a few days later, the Germans crossed the Seine near Rouen; on 14 June they entered Paris. Already on the 10th the French Government under Paul Reynaud had fled to Tours; the day Paris fell, it moved still further south, to Bordeaux.

Both the French nation and the army were, by now, completely demoralized. The German irruption into France a month earlier had come as a fearful shock, having instantly destroyed the 'Maginot Line' illusion on which France had been fed for years. Anyone who, like myself, was in France during that terrible month, will remember the millions of refugees streaming south in trains, in cars, on bicycles, even on foot; and will remember too the distress, anger and bewilderment of an entire nation – anger against the politicians, against the press with its 'Maginot Line' smokescreen, anger against the generals, anger against the English, especially after Dunkirk.[1]

He will remember the demoralization among the soldiers and the same old story of how the officers had 'fled in cars, leaving the soldiers behind'. Realizing, at least after the first week of June, that the war was lost, thousands of soldiers deserted.

Most of the French troops were under-equipped and under-trained, as well as psychologically unprepared to face the massive German tank attacks and the dive-bombers. It is not true, however, that 'the French didn't fight'. Many did not, but there were many who did. They fought well in

---

1. For a graphic description of the French scene of May–June 1940, see, for instance, the author's *The Last Days of Paris*, Hamish Hamilton, London, 1940.

Belgium and round Dunkirk; many soldiers manning the Maginot Line went on fighting even after the Armistice; the future Marshal de Lattre de Tassigny held up the Germans for many days at Rethel on the Aisne. And Colonel de Gaulle, having scraped together a couple of hundred tanks, effectively resisted the German pressure and counter-attacked during the whole second fortnight in May – first, at Montcornet, near Laon, then at Abbeville. Amidst the chaos of May 1940, this was, in de Gaulle's own view, a unique performance. Speaking of the Abbeville operation, he wrote, with a mixture of pride and melancholy:

> We failed in eliminating the German bridgehead at Abbeville entirely; we had reduced it, all the same, by three-quarters. ... Our losses were heavy, but less heavy than the enemy's. We captured 500 prisoners, in addition to the 130 already taken at Montcornet, and large quantities of arms and equipment. Alas! where else during the battle of France did the French reconquer a strip of land fourteen kilometres deep, where else ... were hundreds of Germans taken prisoner? (*Mémoires de guerre*, vol. I, p. 38.)

There were, he says, 3,000 tanks in France – as many as the Germans had; but they were scattered throughout the army, and there was no effective strong armoured force along the lines he had proposed which could smash the German onslaught.

Whether, as de Gaulle suggests, the war could have been 'won', had his advice been followed, is, of course, highly doubtful (after all, a year later, the Germans nearly defeated Russia); but the war in France would have lasted longer, and the French army would have given a much better account of itself.

As things were, de Gaulle realized at the end of May that not only his own battle of Abbeville was lost, but that the Battle of France was about to be lost, too. The Belgians had capitulated; the British – and some of the French – were being evacuated to England; one-third of the French army, trapped in Belgium and Flanders, could be written off.

In the course of the campaign, over 120,000 French soldiers had been killed within little more than a month; the German losses had been only 30,000 dead.

Now, after the Belgian capitulation and Dunkirk, the rest of the campaign seemed likely to be a walk-over for the German army. De Gaulle claims that he fully realized this on 30 May, and the question he then put to himself was whether the war would continue 'in the Empire'. Much depended on the politicians, and, even more so, on the army command, particularly on Pétain, now a member of the Reynaud Government, and on Weygand who, on 20 May (i.e. since the German invasion) had been appointed commander-in-chief in place of Gamelin. De Gaulle relates his meeting with Weygand on 1 June; Weygand left him in no doubt that he considered the position hopeless, and that he was preparing to sue for an armistice.

*

Ever since the beginning of the war, Colonel de Gaulle had viewed the situation with the greatest misgivings; he never, needless to say, shared in the official optimism of the 'maginotistes'. He drew up a memorandum in January 1940 – calling for the immediate constitution of heavy armoured shock units and foretelling a German invasion through Holland and Belgium and he sent this document to eighty political and military personalities. Having studied the Polish campaign of the previous September, he now (as distinct from 1934) also stressed the importance to France of an airforce cooperating with the tanks and infantry.

In his *Mémoires*, de Gaulle speaks not only of those who persisted in believing in the Maginot Line, but also of those highly influential persons, including Pétain, then still Ambassador in Franco Spain, who were dreaming of a peace settlement with the Germans. In March, there had been a change of government; Daladier had been succeeded by Paul Reynaud, who had, however, scraped through the Chamber of Deputies with a majority of no more than one. To keep his precarious parliamentary margin, Reynaud had accordingly to include in his cabinet all kinds of people[1] who were defeatist at heart, as well as Daladier, who clung to the post of Minister of War. Reynaud had offered de Gaulle the post of Under-Secretary of State, carrying a key position on the newly-constituted War Committee which consisted of the principal war leaders and ministers, but Daladier had vetoed such an appointment. It went, instead, to Paul Baudouin, an all-out defeatist, as it turned out and as might have been foreseen. After this abortive visit to Paris in March, de Gaulle had returned to his army post.

*

As we have seen, de Gaulle fought the Germans with unusual vigour during the second half of May and was, at that time, promoted 'temporarily' to the rank of Brigadier-General. On 5 June, in reshuffling his cabinet, from which Daladier had at last been eliminated, Reynaud appointed de Gaulle Under-Secretary of Defence. De Gaulle himself clearly saw that, by now, it was no longer a case of winning the war in France, but only of holding out as long as possible and of then continuing the war in North Africa, after transporting

1. In his *Mémoires* de Gaulle stresses that 'these people' in and around the government were far keener on a war against Russia than against Germany; they – among them Weygand – dreamed of bombing Baku from French Middle-East bases, and had wanted to give the maximum aid to Finland while the war there lasted. De Gaulle's arch-enemy Alfred Fabre-Luce claims that de Gaulle himself proposed, at the beginning of 1940, 'to send French tanks to Finland and to make war there on the Soviet Union'. He does not state on what evidence he makes this allegation. (A. Fabre-Luce, *The Trial of Charles de Gaulle*, p. 48, London, 1963). Whether true or not, there is nothing in de Gaulle's published writings to confirm this story.

there what was left of the French army and its equipment. De Gaulle reckoned that 500,000 valid soldiers could still be 'recuperated'. The transportation, however, required British help, and three days later de Gaulle went on his first mission to London. In the interval, he had seen Weygand again, who had dismissed the idea of continuing the war 'in the Empire' as childish. Within a week of the French defeat, he said, the British would negotiate a peace settlement with the Germans.

*

During his brief visit to London on 9 June, de Gaulle saw Churchill for the first time, and immediately concluded that Britain would continue to fight. But Churchill had the gravest doubts about the practicability of Reynaud's plans. Whatever happened later in North Africa, he flatly rejected de Gaulle's request that at least a part of the R.A.F., and particularly its fighters, be moved to the southern half of France.

De Gaulle returned to Paris that same night, his plane making an uneasy landing at le Bourget which had, shortly before, been bombed by the Germans. While he was conferring with Reynaud, Weygand suddenly burst in and declared that France must immediately sue for an armistice. 'There are other possibilities,' de Gaulle declared. In a mocking tone, Weygand then said: 'Have you anything else to propose?' 'The government,' de Gaulle replied, 'has no proposals to make; it has orders to give. I expect you will be given these orders.' Finally, Reynaud sent him away. 'We parted in a stormy atmosphere. ...' (*Mémoires*, vol. I, p. 51.)

On the following night, 10 June, the government moved out of Paris, de Gaulle travelling in the same car as Reynaud. The roads were jammed with cars, and it took them a whole night to reach Orléans. Once there, they received a phone call from Weygand saying that he had asked Churchill to come to his headquarters at Briare at once.[1] De Gaulle was outraged by Weygand's way of acting independently of the government, and urged Reynaud to dismiss Weygand and appoint General Huntziger commander-in-chief. Reynaud at first agreed and got de Gaulle to consult Huntziger, who accepted. But then Reynaud changed his mind. At the Briare meeting, both Pétain and Weygand pursued their defeatist arguments; Churchill, according to de Gaulle, 'maintained towards the French a friendly reserve, and already seemed to contemplate, not without a sombre feeling of satisfaction, the fearful and magnificent prospect of England fighting on, alone on her island, and with him leading her to salvation' (*Mémoires*, vol. I, p. 54). At the dinner that followed the futile discussion, de Gaulle sat next to Churchill:

Our conversation confirmed me in my confidence in Churchill. And no doubt he also grasped that de Gaulle, though helpless at the moment, was as full of resolve as himself.

There was to be another conference with Churchill and other British ministers at Tours two days later. At this 'dreadful conference', as de Gaulle was to call it, the question was squarely raised of releasing France of her pledge of the previous March not to make a separate peace with Germany. According to Churchill, the British declined this request; according to de Gaulle, Churchill 'was inclined' to release France of her pledge, provided that the French Navy did not fall into German hands. He also asked Reynaud to ensure that the 400 German airmen in France (most of them shot down by the R.A.F.) be handed to Britain.

M. Reynaud willingly gave this promise, but soon he had no power to keep it. . . . In the Battle of Britain we had to shoot them down a second time. (Vol. 2, p. 161.)

At the end of the Tours meeting, Churchill, as he tells the

1. According to Churchill (vol. 2, p. 135) it was Reynaud himself who had asked him to come to Briare.

story, went up to de Gaulle, 'standing stolid and expression-
less in the doorway. Greeting him, I said in a low tone, in
French: "*L'homme du destin*". He remained impassive.'

One can only wonder whether this pretty story is strictly
true. There is no mention of it in de Gaulle.

On the 14th, the French Government moved from Tours
to Bordeaux. Most of the government had by now been
converted to Pétain's and Weygand's defeatist outlook.
Reynaud, physically exhausted, was losing his grip. His
S.O.S. to Roosevelt, sent at Churchill's suggestion, had
produced kind words, but nothing else. At Bordeaux, de
Gaulle urged Reynaud to go to Algiers at once and continue
the struggle. Meantime he (de Gaulle) would go to London
the next day to arrange with the British about troop trans-
ports across the Mediterranean. That evening, at the Hotel
Splendide, he saw Pétain having dinner; he went up to him.
They shook hands in silence. 'I was never to see him again,
never.' (*Mémoires*, vol. I, p. 60)

*

Travelling by car to Brest, and then by French destroyer to
Plymouth, de Gaulle did not arrive in London until the
morning of 16 June. This was to prove a historic day, at the
end of which Pétain became head of the French Government. There is still some contradictory evidence on what
exactly happened in London. While de Gaulle was on his
way there, Reynaud had again asked Britain to relieve
France of her pledge. An answer was sent to Reynaud at
12.45 p.m. saying that France was free to inquire about the
German armistice terms, on condition that the French Navy
sailed forthwith to British ports, pending negotiations.

According to Churchill, early in the afternoon a second
message, 'in similar terms', was sent to Reynaud via Sir
Ronald Campbell, the British Ambassador. Now, there is
some mystery about this second message which, Churchill
says, was equally 'stiff'. De Gaulle tells a different story.

During his lunch with Churchill at the Carlton Club, he expressed to the Prime Minister his 'very unpleasant surprise' at the readiness that Churchill had shown at Tours to 'write off' France as an ally, provided that the French Navy was saved. He argued that, while it was unlikely that Darlan or Pétain would ever voluntarily surrender the Navy, there could be no guarantee, unless France 'remained in the war'. Churchill, de Gaulle maintained, had as good as encouraged France to capitulate. He then tells in his *Mémoires* that Churchill was 'badly shaken' by this, and had a quick talk with his secretary, Major Morton.

That may well be why, half-an-hour later, the British Ambassador at Bordeaux withdrew from Reynaud the Note that had been handed him earlier, allowing France to inquire about the German armistice conditions. (*Mémoires*, vol. I, p. 64.)

There is certainly nothing in Churchill to indicate that he had been 'badly shaken' by de Gaulle's criticism of himself during that Carlton Club lunch. Would, indeed, Churchill have made such an admission even if it were true? Instead, Churchill links his further communications with Sir Ronald Campbell at Bordeaux with something quite different; he says that he instructed Campbell to 'suspend' his earlier message (or messages), not because he had been 'shaken' by de Gaulle's criticisms, but simply in order to give a chance to the 'Declaration of Union' which he had also discussed with de Gaulle during that lunch.

Now the idea of this Anglo-French Union had originally been neither de Gaulle's nor Churchill's; it had been concocted by Ambassador Corbin, M. Monnet, Vansittart and a few other people, and was presented to de Gaulle by Monnet and Corbin on his arrival in London. His first reaction was unfavourable, as was Churchill's. But it was reckoned that such a *coup de théâtre* might help Reynaud. Much to Churchill's surprise, the British cabinet was enthusiastic about the scheme. De Gaulle, according to Churchill, 'read the final draft with unwonted enthusiasm' and hastened to phone it to Reynaud. De Gaulle also seemed to think that, though unrealistic, the scheme might create just the kind of 'psychological shock' that would help the hard-pressed Reynaud to stick to his guns. Later – though much later – he attributed the authorship of this 'absurd' idea of 'merging King George VI with President Lebrun' to M. Jean Monnet.

As it turned out, the 'Declaration' met with almost unanimous opposition from the French cabinet which met that evening. In retrospect, Churchill, too, regretted this move. The French cabinet might, he argued, 'have accepted our primary condition about sending their Fleet to Britain'. In other words, he blamed de Gaulle for having inflicted the 'Declaration of Union' on him. It had only precipitated Reynaud's downfall. Churchill, who was to meet Reynaud at Concarneau in Brittany, the next day, was in his special train at Waterloo when his private secretary arrived breathless with a message saying that the 'ministerial crisis had opened at Bordeaux'. Churchill returned to Downing Street 'with a heavy heart'.

*

De Gaulle had meantime flown to Bordeaux in a plane that Churchill had lent him. 'We had agreed that the aircraft would remain at my disposal in case anything happened that would make me return to London'. On one of the essential objects of his visit – namely, the organization, with British help, of the transportation of the French Army to North Africa – no conclusion had been reached. He found that the British were willing to help, but that, until further notice, 'they remained highly sceptical about any upsurge on the part of official France'.

They had good reason to be sceptical. On arriving at Bordeaux, de Gaulle received confirmation that Reynaud

had resigned, and that Pétain was forming the new government. This, obviously, meant capitulation. He went to see
Reynaud. The ex-premier had no illusions about Pétain; at
the same time, he looked like a man who had suddenly been
relieved of an unbearable burden. There follow here, in de
Gaulle's *Mémoires*, two pages on Reynaud which are perhaps
the most moving tribute he rendered to any man – to his
intelligence, his stoicism, his powers of endurance in the face
of calamity:

Only those who saw him can measure the ordeal of power in
those days of calamity. No respite during the day, no sleep at
night for weeks on end. .... As head of this government he had
received the full impact of all the disasters: the German breakthrough at Sedan, the Dunkirk disaster, the surrender of Paris,
the collapse at Bordeaux. He had become head of the government
on the eve of these disasters, without having been given a moment
to prepare for them, and after having, for years, advocated a
military policy that would have spared us all this. .... Yet never,
during those tragic days, did he lose his temper or his nerve, or
become indignant or plaintive. It was a tragic sight to see this
man of outstanding merit mercilessly crushed by events beyond
his control. ....

Everything around him had collapsed – the régime, the
people, the allies, the army, and the most illustrious
generals. There was, in the end, no other choice than between
continuing the war at all costs in Africa, come what may
to France, and surrender. Did Reynaud hope, in the last
resort, that the Armistice terms would be so harsh that
France would rebel and resume the struggle?[1]

1. This generous and touching tribute to Reynaud is, of course,
wholly at variance with accounts by other witnesses, for instance
General Sir Edward Spears (*The Fall of France*, London, 1954) in
which Reynaud figures as a weak man wholly under the thumb of his
friend Mme de Portes, an ugly and poisonous woman working hand-in-
glove with the defeatists. Under her influence, much more than for
parliamentary reasons, which scarcely counted during the Invasion,

De Gaulle's question can only be answered in the negative. Reynaud was clearly finished. Pétain and, with him, practically the whole of France now wanted peace – wanted, above all, to *survive*. Pétain seemed best fitted for working the trick. It was, in a sense, a masterpiece of expediency, of let's-save-what-can-still-be-saved. A desperate gamble perhaps, but one worth trying. Perhaps Hitler would 'destroy' France, as he had promised in *Mein Kampf*; but what if he did not? Yet in terms of world politics, such a gamble was something unpardonably shabby, and de Gaulle knew it better than anyone. If Hitler won the war, he reflected, both he (de Gaulle) and Pétain would be destroyed; if Hitler lost, then Pétain would lose, too, but de Gaulle would triumph. So, on the morning of the 17th, de Gaulle took the plunge and flew to London. He was accompanied by General Spears and by Lieutenant de Courcel, his own a.d.c. Paul Reynaud had given him 100,000 frs.; de Gaulle asked that part of this money be sent to his family in Brittany so that they could sail to England by the last ship. As distinct from Spears's exciting story, de Gaulle says that the departure took place 'without any romance or difficulty'.

Would he have stayed with Pétain in France if Weygand had not crossed him off Pétain's government list at the last moment – a veto of which de Gaulle had learned before he had decided to leave for England? The story is told by Alfred Fabre-Luce. It seems hopelessly out of character.[1]

---

he filled the government with men from the 'enemy' camp, Georges Mandel remaining to the bitter end one of the few ministers still wholeheartedly opposed to the Armistice.

1. This whole story was to be denied by Weygand himself. (Tournoux, op.cit., p. 442.)

CHAPTER 4

THE FREE FRENCH EPIC

1. One-Man Show in London

LONG after it was all over, Churchill wrote this celebrated passage on Charles de Gaulle:

In these pages various severe statements based on events of the moment are set down ... and certainly I had continuous difficulties and many sharp antagonisms with him. There was, however, a dominant element in our relationship. I could not regard him as representing captive and prostrate France, nor indeed the France that had a right to decide freely the future for herself. I knew he was no friend of England. But I always recognized in him the spirit and conception which, across the pages of history, the word 'France' would ever proclaim. I understood and admired, while I resented, his arrogant demeanour. Here he was – a refugee, an exile from his country under sentence of death, in a position entirely dependent upon the goodwill of the British Government, and also now of the United States. The Germans had conquered his country. He had no real foothold anywhere. Never mind, he defied all ... It was said in mockery that he thought himself the living representative of Joan of Arc ... This did not seem to me as absurd as it looked. Clemenceau, with whom it was said he also compared himself, was a far wiser and more experienced statesman. But they both gave the impression of being unconquerable Frenchmen. (*The Second World War*, vol. IV, p. 611.)

This passage is typical of that love-hate relationship that established itself over the years between Churchill and de Gaulle – two men who had so very much in common. Everybody knows Churchill's wisecrack: 'The Cross of Lorraine was the heaviest cross I have ever had to bear.' Yet, cursing and swearing, he still carried it to the end, and did not abandon it by the roadside, though he was often tempted to do so. And although, on one occasion, he told de Gaulle that if he ever had to choose between him and Roosevelt, he would always choose Roosevelt (a phrase that was to rankle with de Gaulle for the rest of his life, right up to the Common Market crisis – when he vetoed Britain's entry into 'Europe' – and beyond) Churchill still did what he could to narrow the gulf between the Free French and the United States.

And just as Churchill saw in de Gaulle a symbol of French Resistance as Pétain was busy suing for the Armistice, so, to de Gaulle, Churchill personified the British will to continue fighting. That Britain was going to fight on seems self-evident now. But was it in those grim days of June 1940? Weygand had said to de Gaulle only a few days before that, within a week, England would make a peace settlement with Germany; on another occasion, he had said that England 'would have her neck wrung like a chicken'.

De Gaulle did not take this eventuality very seriously. Before finally flying to London on 17 June he had seen Churchill three times, and was convinced that Britain would fight, and that the danger of a German invasion was not immense. At heart he approved of Churchill's refusal to send the R.A.F. back to France, for it was not the R.A.F. that was going to turn the Weygands and Pétains into *lutte à outrance* men . . .

Not that the future was by any means clear the day de Gaulle landed in London. He was embarking on an unpredictable adventure. The word 'adventure' often recurs in what he wrote and said, both then and later. As he was to write in his *Mémoires*:

Here I was, alone and deprived of everything, like a man on the shore of an Ocean he was now going to swim . . .

And, a few pages down:

At the age of 49, I embarked on the adventure, like a man whom fate had cast out of all human categories ...

There can be no doubt that de Gaulle thought of himself already then as a Man of Destiny. But it would be very wrong to think that he imagined from the very outset that the Free French Movement would for a long time be little more than a One-Man Show.

Not for a moment, [he later wrote] did I think in terms of a handful of Frenchmen simply helping England.

In fact, he did not give a hang for England as such and he made this quite clear both then and later. English resistance to Hitler was absolutely essential to de Gaulle's design; but what was at stake for him was something quite different:

What I was determined to save was the French Nation and the French State. What I had to bring back into the war was not just Frenchmen, but France.

And to this he added laconically:

Winston Churchill placed the B.B.C. at my disposal.

*

De Gaulle's famous first broadcast on that 18th of June (though very few people in France heard it at the time) was, when one comes to think of it, an extraordinary intervention. It started with a frontal assault on the Weygands and Pétains – 'the men who, for many years, had been at the head of the French armies, and who have now formed a government'. And this government was now planning to end the struggle. German tanks, planes and tactics had overwhelmed the armies under their command, rather than actual numerical superiority. (In other words, these people were incompetent.)

'But has the last word been said? Must hope disappear? Is our defeat final? No ... For France is not alone. She is not alone. She is not alone. She has behind her a vast Empire. She can join

with the British Empire which rules the seas and is continuing
the struggle. Like England, she can draw without limit on the
immense industrial might of the United States.

'This war is not limited to the unhappy territory of our
country. The outcome of this war has not been settled by the
battle of France. This is a world war...'

'I, General de Gaulle, now in London', then called on
French soldiers and officers, engineers and armaments
workers who were in England, or might come to England,
to put themselves in contact with him. And he concluded:

'Whatever happens, the flame of resistance must not go out,
and it will not go out.'

The broadcast was prophetic, but almost to the point of
recklessness: it was not true at the time that France (or
Britain, for that matter) could draw 'without limit' on the
resources of the United States; but, to de Gaulle, lend-lease
(or its equivalent) already appeared inevitable, as did
America's – and almost certainly Russia's – entry into the
war, (a series of events implied by the phrase 'world war').
Russia, as the only remaining great power outside Germany
on the continent of Europe, already held a very special
place in de Gaulle's view of the world, and the German
invasion of Russia in June 1941 was to be hailed by de
Gaulle as an event which left no doubt that France was now
on the winning side. Significantly he refrained from attacking Russia, both then and later.

The first recorded French reaction to de Gaulle's broadcast was a telegram from Weygand to the French military
attaché in London ordering the General to return to
France immediately.

In reply, de Gaulle wrote Weygand a private letter, urging
him to go to North Africa to head the Resistance there; this
letter was returned two months later with a slip declaring
that if de Gaulle wished to communicate with Weygand, he

must do it 'through the regular channels'. In the interval he had received a second summons to return to France and to appear before a military tribunal. He returned it to the French Embassy with a note saying that it was 'not of the slightest interest' to him. Soon afterwards he was sentenced to death *in absentia* as a deserter by a military court in Vichy France.

The ten days following the first broadcast were crucial. On 19 June he broadcast again, now speaking 'in the name of France, as a soldier and military chief'. More important, he wired General Noguès, the commander-in-chief in North Africa, declaring himself ready to serve under him 'or any other personality willing to head the Resistance'. This, in itself, is significant. De Gaulle did not consider himself the automatic leader of the French Resistance; if more prominent figures than he were willing to head it, he would serve under them. On 22 June the Bordeaux Government signed the Armistice with the Germans, and on the following day the British Government declared that it could not consider the Bordeaux authorities as those of an independent country, and that it was ready to recognize a Provisional French National Committee which would pursue the war. With this end in view de Gaulle sent further messages to Noguès; then to Puaux, French High-Commissioner in Syria and the Lebanon; to General Catroux, Governor-General of Indo-China; and Peyrouton, the French Resident-General in Tunisia. At first, none responded, and it was not until some weeks later that Catroux joined the Free French. The other 'proconsuls' decided to submit to the Bordeaux Government, which soon became the Vichy Government. Thus, de Gaulle started with what was in effect a triple failure: he had not prevented the Armistice; he had failed to persuade the French military and civil chiefs of the French Empire, and particularly in North Africa, to join the Free French; and the number of Free French troops in England was miserably small. After the Provisional French National Committee had come to nothing, the British Government could do no more than merely recognize General de Gaulle 'as the leader of all the Free French, wherever they may be, who will rally to him in the defence of the allied cause'. This happened on 28 June.

There were many thousands of French troops in England at the time – men who had been brought there at the time of Dunkirk and had not yet been repatriated; men who had fought at Narvik; others who had been evacuated from Brest and Cherbourg; and about 10,000 sailors and seamen. But most of them wanted to go home. De Gaulle was not given much opportunity to persuade them to stay. The British Government, while determined to seize all French ships in British ports and anxious to keep their crews, was not interested in French soldiers; it had plenty of manpower, but was, after Dunkirk, desperately short of arms. Much to de Gaulle's indignation, the British military authorities persuaded thousands of French soldiers to go home, and almost forcibly repatriated some of them, particularly 1,500 Senegalese troops, who had wanted to stay but were shipped back to Africa. By the middle of July, the Free French Forces in Britain, including the sailors, amounted to only 7,000 men.

It must be added that the tragedy of Mers-el-Kebir, the naval base near Oran, at which, on 3 July, a British squadron sank and damaged numerous French warships, killing some 1,500 French sailors, had a devastating effect on many of the French still in England, and turned them sharply against the British – and the Free French. There was a deep drop in the number of Free French enlistments. De Gaulle himself seems to have been much distressed and perplexed by Mers-el-Kebir; in his broadcast that day he expressed his great 'anger' at what the British had done, but concluded, nevertheless, that it was better that the French warships should be destroyed than that, manned by Germans, they should some day 'shell British harbours, or Algiers, Casablanca and Dakar'. It was one of de Gaulle's most awkward moments; Vichy redoubled its anti-British and anti-de Gaulle propaganda. In private conversations, de Gaulle expressed great doubt over whether the Mers-el-Kebir massacre was really necessary.

*

De Gaulle in his first broadcast had raised the banner of French Resistance; but France, stunned and bewildered by what had happened, was not yet in a mood to resist. A few members of the now defunct Reynaud Government – among them Mandel and Campinchi, the Minister of Marine (but not Reynaud himself) – along with a number of deputies and senators, sailed to Morocco on board the *Massilia*, only to be interned by Governor-General Noguès who, after some hesitation, had decided to submit to the Pétain government once the Armistice was signed.

Once again the political leaders of the Third Republic failed to take any bold initiative; after playing with ideas about going to North Africa, they all made some mental excuse for 'staying with their people', whether a socialist like Vincent-Auriol, who was consistently anti-Pétain, or Herriot, who, for all his 'pure republicanism', still called on the French people to 'Rally round the Marshal'. All the deputies and senators present at Vichy on 10 July voted for Pétain's plenary powers, except eighty; and even these implicitly agreed that the Armistice was necessary.

The truth is that, during the first few months following the Armistice, all these people and, with them, the bulk of French opinion seemed convinced that Hitler had won the war, and that France had better adapt herself as best she could to the new situation. The prevalent view was that Pétain was in the best position to limit the damage to the minimum. The Vichy régime which was set up in July was

wholeheartedly supported by the entire Right, and also
served, in a spirit of opportunism, by the Centre and even
part of the Left. There had never been such a cult of the
military uniform as among the Weygands and the other
runaway generals of Vichy, and such an orgy of tricolour
flag-waving as in the artificial 'capital' of the Free Zone –
which the Germans had, for reasons of their own, decided to
tolerate for the time being. The very existence of this Free
Zone was comforting to millions of Frenchmen, who sin-
cerely believed that they owed its existence to the legendary
personality of the 'Victor of Verdun'. For the Right, and
particularly for Charles Maurras and the *Action Française*,
who set themselves up as the official ideologists of Vichy,
Pétain's 'National Revolution', with its curious mixture of
fascism and slobbery 'old-French' pietism, was their
revenge on the Republic and, in particular, the Popular
Front. Broadly, the Vichy personnel fell into two groups –
the *attentistes* favouring, in foreign policy, a wait-and-see
attitude; and the collaborators, who believed that they could
get better terms from the Germans by integrating France
wholeheartedly into Hitler's New Order. In October, the
Montoire meeting between Hitler and Pétain marked a
temporary consecration of the 'collaboration' policy; the
dismissal of Laval in December seemed to signal a temporary return to *attentisme*; but when, in February 1941,
Admiral Darlan succeeded Laval as head of the government, the collaborationist tendencies of Vichy became
even stronger than they had been under Laval. Darlan,
frantically anti-British, favoured military cooperation with
the Germans – which is more than Laval had ever contem-
plated.

With few exceptions, Vichy was supported by the Church
hierarchy and by the conservative *élite* of France; practically
the entire French Academy, apart from François Mauriac,
was pro-Pétain, with Valéry and Claudel among the most

relentless admirers.[1] To a man like de Gaulle this Vichy hothouse which was thriving, as Mauriac put it, 'so long as the Germans were there', was intensely nauseating. At heart he no doubt agreed that Vichy was a 'realistic' device for saving France – at least for a time – from physical destruction, but the sight of generals representing France's most shameful defeat as a 'victory of the French spirit' was hard to stomach.

*

In a way, the stay-at-home mood of the French political and military leaders helped de Gaulle to build up the Free French movement as a specifically *Gaullist* one: it might have developed along different lines altogether if political leaders of weight, such as President Lebrun, Reynaud, Herriot, or Mandel had come to London to share in the leadership of Free French resistance, or General Noguès had supported it in North Africa. But they were either (like Mandel) prevented from coming, or (and this was true of nearly all the others) just did not want to come. The only politician of some importance who wanted to 'join' de Gaulle was the former Minister of Air in the Popular Front governments, Pierre Cot, but de Gaulle refused to have him. He was 'too obvious', as de Gaulle later put it. Cot had been the object of some particularly vicious press campaigns in France, as the man who had allegedly 'ruined the French air-force', and so on. De Gaulle did not wish to see his name coupled with Pierre Cot's; it would make the wrong impression in France.

In his *Mémoires* de Gaulle also writes with some bitterness of certain Frenchmen in London who refused to join him – Ambassador Corbin, who resigned from the diplomatic service at the time of the Armistice, but who declared himself too old 'to enter a dissident movement' and later returned to

1. Claudel's *Ode to Pétain* of 1940 was to be succeeded by an equally cringing *Ode to de Gaulle* in 1944!

Vichy France with the entire Embassy Staff; Roland de Margerie, Reynaud's *chef de cabinet*, who was appointed Consul-General at Shanghai by the Pétain government and told de Gaulle that he preferred to 'serve France in his own way'; M. Jean Monnet, who thought it a mistake to start a French Resistance movement on English soil; René Mayer, who thought it his 'duty' to return to France and share the fate of his fellow-Jews. Another Jew, André Maurois, while preferring not to stay in France, would not come to London either, and went to the United States – which produced a famous Churchill wisecrack. Other well-known writers and journalists – Kerillis, Mme Tabouis, 'Pertinax' (André Géraud) – perhaps scared, as de Gaulle suggests, of German bombs or a German invasion, also preferred to go to the United States, rather than support de Gaulle in London.

All in all, [de Gaulle later wrote] this almost general abstention of French personalities *vis-à-vis* my enterprise did not raise its credit in the eyes of the world. For a time, I had to postpone the constitution of my committee. (*Mémoires*, vol. I, p. 84.)

Nevertheless, in July and August, a Free French organization of sorts gradually crystallized in London. In August the Free French were given headquarters at Carlton Gardens, and here one could meet some of de Gaulle's principal assistants – Prof. René Cassin, his top jurist; Escarra, Hackin, and Lapie (the last a Socialist deputy) on the foreign relations side; Pleven, in charge of 'our minute finances' (as de Gaulle was to put it); Massip, in charge of Information; Bingen[1] in charge of matters concerning the French merchant navy; Maurice Schumann, the principal speaker (apart from de Gaulle himself) for the Free French programme on the B.B.C. The Free French navy was under the command of Admiral Muselier, assisted by Captain Thierry d'Argenlieu; Magrin-Verneret and Koenig were organizing the Free

1. When later Bingen went to occupied France as a de Gaulle 'delegate', he was caught by the Gestapo and committed suicide.

French land forces; Pijeaud, the little Free French air-force which was, before long, to take part in the bombing of Germany. De Gaulle's own general staff included Tissier, Dewavrin (the future 'Colonel Passy'), and Geoffroy de Courcel, his A.D.C. who had come with him from Bordeaux.

These members of my entourage, [de Gaulle later wrote] were what hostile propaganda persisted in denouncing as a bunch of traitors, mercenaries and adventurers. But these people, inspired by the loftiness of our task, remained faithful to me, for better or for worse. (*Mémoires*, vol. I, p. 85.)

There is no doubt that de Gaulle's inner circle had a bad reputation, both then and – especially – later, at the height of the 'Muselier crisis'. As M. Henri Michel says:

Among those who joined de Gaulle, there were not many men of the 'Left'... There was a marked preponderance of men of the extreme Right, of the *Action Française* and the Cagoule. Later, when colonial territories rallied to de Gaulle, his followers included many *colons* and colonial officers. Inevitably, any adventure (like de Gaulle's) also attracted a certain proportion of thugs. (*Histoire de la France Libre*, Paris, 1963, p. 29.)

During those early days, de Gaulle, thoroughly disgusted with the Third Republic, was very vague about the kind of future France he had in mind, and avoided the use of words like 'Republic' and 'democracy'. An opposition of sorts rapidly developed in London, and a good deal of angry whispering against de Gaulle could be heard, for instance, from a small group – headed by Pierre Comert, a former French foreign office official, the two Gombaults (*père et fils*) and Louis Lévy – which claimed to represent the 'republican conscience' of France, and had friends in the Labour Party. Comert and the Gombaults ran a daily paper called *France*, which was subsidized by the British Ministry of Information and which was by no means 'Gaullist' in tone. Much of the whispered propaganda against de Gaulle was mischievous and shortsighted.[1] Later, André Labarthe, who was at first de Gaulle's 'science expert', also turned against him, as did Admiral Muselier. But these defections were relatively few; and even as early as July–August 1940 something of a 'de Gaulle mystique' had developed among the Free French. British opinion, on the whole, was favourably impressed by de Gaulle; Churchill and Eden were friendly, and the Royal Family showed a sympathetic interest in the Free French movement.

*

On 7 August, a de Gaulle-Churchill agreement laid the administrative and financial foundations of the Free French; although de Gaulle was the 'supreme commander' of the Free French forces, he agreed to follow the 'general directives' of the British; the financial aid to the Free French was in the nature of a loan.

So, in theory, a little French independence was thus safeguarded; 'Free France' was not just a Foreign Legion in the service of the British. Nevertheless, de Gaulle was the head of a French force which was dependent on the country where it had sought refuge. Since the British were responsible for the arming and upkeep of the Free French, they inevitably tended to regard them as subservient to them.[2]

By July 1940, de Gaulle was already itching to find for the Free French a 'territorial base' of their own, and his eyes inevitably turned to French Africa. He was extremely conscious of not representing France at London in the way

1. I remember one occasion when they tried to plant a particularly vicious anti-de Gaulle article on the *New Statesman*. Although Kingsley Martin's judgement was not always infallible, his reaction this time was sound: 'No,' he said, 'de Gaulle may have his faults, but, damn it, he represents something very big, which these pipsqueaks certainly don't. We are not going to attack de Gaulle and play into the hands of Hitler and Vichy.'

2. Henri Michel, op. cit., p. 13–14.

that the Dutch, Belgian, Norwegian, Czechoslovak, and Polish governments represented their countries. These were more-or-less, regular Governments-in-Exile, whose countries were 'temporarily' under German occupation. The Belgian government controlled the Congo; the Dutch, Indonesia; and though the others had no territory under their control, the Norwegian government, like the Dutch, had a substantial merchant navy, the Polish government had a large number of regular troops under its command, and the Czechoslovak government controlled some smaller units as well as an important intelligence network in Central Europe. In comparison with all these governments, de Gaulle was at a great disadvantage. Though it was not 'recognized' by Britain, there *was* a government in France, which maintained diplomatic relations with numerous countries, including Canada, the United States and the Soviet Union. De Gaulle denied its legality, but that, in itself, was insufficient. Therefore, so long as the Free French movement was confined to a handful of little-known people and to a few small military and naval units stationed in England, its position was very weak. True, its B.B.C. broadcasts[1] were 'fanning the flame of Resistance in France';

1. It is important to distinguish between the French service of the B.B.C. – and this included the famous programme 'Le Français parlent aux Français' – run by Frenchmen like Duchesne, Oberlé, Jean Marin, Maurice van Moppès etc., – and the Free French programme proper. Whereas the former had practically the whole night and day at its disposal, the Free French had only a total of 10 minutes a day – twice five minutes. The principal Free French speaker was Maurice Schumann, with de Gaulle himself speaking usually once or twice a week. The Frenchmen employed by the B.B.C. closely followed the de Gaulle line at first, but, being B.B.C. employees, had to follow certain British instructions. In periods of tension between de Gaulle and the British government, the French service of the B.B.C. was very far from following the de Gaulle line; this was particularly true at the time of the Syrian conflict in the summer of 1941 and, even more so, at the time of the American landing in North Africa in November 1942.

but, during the months immediately following the Armistice, there was, in reality, no flame in France, and only a few glowing embers.

In private, de Gaulle would often bitterly complain during those early days that the French people were 'sheepish and gutless', and had been taken in by the swindles and eyewash of the Vichy Government. It was, in fact, not until the failure of the German invasion of England in the autumn of 1940 that very many people in France began to listen regularly to the B.B.C.

If de Gaulle had the poorest opinion of the French, in the late summer of 1940, what did he think of the British? There are a couple of striking pages on this in de Gaulle's *Mémoires*, which can be summarized as follows: the English people were extremely kind and friendly to the Free French; and their morale was quite admirable; but this was simply because they hadn't the foggiest idea of what they were up against; if the Germans had succeeded in invading England, it would have been like France, or even worse. There was only one thing that could save England, and that was her Fighter Command. In their amateurish way, the people were ready to 'fight on the beaches'; but the more informed knew that this would be useless if the Germans ever gained a foothold in England, and it was *they* who 'whispered the names of politicians, churchmen, writers and businessmen who would come to terms with the Germans' – after the government and the Royal Family had been evacuated to

There was also a marked tendency on the part of the British to censor the Free French programme proper, and particularly to discourage, especially after Dakar, any personal attacks on Marshal Pétain. This (more or less discreet) interference with the Gaullist broadcasts was one reason why de Gaulle was desperately anxious to set up, as soon as possible, a powerful broadcasting station at Brazzaville, in 'purely French' territory. This did not, however, materialize until the spring of 1942, and the necessary equipment was bought, not without some difficulties, in the U.S.A.

Canada. (*Mémoires*, vol. I, p. 87.) He describes an extra-ordinary meeting with Churchill at Chequers in August, when the Prime Minister seemed desperately anxious for the Germans to strike. He was sure that if the Germans bombed England, it would bring the United States into war. 'Sooner or later, the Americans will come in. But the main thing for us is to hold out. That is why I am thinking of our fighters all the time.' And he added:

'You see now how right I was to refuse you these fighters at the end of the Battle of France. If they had been lost, it would have been the end of everything for both you and us.' De Gaulle replied, without much conviction, that the R.A.F. in France might *perhaps* have revived the alliance.

2. The African Base – Dakar

In July and August, de Gaulle had two immediate objec-tives – to secure a 'territorial base' for the Free French, and get the French to fight again in the war. His underlying ambition was to win over the *whole* of the French Empire for the Free French. Hence the Dakar adventure of 23–5 September.

As has been seen, France's 'proconsuls' in North Africa had all rejected de Gaulle's appeals at the end of June, and had opted for Pétain. Mers-el-Kebir had smothered, in de Gaulle's words, any remaining temptation to join the Resistance. Why was French North Africa, and particularly Algeria, willing and, indeed, anxious to follow Pétain? As we know, it was to remain mainly Pétainist even after de Gaulle had established his provisional capital at Algiers in 1943, continuing to be 'Vichyite' and largely anti-de Gaulle during the post-war years, with its leading *colon* ideologist, Alain de Sérigny, making no secret of his Pétainism even after allying himself with the Gaullists in 1958 at the time of the Algiers *putsch*. In 1940, as de Gaulle himself correctly describes the situation:

People there felt, not without a touch of cowardly relief, that the Armistice had left North Africa outside the German occupation zone; French authority was reaffirmed under an emphatic military form which could only reassure the *colons* ... Moreover, various aspects of Vichy's so-called 'National Revolution' appealed to many: the appeal to the *notables*, the increased authority given to the administration, the war veteran parades, the display of anti-semitism ...

This anti-semitism appealed to both *colons* and Arabs.

The situation, however, was more promising in Black Africa. Here the French settlers were 'younger', more adventurous and enterprising; many were outraged by the Armistice. Furthermore, the Cameroons had been a German colony before the First World War, and the Africans did not doubt that the Nazis intended to take the country over as soon as possible. This had repercussions among the African populations in the neighbouring colonies who infinitely preferred the French to the *Herrenvolk*. Significantly the French-Guiana-born Negro governor of Chad, Felix Eboué, was the first to respond, as early as 16 July, to de Gaulle's appeal. But even before that, there had been pro-Free French demonstrations at Dakar, Abidjan, Conakry, Douala, Brazzaville, and other Black-African cities, as well as in Madagascar.

On 23 August, de Gaulle sent Pleven to Fort-Lamy, the capital of the Chad territory, and three days later, Eboué and the local military commander, Colonel Marchand, declared the colony 'Free-French'. The same happened at Douala, the capital of the Cameroons, after Colonel Leclerc, with a handful of soldiers, had seized the main buildings. There was no resistance from the Vichy authorities. Brazzaville, the capital of French Equatorial Africa, was also captured in a similar way by Colonel Larminat, with the help of an infantry battalion rushed there from Fort-Lamy; Larminat declared himself 'Head of Free French

Africa until the Liberation of Metropolitan France'. The British Government approved of these developments, since the arrival of the Germans in the Cameroons might well have constituted a danger to Nigeria and the Gold Coast. Churchill's support for de Gaulle's proposal to capture Dakar sprang from the same reasons.

Even before the abortive Dakar expedition, the Free French, acting on de Gaulle's behalf, had secured control over substantial areas in both French Equatorial Africa and in the Chad Territory, which bordered in the Sahara on what was technically part of Italian Libya. This, in itself, provided possibilities for future Free French operations against the Italians, despite the enormous distance between Chad and the vital Mediterranean ports of Libya. The 'greater part of Equatorial Africa' had been won over by the end of August 'without a single drop of blood being shed', de Gaulle later noted with satisfaction. (True, there was still the 'hostile enclave' of Gabon, firmly controlled by a Vichy governor. But this was to be taken over by the Free French – after some fighting in which they lost twenty men – in October–November, after the failure of the Dakar attempt.)

The ease with which the greater part of French Equatorial Africa had fallen into de Gaulle's lap had encouraged both him and Churchill to go ahead with their attempt to 'win over' Dakar, the great port of French West Africa. Dakar, being the point closest to the American continent, and one of the most important naval bases in Africa, was of great strategic interest to the British Battle of the Atlantic. Churchill dreaded the establishment of German U-boat bases, with Vichy's connivance, along the whole West-African coast.[1] To de Gaulle himself, Dakar was, above all, of political importance. If Dakar, he argued, joined him, the Free French 'contagion' might well spread to all the rest of the French African possessions, including Morocco,

1. Churchill, op. cit., vol. 2, p. 421.

Algeria, and Tunisia. He had convinced himself that a man
like General Noguès in Morocco had only very reluctantly
subscribed to the Armistice, though he did not underrate
the Vichyism of Governor Boisson at Dakar, who had
already ordered the arrest of many Free French supporters,
such as the Administrator of the Upper-Volta Territory.
Militarily, Dakar was well-defended, with fortifications facing the sea, coastal batteries, submarines and warships. To
make matters worse, by the middle of September three
French cruisers had slipped from the Mediterranean
through the Straits of Gibraltar to reinforce Dakar's
defences. Churchill himself attributes this unfortunate
development to the indiscreet talk about Dakar among the
Free French in England, long before *Operation Menace* was
begun.

It is unnecessary here to describe this familiar Anglo-
French operation, except to say that de Gaulle's and
Churchill's accounts of it differ not so much factually from
each other as in the different emphasis they place on various
aspects of the venture. Churchill strongly stresses the leak-
ages in England, which led Vichy to send warships and troops
to reinforce Dakar; de Gaulle's persuasion of the British
naval commanders to proceed with the landing at Dakar,
despite unfavourable last-minute developments; and, finally,
'bad luck' – such as the thick fog on 23 September which
cloaked the appearance before Dakar of 'the Anglo-French
Armada' and prevented it from producing that psychological
effect on the city's authorities and population on which
Churchill had counted so much.

De Gaulle, on the other hand, emphasizes that he was
opposed from the start to a 'direct attack on Dakar' and
wanted, instead, to land troops at Conakry who would then
march on Dakar; on their way there, they would be protected
by the British Navy. Churchill rejected de Gaulle's proposal
on the ground that, with the Battle of Britain at its height, he

could not immobilize important British naval forces in West African waters for any length of time.

After the failure, on 23 September, to land Free French emissaries at Dakar and reach a settlement with the authorities there (the emissaries were captured or fired upon), the further failure to land troops successfully at Rufisque, some distance away, and a somewhat aimless all-day shelling of Dakar on the 24th, de Gaulle proposed that Admiral Cunningham on the 25th stop shelling Dakar and simply blockade it; meantime, French and British troops would be landed somewhere else, perhaps at St Louis, some 150 miles north of Dakar. Admiral Cunningham and General Irvine agreed to this plan. Meanwhile, however, according to de Gaulle (and here his story begins to differ considerably from Churchill's) the Prime Minister had grown restive and impatient at the absence of any favourable results.

He ordered Admiral Cunningham to go back on what had been agreed upon (by Cunningham, Irvine and myself). He had been impressed by all the agitation caused in London and Washington by Berlin and Vichy broadcasts. Moreover, the fog had lifted, and the shelling (of Dakar) seemed to have a better chance. *Without anybody consulting me this time*, the battle was resumed at dawn ... The *Resolution* was torpedoed by a Vichy submarine and had to be taken in tow; several other British warships were hit, and four aircraft from the *Ark Royal* shot down. (*Mémoires*, vol. I, p. 108.)

True, Vichy also suffered heavy losses; the battleship *Richelieu* was badly damaged, and could not be repaired at Dakar, while a Vichy destroyer and two submarines were sunk. But the Dakar forts continued their deadly shelling, and on the morning of the 26th, Admiral Cunningham called off the whole operation.

*

It was a fearful blow to de Gaulle. All his hopes of rallying

West Africa and, after it, North Africa to the Free French
went up in smoke. He was made the scapegoat of the fiasco
both by the British press and in Washington; Churchill, too,
was subjected to some severe criticism for having allowed
himself to be led astray by de Gaulle's 'lunatic' scheme.
True, Churchill had the good grace not to disavow de
Gaulle; in the House of Commons on 28 September he
declared that his confidence in him was as great as ever.
Vichy, for its own part, made the greatest political capital
out of the 'great naval victory' of Dakar, with the heroic
stand taken by its troops and by Governor-General Boisson,
and did its utmost to impress upon the Germans that it
could be depended upon to defend Africa against the Free
French.

Although Churchill did not repudiate de Gaulle and
readily admitted that he shared responsibility with him for
what had happened, relations between the two men were
never quite the same again. This was largely due to the very
bad press de Gaulle had in the United States, and the great
hostility and distrust shown him, after Dakar, by the U.S.
Government, which was determined to maintain the closest
possible relations with Vichy and continued to treat it as the
legal popularly supported government of France. It was very
largely owing to Dakar, where the 'Vichy French' had
sharply resisted de Gaulle, that the Free French were to be
wholly excluded from Operation Torch – the North-Africa
landing – two years later.

*

In the long run, Dakar caused de Gaulle the greatest damage.
But the immediate sequel to Dakar was, on the contrary,
reassuring. The Free French, established in the Cameroons,
in Equatorial Africa and in Chad,[1] with 20,000 troops, had
not been unduly discouraged by the Dakar fiasco; the British

1. These, it is true, were very poorly armed. (De Gaulle to Churchill,
quoted by Admiral Muselier, *De Gaulle contre le gaullisme*, p. 118.)

Navy, as Churchill wrote, 'succeeded in arresting the on-
ward progress of the (Vichy) French cruisers and frustrated
their determined efforts to suborn the garrisons in French
Equatorial Africa'. Escorted by British warships under the
command of Admiral Cunningham, a small Free French
naval force, with de Gaulle on board, landed on 8 October at
Douala, in the Cameroons, and de Gaulle was welcomed by
Colonel Leclerc. There followed a military parade of local
troops and of troops just landed from England, and a
reception at the Government Palace which flew the Free
French Cross-of-Lorraine flag.

The officials, the French *colons*, the African personalities whom
I met there were in a state of patriotic euphoria ... But regardless of various economic and other difficulties, the moral unity
of the Free French, whether they had joined the movement in
England or here in Africa, was complete. (*Mémoires*, vol. I,
p. 111.)

After a visit to Chad, where his presence aroused great
enthusiasm, de Gaulle went on to Brazzaville. Meantime, in
France, the Montoire meeting had taken place between
Hitler and Pétain, and from this de Gaulle drew certain
important political conclusions. Now it was clear 'once and
for all' that Vichy had no claim to 'legitimacy', and he
decided that the time was ripe for him to 'establish himself as
the caretaker (*gérant*) of France's interests and to exercise
in the liberated territories the functions of the head of a
regular government'.

At Brazzaville, in French territory, on 27 October 1940, I thus
came to define my national and international position by a
manifesto, two ordinances and an organic declaration ... I there
set up the *Conseil de Défense de l'Empire*.

To begin with, this consisted of de Gaulle himself and
eight members – among them General Catroux,[1] Admiral

1. Catroux, a five-star general, was governor-general of Indo-China
at the time of the Armistice, but soon afterwards the Vichy Government

Muselier, Cassin, and Colonels Leclerc and Larminat. Eboué was appointed Governor-General of Equatorial Africa and Larminat High Commissioner of all the Free French territories in Africa. The 'hostile enclave' of Gabon was conquered by the Free French soon afterwards, though not without some bloodshed between 'Free' and 'Vichy' French; but the Upper Volta and Niger territories further north remained stubbornly Vichyite. Although de Gaulle was not entirely satisfied with what he had achieved in Africa, a very substantial 'territorial base' had, nevertheless, been secured. This Free French control of Central Africa was also of some value to the British, particularly for their air communications with the Middle East,[1] and although the Council for the Defence of the Empire had been set up without first consulting the British Government, the latter recognized it on 27 December. Elsewhere in Africa de Gaulle was less lucky; although the French Commander in French Somaliland, General Legentilhomme, went over to the Free French, the 10,000 French troops there remained loyal to Vichy and, much to de Gaulle's disgust, failed to play any part in Britain's Abyssinian campaign during the following spring.

3. Malaise *in London*

Having set up his 'empire' in Central Africa, de Gaulle returned to London on 17 November 1940, with the blitz on England at its height. For the British, de Gaulle later wrote, that end of 1940 was 'the blackest stretch of the tunnel', and

1. Churchill, op. cit., vol. II, p. 437.

---

replaced him by Admiral Decoux and he joined the Free French. Though of a much higher rank than de Gaulle, he agreed to serve under him, since the de Gaulle case, in his view, was not subject to the usual 'hierarchical considerations'. Nevertheless, according to de Gaulle himself, Churchill had, shortly before Dakar, toyed with the idea of replacing de Gaulle by Catroux at the head of the Free French! (*Mémoires*, vol. I, p. 113.)

they were in a jumpy and nervous state. Worried by the blitz, by their shipping losses and the fearful drain on their financial assets (for lend-lease had not yet been granted) the British showed remarkably little interest or enthusiasm for de Gaulle's territorial, military, or political ambitions.

Though financially dependent on them, de Gaulle continued to be arrogant and ungracious to the British, explaining on more than one occasion to Churchill that if Britain could afford to bow and cringe to America, it was because she was a strong and independent country; but de Gaulle was too poor to cringe to anybody. It was, apart from anything else, a curious technique which, somehow, paid.

What added to de Gaulle's annoyance during that winter of 1940–41 was that Churchill was determined to maintain some kind of semi-official relations with Vichy, through the British Embassy in Madrid, or through the Canadian and American representatives at Vichy itself.[1] It certainly made de Gaulle squirm when Churchill greatly welcomed the appointment of Admiral Leahy as American Ambassador to Vichy in December 1940. Leahy was wholly in sympathy with the Vichy French, thought he could influence them, paid Pétain the most extravagant compliments, and represented the most extreme anti-de Gaulle faction in Washington. Worse still, he enjoyed Roosevelt's fullest confidence.

For the Free French, the general prospect during that winter was dismal. As de Gaulle now himself admits, more and more people in France listened to the French B.B.C. programme and especially to his own and Maurice Schumann's broadcasts; there were even one or two 'Gaullist' demonstrations in France, as the one on 11 November, when a handful of students marched up the Champs-Elysées

1. It was also in October 1940 that Churchill received (as he put it) 'a certain M. Rougier, who represented himself as acting on the personal instructions of Marshal Pétain'. (op. cit., vol. II, p. 450.)

carrying a couple of fishing-rods ('deux gaules'); but 'in both Zones, opinion continued to be passive', and there could be little doubt about the Marshal's popularity.

During the winter and the spring of 1941 the Free French took part in some minor military operations. A battalion distinguished itself in Wavell's offensive at Sidi Barrani on 11 December, and Colonel Leclerc at the end of January captured Kufra, a fortified Italian oasis in Southern Libya, 700 miles north of his Chad base. 'I was then steering a very small boat on the great ocean of a world war', de Gaulle later wrote with an unusual touch of modesty. All he could do, in effect, was to make the Free French 'play a part' wherever possible; but the possibilities were limited, not only for the Free French, but even for Britain. Everywhere the initiative continued in the hands of the Axis Powers. But how determined de Gaulle was to have the Free French 'talked about' may be seen from his abortive attempt at persuading General Wavell to transport a Free French token force to Greece when that country was invaded by the Germans in April 1941.

In London, during the winter of the blitz, many of the Free French were beginning to suffer from a feeling of frustration; victory – if possible at all – seemed infinitely far away. That winter was marked by all kinds of absurd incidents and sordid quarrels and intrigues among the Free French in London. There were the whispering campaigns, already referred to, against de Gaulle and his entourage, by a number of French 'republicans' in London; there was the 'desertion' (de Gaulle's version) or 'ousting' (Muselier's version) of André Labarthe; there were bitter rivalries between the Free French and the British secret services. British attempts to 'steal' any French agents coming to England from France on the excuse that 'England and de Gaulle are the same thing' particularly infuriated the General. (*Mémoires*, vol. I, p. 130.) And then there was the

Muselier Affair, or rather, the first of the Muselier Affairs, when the Admiral at the head of the Free French navy was arrested on 2 January 1941 by the British authorities as a 'Vichy agent' and kept in prison for over a week. A forged document, manufactured by one Colin, with the help of the 'Vichy' consulate then still in London, and planted on the British by a certain 'Howard', whom de Gaulle had promoted to one of the most responsible posts at Carlton Gardens – the head of his Security Service – was at the bottom of this hair-raising incident. In the end, Muselier was released, received heart-felt apologies from both Eden and Churchill, and was received in audience by the King. According to the Admiral himself, de Gaulle, under the influence of the 'gang', had been very slow in reacting to his arrest, and had shown a singular lack of loyalty to his colleague. In his book, *De Gaulle contre le Gaullisme*, published in 1946, Muselier described in great detail the sordid atmosphere of intrigue and double-dealing, complete with Vichy spies and all kinds of double agents, that existed during that winter at de Gaulle's headquarters in London – 'a most odious *basse-police* and Gestapo atmosphere', as he put it. The two culprits were, owing to de Gaulle's indifference, let off lightly by the British Courts, and many of the 'crooks and gangsters' continued to play an important part in de Gaulle's immediate entourage. De Gaulle's own account of the affair is rather different. He attributes the 'lamentable' incident, first and foremost, to 'British Intelligence' which planted the two crooks – Colin and Meffre ('Howard') – on the Free French during his own absence in Africa. Muselier's allegation that 'Howard' was the top protégé of Colonel Passy, the head of de Gaulle's Intelligence Service, is passed over in silence in the General's story, as is also his rejection of Muselier's demand that he sack Passy and Fontaine, the two big shots at Carlton Gardens who had patronized 'Howard'. Instead he stresses that, after the unfortunate Muselier affair, the Admiral became a British stooge. (*Mémoires*, vol. I, p. 126.)

The Muselier affair is, in fact, one example in a hundred of the strained relations between de Gaulle and the British. The first thing he demanded from them, after the Muselier incident, was that Free French military courts be set up in England; and the British, embarrassed by what had happened, agreed to this, though 'Howard' and Colin, having been expelled from the Free French organization, were actually tried by British Courts.[1] Of the British, de Gaulle later wrote:

Once the British machine had made up its mind to obtain something, it took a mighty effort to resist it ... Without having experienced it, it is hard to imagine the insistence, whether gracious, pressing, or threatening, the English used to achieve their own ends. (ibid., p. 139.)

*

The only favourable development during the winter and early spring of 1941 was Churchill's early-morning phone

1. The Muselier affair did not end there. Vice-Admiral Muselier, with a substantial number of warships and merchant ships which he had 'contributed' to the British war effort, was very conscious of having a higher military rank than de Gaulle, and he had some friends and supporters in the British Government, particularly at the Admiralty. Much of the whispered propaganda against de Gaulle came from him and his friend Labarthe, and, in March 1942, soon after the Free French navy's successful capture of the St Pierre and Miquelon islands off the Canadian coast, a major conflict broke out between Muselier and de Gaulle. In the end, Muselier's attempt to shake off de Gaulle's tutelage over the Free French navy (and to make himself the *de facto* head of the Free French movement, as de Gaulle was to allege) was nipped in the bud by de Gaulle himself through the appointment, in Muselier's place, of Admiral Auboyneau, who had been brought to London from the Pacific. Muselier, who expected the French sailors to support him against de Gaulle, found that he had wholly underrated de Gaulle's personal prestige among the overwhelming majority of them. (De Gaulle, *Mémoires*, vol. I, p. 221.)

call to de Gaulle on 9 March when, 'literally dancing with joy', he informed him that Congress had approved the Lend-Lease Bill.[1] This meant, in de Gaulle's phrase, that the United States had 'made a giant step towards entering the war'. Nevertheless, during that period, de Gaulle, despite his Equatorial 'empire', was, quite as much as Britain, in the 'blackest stretch of the tunnel'. Only America's entry into the war seemed capable of ending that military *impasse* in which Britain – and, with her, the Free French – found herself. Churchill, it is true, thought – or at least said he thought (for instance, in his memorandum to Roosevelt of 8 December 1940) – that the heavy bombing of Germany would, more than anything else, 'shatter the foundations of German military power'.[2] What did de Gaulle think of this? I remember a brief conversation with him in January 1941, when I put this question to him. 'It's important,' he said, 'but remember that the Germans can play at that game, too; and something quite, quite different is needed to smash Germany.' 'What?' He shrugged his shoulders. '*On verra bien; nous ne sommes qu'au début d'une très grande guerre*'.

*

In France, meantime, there was still no serious Resistance movement to speak of, and de Gaulle seemed very conscious of this; worse still, the Vichy government, now under Darlan, appeared to be more 'collaborationist' than it had been even under Laval. On 11 May, Darlan visited Berchtesgaden and made a deal with Hitler laying the foundations for that *military* collaboration against the British, which was soon to have a sequel in Irak and Syria.[3]

1. Later, the Free French were to receive some American Lend-Lease aid, though *via* the British.
2. Churchill, op. cit., vol. II, pp. 499–500.
3. See chapter on 'The Forgotten Admiral' (pp. 78–92) in the author's *France 1940-1955*, with its account of Darlan's visit to Hitler.

4. Syria

In the spring of 1941 the Free French were not in an enviable position. The war was going badly. In April the Germans overran Yugoslavia and Greece; and, with the spectacular German capture of Crete, the war seemed to be moving to the Middle East. After the Hitler-Darlan meeting of 11 May, the Germans made a deal with Vichy France whereby they could land their planes in Syria (a territory under French Mandate) on their way to Irak, where Rashid Ali had started a rebellion against the British. It was then thought possible that the German planes would be followed by German troops, which would turn Syria into a springboard against Egypt and Suez. The great problem facing both the British and the Free French was whether the German planes – and, eventually, troops – would meet with any opposition from the 30,000 Vichy French troops in Syria and the Lebanon under the command of General Dentz.

During the previous months, the Free French had been participating on a small scale in General Wavell's operations in Africa. A small French unit, brought from Cyprus, had fought with distinction at Sidi Barrani during the previous winter, and Free French troops also took part in the British operations in Eritrea against the Italians. But Syria being 'French territory', de Gaulle strongly felt that the campaign there, following the lack of resistance to the Germans by the Vichy troops, should be primarily a Free French affair. Unfortunately, all the Free French could scrape together was 6,000 men, with eight guns and ten tanks. Although de Gaulle thought at first that the Vichy French troops could simply be won over by propaganda, this proved illusory. They were five times more numerous than the Free French, and were well-equipped. On the other hand, Wavell, after all his disasters in Greece and Crete, could not (or would not) send many troops to Syria. De

Gaulle and Catroux realized that a bloodless victory could be achieved in Syria only if the Free French were supported by very large British forces. With Wavell sending to Syria only a bare minimum of British troops, the stage was set, on 26 May, for what de Gaulle was to call 'the great fratricidal tragedy'. There was over a month's heavy fighting between the British and Free French on the one hand, and the Vichy French on the other, with the first losing over 4,000 killed and wounded, and the second over 6,000. It was not till 12 July, after the British had brought more reinforcements from Irak (where the rebellion had meantime been crushed) that the Vichy commander proposed a cease-fire to the British. (There were no direct dealings with the Free French, as these were, technically, under British command.)

Now the real trouble started. The St Jean d'Acre agreement was, as de Gaulle was to say, 'worse than anything we had dreaded'. It provided for the repatriation of the Vichy French forces, complete with their equipment, to France and, as de Gaulle interpreted it, 'transferred the Levant countries, purely and simply, to the British'. No chance was given for the Free French to 'win over' the Vichy troops.

In de Gaulle's view, this was the worst piece of British double-crossing, engineered by men like Glubb Pasha, General Spears, General Maitland Wilson, and other *arabisants* of the Colonial Office 'who were now carving up the Arab world according to their own appetites and without any regard for French sovereignty or suzerainty'. De Gaulle was so infuriated that he ordered General Catroux and the Free French forces in the Levant to ignore the St Jean d'Acre agreement, to take no further orders from the British, and to act 'independently', even at the risk of fighting the British! Finally, after long and stormy discussions between de Gaulle and Oliver Lyttelton in Cairo, it was agreed that only France, not Britain, could grant

independence to Syria and the Lebanon, and that the Free
French should try to win over the Vichy forces. But it was
now, according to de Gaulle, too late; many of the Vichy
forces had already sailed for France, and, in the end, the
Free French won over only 127 Vichy officers and 6,000
men. But for this British 'sabotage', says de Gaulle, the
Free French could 'undoubtedly' have won over most of
Dentz's 30,000 troops. It is perhaps one of his most dubious
assertions, since it minimizes not only the prestige Pétain
still enjoyed with the Vichy army, but also the great reluctance of most Frenchmen to 'leave home', especially at a time
when a British victory still looked highly doubtful. Moreover, they had only just fiercely fought against the Free
French. In any event, the wretched episode embittered de
Gaulle still further against the British; it was not until the
following November that they recognized Syria and the
Lebanon as French Mandated territory, provisionally under
de Gaulle's authority. During the rest of the War, British
and French continued their uneasy co-existence in the two
Levant countries. General Catroux stayed there for a time as
the Free French plenipotentiary and commander-in-chief,
while de Gaulle's old friend, General Spears, established in
Beirut as Minister Plenipotentiary to the Syrian and Lebanese Governments, continued, in de Gaulle's view, to conduct
a strongly anti-French policy. It was also his friends
who undertook to oust the French finally out of the
Levant soon after VE day in 1945 – a course which was to
lead to de Gaulle's first great clash with the British after the
war.

It is significant that while, in retrospect, de Gaulle devotes
a long and very angry chapter to the Syrian campaign, this
should be dealt with only very briefly in Churchill's *Second
World War*, and with practically no polemics against de
Gaulle, except for a vague reference to 'detestable difficulties' in a letter to Eden on 9 July.

Was Churchill's conscience not quite clear this time? In any case, British relations with the Free French were to remain strained for a long time after their joint Syrian victory, and this largely accounts for the enormous eagerness with which de Gaulle sought to establish contact with his new – and very different allies, the Russians.

5. Enter the Soviet Union

The failure of the Free French to win over most of the Dentz army in Syria was, in a sense, as great a blow to de Gaulle as Dakar had been. To have 30,000 or even 20,000 fully-trained and well-equipped new troops under him would have decisively strengthened his hand in relation to the British, and would have had enormous repercussions inside France. Instead, the British were in a foul mood after all the bickering over Syria, and were in no hurry to arm the Free French in the Middle East and Egypt. Whereas the Free French embarked on a land blockade of Djibouti, the capital of French Somaliland, the British naval blockade was half-hearted, allowing Vichy to supply the city and its 10,000-strong Vichy garrison, whom de Gaulle had hoped to starve into surrender. It was not till July 1942 that the Free French forces were able to distinguish themselves again in any major military operation; but even after their gallant defence of Bir Hakeim under General Koenig, they continued to be neglected. Later, at El Alamein, Montgomery reduced to a minimum the role played in that important battle by the Free French.

*

In June 1941 de Gaulle became acutely conscious of the fact that the *real* war against Germany was now being fought in Russia, and not in Africa, and that both Africa and the Middle East might well have been lost to the Germans if they had not engaged the bulk of their forces against Russia.

Russia's entry into the war meant for de Gaulle that the *impasse* in the British and Free French struggle against Germany was at last at an end.

On 10 August 1941 Mr S. Vinogradov, the Soviet Ambassador in Ankara received a visit from M. Géraud Jouve, an emissary from General de Gaulle, then in Beirut.

'I must tell you,' [said Jouve] 'that General de Gaulle has lately been talking a great deal about the Soviet Union. Her entry into the war is for us, he said, an undreamed-of opportunity. One cannot say exactly when victory will be won, but de Gaulle is now absolutely convinced that the Germans will, in the end, be smashed.'

On de Gaulle's behalf, Jouve proposed that the Free French should send to Moscow two or three representatives; this need not imply the official recognition of the Free French by the Soviet Union, but it would mean a direct contact between de Gaulle and the Russians, rather than via the British, as hitherto.

'General de Gaulle,' [he said] 'thinks this very important, since France and the Soviet Union are continental powers, and have therefore different aims and problems from the Anglo-Saxon countries ... Victory over Germany will create for two continental powers like ours a number of problems, which the Anglo-Saxon countries will neither understand nor consider ...'[1]

Thus, almost from the beginning of the Soviet-German war, de Gaulle began to see the whole progress of events in an entirely different perspective. His temptation to break away from British tutelage was almost irresistible; France, in de Gaulle's view, was no longer condemned to the invidious role of Britain's junior partner, and the future opened up some exciting and almost undreamed-of possibilities. To begin with, de Gaulle was anxious almost at once

1. *Sovetsko-Frantsuskie otnosheniya vo vremya ... voiny (Soviet-French relations during the War)*. Moscow, 1959, pp. 43–44.

to associate the Free French directly with the war in Russia. During the first visit that de Gaulle's representatives, MM. Cassin and Dejean, paid to Mr Maisky, the Soviet Ambassador in London on 8 August, they stressed that de Gaulle had now an army of about 80,000 men,[1] and that he was seriously considering transferring the Free French headquarters from Brazzaville to Beirut,[2] i.e. to a point geographically as close as possible to the Soviet Union.

A few months later, in November, the question of French troops in Russia was to be officially raised.

What is more, it did not take long for de Gaulle to realize that the Soviet-German war was going to have enormous repercussions inside France, and it was this, more than anything else, that determined de Gaulle's 'leftward' drift – though this did not become very marked until much later. In their conversations with the Russians, de Gaulle's representatives never stopped complaining, not only of the Americans, but also of the British with their backing of the reactionary and 'pro-German' Vichy régime.[3]

No doubt it was difficult for de Gaulle to decide on a clear line of action in relation to Russia during the first few months of the war there. The Russians were suffering disastrous reverses. But after the Battle of Moscow he was fully reassured about Russia's chances of victory. There are two highly significant dispatches from Ambassador Bogomolov to his government reporting his meetings with

1. These, in fact, included a high proportion of 'colonial' troops – Africans, Syrians, etc.

2. ibid, p. 43.

3. Thus, on 21 August 1941, reporting on a further conversation with Jouve, Vinogradov wrote to his government: 'The great differences between de Gaulle and the British arise from their different attitudes to the Vichy government. The British still continue to hope that they may come to some agreement with it, whereas de Gaulle is convinced that Vichy is finally committed to collaboration with Germany.' (ibid., p. 47.)

de Gaulle on 25 November and 9 December 1941.[1] In the first he wrote:

De Gaulle said that the fate of the world was being decided in the war between Russia and Germany, and there was nothing he wanted more than that Frenchmen should fight in Russia.

He further urged that Free French representatives be allowed to go to Russia to establish liaison with the Soviet authorities.

In the second, Bogomolov wrote:

De Gaulle informed me, in reply to our agreement to his previous request, that he intended to send three representatives to Russia – two civilians and one soldier, the head of the mission being Roger Garreau. He also wants to send to the Soviet Union one of the two French divisions in Syria, complete with guns, tanks and ammunition for five or six months. He could have them transported to Tabriz ...

Speaking of the British setbacks in Libya, de Gaulle remarked that the British command didn't understand anything about the military tactics of armoured formations, and was only now beginning to learn. *Only the U.S.S.R., he said, could defeat Germany. The British could never manage it.* All things being equal, he would now much prefer to help the Russians than the British, for both political and military reasons. If the British were now on their way to Tunis, he would gladly help them ... but now they had got stuck, and would remain stuck for several months.

Returning to the question of the division in Syria that he wanted to send to Russia, de Gaulle said it was to the extent of 40 per cent composed of Senegalese, and had better go there in the spring. Both this and the other French division in Syria were, however, under the command of the British,

1. After the Soviet recognition of the French National Committee upon its formation in September 1941, the Free French dealt officially with Mr Bogomolov, Ambassador to the various governments-in-exile in London, and no longer with Mr Maisky, Ambassador to the U.K.

but he did not think they would raise any objections. (ibid., pp. 50–52.)

The British, however, did raise objections, and Maisky wrote on 3 February 1942, that General Auchinleck had, in fact, vetoed the whole venture.

There are very few references in any British and American memoirs and histories of the war to the relations between de Gaulle and the Soviet Union, and they are also glossed over in de Gaulle's own *Mémoires*. Yet it is quite obvious from the diplomatic documents published by the Soviet Foreign Ministry in 1959 that Russia was in the very centre of de Gaulle's attention; that, in his opinion, the future of France would largely be affected by the role Russia played in the defeat of Germany; and that, while the war was in progress, it was important for the Free French to remain on the very best terms with Moscow, using, whenever possible, Moscow's good offices to relieve British and American pressure on them. A very large part of the statements which de Gaulle's representative in Moscow, M. Garreau, made to Molotov, Vyshinsky, or Lozovsky is concerned with French complaints against the British and the Americans. By the end of 1942, though not so much before that, Garreau also went out of his way to assure the Russians that French Resistance was mounting inside France, that the Communists were being particularly active in it, and that de Gaulle was anxious to secure their full support.

Not that, in 1941 or early in 1942, the Russians could see quite clearly yet what kind of 'future France' de Gaulle had in mind. There is an astonishing report by Maisky, dated 29 January 1942, in which he describes de Gaulle's future plans as 'tinged with Italian fascism':

Although de Gaulle told me that the future Constitution of France should be decided upon by a Constituent Assembly, he personally thinks it should be based on two basic 'ideas' – 1) a strong executive and 2) the concentration on social and economic, rather than political, problems ... He told me he thought in terms of a 'corporative parliament' consisting of a number of curiae, agricultural, industrial, etc. ... Military and foreign policy questions should be settled by the government; though on how this government is to be formed, de Gaulle did not seem to have any very clear idea, except that it should be much stronger than any government of the Third Republic ... He is not against the nationalization of heavy industry, favours a minimum wage and state arbitration of disputes, etc. Thus, there appear to be a good many Italian-Fascist elements in his programme. However, in reply to my question whether the 'corporative parliament' could cope with national problems, de Gaulle agreed that deputies elected in the ordinary way might be added to it ... What he said pretty well confirmed what I had already heard about him before. On the whole his political attitude savours of a modernized kind of Bonapartism, though, in fact, he lacks any firm political views. (ibid., pp. 60–61.)

The complaints against the British and the Americans which the Free French transmitted to Moscow were almost continuous. On 3 January 1942 Dejean complained to Bogomolov of the American attitude to the Free French seizure of St Pierre and Miquelon[1] and of the American desire to maintain the French Empire in a state of passivity and inertia. After the British landings at Madagascar in May, about which the Free French had not been consulted, and in which they had not been asked to participate, Garreau bitterly complained to Vyshinsky of British 'co-operation' with the Vichy authorities on the island; he described British policy as 'disloyal and inadmissible'.

When Molotov visited London in May 1942, he had a long meeting with de Gaulle, who complained of British

1. This essentially very minor episode, which was, however, liable to upset the arrangements made between Washington and Vichy concerning the 'neutral' status of French possessions in the Western Hemisphere, was to infuriate the State Department and especially Cordell Hull, who caused a major uproar on that occasion by referring to 'the so-called Free French'.

policy in Madagascar, and the general attitude of Britain and the U.S.A. which 'were doing all they could to reduce the Free French to a purely military organization, without giving the movement any political significance ... They had also given themselves a completely free hand in the French colonial possessions as could be seen from the cases of Madagascar and Martinique.' This kind of attitude, de Gaulle said, discredited his movement in the eyes of French opinion inside France.

Molotov could do no more than promise to 'show an interest' in these colonial questions when talking to the British and Americans; he would have to see then how they reacted to this Soviet 'interest'.

De Gaulle then came to the burning question of the Second Front, and assured Molotov that he was in favour of such a course; the Gaullists, he said, had recently undertaken various military actions which would facilitate a landing in Northern France; but, unfortunately, he added, the British were not helping much materially – there was a shortage of arms, newspapers and leaflets on the Free French side. Nevertheless he was pressing for the 'very earliest' opening of the Second Front. The Soviet resistance against Germany had made 'a gigantic impression' on the people inside France, and the great majority of them were anxious to give the Red Army the fullest support. (ibid., pp. 80–81.)

During the de Gaulle-Molotov meeting the possibility was discussed of sending to Russia a token force of thirty French airmen and thirty ground staff as a beginning.

*

Although de Gaulle had complained angrily to Molotov about the 'free hand' that the British and Americans had given themselves in the French Empire, it is doubtful whether Molotov, with far more urgent problems to worry him – such as the Second Front and the ominous military situation

in Russia during May and June 1942 – did much about it.
But with de Gaulle this 'free hand' became something of an
obsession, and on 6 June 1942 he was prepared to break with
the British and move, together with his armed forces, to
Russia!

There is no mention of this in de Gaulle's *Mémoires*, but
Bogomolov sent on that date the following dispatch to
Moscow:

Had a talk with de Gaulle. According to his information, the
Americans are preparing to occupy Dakar, and the British the
Niger, without any participation by the Free French. If this
happens de Gaulle intends to break with the British. He asked
me, whether, in the event of such a final breach, the Soviet
Government would admit him and his forces to its territory.

Nine days later, however, de Gaulle seems to have had
second thoughts about such a step. Dejean called on Bogomolov and 'said right away that, in his last conversation with
me, de Gaulle had unwittingly exaggerated his differences
with the British Government and had unnecessarily raised
the question of moving the Free French to the Soviet
Union'. (ibid., p. 82.) De Gaulle received assurances that
nothing would be done about Dakar without the Free
French being consulted. Nevertheless he remained in a bad
mood. In his talk with Bogomolov on 26 September – i.e.
when the Battle of Stalingrad was at its height – de Gaulle
said that he was anxious to rally round himself 'all Frenchmen willing to fight the Germans', and if a prominent
Communist joined him, he would gladly accept him, whether
the British liked it or not. He continued to complain of the
British, who, he said, were trying all the time to displace him
by somebody else. Their own authority had fallen very low
since the fall of Singapore and the surrender of Tobruk,
especially in view of their inactivity in Europe. In Syria they
were trying to substitute themselves for the French administration, but without success so far. The British and American

generals had been talking about the Second Front; but he was not invited to these talks, since they knew he was favourable to such a course, while they themselves preferred to remain inactive.

These Free French complaints to the Russians, as we shall see, were to reach a high pitch of fury after the North Africa landing of November 1942, and over the American policy of favouring the 'crypto-Vichyite' General Giraud, instead of de Gaulle, as the top French leader.

6. Free French and Home Resistance

It may be useful at this point to look back on the first two years of the Free French Movement. It had, in a sense, done both very much and very little. Thanks to de Gaulle – 'the only Frenchman', as Churchill was to say, 'who believed in 1940 in England's victory' – France had remained in the war against Germany. This was of immense moral and, potentially, of enormous political importance. De Gaulle had started with a series of failures, and, for a time, his movement had remained a small one-man show. Yet despite the failure at Dakar, he had built up a Free French 'empire', which included most of Central Africa, the French possessions in India and the Pacific, and – at least nominally – Syria and the Lebanon. He had infuriated Washington by grabbing St Pierre and Miquelon, but had, thanks to British support, got away with it.

On 24 September 1941 a full-fledged French National Committee, looking singularly like a regular government, was established, to be recognized in identical terms by Britain, Russia, and several other countries (though not the U.S.A.). Its leader was de Gaulle, and its ministers (provisionally called *commissaires*) included Pleven (economic, financial, and colonial affairs); Dejean (foreign affairs); Cassin (legal affairs, education, etc.); Legentilhomme (army); Muselier (navy and merchant fleet); Diethelm,

newly arrived from France, who dealt with labour, information and relations with Metropolitan France. General
Catroux and Captain d'Argenlieu were also members of the
committee, though they were stationed overseas, one in the
Levant, the other in the Pacific. Everything went reasonably
smoothly until Muselier's 'rebellion' in March 1942, when
he tried to make himself the independent head of the Free
French navy; but, despite the support he was receiving from
the British Admiralty, de Gaulle made short shrift of him,
and simply replaced him by Admiral Auboyneau, who was
brought to London from the Pacific. There was no anti-de
Gaulle revolt in the Free French navy, and only a handful
of officers followed Muselier into retirement. Muselier was
to be taken up later at Algiers by General Giraud.

What had the Free French contributed to the war effort
against Germany? The Free French navy, though virtually
integrated into the Royal Navy, and partly manned by
British crews, represented some fifty vessels by the middle
of 1941, and included the old battleship *Courbet*, several
submarines, and a number of destroyers and minesweepers.
There were over 3,000 Free French sailors, and this navy
played an important part in the Battle of the Atlantic.

More important still was the Free French merchant fleet,
totalling 170 ships or 700,000 tons, of which about one-third
was manned by the 580 Free French officers and 4,300
seamen. The liner *Ile-de-France* was used as a troop carrier
between Australia and Suez. Both the Free French navy and
merchant fleet suffered very heavy losses, and about one
quarter of the crews had died at sea by the middle of 1942.

In various parts of the world Free French airmen were also
active, mostly flying British planes. It is claimed that between
the beginning of 1941 and the middle of 1943 the Free
French brought down 300 enemy planes for the loss of 412
airmen. Of great symbolic and political significance were
the airmen of the Normandie Squadron in the Soviet

Union – though these did not arrive there until the end of 1942.

In the middle of 1941 de Gaulle claimed to have 70,000 French troops, though of very unequal quality, and scattered throughout the Free French 'empire', besides those in Egypt, Eritrea, Libya, and Britain. The first outstanding major operation to be fought by the Free French against Germans was not, however, to take place until June 1942, when General Koenig fought against Rommel his famous battle of Bir-Hakeim, in which he lost 1,000 of the 5,000 men in his 1st Light Division. It was a glorious defeat, rather than a glorious victory, but at least it contrasted nobly with what de Gaulle was to call 'the incomprehensibly hasty surrender' of Tobruk, with its 35,000 British troops, about the same time.

Before that, in 1940 and 1941, the Free French had taken part in a variety of minor operations in Central Africa, in Libya, and in Eritrea, besides the campaign against the Vichy French in Syria. But all this was still relatively small stuff, and what ultimately mattered to de Gaulle was the liberation of North and West Africa, still in Vichy hands, and of France itself.

He had no means of doing anything about North and West Africa. But the Free French in London were determined, from the outset, to develop their contacts with Metropolitan France. Although much intelligence work was done in France by the British and the Free French, large-scale resistance in France did not develop until the end of 1941 or, rather, the start of 1942. The highly intricate story of the French Resistance cannot be dealt with here; it is enough to say that, although de Gaulle and the Home Resistance leaders were far from having identical aims, de Gaulle did his utmost, through his B.C.R.A. secret service and an emissary like Jean Moulin, to 'unify' the Resistance and make it accept de Gaulle's albeit 'symbolic' authority. The largest and most active single group among the *résistants* were the Communists. Although de Gaulle disapproved of their 'direct action' methods (such as assassinating Germans), which could only lead to the most merciless reprisals, he was anxious for them to accept his 'authority', too.

An important landmark in this process of giving the whole Resistance a Gaullist 'capping' was de Gaulle's decision in July 1942 to give the Free French movement a new name – that of 'Fighting France' (*France Combattante*). Significantly, the Soviet Government gave this move its wholehearted support. It recognized 'Fighting France' as 'the totality of French citizens and territories not recognizing the capitulation and contributing anywhere and by every means to the liberation of France'. At the same time, it recognized the French National Committee as 'the only body with a right to organize the participation in the war of French citizens and territories' and to represent their interests with the U.S.S.R. This meant in effect that *the Russians recognized de Gaulle's authority over the Home Resistance, including the Communists.*[1] This was a very important achievement for de Gaulle, all the more so as the wording of the British and American recognition of 'Fighting France' was much less explicit. The Americans merely treated it as a 'symbol'.

During 1942, more and more Resistance leaders in France, most of them belonging to left-wing movements or parties, made contact with the Free French. Many settled in or visited London, among them Socialists like André Philip (who became a member of de Gaulle's committee), and Pierre Brossolette, who later returned to France and, caught by the Gestapo, committed suicide. Other left-wingers also

1. As de Gaulle saw it, this also meant, in the Russian view, that there were a) Vichy and b) the Free French, including the Resistance, but no 'third solution' which, he had strong reason to suspect, was precisely what Britain and the United States were trying to find.

came to London – Emmanuel d'Astier de la Vigerie, Christian Pineau, Mendès-France, Henri Frenay, etc. In January 1943 Fernand Grenier arrived with a message from the Communist Party associating itself unreservedly with Fighting France. By this time de Gaulle was in deep trouble over North Africa, and was only too glad to accept the helping hand of the Communists, the most dynamic and influential Resistance group in France. In fact, as we have seen, he had told the Russians long before that he wanted the Communists in France to cooperate with him. Finally, in May 1943, the C.N.R. (Conseil National de la Résistance) was set up in Paris as a result of Moulin's[1] endless efforts. It comprised not only all the Resistance movements, but also the trade unions and all the 'anti-German' political parties. Although some of these centre and right-wing parties were essentially Vichyite, they were still represented on the C.N.R. by a few individuals. This was no doubt a subterfuge, but was intended to impress on Britain and the U.S.A. that de Gaulle 'had the whole of France behind him'. The message sent by the C.N.R. demanding 'the formation of a provisional government under General de Gaulle' strengthened de Gaulle's hand enormously in the laborious battle he had to wage, through the greater part of 1943, against General Giraud and his American protectors.

7. De Gaulle versus Roosevelt and Giraud

'Operation Torch' – the North Africa Landing – in November

---

1. Jean Moulin, one of the greatest of the 'Gaullist' Resistance heroes (whose remains were to be reburied at the Pantheon in de Gaulle's presence in 1964) had been a member of the Prefectoral Corps. In 1940 he was arrested by the Germans and tortured. He later escaped to London and, well-supplied with funds, returned to France at the beginning of 1942, where he did his great 'unification' work among the Resistance groups. His work culminated in the formation of the C.N.R. Soon afterwards he was captured by the Germans in mysterious circumstances and tortured to death.

1942 very nearly wrecked de Gaulle's Free French enterprise. After Dakar and Syria, where the Vichy troops had
stubbornly fought against the Free French, the Americans were determined to keep de Gaulle out of the project
at any price. Largely under the influence of men like Admiral
Leahy, the former U.S. Ambassador to Vichy, and Robert
Murphy, the U.S. Consul-General at Algiers, who had been
working hand-in-hand with the so-called 'North African
Resistance' composed of Vichyites now ready to jump on
the American bandwagon, the U.S. Government had made
plans from which, at least for the time being, de Gaulle was
to be left out altogether.

After the trouble with the British in the Levant, his relations with the British Government were also as bad as they
could be, and on 29 September he had one of his stormiest
meetings with Churchill and Eden. As de Gaulle tells the
story, it started with an angry discussion about Syria and the
Lebanon; the British ministers demanded that an election
take place there at once, while de Gaulle firmly refused; then
Churchill said that he was determined not to associate the
Free French with Madagascar – 'I don't see why, in view
of your attitude to the Levant, we should go out of our way
to set up a Gaullist command in Tananarive'. One thing led
to another, and, in the end, Churchill lost his temper completely. 'You keep on saying that you are France! I do not
recognize you as France! *Where* is France? No doubt the
Gaullists are a respectable and important part of the French
people. But we can, without any doubt, find another,
perfectly valid, authority outside the Gaullists.' For several
weeks relations were strained as never before. Then on 6
November, Mr Eden, 'all honey', proposed that the British
and Free French publish a joint communiqué saying that
Legentilhomme, the Free French general, had been
appointed High Commissioner in Madagascar. De Gaulle
immediately concluded that this was a minor sop to keep

the Free French quiet while North Africa was invaded by
the Anglo-Americans. (*Mémoires*, vol. 2, pp. 45–6.)

The Americans had indeed, with British consent, discovered that 'other perfectly valid French authority outside
the Gaullists' to which Churchill had referred, six weeks
before. Distrustful of de Gaulle, whom Roosevelt regarded
as a man of infinite personal ambition with dictatorial
leanings, and whom the State Department treated as an ally
of the Communists inside France, the Americans preferred
to back certain French elements who, though associated in
the past and even now with Vichy, were much more likely
than de Gaulle to obey their instructions.

Their man was five-star general Henri Giraud who had
been taken prisoner by the Germans in May 1940 and had,
in the spring of 1942, escaped from the fortress of König-
stein to Vichy, where he had declared his allegiance to
Pétain.

According to Giraud himself, he did not take the Gaullist,
or any other resistance movement in France seriously, but
considered Vichy's own Armistice Army of 100,000 men his
'biggest trump'. Soon after his return to France he was
contacted by American agents, and, according to him, the
question arose whether there should be an Allied landing in
North Africa or one (which he himself urged) in the South of
France during the spring of 1943 – by which time, he
claimed, the Armistice Army would be ready to support the
Allies. It is hard to say whether the Armistice Army would
indeed have fought the Germans had the Allies landed on
the Provence coast; certainly the Armistice Army (with a
few isolated exceptions) put up no resistance at all to the
German occupation of Vichy France after the Allied North
African landing, and allowed themselves to be disarmed.

In any case, Giraud's services were not required in France,
but in North Africa; and Mr Murphy, working hand-in-
hand with the 'Vichyite' North African resistance, headed

by Lemaigre-Dubreuil, arranged that Giraud be brought to North Africa in time for Operation Torch.

De Gaulle was kept strictly out of it all. Although later de Gaulle was to treat Giraud's war record with devastating irony in his *Mémoires*, he wrote to him in the middle of 1942 and urged him to join the Free French. This invitation, however, met with no response, and the Gaullists then started treating Giraud with the greatest contempt, even alleging that he had had some highly suspect dealings with the Germans and Laval at Vichy, and that there was something rather shady in his spectacular escape.

In the early morning hours of 6 November, a British submarine picked up Giraud on the south coast of France; but, instead of taking him straight to North Africa, it sailed towards Gibraltar where, after various mishaps, Giraud finally landed on the afternoon of the 7th. Here he conferred with Eisenhower, only to find that there had been some confusion over the exact role he was expected to play in North Africa. He stayed in Gibraltar all the next day, when the news started coming in of the Anglo-American landings between Mogador in Morocco and Bone in Eastern Algeria.[1] Nearly everywhere the Vichy French were putting up a strong resistance. Worse still, it was now learned that Admiral Darlan was in Algiers. Finally, Giraud was not flown to Algiers until the 9th, i.e. at least thirty-six hours too late 'to stop the fratricidal struggle'.

*

The arrival in Algiers of Darlan who, as head of the Vichy Government for over a year, had collaborated with the Germans even more thoroughly than Laval had done, had upset both Giraud's and the Americans' plans. Darlan had

1. Giraud claims already then to have pointed out to Eisenhower the folly of not occupying Tunisia, and so forestalling a German–Italian landing there. (Giraud, *Un seul but, la victoire*, Paris, 1949, p. 24.)

ostensibly come to Algiers to visit his son, who was seriously ill. But, as head of the French Fleet, he continued to 'represent the Marshal' and, in the circumstances, the Americans calculated that he alone could put an end to the stiff resistance of the Vichy French. Furthermore Darlan alone seemed able to order the French navy at Toulon to set sail for Africa.[1] A deal was therefore made with him that succeeded in stopping the Vichy French resistance, but also made the *collabo* Admiral the top French authority in North Africa. Three days after the North African landing, the Germans occupied Vichy France; but just before that, General Noguès, the French commander in Morocco, received a telegram from Pétain appointing him 'sole representative in North Africa of the Marshal, Head of the State', and two days later, Noguès handed these powers over to Darlan. The American military, thoroughly briefed by men like Mr Murphy, did not think this such a bad arrangement, all the more so as both the European population in North Africa and the Vichy forces there were thoroughly *maréchaliste*, having almost wholly approved of Pétain's 'National Revolution', concentration camps, and anti-Jewish legislation.

Darlan was behaving with his usual arrogance, and it took Eisenhower three days to persuade him and General Noguès to have Giraud appointed French commander-in-Chief, with Darlan himself remaining civilian overlord in North Africa. Darlan had nothing but contempt for Giraud. 'He is not your man,' he told Murphy. 'Politically he is a child. He is a good divisional commander, nothing more.'[2]

1. The navy at Toulon, as we know, did not escape to North Africa but, rather than fall into German hands, scuttled itself on 27 November. This greatly reduced Darlan's value in the Allies' eyes. De Gaulle, far from paying tribute, like so many others, to the 'heroism' of the French navy, thought its end lamentable and 'idiotic'.

2. Robert E. Sherwood. *The White House Papers of Harry Hopkins.* London, 1949, p. 646.

Although, as we now know, Stalin thought it very clever of the Americans to have 'used' Darlan to stop the resistance – 'in such a political-military situation,' he wrote to Churchill, 'it is right to use not only the Darlans, but even the devil and his grandmother' – the American deal with the Admiral caused the greatest consternation in Britain and the United States. Roosevelt felt obliged to explain some time later that the deal with Darlan should be regarded as no more than a 'temporary expedient' which had had its value. For instance, thanks to Darlan, Governor-General Boisson of Dakar had been won over, without a single shot having to be fired. This implied that it was more profitable to deal directly with the Vichy proconsuls than to allow the Free French to launch naval attacks on them.

Yet the situation in North Africa was absurd with Darlan virtually the supreme ruler. Military operations were not going too well (for, on orders from Vichy, Admiral Esteva had allowed the Germans and Italians to occupy Bizerta and Tunis without putting up any resistance). Then, on 25 December, Darlan was assassinated at Algiers by a young man, Bonnier de La Chapelle. Whether he was a royalist (as Giraud alleged)[1] or a Gaullist has never been clearly established, but, in any case, Giraud had him summarily tried and shot immediately afterwards. The 'Imperial Council', composed of the Vichy proconsuls, then appointed Giraud as Darlan's successor, with the absurd title of 'Civil and Military Commander-in-Chief'. What followed under Giraud was a worse police terror than even Darlan had unleashed. René Capitant, head of *Combat*, the Gaullist resistance group in Algiers, escaped; but dozens of

1. The Count of Paris, the French Pretender, was in Algiers at the time, and pleaded with Giraud for the young man's reprieve. The Gaullists claimed that Giraud himself was a royalist – which suggests that Giraud had something to do with Darlan's assassination, but that Bonnier was an awkward witness to have around.

other people suspected of Gaullist sympathies were arrested or (like M. Louis Joxe) exiled. All official premises continued to be adorned with Pétain's portrait, and Giraud showed himself more than reluctant to release the 50,000 people held in concentration camps (Gaullists, Spanish Republicans, Communists, etc.) or to repeal any of the Vichy legislation. Giraud excused the new arrests by claiming a Gaullist plot to murder Mr Murphy! Strict orders were also given to the French officers that no mention should ever be made of the Free French, de Gaulle, Leclerc or Larminat.[1]

Officially, Giraud declared that 'victory over Germany' was all that mattered; that everybody – the Vichy proconsuls, de Gaulle, and the Vichy army in North Africa – should cooperate; and that it was wrong to try and set up a French government before the liberation of France. Meantime, to please the Americans, he declared that the 1875 constitution could be considered as valid.

*

Giraud's argument that a French Government was 'unnecessary' contradicted the whole policy of de Gaulle, who regarded the political manoeuvres in North Africa as unspeakably squalid. He was himself acutely conscious that the apparent triumph of the Vichyites and their friends represented a deadly danger to the Free French. He dwelt on the absolute 'immorality' of ganging up with the Darlans and Boissons, and even argued that if this kind of thing continued, there would be a Communist revolution in France. He urged Giraud to meet him on French territory, away from American or British tutelage, but Giraud was evasive. De Gaulle's broadcasts had, meanwhile, at the request of the Americans, been stopped on the B.B.C., and it was not till the middle of January that Churchill summoned de Gaulle to Anfa, near Casablanca, where he was in conference with

1. J. Soustelle, *Envers et contre tout*. Paris, 1950, vol. 2, p. 104.

Roosevelt. De Gaulle at first refused to go. Then came a
second summons from Churchill, declaring that this one was
being sent on Roosevelt's behalf as well, and threatening to
wash his hands of de Gaulle altogether if the latter still
refused to come. This time de Gaulle submitted.

De Gaulle's first meeting with Giraud at Anfa 'behind
American barbed wire' – 'most humiliating', he found it –
was far from cordial. He upbraided him for not having
joined the Free French after his escape from Germany;
objected to his collaboration with 'traitors' like the Vichy
proconsuls; and reminded him that the Free French were the
only Frenchmen to have fought the Germans since the
Armistice.

If Churchill found it necessary to bring de Gaulle to
Anfa, it was because there were large territories still under
the Free French, and important forces like Larminat's and
Leclerc's fighting in Africa. But de Gaulle would not associate himself with the Algiers arrangement on Giraud's or
the Americans' terms; and the only tangible sign of a
'reconciliation' between the two generals was the absurd
photograph taken of them shaking hands, with Roosevelt
and Churchill smiling benignly in the background. De
Gaulle had agreed to pose, merely to please Roosevelt. 'I
shall do that for you,' he said to the President. But it meant
nothing, and de Gaulle hastened to return to London.[1]

De Gaulle now seemed in a worse position than ever. But
he did not give up the struggle. He still had his territories, his
armed forces, and public opinion, especially in France,
behind him, while the Algiers arrangement was being more
and more severely criticized in Britain and the United States.

De Gaulle's next move was one of extreme 'radicalism'.

1. The American secret services were so suspicious of de Gaulle that
during the latter's first meeting with Roosevelt, Murphy and several
armed cops were hiding behind a curtain, ready to shoot if de Gaulle
bodily assaulted the President!

For it was by 'radicalizing' his movement, by speaking of the coming French 'revolution' and by generally assuming a left-wing attitude rigidly hostile to everything 'Vichyite' that de Gaulle could appeal most effectively to the Resistance in France and wreck any American designs of setting up a quasi-Vichyite régime there. The first thing to do was to undermine Giraud and, ultimately, seize power in Algiers.

Significantly, between November 1942 and the following autumn, de Gaulle did his utmost to secure Russian support. In his own conversations with Ambassador Bogomolov and in Garreau's numerous talks with Molotov, Vyshinsky and Lozovsky, the same themes recur over and over again. *But for Russian support*, Garreau told Molotov on 26 March, *the Free French might not have survived the November crisis*, when an attempt was made to create a new kind of authority in North Africa. Garreau, in particular, frequently stressed that Giraud was a highly shady character; that there was something very curious about his escape from Germany and his subsequent negotiations with Laval and the German Ambassador Abetz; that the Americans were trying to set up a Vichyite régime in France; that everything was being done to get de Gaulle to submit to Giraud. On 30 March, Bogomolov reported a conversation he had with de Gaulle. Having refused all the offers made to him at Anfa, de Gaulle said, he had now received a visit from Cardinal Spellman, who, obviously acting on Roosevelt's behalf, had asked him, politely, to submit to General Giraud, and warned him that otherwise Free France would be excluded from playing any part in future developments. Garreau also stressed to the Russians that the American troops in North Africa were incompetent; that the Vichy troops, with a few exceptions, were showing no eagerness to fight the Germans; and that Leclerc's Free French division was the only good French unit. Later, during the battle of Tunisia, Garreau declared that if 50,000 troops under Giraud were taking part in the operation, there were also 30,000 Free French troops under Leclerc, though these received no credit or acknowledgement from the Americans. On 11 May, Garreau told Lozovsky that Giraud was planning to become French dictator; to smother the Resistance movement in France with the help of colonial troops; and, under the guise of 'republicanism', to maintain the Vichy régime and the Vichy personnel, so saving all those who had collaborated with the Germans. De Gaulle, on the other hand, was anxious to set up, as soon as possible, a regular government in Algiers, complete with a Consultative Assembly. Finally, after de Gaulle's arrival in Algiers at the end of May, Garreau reported to Lozovsky de Gaulle's latest statement that the Free French would not tolerate anyone associated with Vichy or the Germans having any say in the future running of France.

De Gaulle's extreme 'radicalism' during this period, and his constant search for Soviet support proved to be of the greatest value to him. He became something of an anti-Vichy hero in the eyes of French opinion. And his task was made all the easier because Giraud (one has merely to read his memoirs!) was not only a hidebound reactionary, but also a remarkably stupid man.

To the Americans Giraud was becoming a liability. With his concentration camps and his Vichy legislation, he had, somehow, to be made more respectable – in short, to be 'democratized'. In March 1943 Monnet, at the Americans' request, went to Algiers to re-educate Giraud and to prepare, if possible, a reconciliation with de Gaulle. As Giraud himself wrote in his memoirs, (op. cit., p. 121) 'on 14 March, I made the first democratic speech in my life' – under the influence of Monnet, and in order to please the Americans, on whom he was dependent for arms and supplies. All he achieved, in fact, was to annoy the countless Vichyites in the army, who regarded his speech as 'a betrayal of the Marshal'.

Apart from Monnet, General Catroux also went to Algiers and spent two months trying to convert Giraud. Finally, Giraud had to agree to de Gaulle's coming to Algiers: 'It was difficult not to do so since a few thousand Frenchmen under Leclerc had taken part in the battle of Tunisia.' It was a mistake, he later ruefully remarked, 'but I was perfectly incompetent in politics'. (ibid., p. 160.)

De Gaulle, accompanied by some of his closest London associates, arrived in Algiers on 30 May, and the real trouble started for Giraud. On the very first day, de Gaulle pointedly laid a Cross-of-Lorraine-shaped wreath at the foot of the war memorial, and although the majority of the Europeans in Algiers continued to be *maréchaliste* at heart, there were enough people present to give him a 'mass ovation' – though not without some previous prompting from *Combat*, the semi-clandestine Gaullist organization in Algiers.

Later de Gaulle was to write that although, at that time, 'the army, the police, the administration, the press, radio and everything' were 'dependent on the Civil and Military Commander-in-Chief' (i.e. Giraud), he felt from the general atmosphere at Algiers that 'already then everybody knew who was on the rise and who was on the decline, and how it would all end'. Significantly, on that very day, de Gaulle (and not Giraud) received a letter of resignation from M. Peyrouton, the Giraud-appointed governor-general of Algeria, who now asked to be drafted into the Army. Peyrouton, one of the hardest colonial bosses both under the Third Republic (when he set up a concentration camp in Tunisia) and under Vichy, was one of the Vichy proconsuls, whose cooperation Roosevelt and Churchill had thought particularly valuable.

*

The rather absurd 'bicephalous' Committee of National Liberation, with de Gaulle and Giraud as co-presidents, was

set up on 3 June. It was at first composed of only seven
members – its two presidents; General Georges (whom the
British had smuggled out of France and who was entirely on
Giraud's side); André Philip and Massigli (who were de
Gaulle's men); and Monnet and General Catroux (who tried
to act the honest brokers). A Declaration, chiefly drafted
by de Gaulle, announced that this Committee was 'the
central French authority' which 'directed the French war
effort everywhere and in all forms' and that its authority
extended to all territories hitherto under the authority of de
Gaulle and Giraud. Finally, it said that, pending the transfer
of its authority to 'the future Provisional Government of the
Republic', it undertook to 'restore French freedoms, the
laws of the Republic and the Republican régime,' and to
destroy the 'arbitrary and personal régime' of Vichy. It was
a lot for Giraud to swallow. Moreover, de Gaulle insisted at
the very first meeting of the Committee that the Vichy proconsuls (Boisson, Noguès, etc.) be dismissed.

The U.S. authorities were not too pleased with this display
of 'French sovereignty', and their censorship actually 'sat'
on the Declaration for several hours. Nevertheless, on
Algiers radio, 'to which the Gaullists had now access' (de
Gaulle, *Mémoires*, vol. 2, p. 153), de Gaulle went even
further and announced to France that a French Government had been set up in Algiers, pending its arrival in
Paris.

There were inevitable complications at first. Churchill and
Eden unexpectedly arrived in Algiers, and asking Giraud and
de Gaulle to a picnic, expressed their disquiet.Churchill said
to de Gaulle that, although he did not want to interfere in
French internal affairs, His Majesty's Government could not
remain indifferent 'supposing de Gaulle decided to devour
Giraud'. There was also a great deal of friction with
Eisenhower, who was much more favourable to Giraud
than to de Gaulle. There followed various threats of resig-

nation from de Gaulle and other crises. The Committee of
Seven was increased, first to fourteen and then to sixteen
members, and de Gaulle's position grew much stronger as a
result. Giraud, for his part, had played his hand extremely
badly. To please the Americans, from whom he needed
armaments, he had made that 'democratic' speech in March,
and this had deeply annoyed both the European population
of Algiers and, worse still, the North African army, which
was still imbued with the authoritarian cult of Pétain. De
Gaulle, on the other hand, made most of the audience he
had in occupied France, spoke of 'revolution', and pressed
for the early calling in Algiers of a Consultative Assembly,
largely representing the French Home Resistance.

If de Gaulle was defiant towards the Allies, Giraud, on the
contrary, always wanted to make the best impression on
them. In July, ostensibly for 'purely military purposes', he
went on his ill-fated tour to the United States, Canada, and
England; but he aroused very little interest, and annoyed
all the pro-Gaullist elements by saying repeatedly that he
was 'only a soldier fighting on the side of the Allies', by
never referring to the Algiers Committee, and by suggesting
that 'France did not yet exist' and that 'nobody could speak
in the name of France'. 'Everybody concluded,' de Gaulle
later wrote, 'that in the destiny of France he could never
play anything but a secondary role.' (*Mémoires*, vol. 2,
p. 148.) Meantime, de Gaulle was building up the National
Committee, going on 'triumphal' trips all over North
Africa, and agitating for recognition of France's great power
status – for instance in relation to Italy, where Mussolini had
just fallen, and which was about to be invaded by the Allied
armies, including the French under General Juin. 14 July in
Algiers was a sort of apotheosis for de Gaulle; in the presence
of an enormous crowd in the Algiers Forum, he spoke of the
'new road, the new destinies' of France, of the 'profound
feeling of the French masses which had to be taken into

consideration'. The French forces, he suggested, were
nobody's mercenaries.

His patriotic and ultra-nationalist speeches made a considerable impression, especially on the forces, and there
began that very curious process whereby the 'Vichyite'
elements in the Army – not only the privates, but also a high
proportion of the officers – went 'Gaullist'. The reasons for
this were, after all, elementary: it was felt, more and more,
*that de Gaulle was a real leader, whereas Giraud was not;
to join de Gaulle was to join the winning side. To remain 'loyal
to the Marshal', now that the Marshal was little better than
a prisoner of the Germans, required some extremely tortuous
reasoning.*

This process, as we shall see, was also going to have a very
important effect on de Gaulle. He had been a 'rebel general'
in 1940; he had been sentenced to death by Vichy as a
deserter; now the former Vichyites in the Army were rallying
to him. As a result, he was to find himself, more and more,
in his own social environment. The Army that was being
built up was largely composed of former Vichyites. A very
strong case of 'collaborationism' – not merely with Vichy,
but with the Germans – could be made out against a man
like General Juin. De Gaulle preferred to turn a blind eye to
it. And, once he had got rid of Giraud, he underwent a
gradual, but unmistakable process of *de-radicalization*. This
became particularly apparent once he had landed in France
after D-Day.

Paradoxically, it was Giraud who, as French Commander-
in-Chief, succeeded in liberating Corsica from the Germans
and Italians in the course of September, and he did this with
the help of the local Resistance organizations, which *were
very largely Communist*. It was a great achievement, but was
not at all to de Gaulle's liking. According to Giraud, de
Gaulle was jealous of the man who had, after all, successfully liberated the first *département* of Metropolitan France

at the cost of only 72 dead and some 200 wounded. 'He has stolen my Corsica', de Gaulle is supposed to have said, and it was as a result of the Corsican victory that he made up his mind, there and then, to eliminate Giraud from the Committee of National Liberation. (Giraud, op. cit., p. 260.) De Gaulle took the line that Giraud had acted in his Corsican venture independently of the Committee, and that, moreover, he had given a completely free hand to the Communists to set up local administrations of their own throughout the liberated island. This, in de Gaulle's view, was 'a desperately dangerous precedent to establish' (*Mémoires*, vol. 2, p. 179). He visited Corsica, and appointed a Prefect who 'put everything right'. Back in Algiers, he hastened to draw up an *ordonnance* allowing the Committee of National Liberation to have henceforth only one president. The elimination of Giraud had begun. He was still commander-in-chief, but under the strict orders of the Committee. If Giraud signed the *ordonnance*, it was, according to de Gaulle, because, with the dispatch of a French expeditionary corps to Italy in the offing, he 'could already see the Allies appointing him commander-in-chief there' (*Mémoires*, vol. 2, p. 181). In reality, Giraud was simply to be sacked by de Gaulle's committee six months later.

During the weeks that followed, de Gaulle reorganized the committee, including in it a few former Ministers of the Third Republic like M. Queuille, some deputies like Pierre Mendès-France, and representatives of the Home Resistance who had come to Algiers like Emmanuel d'Astier, de Menthon, and Henri Frenay. Giraud supporters like General Georges were eliminated. Later, in April 1944, de Gaulle also included two Communists on the Committee – Billoux and Grenier. This was an important sop to the Home Resistance, though it greatly alarmed Churchill.

A Consultative Assembly was established, and this met for the first time on 3 November; it included several deputies who had not voted for Pétain in 1940, several Communist deputies whom Giraud had only recently released from concentration camps in North Africa, and representatives of the 'External', 'Home', and 'North African' Resistance, together with a few Algerian notabilities. It held some fifty meetings of which twenty were attended by de Gaulle himself. De Gaulle made 'revolutionary' speeches before the Assembly, and exalted the Resistance as the quintessence of the French spirit; but, at the same time, he felt that the Assembly was much more 'extreme' than himself:

There were a few who simply wanted to return to the institutions of the Third Republic. But, to the great majority, this *ancien régime* was doomed ... And numerous were those who wanted to leave to demagogy ... even more room than under the Third Republic ... Many daydreamed about a 'sole and sovereign assembly', a sort of Convention ... in which most of the politicians who had emerged from the Resistance would find a place ...

The Senate, these people thought, would be abolished; the role of the President would be purely decorative; and the government would be wholly subservient to the Assembly. De Gaulle's *ordonnance* of 21 April 1944 provided that nothing would be settled until the government had returned to France; then, after the repatriation of the war prisoners, there would be local elections, followed by the election of a National Assembly whose role and composition would not, however, be decided until later. Meantime, there would be an enlarged Consultative Assembly in France, and the franchise would be extended to women. The *ordonnance* also made important provisions for the transition stage in France.

It was obvious that, pending all these elections *after* the war, there could only be a government in France under de Gaulle. This, according to de Gaulle's version of the story, did not suit the Allies at all. 'Since they could no longer count on Giraud to counterbalance de Gaulle, they started thinking up all kinds of other expedients', de Gaulle was to write later; and he makes much of the plan 'hatched in London and Washington' to fish out President Lebrun, who had not officially resigned, and to smuggle him to Algiers. Fortunately for de Gaulle, Lebrun did not lend himself to the scheme, and soon afterwards the Gestapo deported him to Germany. Later, as we know, just before the liberation of Paris, an American attempt was to be made to summon the Chamber of Deputies with the help of Herriot and – Laval!, so spoiling de Gaulle's return as 'the conquering hero'.

*

Relations with the Allies between August and the following spring underwent some curious changes. In August 1943, rather to the disgust of the U.S. and British Governments, the Soviet Government gave the French Committee more straightforward and wholehearted recognition than either London or Washington were prepared to do.[1] During his 'radical' phase, when courting the Russians, de Gaulle offered to send a French infantry division to Russia, create a direct Moscow–Algiers airline, and generally establish a variety of links quite independently of the 'Anglo-Saxons'. (Nothing came of the airline, since it had to cross British-controlled territory.)

The Western Allies did not much care for these secret talks, and practically prohibited the visit to Algiers of Ambassador Bogomolov. De Gaulle's representative in Moscow, M. Garreau, however, was able to spend two months in Algiers. All seemed to be going well until suddenly de Gaulle discovered that, during the Foreign Ministers' Conference at Moscow in October 1943, it was Stalin who had opposed the inclusion of the French in the European

1. It recognized it as 'the representative of the State interests of the French Republic and the leader of all French patriots fighting against Nazi tyranny'.

Advisory Commission. (*Sovietsko-Frantsuskie otnosheniya*, p. 225.) A few days later, the Russians informed Garreau that it was the British and Americans who, 'for the time being', had excluded the French from the E.A.C. Whichever version was strictly correct, the Americans continued to look upon de Gaulle with much distrust. In a conversation with Vyshinsky on 13 November, Ambassador Averell Harriman commented on Giraud's exclusion from the C.F.L.N.:

We expected him to exercise some political activity, but our hopes were deceived. However, his departure may consolidate the Committee. Unfortunately de Gaulle is thinking more of how he is going to rule France than of the ways of liberating her. That is his great flaw. Also, he is extremely vain and imagines himself a sort of Joan of Arc, and that makes work with him difficult. No doubt de Gaulle did a useful job in unifying the Resistance forces. But there are stronger and more acceptable people on the French Committee, for instance Monnet and Massigli. (ibid., p. 232.)

The ousting of Giraud marked the real beginning of de Gaulle's 'de-radicalization' process. More and more representatives of the 'old society' and of the old 'general staffs' (military, administrative, political, economic) who had supported Giraud, now saw no alternative to supporting de Gaulle. Many of these people had much more practical experience than the Free French 'amateurs', and they began to convert some of the Free French round de Gaulle to their own way of thinking; the extreme 'radicalism' of the Resistance, strongly influenced by the Communists, scared many Gaullists, and they began to create round de Gaulle himself a new political atmosphere which was different from the 'pure Gaullism' of the London days, with its uncompromising hostility to Vichy. More important still was the Army; there were about 400,000 French troops (though only about half of them armed) outside France, and most of them had originally been 'Vichyite' and not 'Free French'. Even in the famous Free French Division under General

Leclerc, which was the first to enter Paris, less than half of all the officers and soldiers were originally Free-French; the rest were mostly ex-Vichyites. Very significantly, in a Washington dispatch of 25 February 1944, Ambassador Gromyko noted that the State Department had lately been more tolerant of the Algiers Committee:

> This can be attributed to the fact that, in the American view, de Gaulle *has been gradually departing from his former radicalism. His much softer treatment of former Vichyites is, in the eyes of the State Department*, a welcome development. (ibid., p. 241.)

*

But although de Gaulle had made peace with many former Vichyites, this did not mean that he could be anything but wholly hostile to the Vichy régime. Its absolute disappearance was the pre-condition for the future France he himself had in mind. D-Day was approaching, and de Gaulle was worried by the military role that the French themselves were to play in the liberation of their country – both as soldiers and as the Home Resistance; by the necessity of having France administered by Frenchmen, and not by A.M.G.O.T., after the unfortunate model of Italy; and by the problem of how the Home Resistance, once it had outlived its usefulness, could be made to conform with the requirements of that central authority which he was determined to create.

*

To make quite sure that they were not going to be forestalled by anybody else in France after the Allied landings there, the Algiers Committee declared themselves, on 3 June 1944, three days before D-Day, the Provisional Government of the French Republic. They were not, however, to be recognized as such by the Allies until long after the Liberation of Paris. To achieve this aim, it was absolutely essential for de Gaulle to show that France had 'accepted' him as her leader.

CHAPTER 5

THE LIBERATION

1. De Gaulle's Paris Apotheosis

THERE was a somewhat childish and petulant 'me-too' attitude on the part of de Gaulle which annoyed, irritated, and sometimes amused the British, the Americans, and even the Russians. These were the Big Three who were fighting the war – Britain principally with her navy and air-force; the U.S.A. above all with her vast economic resources; Russia, with millions of soldiers and a gigantic economic effort. There could have been no Liberation of France but for the combined effort of the Big Three. Not only in his memoirs, written long after the event, but also at the time, de Gaulle admitted this fundamental fact of the war situation only very grudgingly. When, at the end of 1944, he visited Stalingrad, he described that battle as 'the symbol of our joint efforts', which made the Russians on the spot raise their eyebrows.

As has been seen, the armed forces that the Free French contributed to the British war effort while de Gaulle was in London were of some value, but they were still very small stuff. Later, in North Africa in 1943–4, when the 'Vichy' troops there had become available, the French armies (including a considerable proportion of Algerian and other colonial troops) did not exceed 230,000, of whom 120,000 were to fight in the Italian campaign under General Juin (*Mémoires*, vol. 2, p. 304). There were, moreover, some 150,000 troops which de Gaulle describes as '*forces de souveraineté*', i.e. French troops stationed in the various colonies and protectorates. With characteristic petulance de Gaulle was to write later:

We were never consulted on strategic questions ... The Anglo-Saxons never really treated us as real allies. Whether as a matter of policy, or merely because it was expedient, they used the French forces in operations where they themselves had taken the decisions, just as if the French forces belonged to them, merely because they had helped to arm them. (ibid., p. 317.)

De Gaulle severely criticized Churchill's 'Mediterranean strategy', and was much relieved when 'under Russian pressure' *Overlord* was finally agreed upon in Teheran at the end of 1943. But even then he had considerable trouble in obtaining the assurance that French troops would be used in the subsequent landing on the south coast of France, and, above all, in the operations across northern France, following the Normandy landing. For one thing, there were no French troops available in England for the purpose, and General Leclerc's 2nd Armoured Division had to be taken by sea all the way from Algeria to England. As regards the Provence Landing, de Gaulle was very worried for a long time that the French troops fighting in Italy might be used not for liberating southern France, but for Churchill's schemes of forestalling the Russians in the Balkans, Hungary, and Austria. By and large, through sheer persistence, de Gaulle received satisfaction, though the Normandy Landing was, in fact, carried out practically without French participation, except for some ships and airborne troops. This was to rankle with de Gaulle so deeply that, even twenty years later, when commemorative ceremonies were held on the Normandy beaches, the President of the Fifth Republic refused to attend them.

*

At the time of the Normandy Landing, the internal situation in France could not have been more confused. The Vichy government was still in existence, though more and more a prisoner of the Germans. And yet, in the spring of 1944,

Pétain had visited Paris, and had received a rousing welcome from the population; a film of the visit was shown to de Gaulle, who did not like it at all, though he tried to console himself with the thought that this was 'perhaps the only way many Parisians thought they could protest against the Germans'. De Gaulle himself did not yet see very clearly how he could impose himself on France as the head of the government. There were several dangers, as he saw it. The Allies might impose, for the time being, a sort of occupation régime of their own, and he violently protested against the use of American-made bank-notes by the Allied troops. And what if the Vichy régime was to perpetuate itself in some way? Or an attempt was made by the Americans to revive the Third Republic by some shabby trick? Finally, was there not also a danger that the Resistance, 'under Communist influence', might try to set up a revolutionary régime of its own?

On D-Day (6 June) and for several days afterwards, de Gaulle was virtually marooned in England, but busy protesting against the establishment of a military administration in the small liberated areas of France. Then, between 8 and 20 June, de Gaulle was suddenly given a helping hand by several governments-in-exile – Poles, Belgians, Yugoslavs, Norwegians, Czechoslovaks, who recognized the French Provisional Government, despite American and British objections. Almost surreptituously on 13 June, de Gaulle and a small group of his assistants, went on a short visit to Bayeux, on the Normandy beachhead; among the persons accompanying him was a M. Coulet, whom he hastened to appoint *Commissaire de la République* for Normandy, so establishing a Gaullist governor. Although there were still numerous portraits of the Marshal at Bayeux, de Gaulle received a rousing welcome from the population, and the sub-prefect 'submitted to him' and – took down the Marshal's picture – to which the Allies had, apparently raised no objections. In his subsequent dealings with the British and Americans, de Gaulle was to make much of his popularity with the 'French people', as shown by the Bayeux sample. There was another important fact which was now playing in his favour. The French Resistance, including the French Home Forces (F.F.I.) under the command of General Koenig, were contributing nobly to the Allied war effort, tying up substantial German forces in Brittany, and dislocating German rail and even road transport throughout the greater part of France.

De Gaulle did not stay more than a few hours in France. On his return to London he learned that Roosevelt was anxious for him to come to Washington, maybe to get him out of the way. So while the Battle of France was in progress, de Gaulle first travelled to Algiers, then to Italy, and finally to the U.S.A. In Rome, he was received in audience by Pope Pius XII. Although (he wrote) 'in his infinite caution, the Holy See had hitherto ignored Fighting France and the Algiers Government' and had maintained diplomatic relations with Vichy, 'the Holy Father desired the defeat of Hitler'. He was, of course, very concerned about Communism. Germany 'which, in many ways, was particularly dear to him, was in the centre of his preoccupations'. 'Poor people,' His Holiness said, 'how much they will suffer!' Although, in conclusion, de Gaulle says that Pius XII deeply impressed him by 'his piety, pity, and political sense in the highest sense of the word' (*Mémoires*, vol. 2, p. 286), his account of the Pope is, in fact, a little masterpiece of *vacherie*.

De Gaulle's visit to Washington did not go too well. Roosevelt was much more cordial than ever before, but de Gaulle was taken aback by the President's ideas of running the world through a sort of Four-Power Directorate composed of the U.S.A., Russia, Britain, and China, and of turning Western Europe into an American sphere of influence. It was not till after de Gaulle's return to Algiers that a communication was received from the State Department saying that the French Committee of National Liberation was 'qualified to administer France'. This did not, however, prevent certain American authorities from trying out some quite different solutions – with the help of Herriot – and even Laval.

*

De Gaulle did not return to Normandy until 20 August, i.e. after the Paris insurrection against the Germans had already begun. At Eisenhower's headquarters, as he tells the story, he was startled to find that the commander-in-chief seemed cagey and embarrassed, claiming that the insurrection had 'started too soon', and showing himself in no hurry to send the Leclerc Division into Paris, though it was available. De Gaulle's explanation is that Roosevelt was still hoping that the Herriot-Laval combination would, somehow, succeed. On the 21st it was learned that, although they had both had a farewell lunch with Abetz, the German Ambassador, at the Hotel Matignon, the Premier's office, on 18 August, nothing had come of the plot to call the old Parliament and thus 'revive' the Third Republic. Laval had been taken east, and Herriot, the President of the Chamber, re-arrested. At Vichy, meantime, Pétain was about to be deported by the Germans, too.

Politically, this suited de Gaulle perfectly. *A political vacuum had been created in France, thanks to the Germans themselves.*

The story of the Paris Insurrection is highly complex, with its 'direct-action' enthusiasts, headed by Communists like Rol-Tanguy, and its more cautious men like de Gaulle's delegates, Parodi and Jacques Chaban-Delmas who, at one stage, even negotiated a temporary truce with the German commander of the Paris garrison, General von Choltitz, through the offices of Mr Nordling, the Swedish

Consul-General. Under pressure from the 'extremists', and partly in order to create the illusion that 'the people of Paris had liberated themselves', they agreed, however, on 23 August, to resume their battle against the Germans. In a sense Paris did liberate itself; but it did so with the Leclerc Division already on the point of entry and with the helpful attitude of the German general, who had made up his mind to ignore Hitler's order to destroy the city. There was some fighting in Paris all the same, both before and after the 'truce'; some 3,000 resisters were killed and 7,000 wounded.

De Gaulle claims great credit for having, with much difficulty, persuaded Eisenhower to rush Leclerc's Armoured Division – and not any other – to the aid of the Paris Insurrection. Eisenhower, who had intended to outflank and surround Paris, had had his hand forced by this Insurrection; but, as he himself says, Bradley had already chosen Leclerc's Division 'for the honour of first entry'.[1]

The veterans of this organization had started at Lake Chad three years before, made an almost impossible march across the Sahara, joined the [British] Eighth Army to participate in the latter part of the African campaign, and now its commander received, on 25 August, the surrender of the German general commanding the Paris garrison.[2]

Once Paris had been captured, Eisenhower notified de Gaulle that he 'hoped he would quickly enter the capital'. 'I desired that he, as the symbol of French Resistance, should make an entrance before I had to go through it.' (ibid., p. 325)

Eisenhower was later to speak with great warmth of the French Resistance.

1. This was an American gesture which unquestionably helped de Gaulle. The effect would not have been the same if he had followed an *American* division into Paris.

2. Dwight D. Eisenhower, *Crusade in Europe*. London, 1948, p. 325.

They had been of inestimable value in the campaign. They were particularly active in Brittany, but on every portion of the front we secured help from them in a multitude of ways. Without their great assistance the liberation of France ... would have consumed a much longer time. (ibid.)

For de Gaulle himself, the Resistance was more a major political problem than a military one. Even before entering Paris he had decided *not* to go straight to the Town Hall where the National Resistance Council and Paris Liberation Committee were in session, and where the Resistance were expecting him 'to proclaim the Republic'. He had decided instead to go to the Ministry of War, 'the obvious seat for the French Government and the French Command'. In other words, he was determined not to accept any kind of 'investiture' by the Resistance Organization; if there was to be any such 'investiture', it could only be from 'the crowds'. (*Mémoires*, vol. 2, p. 368).

That day he had been badly upset by a proclamation of the Resistance organizations expressing their 'revolutionary will', declaring that the Resistance Charter would now be solemnly handed to the head of the Provisional Government, but not mentioning de Gaulle by name. De Gaulle had already decided that the State (which he represented) was going to dominate the Resistance, and not *vice versa*. Finally, after establishing his headquarters at the Ministry of War and paying a visit to the Prefecture de Police (another stronghold of *governmental* authority) he arrived at the Hôtel de Ville. Here he was welcomed by one of the Communist leaders of the Paris resistance, Georges Marrane, and by Georges Bidault, President of the National Resistance Council. But in his speech, he said nothing about the revolutionary nature of the Liberation, and merely dwelt on 'national unity' and on the war against Germany that was continuing. Nor did he have the members of the C.N.R. presented to him. And when Bidault proposed that de Gaulle proclaim the Republic from the balcony of the Hôtel de Ville, the general replied: 'No, the Republic has never ceased to exist.' And he added that it had been embodied in the Free French Committee, in Fighting France and in the present Provisional Government.

So that was that. On the following day came de Gaulle's apotheosis – his famous procession across Paris, from the Arc de Triomphe to Notre-Dame. According to himself, two million Parisians had come to cheer him – *a peculiar kind of referendum to which de Gaulle – then, as later – attached the greatest importance.* The C.N.R. had not been invited to take part in the procession, and de Gaulle continued to cold-shoulder the Resistance Council, conveniently forgetting the decisive help it had given him, back in 1943, in his struggle against Giraud. The C.N.R. had asked to be given a government building as its headquarters; this also de Gaulle refused. When, ten days later, he deigned to receive the members of the C.N.R., it was only to stress to them that there was no room for them in the French State. He offered them several government posts, but only Georges Bidault accepted, and became Foreign Minister.

In any event, the 'apotheosis' had been a great personal triumph for de Gaulle, despite some confusion, some mysterious rifle shots, even in and around Notre-Dame, and despite de Gaulle's request to Mgr Suhard, the Archbishop of Paris, to refrain from coming to the Cathedral where, only a few months before, he had received Pétain in great pomp, and had also officiated at the funeral of a French traitor, Philippe Henriot, assassinated by the Resistance.

In de Gaulle's account of all these happenings, the Liberation of Paris and the disputes and unpleasantness that followed it, appear all as a purely French affair. What he does not say is that (if one is to believe Eisenhower) he also wanted the Americans to help him to restrain the excessive revolutionary ardour of the Resistance.

He asked me for a temporary loan of two American divisions to use, as he said, as a show of force and to establish his position firmly. (Eisenhower, op. cit., p. 326.)

Ike did not have any divisions to lend him, but arranged, all the same, that two of them, on their way to the Front, should march through Paris, with de Gaulle and General Bradley on the reviewing platform 'to symbolize Allied unity'. 'I felt that this show of force ... would accomplish all that he sought.' Eisenhower comments with some humour on 'the symbol of Liberation having to ask for Allied forces to establish ... its position,' – which was something de Gaulle had never done while in Africa ...

He also recalls that de Gaulle asked him for 'thousands of uniforms for the Free French Forces, so as to distinguish them from the disorderly elements'; as well as for food and various supplies, which were lacking in Paris.

The war against Germany was still continuing, and, before long, France's large-scale participation in the final stages of this war was to become one of de Gaulle's principal concerns.

2. De Gaulle versus the Resistance

26 August, the day of de Gaulle's apotheosis in Paris, was a day of patriotic exaltation and national rejoicing. For a few hours all differences seemed to have been sunk, all difficulties seemed to have been forgotten. Paris belonged to France again, and the four years of the German occupation were over at last. With skill and persistence de Gaulle had remained at the head of the 'external resistance', and had built up a Government machine, despite the opposition he had met from both the Allies and the Vichyite elements in North Africa. With equal skill, he had also persuaded the Home Resistance to sponsor him as head of the Provisional Government. Finally, he had seen to it that the Liberation of Paris should be made to look an exclusively French affair;

the American and other allies were, somehow, kept out of it.

It was the Germans who first brought Paris back to earth on the very night following de Gaulle's apotheosis, by inflicting on the capital a particularly savage 'revenge' air-raid, in which over a thousand people were killed and several thousand wounded.

Nor was that all. General living conditions in Paris during the weeks following the Liberation were even worse than under the German occupation. Transport had broken down, and even the highly-organized black market was experiencing the greatest difficulty in bringing supplies to the capital. Many of the most elementary public services were at a stand-still; the Metro itself did not begin to run again until three weeks after the Liberation on 11 September. Railway and road transport had been virtually paralysed all over France; all the bridges on the Seine between Paris and the sea had been destroyed, and the same was true of the Loire and the Rhône. Of 17,000 railway engines less than 3,000 were left, and rolling stock was down to thirty-five per cent of the pre-war total. By the end of the war, nearly half-a-million houses were to be destroyed and 1½ million damaged; the output of electricity in September 1944 was down to one-half, and that of coal to one-fifth of the 1938 level. No doubt, the destruction in France was mild compared with that suffered by Poland or Western and Southern Russia; the number of livestock had diminished to a surprisingly small extent; and although, owing to the shortage of man-power, machinery, and fertilizers, the soil of France was yielding less than before the war, France managed, even in the wholly abnormal conditions of 1944, to harvest 6.4 million tons of wheat, or about eighty per cent of the pre-war average. But since the transport system was in ruins, some parts of the country were bursting with food, while Paris itself was starving, with adult rations down to 1,050 calories. Although vegetables and other unrationed foods could be bought in the open market, wages had scarcely doubled since pre-war, while the currency inflation had reduced the franc to one-fifth of its pre-war value. The working class were suffering worst of all and they were far angrier with the Germans and the profiteers than others, like the farmers, who had been hit less severely by the war and many of whom had even made large fortunes. With a certain Machiavellian cunning, de Gaulle hastened to appease the working class by giving the Communists a share of power in the government.

In the uneasy atmosphere of 1944–5 de Gaulle succeeded – at least for a time – in representing a curious compromise between two parallel and sometimes conflicting tendencies in the France of the Liberation days: on the one hand, the idealistic reformism of the Home Resistance, as embodied in the C.N.R. (National Resistance Council) Charter, and, on the other hand, the desire of a very large part of the population – the *petite bourgeoisie*, the government officials, the peasantry among them – to 'get back to normal'. The main provisions of the C.N.R. Charter were:

The establishment of the government of the Republic under de Gaulle, as a government which would defend the political and economic independence of France and re-establish her greatness and prestige;

Traitors should be punished, and those actively associated with Vichy should be eliminated from the administration;

The property of traitors and black-market profiteers should be confiscated, and wartime profits heavily taxed;

There should be universal suffrage and complete freedom of thought; freedom of the press and its independence *vis-à-vis* the government, vested interests and foreign Powers; freedom of association; respect of the human person, etc.;

A true economic and social democracy should be established, independent of any of 'the great economic and financial feudal forces';

Production should be intensified in accordance with a State Plan, after consultation with all those concerned;

There should be nationalization of 'all the great monopolies; of the sources of power; of mineral wealth; of insurance companies and the big banks';

There should be a share of responsibility for the workers in the economic direction of enterprises;

There should be an adequate rise in wages, and the protection of purchasing power on a national scale leading to monetary stability;

The re-establishment of independent trade unionism; a complete plan of social security; and various measures in favour of remunerative agricultural prices;

Political, social and economic rights should be extended to colonial populations;

There should be the fullest educational possibilities for all French children, and the creation of 'an élite of merit instead of an élite by birth'.

This was by no means a revolutionary programme; at most it corresponded to what Bidault, head of the C.N.R., had called '*la révolution par la loi*' – a partly socialist, partly New Deal kind of programme in which nationalizations and *dirigisme* (planning) held an important place. The Communists themselves accepted it as a bare minimum. Some of its features, such as a press 'completely independent of the great financial interests' were, of course, to prove a delusion; nevertheless, de Gaulle personally favoured some of the measures in the C.N.R. Charter, including the nationalization of mines, electric power, gas, railways, civil aviation, some of the Merchant Navy and a number of major enterprises, whose management had greatly helped the Germans, such as the Renault Works of Boulogne-Billancourt. The nationalization measures were also to be extended to some of the bigger banks and insurance companies.

But all this came later. In August–September 1944, with the war against Germany continuing, de Gaulle's immediate problems were (1) to reconstitute his government, now that it had moved from Algiers to Paris; (2) to secure this government's full recognition by the Allies; (3) to take at least a bare minimum of economic and administrative measures to normalize, as far as possible, ordinary everyday life, especially in Paris; (4) to raise a large French army which would play as great a part as possible in the final stages of the war; (5) to normalize promptly relations between the central government and the Resistance – in other words, *reduce the role of the Resistance organizations throughout the country to a purely auxiliary one, pending their complete disappearance.*

The Government of 'National Unanimity', as it was significantly called, was formed a fortnight after the Liberation of Paris and was composed, in the main, of former members of the Provisional Government in Algiers (these included some of the original London 'Gaullists'); of some members of the Home Resistance; and of the representatives of four of the political parties – the Radicals, the Demo-Christians (later called M.R.P.), the Socialists and the Communists. The two Communists in the government were Billoux, Minister of Health, who had already been a member of the Algiers Committee, and Tillon, Minister of Air, who, as head of the Francs-Tireurs-Partisans, had been one of the most active members of the Home Resistance. This very mixed company (from which, however, anybody even remotely connected with Vichy was excluded) was, above all, held together by the personality of de Gaulle. When conflicts arose, as they were bound to do, it was de Gaulle who decided who was right and who was wrong. The most famous clash during the first year was to be over monetary policy, when the drastic reform proposed by Mendès-France, Minister for Economic Affairs, was rejected in favour of the more orthodox and easy-going policy advocated by Pleven, the Minister of Finance.

The Home Resistance had rendered de Gaulle an immense service back in 1943 by strongly backing him against Giraud. But already, on the evening that de Gaulle arrived in Paris, he had made it painfully clear that France would henceforth be run by its central government, and not by the Resistance organizations. These, and particularly the local Liberation Committees, would at most play a consultative and auxiliary role in 'assisting' the government-appointed Prefects to purge local authorities of their collaborationist or outspokenly Vichyite elements. The whole machinery for purging or replacing the *conseils généraux* and other local assemblies was carefully supervised; the Liberation Committees themselves, composed of representatives of the Resistance organizations and of parties affiliated with the C.N.R., were to 'assist the Prefect, but cease their function after the re-establishment of the *conseils généraux*'. The reconstitution of local councils by the Prefects with the help of the Liberation Committees, and the subsequent fading-out of the latter, had, indeed, already been outlined in the Algiers Committee's famous *ordonnance* of 21 April 1944. This *ordonnance*, it is true, provided that priority should be given in the new local government organs to men who had 'remained faithful to their duty', and to members of the Resistance. But the Resistance organizations, and particularly their numerous Communist members, were reluctant at first to hand over all their authority to the Paris-appointed Prefect. Furthermore there was the problem of the *milices patriotiques*, the para-military formations which had sprung up all over the country in the course of the great anti-German rising by the Resistance during May–June–July 1944, and which were largely composed of Communists. These para-military formations were dissolved by the de Gaulle government on 28 October; but there followed, soon afterwards, a decree amnestying Maurice Thorez, then still in Moscow, for having 'deserted' from the French army in

1939 when he was certain to be arrested and probably murdered! On 30 November Thorez made his first great speech in Paris saying that the war against Germany was, 'for the present', the only task; and on 21 January 1945, he openly approved before the Communist Party's Central Committee, de Gaulle's decision to dissolve the *milices patriotiques* and other para-military formations that had emerged from the Resistance.

To 'tame' the Communists, the most dynamic part of the Resistance, while making the fullest use of them in winning the war against Germany and in keeping the working class under control was one of de Gaulle's principal aims in 1944–5, and he succeeded completely, though not without a great deal of angry grumbling from the Communist rank-and-file.

In France, as was to be expected, central as well as local government machinery fell into place with remarkable speed; the bulk of public opinion, whether in the towns or in the villages, was anxious for a return to 'law and order'. The peasants, in particular, having in the main accommodated themselves perfectly to the Pétain régime, were equally willing to accommodate themselves now to a de Gaulle one; in many parts of the country their 'cooperation' with the Resistance *maquis* had been forced, rather than voluntary. Needless to say, with Pétain's *État Français* having, at least nominally, ruled France for four years, a very high proportion of 'Vichy' officials had to be left in place; practically all of them hastened, however, to adapt themselves to the new order, and even to claim always to have been 'on the side of the Resistance'. The great tragi-comic joke of France in 1944 was that *everybody* had been 'in the Resistance'.

In reality, of course, the active resisters had been only a tiny minority; Soustelle in 1943 put the 'active Resistance' at one per cent of the adult population. After D-Day, the number of genuine resisters grew enormously, partly because they were at last being supplied with arms; but even before that, the Resistance had greatly interfered with the Germans, particularly by the railway sabotage which became increasingly effective during the first half of 1944. And the F.F.I. (the French Forces of the Interior) had been of considerable military help to the Allied and regular French forces by often liberating whole towns, cities and areas shortly before the arrival of these regular troops. In de Gaulle's view, the F.F.I. were now, as far as possible, to be drafted into the regular French Army, while the rest of the resistance fighters were to be demobilized.

*

Altogether, relations between de Gaulle and the Home Resistance (including the non-Communist Resistance) were far from cordial. In *France 1940–1955* I quote a significant conversation with Lucie Aubrac, a highly active member of the Resistance and wife of the Raymond Aubrac who, in 1944, was *Commissaire de la République* at Marseilles:

'The C.N.R., as you know,' [she said] 'was created towards the *end* of the Resistance, and just in order to give the world the idea that de Gaulle had "the whole of France behind him" ... For a long time the Resistance didn't know much about him. In Normandy, before he arrived, they used to ask: "What's he like – big or small, thin or fat?" During his "triumphal" journey through France in the autumn of 1944, he behaved most unpleasantly. At Marseilles he was given a truly exuberant reception. You know what our Marseillais are like. There was a tremendous parade of the Maquisards, wearing tattered civilian clothes – real *sans-culottes*! – most of them with open collars, for it was a very hot day, and with flowers tied to their rifles. And they dragged along a German armoured car, and on top of it were a lot of young Marseille women in somewhat frivolous and not very modest summer dresses, screaming and waving flags – a really nice bit of Mediterranean exuberance. And, do you know, de Gaulle took it very badly indeed; he sat there glumly, muttering: "*Quelle mascarade, quelle mascarade!*" His anti-plebeian instincts came out with a vengeance that day. And, on another occasion, at Lyon, he wanted to sit at a banquet between the Prefect and the *Commissaire de la République*. Instead, we put him between two leaders of the local Resistance. He took it very badly; looked like thunder, and didn't address a single word to them throughout the meal.'

In a sense those journeys around liberated France were triumphal; but de Gaulle made it quite clear that the government was master now, and that the Resistance organizations had outlived their usefulness. As the non-Communist Resistance paper, *Combat*, was to write soon after the Liberation of Paris: 'All the Resistance has now left is its movements and its press'. The two principal movements – the mainly non-Communist 'federation', the M.L.N. (*Mouvement de Libération Nationale*), and the predominantly Communist or near-Communist *Front National* – with their inflated membership (largely composed of last-minute or even post-Liberation 'resisters') were to disintegrate completely within the next year and to be, in effect, replaced by the parties. As for the Resistance press – and practically all the papers in August 1944 represented some Resistance organization – it also changed its character very quickly. Owing to financial difficulties, many of these papers simply disappeared; others became party organs; and still others went 'commercial'. *Défense de la France* was turned into *France-Soir* within a very short time, while *Le Figaro*, never even nominally a 'Resistance' paper, became more or less openly conservative, with a soft spot for Vichy. *Combat* tried longer than any other paper – indeed, till 1949 – to keep alive something of the Resistance *mystique*. De Gaulle, it is true, had adopted part of the C.N.R. Charter, complete with nationalizations and a variety of social reforms; he had no serious objections to these, and they kept the Socialist and Communist members of his government happy – or at least quiet. But the Resistance *mystique* died very soon for a large number of reasons, of which the lack of revolutionary enthusiasm (except among the Communist rank-and-file and a number of intellectual groups) and a desire to 'get back to normal' were perhaps the most important.

3. De Gaulle Wants a Big Army, but –

Significantly, de Gaulle had tried to persuade himself soon after the Liberation of Paris, and while he was presiding over a government composed of both pro-American and pro-Russian elements, that France had a special place to hold in the world – facing 'both east and west', and acting as a link between the two worlds. The idea that she could become *the centre of a sort of international Third Force* was already obviously at the back of his mind. Both he and Bidault, his Foreign Minister, kept on repeating in 1944–5 that they were not in favour of a 'Western Bloc', and that 'it would be wrong to separate Western Europe from the rest'. De Gaulle also wanted a separate status for the left bank of the Rhine, and for the Ruhr, the former to be more or less openly incorporated in French territory – a curious 'Poincaré', not to say 'Maurras' approach to the German problem. He was ready to agree to the Oder-Neisse Line as Germany's eastern frontier, while the rest of Germany was to be organized on 'federal' lines without a central government – a project equally in the Maurras-Bainville tradition.

He received no encouragement from either Britain or the United States, and Churchill's first visit to Paris after the official recognition of the de Gaulle Government by the Allies at the end of October (Roosevelt had been particularly reluctant to give his assent) was much less cordial than it appeared on the surface. The story is even told that, as Churchill was being loudly cheered in the Champs

Elysées, de Gaulle muttered: 'Fools and cretins! Look at
this rabble (*cette canaille*) cheering the old bandit!'[1] He was
particularly displeased with Churchill, who seemed to him,
more than ever, under the American thumb, who would not
commit himself to de Gaulle's Rhineland proposal, and showed himself in no hurry to have arms sent to the French Army.

To de Gaulle the French Army presented a dual problem.
One was the amalgamation of the regular army (much or
most of it brought from North Africa, and including a large
proportion of soldiers and officers who had served Vichy),
and the French Home Forces, the F.F.I. Although there
continued to be some inevitable antipathy between many of
the ex-Vichyite officers and the Resistance 'upstarts' with
their somewhat arbitrarily adopted ranks of major, colonel,
and even general, the amalgamation, nevertheless, succeeded
reasonably well in accordance with a government decree of
23 September. Many of the F.F.I. officers were given addi-
tional training in the use of modern weapons, and were
allowed to keep their ranks.

Much more serious was the question of equipping the new
French Army. On 26 October, at a press conference, de
Gaulle bitterly complained of the Allies' failure to supply
France with arms. 'Not a single major army unit could be
properly constituted since the Liberation,' he said, and he
denied that the shortage of landing facilities was the only
reason for this. In another speech during the same week he
declared that the F.F.I. were mostly young people of the
highest quality, and that they and the old army would make
an excellent mixture. But the Allies were in no hurry to help.

1. J. R. Tournoux, op. cit., p. 329. Although de Gaulle himself
needed – and sometimes even desperately needed – popular acclaim
(thus his Paris apotheosis of 26 August was of the greatest political
value to him) – he frequently used the word *canaille* – rabble. No
doubt even at the height of his Paris apotheosis he remembered that,
only a few months before, the *same* people had given almost the same
kind of rousing reception to Pétain.

To the French, it was, indeed, becoming very like another 'phoney war'. During the Rundstedt offensive, there were no French troops in the field except the de Lattre Army, the Leclerc Division and the Alsace–Lorraine Brigade, with some 20,000 F.F.I. drafted into them; some 70,000 F.F.I. were being used for besieging St Nazaire and other ports still in German hands, but they were so poorly armed that they could not do much. The others were idle.

Even with V.E. Day approaching, things were far from good if France was to hold a worthy place among the victorious nations. On 1 March 1945 de Gaulle complained that although there were now 1,200,000 French troops, their equipment was wholly inadequate; the first French tanks, he said, could not be produced until the following September. There was the strongest suspicion in France – and one shared by de Gaulle – that, just as the Allies had been in no hurry to arm the French Resistance, so they were not at all anxious to arm a large French army including so much 'revolutionary material'. There had been enough trouble in Greece with E.L.A.S., as well as some in Belgium, Italy, and elsewhere . . .

To de Gaulle, the status of a very minor partner in the final defeat of Germany was particularly galling; he was also conscious of the fact that, as distinct from 1939, a large part of France was now genuinely anxious to fight the Germans, and was being denied this opportunity.

He deeply resented this British and American attitude to France, and although Russia was in no position to send him military equipment, he decided to go to Moscow in December, partly in order to break away from France's entire dependence on the 'Anglo-Saxons'.

*

4. Horse-Trading with Stalin

The chapter in de Gaulle's *Mémoires* on his visit to Moscow in December 1944 is one of the more unfortunate examples of his peculiar technique in writing history. On closer examination one finds that here, as elsewhere, he is usually concerned with his apologia of de Gaulle. Here, as elsewhere, de Gaulle nearly always turns up trumps. If there are any awkward moments, these are either presented in a slightly twisted way, or are not mentioned at all. I happened to be in Moscow at the time, and followed all the goings-on as closely as possible. On the morning of de Gaulle's arrival in Moscow, a large crowd had gathered, attracted by the large number of official cars outside the Kursk Station.

This is how de Gaulle describes the scene:

> As we came out of the station, I saw that a considerable crowd had assembled, from which rose a hum of sympathetic voices.

This is not, however, at all what happened. De Gaulle stared at the crowd, and the crowd stared back, scarcely knowing who he was; there was certainly no 'hum' of any kind. Bidault later, indeed, told me that he and de Gaulle had been greatly perplexed by the total indifference shown them by the Russian crowds. De Gaulle was a very great man in France, and he was surprised at not being treated in Russia accordingly.

This is, of course, only a small detail, but a significant one. Moreover, de Gaulle, in his *Mémoires*, makes out that 'M. Bogomolov ... took every occasion to urge me to visit Moscow'. In reality, as clearly appears from the diplomatic documents published by the Russians in 1959, and particularly from Bogomolov's dispatch of 8 November 1944, it was de Gaulle who fished for an invitation; this was sent to de Gaulle ten days later, 'in view of the desire General de Gaulle had expressed, in his recent conversation with A. E. Bogomolov, to visit the Soviet Union'.

No doubt de Gaulle had, at that time, every reason to be satisfied with the Russians. They had shown greater eagerness than either the British or the Americans to recognize the

French Provisional Government; and it was also they who had persuaded the other two to admit France as a fourth member to the European Advisory Commission.

De Gaulle's telegram to Kalinin on the anniversary of the October Revolution was particularly gushing and spoke of the Russian people fighting for common victory 'under the guidance of their leader of genius'. ('*sous la conduite de leur chef génial*').

The Russian minutes of de Gaulle's conversations with Stalin are of the greatest interest, especially when one compares them with de Gaulle's own account of these meetings, so silent about the first half-hour or so when Stalin made it pretty clear that he considered France a poor relation, with very little to contribute to the common war effort. This sample from my summary of the Stalin – de Gaulle conversations, in my *Russia at War* gives the flavour of them.

Stalin: How is the restoration of French industry progressing?

De Gaulle: It is being restored, but very, very slowly. There are terrible transport difficulties and a coal shortage. In order to equip her army, France has to appeal for arms from the Americans and, for the present, they won't give her any. It will take France two years to restore her industry.

Stalin: I find this rather surprising. Russia is not finding the restoration of industry such an insuperable problem. The south of France was liberated without much difficulty, and there was not much fighting in Paris. So what's the trouble?

De Gaulle: Most of the French rolling stock was destroyed ... and what is left is mostly used by the British and the Americans.

Stalin then asked how France was placed for officer *cadres*.

De Gaulle: In 1940 the Germans captured nearly the whole French army and most of the officers. Only a small number were left in North Africa, and these are now fighting in France. Some betrayed their country by collaborating with Vichy. So now a lot of new officers have got to be trained.

Stalin: ... And how do you stand for airmen?

De Gaulle: We have very few airmen and even those we have need complete re-training, as they are unfamiliar with modern planes.

Stalin: Now the French airmen of the Normandie Squadron are doing very well on the Russian front; so if you are so hard-up for airmen, we could perhaps send them back to France?

De Gaulle: No, no, this is quite unnecessary. They are contributing nobly to the common cause while in Russia.

Stalin: I suppose you have very few training schools for airmen?

De Gaulle: Yes, very few, and very few planes.

This was, obviously, not at all a pleasant conversation for de Gaulle, and he prefers to omit it altogether from his account of the Moscow visit. Nor does he emphasize the extent to which he complained to Stalin of the bad treatment he was getting from the British and the Americans. These, he kept on repeating, were not continental European powers, and the two great military powers which could keep Germany in order were obviously only Russia and France; he therefore promptly proposed that Russia should agree that the left bank of the Rhine be 'joined' to France, just as the Oder-Neisse Line would constitute the Western frontier of Poland.

But Stalin did not rise to the bait. Fully conscious of the military and economic power of Britain and the United States, Stalin thought it totally unrealistic to build the future of Europe on a somewhat problematical Franco–Soviet alliance. He immediately told de Gaulle that the question of the Rhine frontier could not be decided except in consultation with Britain and the U.S.A. Significantly, Stalin kept on communicating with Churchill throughout the de Gaulle visit, and even at first supported Churchill's preference for a Three-Power Alliance of Britain, the Soviet Union and France to a straight Franco–Soviet Alliance. De Gaulle declared this to be 'un-French' since, under such a Pact, France would figure as a sort of junior partner, a merely belated adherent to the Anglo–Soviet Pact of 1942. The Russians – to tell the very long story very briefly – decided to take advantage of this French preference for a straight Franco–Soviet Pact, and now urged the French more than ever to recognize the Polish 'Lublin Committee'; if they did that, the Russians would sign the Franco–Soviet Pact, 'even at the risk of offending Churchill'. Having failed to receive satisfaction over the Rhineland, de Gaulle flatly refused to consider the recognition of the Lublin Committee. And during the last night, de Gaulle made a dramatic departure from the Kremlin and refused to sign the Franco–Soviet Pact, since the Russians still persisted in demanding France's recognition of Lublin. In the end, he was brought back to the Kremlin, and the Russians gave way. De Gaulle describes this episode as a great triumph of his diplomacy. In reality, de Gaulle had tried to pull a fast one on the British and Americans by getting the Russians to subscribe to the Rhineland Frontier, while the Russians tried to pull an equally fast one on them by getting de Gaulle to recognize Lublin. Both failed. But there is nothing to suggest that the Russians desperately needed the Franco–Soviet Pact, though it was useful to them in a small way, just as it was to de Gaulle, as part of his 'facing-both-ways' policy. It is a moot question whether de Gaulle would have recognized Lublin if the Russians had agreed to the Rhineland frontier; but in any event they made it clear from the start that they could not agree to this without the approval of Britain and the U.S.A. – who were *the* Allies who really mattered in those final stages of the war.[1]

1. That the French might have recognized Lublin if the Russians had agreed to the Rhine frontier is suggested by Bidault's reply to Molotov when he first raised the question of the recognition of Lublin: 'I did not think the Soviet–French Pact had this *condition préalable* attached to it. But please remember that we also have certain problems we should like quickly settled, for instance that of the Rhine frontier.' (*Sov.–Fran. otnosheniya*, p. 353.)

None of this emerges clearly in de Gaulle's *Mémoires*. He prefers instead to dwell on his great diplomatic triumph, and to draw a satirical picture of Stalin, with his mixture of jovial and sinister buffoonery, during that final Kremlin banquet. One wonders whether, at heart, de Gaulle felt what a French diplomat felt when he told me about it the next day: '*Il avait l'air de se foutre un peu de nous.*'

When it was all over, Stalin commended de Gaulle for his toughness as a negotiator: 'You have played well! Well done!' But if, before the Moscow meeting with de Gaulle, Stalin (in his letter to Churchill of 20 November) saw no objection to the French joining in the next Big Three meeting, 'provided Roosevelt doesn't object', he did not, after the meeting, raise a finger to overcome the President's objections to de Gaulle's presence at Yalta. At Yalta, as we know from Stettinius, he described de Gaulle as 'not a complicated man' (meaning, it seems, a man with a one-track nationalist mind); moreover, he was, on the whole, less charitable to France than Churchill, saying it was nothing but an act of kindness to give the French a zone of their own in Germany.

5. France 1945–6 – Exit de Gaulle

Already in April 1944 the National Committee at Algiers had decided that there could be no general election in France until after the end of the war and the return of the 1½ million war prisoners together with the hundreds of thousands of workers who had been sent to Germany. The Third Republic had, in fact, voted itself out of existence on 10 July 1940, in favour of Pétain's *État Français*, and this had ceased to exist in any sense by August 1944. De Gaulle had denied the Vichy régime any 'legality' from the outset, and even claimed, at the time of the Liberation, that 'the Republic' had never been abolished, since it had continued to be impersonated by the Free French and then by the Algiers

Committee; at the same time this impersonation was, clearly, not the same thing as the Third Republic. The French Provisional Government of 1944–5 was accordingly not based on any formal or legal title until the constitutional referendum and the election of the first Constituent Assembly on 21 October 1945; between September 1944 and this election France was ruled by a government which had derived its authority from 'history', as it were. This represented the 'new men' who had, in varying degrees, been associated with the external and internal Resistance. But, as we have seen, de Gaulle lost no time in drawing a clear line between government authority and the authority temporarily assumed by the various Resistance organizations in the country. These organizations were soon to disappear altogether. What survived and revived were the parties; and the three main parties, which all claimed to continue the traditions of the Resistance, were the Communists, the Socialists, and the Christian Democrats, now called M.R.P. (*Mouvement républicain populaire*). The Radicals (who were now popularly associated with the worst features of the Third Republic) and the Right (who were associated with Vichy) appeared in 1944–5 to be hopelessly discredited, though there were, of course, a few exceptions; de Gaulle's first government of 'national unanimity' included a number of Radicals such as Mendès-France (who had joined him in London) and René Mayer (who had joined him in Algiers).

The most revolutionary element in France was represented by the Communists, and de Gaulle, as has been seen, did his utmost to 'tame' them by including two Communist Ministers in his 1944 government (with more to come later) and by proclaiming them on numerous occasions to be patriotic Frenchmen. He could not deny the very important role that the Communists had played in the active Resistance, and he could not ignore them at a time when the fullest cooperation of the working class (which was predominantly Communist) was needed for the economic restoration of France. Maurice Thorez, the popular Communist leader, having returned to France at the end of 1944, was of the greatest help to de Gaulle in persuading the French working class to be patient, not to strike and not to make 'unreasonable' wage claims while the war was still in progress. There is little doubt that the top priority given to 'victory over Germany' was what Stalin had recommended to the French Communist Party. But even after the war was over, the Communists intended to remain a permanent government party, lending their 'critical cooperation' to de Gaulle and, later, to his successors.[1] It was the Cold War which was chiefly responsible for eliminating, in 1947, the Communists from the French government. Certainly their value to de Gaulle in 1944–5 was unquestionable, while the Communists in the government had the pleasant illusion that the various structural and social reforms carried out in 1944–5 were largely due to their influence. De Gaulle's own attitude to the Communists was, at that stage, a curious mixture of distrust and admiration; he tended to agree with François Mauriac's famous phrase written during the war: 'Only the working class *as a whole* remained faithful to France in her distress and humiliation'.

*

In the C.N.R. Charter the punishment of traitors and the elimination from government and professional activity of those 'who had been actively associated with Vichy' held a high priority. So 1944–6 was marked by a great variety of purge trials, and the punishment ranged from the death sentence to a few years of 'national unworthiness'. It is generally agreed that the purge was not well conducted; it was too much like a lottery. Depending on the jury, or the

1. See the author's *France 1940–1955*, pp. 263–70, chapter on 'The Communists' ambition to be a permanent government party'.

time that the trial was held, the sentences were often absurdly severe or ridiculously lenient; the later after the Liberation a trial took place, the greater was the chance that the accused would be let off lightly, or even acquitted. The case of the principal all-out German collaborators – the chiefs of the French Gestapo in Paris, of the French Nazi press or radio, of Joseph Darnand, head of the Vichy *milice* – was a simple one; more complex was that of certain Vichy Ministers who invariably claimed to have played a double game and to have worked for the good of France, as they understood it. De Gaulle had mixed feelings about the purge. He was not much interested in the punishment of the 'economic collaborators'. He felt strongly, however, that not only the all-out Nazi collaborators, but also certain important Vichy leaders, including some of the admirals and generals (particularly General Dentz who had fought the Free French in Syria) deserved to be punished. As head of the government and (though unofficially) head of the State, he had assumed the right to commute death sentences.

The two most famous trials in 1945 were those of Pétain and Laval. After being deported to Germany, the 89-year-old Marshal had been allowed by the Germans to go to Switzerland, and de Gaulle unofficially informed the Swiss authorities that he would like Pétain to stay there; but the Marshal decided, of his own free will, to return to France and stand trial. This trial, with its extraordinary procession of witnesses – including Vichy Ministers, Third Republic politicians, generals, and diplomats – ended with a death sentence, but one accompanied by a recommendation of mercy. De Gaulle, of course, hastened to commute the sentence on the aged Marshal.

Unlike the trial of Pétain, that of Laval was conducted in a scandalously unfair manner; but de Gaulle was adamant in not commuting the death sentence, and even refused a retrial. The execution of Laval was, in de Gaulle's view, an indispensable symbolic gesture required for 'reasons of State'. There was a suspicion, though, that, in having Laval executed, de Gaulle was trying to please both the Vichy leaders and the Third Republic politicians who had made Laval their scapegoat and their most convenient alibi.

There was much in these trials that was arbitrary and artificial; both the judges and the public prosecutors were, with very rare exceptions, men who had themselves sworn allegiance to Pétain. There were, indeed, hundreds of thousands of other officials, big and small, who had served under Vichy, including many policemen with highly dubious records who were, without any serious investigation, now incorporated in the C.R.S. and other police forces. And, after all, did not a very large proportion of the regular French army consist of 'Vichyites'? Characteristically, de Gaulle was seldom so infuriated as when Herriot – the kind of Third Republic politician he despised most – raised objections to Vichy soldiers being allowed to keep their decorations for having fought the British and Americans during the North Africa landing in November 1942. These people, though misguided, had, as de Gaulle saw it, after all 'fought for France'. Who was Herriot to object – the very Herriot who had had all those shady dealings with Laval and the Germans and American agents only a few days before the Liberation of Paris? So even then, at the height of the purges, there was an almost inevitable ambiguity in de Gaulle's attitude to Vichy. The leaders had to be more or less severely punished. But what was one to do with the rank-and-file officials who had merely served what they considered to be the established order?

All the same, it was necessary, as far as possible, to exclude the 'Vichyites' from the political life of the nation; and the three main parties, the Communists, Socialists, and M.R.P., all claiming to represent the Resistance, held strong views on the exclusion of Vichyites from parliament. The

Socialists, for example, excluded from the party all those
deputies and senators who had voted for Pétain in 1940; and
the M.R.P. made great political capital out of being the
'party of fidelity to de Gaulle'.

*

Except for the moneyed bourgeoisie, which continued to live
comfortably with the help of the black market, France, and
especially Paris, lived miserably through the winter of
1944–5, and the spring and summer of 1945 were not much
better. De Gaulle's relations with the Allies were far from
satisfactory. Roosevelt had excluded him from the Yalta
Conference, and when, on his return journey, the President –
already a very sick man – asked de Gaulle to meet him at
Algiers, the general bluntly refused. The French army had
played an honourable part in the final stages of the war, but
still only a very small part, since the Allies had been in no
hurry to arm the French. After VE day the French war
prisoners began to return, and so did the survivors of the
Nazi concentration camps. Many thousands had died there,
and many of those who had not, were now brought back to
France in a fearful physical and sometimes mental condition;
all these thousands of human tragedies added to the great
anger against Germany. Apart from the Communists, the
bulk of French opinion was disturbed by the Russian pene-
tration of Eastern Europe; but relations with the Western
Allies were not very happy either. The British attempt to
oust from Syria almost immediately after VE day the 5,000
French troops still there outraged de Gaulle beyond words.
At a press conference on 2 June he fumed against 'Churchill's
ultimatum' that the French troops be withdrawn to a coastal
strip and against the British take-over 'with the help of
British troops marching from Palestine into Syria carrying
swastika banners'. The British, he said, had persuaded Syria
and the Lebanon not to negotiate their independence

treaties with France. The whole thing, he said, 'stank of oil'.

Later in the summer, there was Potsdam, and even though the French had, by then, been given an occupation zone in Germany and a seat on the allied control council, they were not invited to the Big Three Conference.

De Gaulle's brief visit to Washington at the end of August, as the guest of President Truman, was not a success. When Truman bluntly told him that it was high time the French threw the Communists out of the government, de Gaulle politely but coldly reminded him that this was, after all, an internal French affair. In reply, Truman made it plain that, in the circumstances, France need not expect much financial aid from the U.S.A. Nor did he support de Gaulle's plea for French control over the left bank of the Rhine or the internationalization of the Ruhr, and there was some unpleasantness about American bases on French territories in the Pacific. De Gaulle reminded Truman that the Americans were using Noumea, in New Caledonia, as a base, and said that this could only be a provisional arrangement, because France had full sovereign rights over it.

*

Since the Liberation, the only parliament in France had been an enlarged version of the Algiers Consultative Assembly, and though this was full of worthy people, many of them with very fine Resistance records, de Gaulle took very little notice of it. Now at last, in October 1945, the time had come for the constitutional referendum and the election of a Constituent Assembly – unless, of course, the electorate decided in favour of a plain return to the 1875 Constitution, i.e. the Third Republic. In the referendum this was rejected by an overwhelming majority, but the real question remained *what kind* of Constituent Assembly the French people wanted – one with full constitutional powers and no time limit, as advocated by the Communists, or one with powers limited to seven months, after which the Draft Constitution would be submitted to another referendum. This last solution, supported by de Gaulle, the Socialists and the M.R.P. was approved by thirteen out of twenty-one million voters.

The election, run on the principle of proportional representation and of local party lists (though without a national pooling of votes), enormously favoured the three big parties: the Communists (who got over five million votes and 158 seats), the Socialists[1] ($4\frac{1}{2}$ million votes and 142 seats), and the M.R.P. ($4\frac{1}{2}$ million votes and 152 seats). Only one quarter of the seats went to the Radicals and the Right. An enormous number of conservatives and ex-Vichyites voted, of course, for the M.R.P., which they regarded as the most conservative element in the government coalition, despite the M.R.P.'s avowed loyalty to the C.N.R. Charter.

The newly-elected members unanimously elected de Gaulle head of the government at their meeting of 13 November. But when it came to appointing the Cabinet, new complications arose, chiefly from de Gaulle's unwillingness to give any of the key posts (Defence, Foreign Affairs, or Interior) to the Communists, although they were the biggest party of all. It was not till 21 November that the government was therefore finally formed, with the Communists given five out of the twenty-two posts, but none of the 'key' ones. They were, however, given four of the economic departments, and – a great consolation prize – Maurice Thorez figured among the four Ministers of State. They swallowed their pride.

The Constituent Assembly of November 1945 was, in fact, the first parliament with which, as head of the government,

1. Including the small but important U.D.S.R. party, at that time affiliated to the Socialists. Its future ministers in de Gaulle's new government included Pleven, Soustelle and Malraux.

de Gaulle had ever had to deal. The Provisional Government had itself ruled by decrees and ordinances. Not that de Gaulle seemed at first unwilling to play the parliamentary game: he outlined a substantial programme of reforms that would be submitted to the Constituent Assembly, including several nationalization measures (the Bank of France, five of the Big Banks, electricity, insurance, etc.); a variety of other economic reforms; the creation of an Economic Plan, besides the vote of the 1946 Budget; and much else. Several of these reforms were duly passed, but difficulties arose over the Budget, when de Gaulle sharply reacted against the various amendments that the Assembly proposed.

What he did in effect was to reject the idea of 'governing by compromise', and he bluntly declared:

'The Assembly has shown by its attitude that it prefers a régime in which the Assembly governs. It is not a system with which the government agrees ... Is the Assembly in favour of a real parliamentary régime, or of an all-powerful Assembly merely delegating limited powers to the government?'

In short, de Gaulle resented amendments and even criticism from the Assembly as so much *interference* with the government, and there was a widespread feeling in the country that he was blackmailing the Assembly into complete subservience, on the ground that his personal prestige alone held the tripartite coalition together.

It is highly probable that, if he had persisted, de Gaulle *could* have 'blackmailed' the Assembly into such subservience. Instead, barely two months after forming his first regular 'parliamentary' government, he suddenly resigned.

His letter to Félix Gouin, the President of the Assembly, made little sense. He explained that he had meant to retire after the election, but he had been prevailed upon to remain head of the government by the unanimous vote of the Assembly. However, the transition period was now over:

France was no longer in a state of alarm; there were still many problems and hardships, but, in the main, France was on the road to recovery. Economic activity was developing favourably and she had recovered all her overseas territories, except Indo-China, where she had, however, now gained a foothold (General Leclerc had just occupied Saigon and parts of Cochin-China).

He was planning to give a broadcast in which, it was said, he was going to denounce the party system and explain his disagreements with the Constituent Assembly, but he was prevailed upon not to do so.

So de Gaulle went; and, as *Combat* put it, 'there was no cataclysm, and the empty plate didn't crack'.

Needless to say, there was no end of speculation on why de Gaulle had really resigned with such suddenness. The most common explanation was that he had disagreed with the Assembly; but it is quite clear that that was not the real reason or at least not the principal one. There was profound economic discontent in the country (even bread rationing, which had been rashly abolished before the election, had had to be reintroduced); there were inextricable economic difficulties ahead; and so long as the Communists were in the government, no serious help could be expected from the United States. Further, as Couve de Murville's mission to Washington in December had shown, there was no inclination on the part of the Truman Administration to take the slightest notice of France's ideas on the future organization of Germany. Above all, de Gaulle could see the Cold War developing at a terrific speed, and this, in itself, made nonsense of his 'national unanimity' formula. *France was, obviously, heading for a major economic crisis which American help alone could solve. And, worse still, the world was heading for an international conflict in which it would be impossible for France to hold that 'unique and special' position between East and West, so dear to de Gaulle's heart.* Rather than remain head of the government in the midst of this dual crisis, de Gaulle decided to step aside – in order to be able to wait and see, and *to keep himself in reserve.*

Thus came to an abrupt end the highly 'personalist' de Gaulle régime in France which had lasted from August 1944 to January 1946. The French people were puzzled, rather than upset. The 'empty plates' had a great deal to do with the curious indifference that accompanied the great man's departure. He had ceased to be the indispensable national figure he had been at the time of the Liberation. Or so nearly everybody in France thought at the time.

CHAPTER 6

1946-58: OUT OF OFFICE - THE R.P.F.

1. The Uneasy Beginnings of the Fourth Republic

ALL admirers of General de Gaulle grow greatly offended when the 'Rally of the French People' – *Rassemblement du Peuple Français* or R.P.F. – the mass movement he succeeded in building up in 1947-8 is described as 'fascist'. Yet it was in reality as near a totalitarian movement as anything France had ever seen, was marked by some characteristic fascist thuggery, and had even borrowed much of its stagecraft and many of its demagogic tricks from the late Dr Goebbels. François Mauriac, a consistent admirer of de Gaulle's, thought the R.P.F. 'the biggest mistake' he had ever made[1] – a verdict with which de Gaulle himself was later, obviously, to agree. Not only, on the last page of his *Mémoires*, did he dismiss the whole R.P.F. experiment in a couple of nobly-worded sentences, but he was very careful, in 1958, when he returned to power, not to revive any of the extremist features of the R.P.F., such as its absolute anti-Communism or its ambition to abolish the political parties altogether, and to disband the trade unions. Although, at the height of R.P.F. success in October 1947, nearly forty per cent of the French people supported it, de Gaulle was made to realize before very long that this was a flash in the pan and that, funda-mentally, the bulk of French opinion was in favour of preserving at least the semblance of democratic government and freedom. In the great struggle of 1947-9 between de Gaulle's R.P.F. and the Fourth Republic, the latter – repre-sented by the 'Third Force' parties (i.e. the parties other

1. Later, in his *De Gaulle*, published in 1964, he was, oddly enough, to modify this view.

than the R.P.F. and the Communists) – won a resounding victory.

*

De Gaulle's extraordinary R.P.F. experiment would, indeed have been inconceivable outside the peculiar economic and international context of 1947–8 in which it was undertaken.

His sudden resignation on 20 January 1946 was followed by a return to 'normal' parliamentary government, something remarkably reminiscent of the good old days of the Third Republic, except that the parties were more powerful and 'monolithic', and the Communists continued to sit on the government bench. To many, it was almost a relief to see, at the head of the government, not the towering figure of de Gaulle, but a mediocre Socialist politician like M. Félix Gouin. In reality, 1946 and 1947 were to prove the most difficult years in the post-war history of France. Yet despite great problems, the country's economy was being restored; although the general index of production in September 1946 was only eighty-seven per cent of the 1938 level, coal, at over four million tons a month, and electric power (down to very little at the time of the Liberation) were now above pre-war levels. The coal deliveries France was to receive from Germany as reparations, however, were very meagre, and bitter complaints were voiced by all the parties at British and American 'discrimination' against France.

There were great shortages in practically everything, and the black market continued to dislocate the rationing system; thus, one-third of the country's sugar production found its way into the black market and had to be replaced by imported sugar for the benefit of ration-card holders. From where was the money for these imports to come?

Since no drastic monetary reform had been carried out after the Liberation, inflation continued at an alarming rate, with the note circulation in 1946 alone rising by some fifty per cent, and *controlled* retail prices in Paris rising a hundred per cent during the same period; black-market prices rose even more rapidly, while wages lagged far behind.

It was more obvious than ever that only large-scale financial help from the United States could help to overcome France's economic difficulties. Léon Blum was sent to Washington in March 1946 where, in addition to the loan of a few hundred million dollars already contracted in December 1945, he secured a further loan of 650 m. dollars, though on terms that were far from favourable. It was clearly explained to him that France need not expect highly-favoured treatment so long as there were Communists in her government. There was, indeed, not going to be even the promise of Marshall Aid for more than a year.

De Gaulle's policy towards Germany was being pursued by Georges Bidault, who remained as Foreign Minister. He continued to press for a separation of the Rhineland from Germany, for the incorporation of the Saar in France, and for the internationalization of the Ruhr; but he came into collision with the British Labour Government, met with no support from either the U.S.A. or even Russia, and was virtually disavowed even by his Prime Minister, M. Gouin. Ernest Bevin, treating Bidault as 'the dear little man', refused to take him seriously. Mr Byrnes's Stuttgart speech of 5 September finally put an end to French illusions, and Bidault bitterly remarked a few weeks later that 'in the matter of Germany, France was now a voice crying in the wilderness'. Already there were clear signs – such as the creation of the Anglo-American Bizone, that nucleus of the future West German State – that Germany would be divided in two. As the Foreign Minister of a tripartite government, including the Communists, Bidault still clung to his illusion that this division of Germany – and of Europe – could perhaps still be avoided; but in reality the French tripartite governments, symbolizing, as it were, the common victory

over Germany of East and West, were becoming anachronistic and more and more out of harmony with the Cold War.
As early as March 1946 Churchill had made his famous
Fulton 'iron curtain' speech, which had been openly
endorsed by the U.S. Government and also more or less
approved by the Labour Government in Britain. There was
more and more talk of a shooting war.

*

The first Draft Constitution, though approved by a comfortable majority of the Constituent Assembly, was, nevertheless, rejected in the referendum on 5 May 1946, by over
10 million votes to 9.5 million, with some 5 million abstentions. The majority felt that, under this Constitution, the
Assembly was given excessive powers, which might even lead
to the formation, in certain conditions, of a Communist-
headed government.

De Gaulle did not take part in this referendum campaign,
but a few days later he demonstrated his contempt for the
government by disdainfully refusing M. Gouin's invitation
to attend the Victory Day celebrations in Paris on 8 May.
He also kept silent during the June election of the second
Constituent Assembly – an election marked by a rise in the
M.R.P. and Communist vote, and a decline in the Socialist
one; but soon afterwards, on 18 June, he suddenly re-
emerged with a speech at Bayeux welcoming the rejection of
the first Draft Constitution, and advocating a very different
system. Under this, a bicameral parliament would exist in
which the second, 'administrative' chamber – elected by
local government bodies, etc. – would act as a corrective to
the first, 'political' chamber, and a powerful Head of the
State would appoint the premier responsible for the government's policy. The President would act as arbiter among
the parties, and be endowed with an unrestricted right of
dissolution; he would himself be elected by a college far

more extensive than the two houses of parliament. These and several other features of the 'Bayeux Constitution' already foreshadowed de Gaulle's subsequent attempts to 'reform the State'. With its massed Croix de Lorraine banners and its crowds shouting '*de Gaulle au pouvoir!*' (the rally had been carefully organized several days in advance) this Bayeux speech was like a rehearsal for the great Gaullist rallies of the next few years.

In June 1946 Bidault replaced Gouin at the head of another tripartite government, and, during the following months, the second Constituent Assembly composed, after endless inter-party discussions, the second Draft Constitution. This, in fact, differed very little from the first, despite de Gaulle's warning, and speaking before 60,000 people at Epinal, a few days before the referendum on it, de Gaulle proclaimed his opposition, at the same time 'rejecting with iron contempt' all insinuations about his own dictatorial ambitions. The Constitution, he said, did not provide for the necessary separation of powers, gave quite insufficient powers to the Head of State, and 'placed the omnipotence of the Parties above the State'. He called on the electorate, and particularly on the M.R.P. voters, to reject the Constitution – which caused inevitable clashes between de Gaulle (together with his embryonic new 'movement', the *Union Gaulliste*) and the M.R.P. leaders who had always sworn their fidelity to de Gaulle in the past. The hesitations created in the minds of the M.R.P. voters led to an unusually high number of abstentions – eight million – in the Referendum of 13 October 1946. The Constitution was approved by no more than 9.2 to 8.1 million votes; but this majority, small as it was, showed at least that the country wanted to get 'back to normal', even with an imperfect political structure.

The election to the first National Assembly of the Fourth Republic was held on 10 November and was a triumph for the Communists, who scored 5½ million votes; the M.R.P., with 5 million, and the Socialists with 3.4 million votes, lost ground, especially the Socialists. Although Thorez, the Communist leader, was the most obvious choice for premier, the Assembly refused him its investiture, fearing both the internal and the international repercussions that a Communist-headed government in France would produce. In the end, pending the election of the President of the Republic in January 1947, an all-Socialist 'caretaker' government was formed under the premiership of the 75-year-old Léon Blum, which had the unenviable distinction of failing to nip in the bud the Indo-China war that broke out on December 20.[1] Instead, the new administration played into the hands of the French High Commissioner there, Admiral Thierry d'Argenlieu, a de Gaulle appointee, who took up the cause of the extreme colonialist die-hards, and, after helping to provoke the war, sabotaged every possibility of a peaceful settlement with Ho-Chi-Minh, though the Vietnamese leader was clearly anxious to negotiate.

The outbreak of the Indo-China war – which was to last for eight years – added of course to the difficulties of maintaining a tripartite government in France, since the Communists favoured a peace settlement in Vietnam, the Socialists adopted a wait-and-see attitude, and the M.R.P. supported the colonialist die-hards.

After the election (with the help of Communist votes) of Vincent Auriol as first President of the Fourth Republic, the old-fashioned, very 'Third Republic' Paul Ramadier formed the last tripartite government – the one from which, in April 1947, the Communists were to be eliminated. Not that the Communists themselves were anxious to stay on in the government; the war in Vietnam and the intensification of the Cold War in 1947 had made their position on the government bench almost untenable. The announcement of the Truman Doctrine just before the Foreign Ministers' Con-

1. See the author's *France 1940–1955*, pp. 326–47.

ference in Moscow (which hopelessly widened the gulf between West and East) was a prelude to the Communist departure.

Moreover, the Ramadier's government's 'frozen wages' programme (an abortive policy that Blum had initiated in December) was becoming more and more difficult for the Communist Ministers to support, and when, on 30 April, 20,000 Renault workers went on strike, the Communists, after some hesitation, openly came out in favour of the strikers' claims, so giving Ramadier the technical excuse for turning them out of the government.

2. R.P.F. – De Gaulle Turns Fascist Demagogue

Everything during that summer of 1947 combined to create the kind of atmosphere in which de Gaulle had a chance of carrying out a 'national revolution' of his own. The Truman Doctrine; the breakdown of the Foreign Ministers' Conference in Moscow (which meant a complete East-West deadlock); the acute food shortages in France (complete with food riots in May); the violent *anti-dirigiste* movement among the shopkeeper class; a furious wave of anti-Communism that swept the country; and an unprecedented war hysteria were all playing into de Gaulle's hands. The war hysteria – with visions of the Red Army marching into France, where it would be assisted by its Fifth Column, the Communists – lent itself to the most extreme demagogy on the part of de Gaulle. Whether he believed in the imminence of such an invasion, or not, it was as good an argument as any for saying that the National Assembly, with its 169 Communists and ineffectual leaders like Ramadier, represented a kind of 'régime of the parties' which could certainly not cope with a major international crisis, let alone an invasion. Anti-Communism was not only a popular line, but also a profitable one. As Mendès-France remarked later that summer with a touch of irony: 'Thank God for the

Communists! Just because we've got a "Communist danger",
the Americans are going to make a tremendous effort to help
us. We must keep up this indispensable Communist scare'.
Molotov's visit to Paris in June and his attack on Marshall
Aid added to the more-or-less genuine nervousness.

As early as 14 April 1947 a de Gaulle statement was
published announcing the formation of the 'Rally of the
French People' (R.P.F.). And then, during the summer,
came that series of spectacular de Gaulle meetings which,
with their Croix-de-Lorraine flags, and beacons, and thousands of frenzied supporters, seemed like so many little
'Nurembergs'.

The French Führer's speeches (and he *was* beginning to
look singularly like a Führer) were becoming increasingly
violent. He coined a new term to describe the Communists:
they were the 'separatists', who were the agents of a foreign
power in all they did, whether in provoking inflation with
their wage claims, or in undermining the loyalty to France
amongst the colonial peoples. France could be a united
country, and all patriotic Frenchmen and Frenchwomen
were invited to rally round General de Gaulle – except, of
course, the 'separatists' whom he declared to be beyond the
pale. Not that he wanted to exclude the working class from
the French nation; but the working class must stop following
the 'separatists'. He took some trouble to explain why,
during and after the war, he had included the Communists
in his government; they *had* played a part in the Resistance,
and seemed, for a time, to have chosen the patriotic road;
but now this was over. And he went on to talk of the 'mortal
danger' that the Soviet bloc of 400 million people represented
for France – a bloc only 300 miles away. How near de Gaulle
was getting to a wholly totalitarian concept may be judged
from his forecast of 12 November 1947:

The R.P.F. will continue to expand until it *embraces the entire
nation*, with the exception of the separatists, of course (for it is not

their job to form part of the nation), and also a few 'general staffs' without any following, and a few soured and melancholy individuals.

There is, when one comes to think of it, an extraordinary similarity between this speech and Hitler's speeches of February–March 1933 declaring that *all* Germans would, before long, become National-Socialists.

This extremism in de Gaulle's various programmes of the R.P.F. period is particularly striking when one compares it with the caution and moderation he exercised on these very same questions after 1958, when he realized that the essential totalitarianism of the R.P.F. was both politically and psychologically wholly unacceptable to France. But that was some years away. Now, not only were the Communists to be outlawed, but de Gaulle's Number One social objective – the 'Capital-Labour Association' – clearly meant a 'profound reform' and a total 'depolitization' of the trade unions, in fact their abolition. Later, in 1948, he became even more explicit, saying that, under the new Constitution, 'it would not be necessary to recognize the trade unions'.[1]

The trade union organization will have to be subjected to a profound evolution. If we establish the Association, the very nature and appearance of the trade unions will be changed, for there will be no class struggle inside the Association of capital and labour.

This was a curious sequel to those 'Italian-Fascist corporatist ideas' he had already outlined to Ambassador Maisky in London back in 1942!

Altogether, a new Constitution was required, one which would reduce the role of the parties to little, or indeed nothing, since 'everybody' would join the French People's

1. *La France sera la France: ce que veut Charles de Gaulle*, Paris, 1950, p. 136. This book, published by the R.P.F., consists of extracts on every subject from speeches that de Gaulle made, chiefly between 1947 and 1950.

Rally. There must be a powerful executive, a powerful French State.

Even more remarkable, in the light of what happened after 1958, was de Gaulle's line on the colonial territories. It was thanks to him that an expeditionary force of 80,000 men had been sent to reconquer Indo-China; an Indo-China Federation, he said on 24 April 1947, would have to be reconstituted, and must form part of the French Union. Later, in 1948, he stressed that the Indo-Chinese problem could only be handled from 'positions of strength'; that Ho-Chi-Minh was merely an agent of international Communism; and that the Emperor Bao Dai should be given France's full support. Proudly he exclaimed on 11 February 1950, that in all the world, the French army alone was fighting against world communism!

No doubt de Gaulle made the most of the 'liberalism' towards the colonial territories that he had shown, back in 1944, at the Brazzaville conference; but while he was prepared to make minor gestures and concessions (for instance in Algeria), he firmly adhered to the view that in all the territories of the French Union 'the authority of France – yes, I repeat, her authority – must be clearly exercised on the spot'. Algeria, he stressed, was a sovereign French land.[1]

But these were still side issues; the main emphasis in 1947, on the eve of the R.P.F.'s shortlived triumph, was on the necessity of 'unifying the nation' round General de Gaulle; on the need for a new State; on the fearful danger of war, and the threat that the 'separatists' represented.

*

De Gaulle's precise motives in embarking on this venture, remain something of a puzzle. One explanation offered is

---

1. ibid., p. 174. He never referred to the fearful massacres in Algeria during May 1945, when he was head of the movement.

that, having given up office in January 1946, and, with large-scale American aid at last in the offing, he felt that he could now return to power without having to face all the internal economic complications of 1946. Was his anti-Communism intended to make him highly popular in Washington, as he had already become with a part of the American press? *And was there not, in his view, a danger that, with American help, the Fourth Republic would, somehow, settle down, and – de Gaulle would be forgotten?* And did he also try to persuade his public – and perhaps even himself – that war with Russia was inevitable, or at least highly probable, and that, in the circumstances, France had better be ruled by a powerful leader, rather than by a mere Monsieur Ramadier?

De Gaulle was not a demagogue by natural inclination; yet the impression he gave in 1947 was that he was prepared, for various reasons, to go through all the motions of one. Perhaps at some stage, it flattered his vanity that a man with so little natural 'political sex-appeal' could still succeed in carrying the people of France before him.

*

The tremendous popular agitation that de Gaulle had excited during the summer of 1947 culminated in the extraordinary triumph of the R.P.F. in the municipal elections of 19 October, when the 'Rally' got nearly forty per cent of the votes. Paradoxically, the Communists, against whom all the thunder and lightning of the election campaign (not only from de Gaulle, but also from the other parties) had been directed, held their own, while the M.R.P., the Radicals and the Right were almost wiped out. The R.P.F. had simply taken their place by catering precisely to the same electoral clientele! Of the government parties, the Socialists alone suffered relatively few losses. In nearly all the large towns the R.P.F. captured the municipal councils, and in Paris secured fifty-two out of the ninety seats, so that the general's brother,

M. Pierre de Gaulle, became president of the Paris town council.

Interestingly it was the Right, i.e. all that was still more-or-less Vichyite in France, which rallied to de Gaulle – a phenomenon that was to become even more marked in 1948.

*

It was, of course, de Gaulle's bad luck that the October election should have been a municipal, and not a general, one. The vote itself caused a sensation; the papers talked about 'the de Gaulle Miracle'; the *New York Times* described it as 'the victory of the Marshall Plan over the Fifth Column'. Constitutionally, however, nothing had changed. De Gaulle had no claim to power. The National Assembly had been elected in 1946 for five years. Short of the whole Right, Centre, and M.R.P. joining the handful of Gaullists, there was no chance of any 'Gaullist' majority. And the M.R.P. seemed hostile, in the main. Nevertheless, it was all very awkward; although the Communists and Socialists had the same support in the country as before, the rest of the National Assembly no longer seemed representative. There was talk that de Gaulle would demand a referendum or plebiscite, and there was accordingly a temptation, here and there, to reach a compromise with him.

What ruined his chances was his own extreme arrogance. In a statement on 27 October he declared that 'an immense power' had risen in France; that 'the régime of division and confusion' had been finally condemned; that the government now represented only a feeble minority, and if its two main parties – the Socialists and M.R.P. – collected four million votes between them they would be lucky. A general election was therefore necessary, and a drastic reform of the Constitution. The international situation was very serious and France could not wait. The Assembly had the constitutional means of dissolving itself by a two-thirds majority.

Such truculence was too much; and a strange thing then happened, 'profoundly French' as many observers remarked at the time. The de Gaulle 'ultimatum' aroused in the National Assembly on the night of 28 October, something of the old republican *mystique* – with Ramadier and Herriot proclaiming that they would defend the National Assembly against all threats and summonses. Men like Herriot, who knew their provincial France better than de Gaulle, foresaw the disastrous effect that his 'ultimatum' would produce there. As Claude Bourdet was to write in *Combat* the next day:

De Gaulle has shocked the rank-and-file of our people – all those to whom a bad republic is still preferable to a good tyranny. Last night Ramadier, that unwieldy old man, somehow reminded me of all this. His unoriginal words seemed to echo across the decades, and reminded the young of the great crises the Republic had survived in the past.

Thus, bad timing and de Gaulle's mistakes, combined with the impulsive, emotional, and often half-hearted nature of the 19 October vote, produced this strange result: R.P.F. influence began to decline almost from the moment it achieved its greatest triumph. Many were shocked by the arrogance of de Gaulle's message to Parliament; and some began to wonder about the implications of his 'programme'. The suggestion that the Communist Party (with $5\frac{1}{2}$ million votes) might be dissolved could lead to the 'muzzling', before long, of the other parties, too. It was all highly dangerous. Would de Gaulle start abolishing the trade unions to replace them by something singularly like Vichy's *Charte de Travail*? Might not all this create a civil war situation?

There were many also who were becoming alarmed by de Gaulle's war hysteria. Was there any serious evidence that the Russians *were* prepared to invade Western Europe? The government parties – the Right and Centre, the M.R.P. and even the Socialists – could play the anti-Communist game as well as de Gaulle; they were doing it in a different way – though quite drastically enough to please the U.S.A. At the end of 1947, M. Moch, the Socialist Minister of the Interior, supported by the new M.R.P. Premier, M. Robert Schuman, mercilessly crushed a large number of Communist-promoted strikes with the help of armed C.R.S. guards. At the height of the labour turbulence, there were three million strikers; but, by 9 December, the strike movement was broken. The government also actively encouraged the non-Communists to break away from the C.G.T., the Trade Union Federation – a project furthered by American Federation of Labour subsidies, as we know from George Meany, the new head of the A.F. of L. in 1953, who proudly announced that the non-Communist Force Ouvrière was set up, after the December 1947 split, with the help of American funds.

It was also at the end of 1947 that the Schuman government very nearly broke off diplomatic relations with the Soviet Union. On 4 December, Mr John Foster Dulles came to Paris and had meetings both with the French government and with de Gaulle. He declared that what was happening in Paris was 'of the greatest importance', and that he was pleased the French government was getting tough with both the Communists and the Russians. Both Dulles and de Gaulle considered 'the revival of Germany essential'; and that an Anglo–Franco–American military alliance was 'necessary'.

But, as we shall see, the U.S. government, much impressed by men like Schuman and Moch, decided that the Third Force parties, rather than de Gaulle, were best suited to a life of friendship and harmony with the United States.

*

In 1948 the Cold War grew more dangerous, with the Communist *coup* in Czechoslovakia, the breach between Stalin and Tito, and the Berlin Blockade. One would have thought, in such circumstances, that de Gaulle's R.P.F. was bound to make an ever-growing appeal to the French people. Yet this did not happen. For one thing, 1948 marked the turning-point in the post-war economic history of France. Marshall Aid was now arriving on a generous scale, and, for the first time since the war, living conditions were beginning to return to normal. For this improvement the 'Third Force' governments were taking (and getting) the credit.[1]

This did not help de Gaulle. The United States government, despite some hesitation at various moments, firmly decided to support the Third Force, rather than the General, who was arrogant, unreliable, and moody, and might well precipitate a civil war in France. His behaviour throughout 1948 was becoming wilder every day and was beginning to alarm wide sections of French public opinion. Some R.P.F. leaders like André Malraux were now indulging in a sort of cosmic catastrophism, while others, like General de Benouville, almost went as far as to advocate preventive war against Russia. Such 'Free World' zeal was becoming excessive.

Moreover, de Gaulle insistently put forward his own ideas on *grandeur française*, ideas which did not at all fit in with American plans; for instance, when he said:

Since Prague has followed the others into outer darkness, the West must join in economic and military cooperation. The physical and moral centre of this grouping must be France. Germany can work with us, though not as a Reich, but as a series of sovereign federal states ... I would consider it criminal

1. The government of M. Ramadier (Socialist) had been replaced by one under M. Robert Schuman (M.R.P.) in November 1947; in September 1948, after a short-lived government under M. Marie (Radical), M. Queuille (Radical) became head of an administration which lasted for more than a year. All these were coalition governments composed chiefly of Socialists, Radicals and M.R.P., with a few members of the moderate Right.

if our strategy consisted in deliberately abandoning France, first
to invasion, and then to liberation by means of the atom bomb.
(*Combat*, 18 April 1948.)

The London Recommendations of June 1948, which were
to lead to the abandonment of the Ruhr to Germany, to the
early formation of a West-German State and to the absorption of the French zone into the Anglo-American Bizone,
were opposed by de Gaulle with the greatest vigour as being
in every way dangerous to France. He sharply criticized the
whole of U.S. policy, as it was now taking shape over
Germany.

But if he was annoying the United States more and more,
he was also beginning to alarm many people in France who
had been sympathetic to him only a few months earlier. For
one thing, every de Gaulle meeting now tended to assume
the character of a para-military rally, with thousands of cars
bringing supporters from distant parts, and scores of armed
men surrounding the general: at the Grenoble rally in
September there were serious disorders; one Communist
was killed and many other anti-Gaullists wounded by bullets.
Jules Moch, the Minister of the Interior, who had shown how
tough he could be with the Communist strikers during the
previous winter, declared himself equally determined to stand
no nonsense from de Gaulle. He said that all the shooting at
Grenoble had been done by the Gaullists, and that a feature
of these de Gaulle rallies now were the numerous jeeps
crowded with Marseilles gunmen (*nervi*) – precisely the kind
of people who used to surround Jacques Doriot, the thuggish
French Nazi 'Führer', in the immediate pre-war years. Moch
furthermore complained that all these Gaullist rallies were
costing the government a great deal of money and trouble:
numerous police cars and a platoon of gendarmes had to
accompany de Gaulle all over the place, security measures
which had already squandered ten million francs and 57,000
litres of petrol. M. Ramadier, the Minister of Defence,

immediately announced that he was withdrawing from de
Gaulle his usual Guard of Honour: 'let the Minister of the
Interior take care of de Gaulle as of any other citizen'.

All this fuss over the taxpayer's money and the Third Force
government's petrol did not fail to make de Gaulle look
slightly ridiculous, and he was certainly furious at a press
conference that he held a few days later. He kept referring to
M. Moch as *ce personnage* and embarked on a somewhat
absurd piece of arithmetic, arguing that since he had received one million letters from his supporters, each with a
ten-franc stamp, the government had been 'refunded' its
expenses.

He claimed that the R.P.F. had a membership of 1½
millions. And it is true that, in the autumn of 1948, he was
still popular. His meetings drew enormous crowds, and in the
Senate (Council of the Republic) election in November, the
R.P.F. did very well, with 130 of the 320 members either
R.P.F. or members of other parties 'adhering' to it. The
whole 'classical right' had now (temporarily) joined de
Gaulle and, ironically, most of the ex-Vichyites were eager
to join. His public meetings were becoming more and
more like those of the Pétain Legion in the past, with some
Nazi showmanship and Doriot thuggery added. But this
association of 'Gaullists' and 'Vichyites' did not last very
long. On the crucial question of Pétain, interned in a fortress,
de Gaulle tried to steer a middle course which pleased
nobody. He was against abolishing the sentence of life
imprisonment passed on the Marshal, yet pleaded that mercy
be shown to the old man by letting him end his days at home.[1]

---

1. It was in 1948–9 that de Gaulle either said, or was reported to
have said, that Pétain had, after all, served a useful purpose during the
war; France at that time *'had two strings to her bow – one was de
Gaulle, the other Pétain'*; or, better still, *'Pétain was the shield and de
Gaulle the sword'*. The latter remark, allegedly made by de Gaulle, was
quoted by Colonel Rémy, a wartime associate of his.

In 1949 many of the Vichyites turned against de Gaulle. Characteristically, the very conservative and crypto-Vichyite *Figaro* published that year the extremely anti-de Gaulle posthumous *Memoirs* of General Giraud; it was also in 1949 that André Malraux, in a moment of indiscretion, remarked: 'De Gaulle took us full speed to the Rubicon and then told us to get out our fishing-rods.' This question of the 'Rubicon' is, indeed, an interesting one. How, one may ask, short of an armed insurrection, could de Gaulle have 'crossed the Rubicon'? De Gaulle must have known that – even if he had the means of staging such an insurrection, which is more than doubtful – he would merely have plunged the country into a state of chaos, since the working class was, at that time, in an angry and exasperated mood. As for the general public, they were, fundamentally, more interested in peace and quiet, in a 'return to normal' and – in American aid. As for 'crossing the Rubicon' by at least nominally 'legal' means (as de Gaulle was to do with such brilliant success in 1958), conditions simply did not lend themselves to such an operation; the 'Third Force' governments, confident of American support, were totally unwilling to accept his ultimatum demanding dissolution and a new election.

It is said that, in view of its rabid anti-Communism, the R.P.F. was subsidized by American funds. That may be true; but most of the American money – that of the U.S. government – went not to de Gaulle, but to the much more pliable Third Force governments.

De Gaulle's attempts to appeal to the working class failed completely; his audiences were almost entirely bourgeois, with only a small working class sprinkling. His 'corporatist' arguments carried no weight with the working class; and he received no support at all from the Third Force. President Auriol was violently opposed to him, and the Socialists and M.R.P. were determined not to let de Gaulle 'pass'.

3. *The Decline of the French People's Rally, and Why – The Fourth Republic Wins*

Who, then, were the organizers and the active members of the R.P.F.? A high proportion of them belonged to the Free French who had fought under de Gaulle during the war and, above all, to his Intelligence networks, first in London and then in Algiers. Significantly, the secretary-general of the Rally, i.e. the second-in-command, was none other than Jacques Soustelle, who had been head of the B.C.R.A., de Gaulle's Intelligence Service in Algiers.

The Gaullist 'nobility', which the General had created by conferring the title of 'Companion of the Liberation', consisted of just over 1,000 persons, and of these 783 belonged to the Free French Forces, 107 to the Gaullist Intelligence networks, and only 157 to members of the Home Resistance. The backbone of the R.P.F. largely consisted of these 'Companions', and what members of the Home Resistance joined the R.P.F. leadership were a few right-wingers like General de Bénouville, formerly of the *Action Française*. Relative 'liberals', like Edmond Michelet or Debû-Bridel, were few and far between. The R.P.F. also had a certain appeal among the professional classes, particularly medical men, and among some intellectuals, like the eminent jurist Professor Marcel Prélot and (for a time) M. Raymond Aron. The greatest intellectual ornament was André Malraux, the famous novelist, who regarded the R.P.F. as a fascinating new revolutionary adventure. As a florid speaker adept at theatrical effects and luminous with historical mysticism, he was to become the great star turn (next to the General) at R.P.F. rallies. Though not very prominent in the R.P.F. at first, Michel Debré, a close associate of de Gaulle's in Algiers, was to start, like so many others, his great political career as an R.P.F. *notable*. In 1948 he was elected to the

Senate, and there, for years, he was to be the most violent Gaullist spokesman.

One of the weaknesses of the R.P.F. was the comparative lack of support it was getting from Big Business, which preferred to assist the 'classical' and quasi-Vichyite Right. Among the exceptions was M. Marcel Bloch-Dassault, the aircraft magnate, who subsidized the R.P.F. from the outset, in 1951 became a Gaullist deputy, and, after 1958, one of the powers behind the Throne.

By and large, however, the 'classical' Right was distrustful of de Gaulle; despite all the plausible explanations he now gave, he had fraternized with the Communists at the time of the Liberation. Moreover, Marshall Aid was helping to restore France as part of the 'American sphere', and as part of what came to be known as 'the Bankers' Europe'. Between 1948 and the outbreak of the Korean War, which was temporarily to promote a ruinous rearmament drive, France enjoyed relative prosperity. The Communists had, by now, been driven into a sort of political ghetto, and President Truman was very pleased with the French, who had eliminated the Communists from the government, were returning more and more to free enterprise, and were relying on the United States to protect them against Russia.

This dependence on the United States was not to de Gaulle's liking. In 1949–50 he began to think more and more in terms of 'Europe', and as early as 16 March 1950 started his overtures to Adenauer, whose proposal for a Franco–German union he now heartily welcomed.[1] He thought there was 'something almost dazzling' in a union between France and Germany, which would then extend to Africa.

I can see here the possibility of a joint development which would transform that part of Europe which has remained free and even give fresh hope to that other part which has lost its freedom. It would be a case of rebuilding on a modern basis, that is econ-

1. *La France sera la France* . . . p. 298.

omically, socially, strategically and culturally, the Charlemagne Empire.

And this 'Charlemagne Empire', he thought, might well eventually liberate Eastern Europe.

I am convinced that if France, once she is well on her feet and properly governed (i.e. by de Gaulle) called on Europe to reorganize herself, particularly with the help of the Germans, the whole European atmosphere would be changed, all the way from the Atlantic to the Urals, and even the leaders of the Iron Curtain countries would feel the consequences. The key to the liberation of Europe is in Europe.

In Europe, and not in the U.S.A. He favoured, in certain conditions, the rearmament of Western Germany[1] and the creation of a European Confederation. The Atlantic Pact and 'the day-dreaming of the Council of Europe' were producing the very opposite result. Once the Gaullists got into power, he suggested, 'France would take an entirely different road and carry the Continent with her'. (ibid., p. 299)

After the outbreak of the Korean War, de Gaulle was more emphatic than ever that the defence of Europe should be based on a Franco–German *entente*, that there should be

1. He welcomed it, even though, he had only very recently, violently protested against the constitution of a West German State, that 'nucleus of a Reich', which would always be aggressive. With 'two Germanies' in existence, he thought the absorption of Western Germany by a dynamic, totalitarian and Russian-backed Eastern Germany much more likely than the reverse. Without demanding any more the separation of the Rhineland from Western Germany, he still insisted, as late as 1949, on a 'different' solution – the creation of several small federal states of Western Germany, instead of a 'central' German state, with Bonn as its capital. This 'embryo of the Reich' was fearfully dangerous. (Speech on 22 May 1949, see *La France sera La France*, p. 292.) In the same speech he said that the Ruhr should be given a separate 'European' status. He blamed Britain for 'pursuing her instinctive and traditional policy of playing off Germany against France'.

European institutions 'directly elected by the citizens of
Europe and enjoying, in economic and strategic matters, a
part of the sovereign rights delegated to them by the sovereign
states'. Above all –

'There must be a system of common defence, the plans of
which should be normally drawn up by France, and whose chief
should be appointed by France, just as, in the Pacific, the
Americans should be predominant, and, in the East, the British.'
(Speech on 17 August 1950.)

All this sounded singularly unrealistic in 1950. It was the
year of the Schuman Plan, which was first presented to
Parliament in May. Then, after the outbreak of the war in
Korea, there arose the issue of a 'European Army', also on
some kind of supra-national basis. This started with the
'Pleven Plan' of 24 October, itself the outcome of inter-
minable discussions following Truman's and Acheson's
blunt announcement on 11 September that Europe must
have sixty divisions, ten of them German. With their
'Pleven Plan' the French government tried to limit the
damage; but, in reality, the 'Pleven Plan' was already the
embryo of what was later to develop into the abortive
European Defence Community (E.D.C.). Although de
Gaulle had supported German rearmament long before, his
spokesman in the National Assembly, M. René Capitant,
attacked the Pleven project and declared, like de Gaulle a
few weeks before, that the defence of Europe must be led by
France, and no other country (by which he meant, of course,
the U.S.A.).

*

From the American point of view, the Gaullists were becoming troublesome, and the Third Force parties, more and
more dependent on American financial aid, were worried lest
the Gaullists on the one hand and the Communists on the
other make the new Assembly – due for election in June 1951

- utterly ungovernable. A new electoral system was accordingly devised, based on *apparentement*, by which the candidates of parties 'associated' in any constituency got all the seats if they won more than fifty per cent of the votes. It was a thoroughly dishonest system, but it produced the desired result: instead of having just over 300 seats, the Third Force parties (including the 'classical' Right) got nearly 400; the Gaullists, instead of 143, got 117; the Communists, instead of 150, got 101.

*

It is curious to think that, during the election campaign of June 1951, de Gaulle and the R.P.F. should still have been taken very seriously, despite the evidence there was to show that their influence had sharply declined since October 1947. Before the election, it is true, the Gaullists had made some very bad mistakes. General Koenig, the hero of Bir Hakeim, and now one of the Gaullist candidates, had conducted a campaign for a vast French Army, with a standing force of twenty divisions, a possible extension of the military service to three years and the dispatch of large forces to Indo-China; and, on May Day, in the Bois de Boulogne, de Gaulle himself had made a particularly provocative speech in which he spoke of a 'rendezvous in the Champs-Elysées', suggesting a march on the Elysée palace after the R.P.F.'s election victory. All this, to the man-in-the-street, meant violence and revolutionary disorder, especially as the R.P.F. could not possibly 'win' the election in the ordinary sense of achieving a parliamentary majority.

The R.P.F.'s only asset was the personality of de Gaulle himself; but whether he was threatening a 'march on the Elysée', or being petulant in his protestations of republicanism ('it was I who gave you the Republic in 1945') there was something disquieting about him, especially to provincial France. He was not 'adored' the way Hitler or Mussolini had been; his personality was cold and far from magnetic;

and the fact that he surrounded himself with an aura of mystery, seldom appeared in public, and spoke in riddles, cut both ways. *That tremendous propaganda instrument which he was to use with such effect after 1958 – television – was not yet there.* His programme, as outlined in its potted version on those postcards – *les cartes nationales* – which one bought for 100 francs (about 1s. 6d.), and sent to de Gaulle at Colombey with compliments (he collected £40,000 or £50,000 this way) was both very vague and rather alarming. It said that the country was to be 'liberated from the stranglehold of the parties', that these were to be 'done away with'; that the separatists (i.e. Communists) were to be liquidated; that France must have her own Army; that the Atlantic States would be associated with France, but would not be her masters. (This meant complete independence from the United States, but – much greater armaments expenditure.) Finally, the promise to replace the trade unions by 'Labour-Capital Association' appealed neither to the working class, nor to the capitalists. As the *Canard Enchaîné* put it:

The R.P.F. want to make friends at the Bourse, but the Bourse won't hear of it. For if the R.P.F. gets away with it, these gentlemen say, stocks will go down the drain the very next week … At the Bourse they are convinced that the R.P.F. in power will mean undiluted communism in six months' time.

In the countryside the R.P.F. made very little impact, except in Normandy, Britanny, and the East; it did much better in the larger cities like Lyon, Nice and Bordeaux, and also in Paris. But, in any event, it was clearly not the all-embracing 'immense force' that de Gaulle had spoken of in 1947. It was, in fact, no more than another competing *party*; its one hope was it would gain a sufficient number of seats in parliament to win over enough other parties to form a majority (possibly after 'outlawing' the Communists, as

Hitler had done in 1933). In the election campaign de Gaulle (not a candidate) spoke in riddles; Malraux spouted romantic nonsense;[1] in provincial France, many Gaullist candidates were on the defensive, claiming to be good republicans, though advocates of a Republic that would be stronger and cleaner and more prosperous than the Republic of M. Pleven or M. Queuille.

In the end, all the R.P.F. got was 117 seats out of 627, and four million votes – just over twenty per cent, or half its poll in October 1947.

*

It is not surprising that in all the pro-de Gaulle literature published in France during the last few years, the whole R.P.F. experiment should hardly ever be mentioned. It was a failure, despite the four million votes it collected in the 1951 election. Politically, it was inept and amateurish; its programme was a collection of pompous commonplaces, plus some highly explosive proposals. In its foreign policy it was incoherent – both pro-American and anti-American, and successively anti-Bonn and pro-Adenauer in relation to Germany; in home affairs, its programme was thuggish in its anti-Communism and anti-trade unionism. It underrated the widespread French desire to settle down at last to more normal conditions with the help of Marshall Aid, and the general reluctance to have an open fight with the Communists, who by now no longer represented any sort

1. In his pre-election speech at a big meeting in Paris, Malraux proclaimed the Gaullists to be the legitimate heirs of the Great French Revolution. 'Think,' he cried, 'of the soldiers of Valmy and Jemmapes! Those were the days when the whole world gave itself to France! Those were Republicans ind ed! But now look at them – Herriot, Pleven, Marie – bah!' This had nothing to do with more serious matters like the Gaullist plan to disband the trade unions, still less with such prosaic matters as the price of steak. For catching votes, Malraux's grand harangue was utterly useless. (cf. *France 1940–1955* pp. 536–41.)

of real danger anyway. M. Moch, as Minister of the Interior for over two years, had drawn their teeth.

Other factors were unfavourable to de Gaulle. He had hardly any access to radio; television was scarcely in existence; and, apart from the two R.P.F. weeklies and a few local sheets, *practically the entire press was opposed to him.*

He also had bad luck elsewhere. Shortly before the election, the official Vatican paper *Osservatore Romano*, came out with an article virtually calling on all good Catholics in France to vote for the M.R.P., the 'Third Force' Catholics, rather than for the R.P.F. There had never been much love lost between de Gaulle and Pius XII, 'the Nazi Pope', as the General would call him in moments of annoyance. And now the Pope was supporting that Little Europe, dear to the hearts of Schuman and Teitgen, Adenauer and Gasperi.

*

Become a parliamentary party like any other, the R.P.F. was in an awkward spot. Where did it go from here? Since the 'classical' Right, the Radicals, and M.R.P. – all these forming the new government coalition under Pleven – were 'pro-American', it was difficult to see how the R.P.F. could win enough of them over to become the centre of a new government coalition.

At the R.P.F. Congress at Nancy in November, de Gaulle still talked big, declaring that if the R.P.F. 'was the spirit of France, it is now its organization and its strength'. Although he now indicated that discussions should be started with other parliamentary parties, it was not at all clear what the purpose of these could be, since the R.P.F. was uncompromisingly hostile to the Schuman Plan, the European Army, and indeed, the whole of the government's foreign policy, including that European Integration so dear to the 'Europeans' of the M.R.P.

In the ratification debate on the Schuman Plan (the Coal-

Steel Pool) in December, Soustelle, the R.P.F. spokesman, claimed that the whole project 'made us abandon an important sector of our economy to a stateless and uncontrolled autocracy of experts'.

*

And now, in 1952, began the rapid decline of the R.P.F. as a parliamentary party.

In March 1952, after a short-lived government under Edgar Faure, the highly conservative, dull, and respectable M. Antoine Pinay (a former Vichyite) presented himself for the Premiership. He was remarkably vague about foreign policy, but concentrated on France's economic problems, declaring himself to be 'Mr Consumer', head of a society of forty-seven million Frenchmen.

There had been serious discontent in the country over inflation, and now, with the stabilization of prices in the offing, Pinay seemed the right man to handle the country's affairs. So, in the investiture vote, twenty-seven of the 117 R.P.F. members – those belonging to the more 'conservative' and even 'Vichyite' fringe – broke away and supported M. Pinay. The great charm of the R.P.F. was broken. De Gaulle was furious: 'I did not save France to hand her over to this Monsieur Pinay!' he remarked; but that did not stop the rot.

*

During the next few months, in by-elections and local elections, the R.P.F. vote dropped from twenty per cent to a mere ten per cent of the poll. A 'Pinay Legend' had been built up – that of a sensible down-to-earth champion of stability and financial orthodoxy who had at last succeeded in stopping inflation and the rise in the cost of living. In reality M. Pinay had simply been very lucky; it so happened that, after the boom in raw materials due to the Korean war, there had been a sharp drop in world prices, and, by 1952, with a slowing-down in stockpiling, prices became stable for the first time since the war.

The Fourth Republic seemed to be definitely settling down, and the R.P.F.'s strident call for drastic change no longer had any wide appeal. Even the all-out anti-Communists had every reason to be pleased with Pinay; it was under his government that the Fourth Republic came nearest to outlawing the C.P., following the arrest of Jacques Duclos in an all-too-obvious police frame-up.[1] A lesson, by the way, which de Gaulle himself certainly learned from this incident was that French public opinion as a whole was not favourable to outlawing the Communist Party. From now on he stopped speaking of 'separatists'.

Nevertheless, he was still determined to knock down the Fourth Republic. When, on 21 December, Pinay resigned, following various disagreements with the M.R.P. (whose enthusiasm for the 'European Army' he did not share) and the obstructive tactics of the remaining eighty-five Gaullist deputies, de Gaulle declared that it was 'in the public interest' to disrupt any combination of parties 'tending to perpetuate the present system'.[2] Even many R.P.F. deputies thought that such a call to overthrow the Fourth Republic would not help the Gaullist cause. When, after Pinay's resignation, President Auriol called on Soustelle, the R.P.F. parliamentary leader, to form the next government, the latter found all the other parties highly distrustful of him. In the end another right-centre government was formed under M. René Mayer. It was then that the disintegration of the R.P.F. started in real earnest. The municipal elections of April 1953 proved a disaster, the party's votes were down to less than ten per cent of the poll; in Paris only ten Gaullist town councillors were returned as against fifty-two in 1947

1. See chapter on 'Duclos and the Carrier pigeons' in *France 1940–55* pp. 575–86.
2. *L'Année politique*, 1952, p. 94.

and the drop was even greater in other cities. De Gaulle washed his hands of the Gaullist deputies, giving them a free hand in their future activities and withdrawing from them the R.P.F. label. The R.P.F. movement would continue, he announced, but would in no way be associated with the 'disastrous system'.

The remaining eighty-five Gaullist members of parliament changed the name of their party to U.R.A.S. (*Union Républicaine d'Action Sociale*)[1] and now took the line that, thanks to their fairly strong tactical position, they could serve some purpose in treating every problem from a 'national' point of view; in particular, they were going to oppose the European Army with all their might, in alliance with the Socialists, if necessary, and even with the Communists! Up to the January 1956 election, they were indeed to play an important part in opposing the 'satellization' of France and the 'integration' of Europe. For tactical or other reasons some of the former R.P.F. deputies even entered a number of governments, including that of Mendès-France in 1954.

De Gaulle, while conducting his campaign against E.D.C. and against British and American policy, nevertheless felt bitter and frustrated as seldom before. The Left, he said on 6 May, had turned against him since the Liberation, and was busy now building up a new – and even worse – version of the Third Republic, while the Right, having sought refuge against Communism in the R.P.F., had now abandoned him 'under the influence of the feudal lords of Money and the Press', of the 'incorrigible Vichyites', and 'foreign pressure'.[2]

1. Later they abbreviated this to *Républicains sociaux*.
2. *L'Année politique*, 1953, p. 40.

4. De Gaulle against Integrated Europe – His Strange Confession of Failure

The E.D.C. treaty remained in the centre of French political life throughout 1953, first under the Mayer government and then under the Laniel one. Britain and the U.S.A. – though keeping out of it themselves – were demanding with ever-growing persistence that the 'European Army' be ratified by the French Parliament. The French governments were playing for time. De Gaulle, in November 1953, came out with one of his most violent blasts against the 'Anglo-Saxons'. At his press conference he referred to 'this monstrous treaty' which, he said, would rob the French Army of its sovereignty. He blamed this and other 'supranational monstrosities' on M. Jean Monnet who, already in 1940, 'had tried to integrate King George VI with President Lebrun' and, in 1943, 'to integrate de Gaulle and Giraud'. Now he was trying to do the same with France and Germany. In reality, he said, this 'stateless army of Germans and Frenchmen' would be placed at the entire disposal of the American commander-in-chief.

Instead, de Gaulle spoke of a confederation of national armies in which Germany would hold at first only a small and well-controlled place; but it must be a Grand Alliance, comprising Britain. Before anything like this was created, he said, *an attempt should be made to revive the Franco–Russian alliance*, since France was still an ally of Russia against any revival of the German menace.

It should be recalled that, by this time, Stalin had died, and de Gaulle obviously saw some new possibilities in the East; furthermore, he was violently angry at all the pressure to which the U.S.A. and Britain had latterly subjected the French. He attacked the U.S.A. for trying to force France to accept E.D.C., which could only 'condemn her to decay'.

'The encouragement the U.S.A. are giving to Germany to become again the most powerful country in Europe can only lead to war sooner or later.'

He was even angrier with Britain:

'Yes, Britain, too, is demanding that we join E.D.C., though nothing in the world would induce her to join it herself. Abandon your soldiers to others, lose your sovereignty, lose your Dominions – that's fine for Paris, but not for London ... And why? It's because we are the Continent, the "unhappy Continent", as Churchill has already called us ... No doubt there will be a few British soldiers in Germany and a few observers attached to E.D.C. ... Very pleasant, indeed, to be the guest of honour at the banquet of a society to which you pay no dues.'

The memory of Syria was still rankling; if France became involved in a war, would not the British help themselves to the French Empire?

'If France, for the sake of E.D.C., is so determined to separate herself from her overseas territories, well, why not? A world crisis might well create a situation in which all kinds of new possibilities might present themselves to Lord Mountbatten, or to Lord Alexander (*snarl*), *Vicomte de Tunis*, if you please ...'

About his own position, de Gaulle was now deeply pessimistic. Probably for the first time in his life he made at that November press conference this extraordinary confession of failure:

'Think by how many failures my life has been marked! First I tried to persuade the authorities to endow France with an armoured force that would have spared us the Invasion ... Then, after the disaster of 1940, I tried to persuade the government to go to North Africa ... Again I failed. I failed at Dakar. Then, after victory I tried to maintain the unity I had formed around myself, but in vain. Later, in grave circumstances, I again tried, but in vain ... If these failures had been mine, they would have been of no importance, but they were the failures of France. True, from time to time, there were successes ... And yet, during the darkest moments of the war, I sometimes wondered: Perhaps it is my mission to represent in the history of our country its last upsurge towards the lofty heights. Perhaps it is my lot to have written the last pages in the book of our greatness . . .'[1]

And, a few months later, after another de Gaulle press conference against E.D.C., Mauriac, who was present, felt that here was 'the last Frenchman who had made his country-men believe that they were still a great nation'.

His words, [Mauriac wrote] are like a cold wind, coming from very far and very high . . . No one asked him: 'Do you agree with the (Laniel) government?' because by his presence, de Gaulle makes the dictatorship of Lilliput invisible to the naked eye.

Mauriac also recalled that, at the same meeting, de Gaulle had used this strange phrase – and had used it naturally, almost without arrogance, but with a touch of melancholy pride – *'J'étais la France'*. And no one had protested, be-cause, in a sense, it was true.

The phrase is all the more strange as de Gaulle was saying in 1954 that he *had been* France; he was no longer saying that he *was* France.

*

E.D.C. was the central issue in French politics throughout 1953, and the greater part of 1954 – a year which was, moreover, marked by the dramatic end of the war in Indo-China. On E.D.C. de Gaulle continued to hold the strongest views, and when, after the fall of the Mayer government in May 1953, Mendès-France made his first attempt to form a government, it was de Gaulle who 'advised' the Gaullists in parliament to vote against his investiture, 'since he probably would not have the guts to stand up to the Americans over E.D.C.'.

The position of the Gaullists was very strange. Though

1. *Le Monde*, 14 November 1953.

continuing to be 'against the régime', they entered several governments: Laniel's in June 1953, then Mendès-France's in June 1954; then Edgar Faure's in the following year. Mendès-France himself, shortly before being overthrown, appointed Soustelle Governor-General of Algeria. De Gaulle's views on the colonial problems, seem, during those years, to have undergone considerable changes. He did not protest against the 'surrender' of Indo-China in 1954, and one of the Gaullist Ministers, M. Christian Fouchet, accompanied Mendès-France to Tunis when the Premier granted the Protectorate 'internal autonomy'. But on E.D.C. the Gaullists continued to be uncompromisingly hostile, and when the project was defeated by the National Assembly in August 1954, they continued their sharp opposition to those Paris Agreements under which Germany was to be rearmed in a different way. These were nevertheless approved by the Assembly after a dramatic debate in December 1954, and soon afterwards the Mendès-France government was overthrown, although most of the Gaullists now voted for him.[1]

1. Mendès-France, who was premier between June 1954 and February 1955, was one of the few leaders of the Fourth Republic for whom de Gaulle had a great deal of admiration. Though he doubted that, under the prevailing 'system', Mendès-France could last, he admired his bold style of governing – his settlement of the Indo-China problem, his handling of Tunisia, his challenge to many of the stick-in-the-mud methods of the régime. Significantly, at the end of 1954, Malraux and Mauriac, in statements to L'Express, discussed the possibility of some sort of 'new liberalism' being built up with Mendès and de Gaulle as its main pillars. This, of course, came to nothing. But I remember a conversation with Mendès-France in July 1956 when he clearly suggested that de Gaulle was now the only man who could still settle the Algerian problem. At that time, Mendès was willing to work with de Gaulle wholeheartedly if the latter had a clear programme of action. (See the author's The Strange History of Pierre Mendès-France, pp. 317–18, London, Barrie. 1957.)

5. De Gaulle Retires from Public Life

De Gaulle's speeches and press conferences were now becoming few and far between, and, in July 1955, obviously
frustrated by the failure of the R.P.F., and not very happy
about the ambiguous position in which the Gaullist deputies
were finding themselves (some seemed to have taken a liking
for government posts under the Republic), he suddenly
called a press conference at which he declared that he was
retiring from public life.

In his statement he deplored the way the question of
German rearmament had been settled; spoke rather vaguely
about the future of the overseas territories, mentioning
'association' as a solution in the case of Tunisia and
Morocco, and 'integration, provided it can be sincere', in the
case of Algeria. Of the régime in France, he spoke more in
sorrow than in anger, 'Everything suggests,' he went on,
'that it will be a long time before we meet again. It is my
intention not to intervene any longer in what is called
"public affairs".' He added that he would take 'no interest
at all' in the 1956 election. Maybe he would intervene in
public affairs once again, but 'a rather unusual shock' would
be required for this. And meanwhile, 'I say good-bye,
perhaps for a long time'.

                                    *

Perhaps not nearly enough attention was paid to these words
at the time. It was, somehow, assumed that de Gaulle had
decided to retire for good. He was nearly 65. His R.P.F.
had been a failure. It was known that, having published the
first volume of his *War Memoirs* in 1954, he intended to
continue this work.

His retirement did not help the Gaullists, and the January
1956 election resulted in a complete débâcle for them. Only
sixteen were returned (later five more joined them) and the
total Gaullist poll dropped from over four million in 1951,

to 900,000. Instead, 2½ million votes were collected by a new formation under the right-wing demagogue, Pierre Poujade, representing, on the one hand, the discontented small shopkeeper class, and on the other, colonialist extremism.

But even the handful of Gaullists in the new Assembly were not without importance, as the events of 1958 were to prove. Among them were General Koenig, M. Soustelle, (who soon became the most vociferous leader of the Algerian diehards), M. Triboulet, and, most important, M. Chaban-Delmas, the Mayor of Bordeaux, who, together with Soustelle, and as the Gaullist Trojan horse inside the Gaillard government of 1957–8, was to play a leading part in preparing the Algiers *putsch* of May 1958. In the Senate, M. Debré continued to be the most virulent Gaullist spokesman.

*

And so, from the middle of 1955 to May 1958, de Gaulle stayed in the wilderness, writing his *Mémoires*. In 1956 he went on a long voyage to the French West Indies and the Pacific islands, and everywhere was given a rousing welcome. In his speeches along the way he prophesied a 'great future' for France. Most of the time, however, he spent at Colombey-les-Deux Eglises, writing. Unlike Churchill, he wrote every word himself, though he had one or two assistants to look up documents for him. But it would be wrong to suppose that he was out of touch with public affairs. Certain politicians – among them Mendès-France and some of the leading Gaullists – either visited him at Colombey, or saw him during his weekly visits to Paris. A fairly frequent visitor was Mr Vinogradov, the Soviet Ambassador, who thought de Gaulle's return to power, sooner or later, highly probable. Significantly, some Algerian Moslem leaders also visited him, thinking him more likely than anyone else to settle the Algerian problem. President Bourguiba of Tunisia often publicly referred to de Gaulle as North Africa's 'best hope'.

Paradoxically, however, most of the remaining Gaullists (now called *Républicains Sociaux*) in Parliament, and, above all, their leaders (Soustelle in the National Assembly, Debré in the Senate) took the most extreme colonialist line in respect of Algeria.

It should be recalled here that the January 1956 election resulted in an at least nominal victory of the Left and in the formation of a government under Guy Mollet, the Socialist leader. But Mollet soon quarrelled with the Communists as well as with Mendès-France, the Radical leader, having, barely a month after the formation of his government, surrendered to the colonialists during his famous visit to Algiers on 6 February. He cancelled the appointment of the relatively liberal General Catroux as Minister-Resident in Algeria, and appointed instead Robert Lacoste who, though a Socialist, adopted the extreme colonialist line. It was Mollet, too, who was the chief French instigator of the Suez adventure. He had two Gaullists in his government – Chaban-Delmas was a Minister of State – and his uneasy coalition lasted till June 1957. It was then replaced by a short-lived government under a Radical, Bourgès-Maunoury (the only one with no Gaullist members); and in November 1957 a new government was formed under another Radical, Félix Gaillard, with Chaban-Delmas as Minister of Defence.

Both the Bourgès-Maunoury and Gaillard governments were overthrown on the Algerian issue, the main attack on the cabinet being led in both cases by Jacques Soustelle, who was supported by all the Gaullists, most of the 'classical' Right, and the Poujadists. On the other side of the Assembly, the Communists automatically voted 'against'. There is every reason to suppose that de Gaulle and 'his' representatives in parliament did not see eye-to-eye at all on the Algerian issue. Soustelle and, with him, the whole Right represented perfectly the *Algérie Française* point of view, with its citadels in the North Africa Lobby and – the Army command in Algeria.

And then, in February, 1958, under the unfortunate Gaillard government, the process of finally wrecking the Fourth Republic began. Men like Soustelle, taking advantage of the fact that de Gaulle was 'against the System', allowed it also to be assumed from this that de Gaulle was a supporter of *Algérie Française*. De Gaulle himself was careful, extremely careful, not to disavow Soustelle – and he remained so until some time after the Fourth Republic had gone into voluntary liquidation.

At the age of 67, de Gaulle was now itching to return to power. Soustelle, the Algiers generals and the Algiers teddy-boys, as well as the whole colonialist Right on both sides of the Mediterranean, were going, between them, to create that 'rather violent shock' which, as he had said in his farewell press conference back in 1955, might bring him back to public life.

We saw in the first chapter of this book with what fantastic cunning he handled the desperately dangerous situation of May 1958.

CHAPTER 7

INTO THE FIFTH REPUBLIC

1. De Gaulle and the Army

THE Fourth Republic collapsed under the shock of the Algiers *putsch*. It has since been argued that this collapse was bound to take place anyway. But is this true? As a result of economic difficulties and the Cold War, the tripartite coalition, including the Communists, had broken up in 1947. But, given American aid, the 'Third Force' governments ruled France with reasonable success until 1951, standing up to both the Communists and de Gaulle's R.P.F. It was during the 1951–5 parliament that governmental instability grew more serious, mainly as a result of numerous international complications – the winding-up of the Indo-China war; the open revolt of Tunisia and Morocco; the beginning of the Algerian war; the violent controversies over E.D.C. and German rearmament. Even Pinay's 1952 government, popular with the Right and Centre, and the Mendès-France government of 1954–5, popular with a large part of the Left, did not last more than seven or eight months.

After the 1956 election the possibility of a solid government majority and of a coherent government policy became even more precarious. With uncompromising opposition from the Poujadists on the extreme right and from the Communists on the extreme left, any government was, in effect, dependent on the support of the 'classical' Right and the small Gaullist group, and both these were sharply hostile to any weakness shown in the handling of the Algerian problem. If the first government of the legislature, under the Socialist leader, Guy Mollet, managed to last for over a year, it was only because it pursued a diehard Algerian policy, and even enthusiastically embarked on the Suez escapade. But, by 1957, French public opinion was becoming increasingly weary of the Algerian war, and this was reflected in the policies attempted by the next two governments – those of Bourgès-Maunoury and Félix Gaillard. Both governments were overthrown when the 'classical' Right and the Gaullists – both these representing the Army and the colonialist diehards – withdrew their support.

Government authority had, in 1957-8, reached its lowest ebb. Not only the Army, but even the administration were, less and less, under government control. As André Siegfried put it, 'under the Fourth Republic, France was administered, rather than governed'; but even this was scarcely true during the final stages. The anti-parliamentary demonstrations of the Paris police in February 1958 were highly ominous. But, more significant still, the Army leadership, not only in Algeria, but in France itself, was on the verge of open revolt against the government. Perhaps for the first time in French history, the Army (including most of the generals and the 'activist' colonels) had become something of a political 'party'. The disaster of 1940 was still a fairly recent memory with many of them; the great fiasco of Indo-China rankled even more; and the 'shameful climb-down'at Suez, and the 'surrender' of Tunisia and Morocco, constituted the last straw. They were determined to retain Algeria at any price. Over the years, they had convinced themselves that the Paris governments were too remote from a place like Algeria, and could not be trusted to 'save it for France'. The wretched Félix Gaillard, for instance, had shown how he could be influenced by Murphy or Eisenhower.

The Algiers Rebellion of 13 May was a genuine one which, with its extreme right-wing ideology, aimed not only at saving Algeria, but also at setting up some kind of *salut public* régime in France, anti-communist, anti-parliamentary, and neo-fascist. The professional soldiers in Algeria supported the rebellion, and it soon became apparent that the generals in France were fully in sympathy as well. A few days after the rebellion, General Ely, the chief-of-staff, resigned. The police in Corsica had failed completely to deal with the *putsch* there. The Paris police were an uncertain factor. *M. Pflimlin's Minister of War had no Army; his Minister of the Interior had no police; and his Minister for Algeria could not even go there, since he would have been arrested on the spot.*

Could the Left have reacted effectively against this state of affairs? Perhaps; but for men like Mollet this would have meant the closest cooperation with the Communists, and a revival of the Popular Front. Mollet infinitely preferred the 'de Gaulle compromise' to any such revival, which might, moreover, have precipitated an open clash with the Army and police in France itself.

No doubt if, before the Algiers *putsch*, French opinion had been asked whether it wanted the 'system' scrapped, the answer would have been No. But, faced with the threat of civil war, it readily accepted the 'de Gaulle compromise'. The sudden formation, in May 1958, of a solid government majority, with Communist support, had come too late; in the prevailing circumstances, it was no longer of any practical importance. Especially after de Gaulle's statement of 15 May, the government was completely helpless.

*

De Gaulle was certainly brought back to power by the Algiers *putsch*, supported, as it was, by the Army. By the *professional* Army, it should be added. The ordinary conscripts, not quite understanding what was happening in Algiers, remained more or less neutral at the time, though it would be they, as we shall see, who intervened decisively again the rebellious generals in 1961, so saving de Gaulle's government in Paris.

But was de Gaulle himself at the origin of the Algiers *putsch* in May 1958? The answer would seem to be No, even though certain Gaullists like Soustelle, Chaban-Delmas, and Delbecque played a leading role in preparing it. Algiers was far more fascist and Pétainist than it was Gaullist, and the Algiers mob, as well as the Army, decided to *use* de Gaulle as a means of making 'their' revolution acceptable to France. De Gaulle had only to lend himself to this operation, watching with some amusement how Pinay, Mollet, Auriol and President Coty begged 'the most illustrious of Frenchmen' to help them out and – 'renew the contact between Paris and Algiers', which they had proved incapable of doing.

So, from the outset, de Gaulle set himself three immediate objectives: (1) to recast the internal régime in France; (2) to crush the *ultra* elements in Algeria, first by attacking the Committees of Public Safety; and (3) make the Army wholly obedient to the government.

Paradoxically, by far the most difficult problem for him was to tame the Army. Although, long after becoming President of the Republic, he preferred to be called *General* rather than *President* de Gaulle, it has been correctly remarked that he is a statesman much more than a general. And the truth is that, *for four years, between 1958 and 1962, de Gaulle had to wage his main battle not against the Algiers ultras, still less against the left-wing opposition in France, but against the Army.* As an independent political force the Army had to be destroyed. It was a long and arduous process, and de Gaulle resorted to no end of double-talk and plain double-crossing to achieve his end. But for the sharp opposition he met from important sections of the Army leadership – which, on two occasions, openly challenged him and his régime – the war in Algeria might well have ended long before 1962. In 1960, after the January revolt in Algiers – the famous *Semaine de Barricades* – he had to practise, for more than six months, a policy of plain appeasement towards the Army. In 1961, after the *putsch* of the Four Generals, he had to resort to the emergency powers under Article 16 of the Constitution, employ the fullest support of metropolitan opinion to make the Army an obedient tool in the hands of the government. The contention that 'anybody else' could have made peace in Algeria more quickly than de Gaulle is wholly unfounded. It took all his authority, skill and cunning to *break* the Army; under the Fourth Republic, constantly scared of the Army as it was, the war in Algeria might have gone on to this day.

2. First Contacts with Algeria

The de Gaulle régime – which began on 1 June 1958, but did not become the Fifth Republic until 8 January 1959 – falls into two quite distinct periods: that before the Evian Agreements of March 1962, which put an end to the Algerian War, and the period since.

Looking back on the first months of the régime, one cannot but admire the extraordinary cunning which de Gaulle displayed in handling a highly explosive situation. He got himself *legally* appointed head of the government by the National Assembly, even though parliament was acting under the pressure of a totally *illegal* outside movement. For a time, he succeeded in pleasing *everybody*: parliamentary opinion, French public opinion generally, and even the Army and the *ultras* of Algeria.

Parliament was at first carefully reassured. The Constitutional Bill it was required to pass sounded reasonably democratic. Moreover, the first government that de Gaulle formed was in the nature of a compromise; besides a number of officials and technicians, the Ministers included several of the leading Fourth Republic politicians, among them Mollet, Pflimlin and Pinay; and although the Minister of Justice, who was to play a leading role in drafting the new Constitution, was Senator Michel Debré, with a recent record of extremist views on Algeria, it did not (at first) include anybody, such as M. Soustelle, directly associated with the Algiers *putsch*. The inclusion of representatives of the 'system' perplexed the Algiers extremists, but they tried to console themselves with the thought that de Gaulle had to do a little finessing at the outset.

No sooner had he received from parliament his plenary powers than he went on his first trip to Algeria, and aroused tremendous enthusiasm among the European community there by beginning his first great speech with the words: '*Je vous ai compris . . .*' (I have understood you). But his hosts waited for de Gaulle in vain to speak of either 'integration' or of '*Algérie française*'. Instead, he spoke of the future election, in which both the European and Moslem communities would vote on a perfectly equal footing; and only after that would 'the rest' (i.e. the future status of Algeria) be resolved. Though speaking in riddles, he nevertheless gave the impression that Algeria would, in one way or another, remain 'part of France'. Only in his very last speech (at Mostaganem) did he once use the phrase '*Algérie française*'; and no doubt he derived some amusement from the speculation that followed on whether he had really meant it, or whether it had merely been a slip of the tongue!

The real significance of that first trip to Algeria, however, lay in de Gaulle's blunt statements putting the Committees of Public Safety in their place. General Salan was made the government's top representative in Algeria, and, altogether, de Gaulle stressed that the Army was in command, with the role of the Committees, at best, no more than auxiliary. 'You gentlemen,' he told the Oran Committee, 'will *not* continue to make a revolution. Your job is to win over people's minds to national unity, to the reform of France, and to support for General de Gaulle, without trying to force his hand, and within the framework which I shall set down.'

At the same time, he made it clear that although Salan was the government's representative in Algeria, the real Minister of Algeria was de Gaulle himself – and not, as the *ultras* had hoped, M. Soustelle, the object of so many ovations during the first de Gaulle visit. De Gaulle still spoke of those 'ten million French Algerians' who would 'walk through life hand-in-hand' – as they had already done in the (highly artificial) 'fraternization' rallies during the previous month. Did he believe for a moment that the nine million Moslems could ever become Frenchmen? It seems exceedingly doubtful; but in the atmosphere of 1958 de Gaulle simply could not depart from what was in effect the 'integrationist' concept – even though he carefully avoided the word. In the 1958 setting, too, the use of a word like 'self-determination' – which he was to produce over a year later – would have caused an explosion both among the Europeans and in the Army.

In reality, de Gaulle seems to have had no illusions about 'integration', as understood by either the Army or the Committees of Public Safety. Nor was he at all reassured about having won over the Army during that first visit. So three weeks later, he went to Algeria again, visiting chiefly the various Army headquarters this time. He refused to see any of the Public Safety Committees, and when, on behalf of the principal one, General Massu presented him with a rather peremptory motion, de Gaulle took it very badly. He had already made up his mind to order the generals and colonels to get out of the Committees at the first opportunity. As the *Canard Enchaîné* neatly summed up de Gaulle's second visit:

Throughout the journey, Great Charles seemed in a nasty mood. He had the impression that these Army people were trying to take him for a ride with all their fraternization and integration-of-souls stuff ... Departing from his Bossuet style, he used some plain barrack-room expressions ...

Nevertheless, after this second journey, the General's entourage seems reasonably happy: the Army seems to have 'rallied' to de Gaulle, and will carry out his orders. The wilder men like Colonel Trinquier ... have been transferred *extra muros*. But there are still some doubts about three great military personages and their 'Gaullist loyalty': Goussault, head of the Psychological Action; Lacheroy, head of Salan's Information Service; and – Salan himself, who is being very closely watched from Paris, even though 'the utmost confidence' is being shown him in official communiqués.

The *Canard* might have added that there were many other unreliable generals – notably Massu; but this did not become apparent until after de Gaulle's self-determination announcement in September 1959. And even in July 1958 de Gaulle still found it necessary to appease the *ultras* a little; which explains the appointment of Jacques Soustelle as Minister of Information, and why the paratroopers, as well as some 'tame' Algerians, were allowed, in the 14 July parade, to march down the Champs Elysées, with Generals Salan and Massu – those heroes of 13 May – at their head.

In his first speech at Algiers de Gaulle had made a perfunctory offer to the Algerian 'rebels' to stop all military operations, in other words, to surrender. This meant nothing in practice, and the guerrilla war continued ...

In September, a Provisional Government of the Algerian Republic was set up in Cairo under Ferhat Abbas. Although de Gaulle objected to its being recognized by foreign powers – as indeed, it was by most of the Arab countries, as well as by China – he at heart welcomed this new development: for these were the people with whom, sooner or later, he would obviously have to negotiate ... Rumours were widely current in Paris even then that, in private, de Gaulle, when asked about Algeria, would shrug his shoulders and say: 'Of course, Algeria will be independent in the end. ...'

3. *Eighty Per Cent for de Gaulle*

It was extraordinary how, after the famous Twenty Days in May that shook France, and de Gaulle became head of the government, everything in Paris suddenly seemed to return to normal. If anything, indeed, people seemed less anxious than during the last months of the Fourth Republic. It was generally felt that de Gaulle had greatly mellowed since the R.P.F. days and that, despite his arrogant manner, he was not going to do anything reckless; he seemed to keep his finger on the nation's pulse, and to be fully conscious of its reluctance to see a sharply authoritarian régime established. The way in which he had talked to the *ultras* in Algiers pleased people in Paris enormously, and it looked as if he was the only man capable of putting those generals and 'activist' colonels in their place.

The de Gaulle government did not even hesitate publicly to assail some of the ugliest aspects of the war in Algeria, like the torture so widely used against Algerian prisoners and suspects. Much to the *ultras*' annoyance, André Malraux, then de Gaulle's Minister of Information, referred to the matter in a press conference on 24 June, saying that, 'to his knowledge', no act of torture had been committed in Algeria since de Gaulle's visit there. He even offered to send France's three literary Nobel prizewinners to investigate the matter on the spot; and although this offer came to nothing, it was significant that the de Gaulle government should have formally condemned torture – which was more than any government of the Fourth Republic had ever done. (On the contrary, men like Lacoste were known to have regarded it as 'inevitable'.) Not that, in reality, the paratroopers or the Foreign Legion stopped torture; but the Malraux statement was at least a gesture calculated to please French opinion, which was upset at the thought that many of the French in Algeria were 'no better than the S.S.'.

The Constitution of the Fifth Republic was drawn up between June and August. Without going into its endless details, it is enough to say that, although the government remained 'responsible to Parliament', the legislative scope of parliament was itself greatly reduced; the President had an absolute right of dissolution; he appointed the Premier and the other Ministers; concluded international treaties; had a new referendum machinery at his disposal and could, in certain conditions, resort to his emergency powers under Article 16 – he himself, in fact deciding whether these conditions had been fulfilled. Interpellations, that life-blood of parliamentary discussion, were virtually abolished.

The new Constitution also established a Community – i.e. the association of France and her former colonies which, under the September referendum, could secede if they were ready to abandon all French financial and technical aid. This part of the Constitution dealing with the Community and its elaborate institutions (the Community President, the Community Senate, the Community Law Court, etc.,) was to prove the most ephemeral of all; although the former colonies, except Guinea, voted for the Community in 1958, they practically all demanded independence two years later, and the Community in its original form came to an end.

More important, from the internal French point of view, was the fact that the new Constitution gave the government enormous scope for legislation by ordinance and decree. Two of the main objections raised were that the Constitution said next to nothing about Algeria and that it had been made to measure for de Gaulle; would his successors be able to 'wear' it? Furthermore, the actual *working* of the Constitution was largely left for 'organic laws' (to be passed *after* the referendum on it) to define.

The work on the text of the Constitution had begun as early as 12 June, when de Gaulle presided over an inter-ministerial council composed of the four Ministers of State (among them Mollet and Pflimlin) and M. Debré, the Minister of Justice, who was to become the chief author of the draft. De Gaulle did not write it himself, and at the 12 June meeting merely laid down some of the general principles that he wished incorporated in the text. The preliminary draft was completed on 29 July, was submitted to the newly-created Advisory Constitutional Committee, and, later, to the Conseil d'État. De Gaulle himself appeared several times before the Constitutional Committee, presided over by the 80-year-old Paul Reynaud and composed in the main of others who had been prominent in the lives of the Third and Fourth Republics. As the press reported, he talked to them like 'a half-strict, half-jocular uncle'; 'they ate out of his hand'; 'they were charmed into submission, dazzled and fascinated'. He had, indeed, made it plain from the start that he was prepared to agree to a few minor changes, but that was all. For example, the wish which the Committee expressed that there be a referendum on the voting system to be applied in the November election was simply brushed aside by de Gaulle; he had, indeed, already made up his mind that the government, and only the government, would decide on this, regardless of what Mollet and Pflimlin had promised the old Assembly, ostensibly on *his* behalf.

For all that, the Constitution, like so much else under the new régime, was in the nature of a compromise between de Gaulle's 'presidential' and Mollet's and Pflimlin's more 'parliamentary' ideas. As for Debré, he had, after all, been a senator for many years, and it cannot be said that he was an all-out 'presidentialist'. It was not until later, especially from 1960 on, that the Constitution became, in its application, increasingly 'presidential', with the principal government posts nearly all given to high officials and other non-parliamentary figures.

*

During summer of 1958 there was a pleasant feeling that de

Gaulle had successfully averted in May some terrifying possibilities. The only disturbing intrusion was an intensification of Algerian terrorism in France. Thus, the night of 24 August was marked by fires, explosions and various other acts of sabotage in fifteen different places across France – which suggested that the thousands of arrests made by the police amongst Algerian suspects had failed to decapitate the Algerian terrorist organizations. This Algerian terrorism undoubtedly strengthened that 'safety-first' reflex reflected in the enormous YES vote for de Gaulle in the 28 September referendum. On 15 September an Algerian 'commando' made an attempt on the life of Jacques Soustelle, the Minister of Information and the Ministry of the Interior hastened to turn this (rather suspect) affair into an alleged 'communist plot' – even though de Gaulle himself had, since his return to power, carefully refrained from attacking the Communists, as he had done in the R.P.F. days.

*

The referendum campaign was officially opened by de Gaulle himself at a great 'mass' meeting in the Place de la République, in the east end of Paris, on 4 September, the anniversary date of the Third Republic. The whole idea – thought up by Malraux – of holding this meeting in the east end was an incongruous one, and the Communists in particular regarded it as a deliberate provocation (which, in a sense, it was). So only people holding invitation cards – which were checked by four or five cordons of police – were allowed into the Place de la République at all; and in the side-streets there were some violent NO demonstrations held not only by Communists, but also by a great number of left-wing intellectuals, teachers, and other traditional 'republicans'. The police were extremely rough, and hundreds of people were injured, at least two by bullets. After a particularly florid speech by Malraux, placing de Gaulle in the tradition of the Convention, the Soldiers of Valmy and Jemmappes, Rivoli and Austerlitz, and more nonsense of the same kind, de Gaulle spoke. After paying a few (mostly back-handed) tributes to the Republican tradition in France (the Third Republic had proved its worth in 1914, though not in 1940, and the Fourth had brought France to the brink of disaster), he then spoke of the tasks awaiting France. One of them was to restore peace in Algeria, to develop her economically and settle the question of her place and her stature. In conclusion he asked for a massive YES vote in the referendum, which alone could safeguard the future greatness of France.

After calling on those present to sing the *Marseillaise*, and shaking a few hands, he hastened to drive away. He was fully aware of the beatings-up that were going on in the side-streets, and that evening expressed his extreme dissatisfaction with those – and Malraux in the first place – who had thought up this Place de la République stunt, announcing that he would not face this kind of thing again. Soon afterwards he decided that, during the referendum campaign, he was not going to visit any cities where any serious hostile demonstrations were likely to occur. These would strike, he declared, a very jarring note in that picture of national unanimity he was trying just then to create.

*

During September, there was some discussion – though not much among the general public – on the pros and cons of the Constitution. The Right and Centre, including the M.R.P., were (with a few exceptions like Poujade and some incorrigible Pétainistes) for the YES vote; the Communists and a Socialist minority (including most of the teachers) were for the NO vote; so that the most important question was which way the Radicals and most of the Socialists would jump. The majority of the Radicals at their Congress decided for the YES vote. At the Socialist Congress a heated debate went on for three days; but, in the end, Mollet, supported by Defferre, head of the powerful Marseilles Federation, was followed by the great majority of the Congress. Mollet argued that the Constitution was not undemocratic or anti-parliamentary, and clearly suggested that de Gaulle's defeat would merely lead to an attempt by the Algiers colonels and generals to set up a military dictatorship, with civil war as the likely consequence.

The decisive support given to the YES vote by Defferre was significant. Fully conscious of Defferre's importance at the Socialist Congress, de Gaulle had invited him to his office, and had talked to him for two hours a few days before. He had gone out of his way to use on Defferre all his powers of seduction, and, in particular, to persuade him that he was determined to make peace in Algeria. Defferre came away from the meeting altogether starry-eyed.

At the Socialist Congress he argued that de Gaulle, who had only recently normalized relations with Tunisia and Morocco,[1] could not possibly pursue the diametrically opposite policy in Algeria. The Army had achieved nothing; and de Gaulle alone had a good chance of restoring order in Algeria. The Socialists must help de Gaulle to get rid of the pressures of the men of 13 May; he must be enabled to act without them, and even against them. It was important to negotiate a settlement with the F.L.N.

And Defferre hinted that de Gaulle had promised him that he would soon offer to negotiate with the Algerian 'rebels'.

*

De Gaulle and his government had a virtual monopoly of radio and TV, while the entire press – except for the Com-

1. Soon after becoming Premier, de Gaulle had agreed to lift the embargo on arms to the Tunisian government, and withdraw French troops from Morocco.

munist papers, the important Radical *Dépêche* of Toulouse, and a few 'intellectual' weeklies – was for the YES vote.[1] But even apart from that, there is little doubt that de Gaulle would have got an overwhelming majority in the 28 September referendum. Although prophecies were cautious (the Prefects forecast a sixty-five per cent majority), de Gaulle got nearly eighty per cent. Very few bothered about the finer points of the Constitution – or even about the Constitution *tout court*. People were tired of the instability of the Fourth Republic, and were, above all, frightened of what would happen if de Gaulle was defeated. To very many, the choice lay between de Gaulle and 'the Algiers colonels' or 'Massu's paratroopers'.

Of the 26.6 million voters, only 4 million abstained; 17.7 million (79.25 per cent) voted YES, and 4.6 million (20.75 per cent) voted NO. The YES vote for Paris was 77.5 per cent, and for the *banlieue* (including the 'Red Belt') of Paris over 68 per cent. One of the most striking features of the referendum was that, of the $5\frac{1}{2}$ million Communist voters of 1956, at least one million had voted for de Gaulle, and possibly more. The Communist leadership was very upset about it, and said so openly after a few days' reflection.

Geographically, the vote for de Gaulle was strongest in the more prosperous parts of Paris, in Brittany and Normandy, and in the East; it was, with some notable exceptions, weaker in the 'traditionally republican' southern half of France with the record of NOES held by the Corrèze, which registered only 64 per cent YES votes.

In Algeria, with 3.6 million YES votes and 119,000 NOES, the results had simply been 'cooked' by the Army, and particularly by General Salan – not so much by 'stuffing' the ballot-boxes (as had been done in the past) as by terrorizing Moslem voters (usually transported to the polling stations in

1. *Le Monde*, though a YES paper, published several NO articles, mostly by outside contributors.

army trucks) to vote YES. The Europeans, by voting
YES, were of course voting not for de Gaulle, but for
integration.   *

4. The Last Months of de Gaulle's Premiership

A few days after the referendum, the General went to
Constantine to proclaim his Constantine Programme – an
ambitious plan for housing, agricultural reform and in-
dustrialization in Algeria – and it aroused the fury of the
Committees of Public Safety, especially as de Gaulle failed
to speak of either 'French Algeria' or 'integration'.

But worse was to come. After the Algerian 'referendum',
de Gaulle had sent Salan his 'warm congratulations' on the
'magnificent service' the Army had rendered in making the
referendum such an overwhelming success. But a few days
later, on 9 October, he sent Salan a message in which he
demanded, in a peremptory tone, and with the suggestion
that the referendum had been a swindle, that the November
elections in Algeria be conducted 'in conditions of complete
freedom and sincerity', and that the electoral lists of all
tendencies – 'and I mean *all* tendencies' – be enabled to
compete freely. This implied that even the F.L.N. could run
candidates in the election! And then came another bombshell: de Gaulle demanded that all members of the Army
resign from the Committees of Public Safety, a step obviously
intended to deprive these committees of the prestige that
they derived from Army patronage. Massu and the other
generals and colonels obeyed, though no doubt with a great
many mental reservations. In France de Gaulle's move against
the Committees of Public Safety was heartily welcomed, and
even the Communist press expressed great satisfaction.

De Gaulle did not stop there, however. At his press
conference on 23 October he offered to enter into negotiations with the Algerian rebel leadership and it seemed for a
short time that Ferhat Abbas and two other Algerian

'Ministers' might come to Paris to negotiate with de
Gaulle personally. But de Gaulle still had to consider the
feelings of the Army; and his simultaneous proposal that,
on the local level, Algerians 'carrying a white flag' should
make cease-fire arrangements with the French military
meant that he expected the Algerian rebel troops simply to
allow themselves to be disarmed.

It was the 'white flag' phrase which ruined everything; the
Algerian nationalists refused to consider any negotiations
under such conditions. They interpreted de Gaulle's proposal as a demand for unconditional surrender, and their
natural response delayed any progress in the settlement of
the Algerian problem for many months to come.

The Algerian rejection of de Gaulle's offer delighted the
Army and the Europeans in Algeria; in their view, the only
thing to do was to go on with the 'pacification' of Algeria
till the F.L.N.'s final surrender. De Gaulle had to leave it at
that for the time being . . .

*

At this period de Gaulle had also to consider the strong
ultra influences in Paris. After the referendum, his government had been sharply divided over the character of the
election system. Soustelle, the leader of the Algerian *ultras*
and now Minister of Information in control of radio and
TV, favoured a system which would give the Gaullists and
the 'classical' Right an overwhelming majority in parliament. Finally, de Gaulle, supporting Mollet and Pflimlin,
decided in favour of the *scrutin d'arrondissement*, the two-
ballot, single-member, system which, he thought, would
produce a more evenly-balanced parliament, with a fairly
strong contingent of Centre and Socialist deputies.

The election itself was a repeat performance of the
referendum, with practically every party, except those on the
extreme left, claiming to be more-or-less 'Gaullist', and even
the Socialist leader, Guy Mollet, waving before his voters an

autographed photograph of de Gaulle! But, though not officially – for de Gaulle had prohibited the use of the 'Gaullist' label – the most obviously 'Gaullist' party was still the newly-formed U.N.R. (*Union pour la Nouvelle République*), a party in which former worthies of the R.P.F., as well as some Algerian *ultras*, were still highly prominent, together with a certain new 'technical élite' element, represented by men like M. Albin Chalandon. Behind the scenes, some sharp rivalries existed amongst its leaders, particularly between an *ultra* like Soustelle and an 'unconditional Gaullist' like Michel Debré.

Despite its 'Gaullism', the U.N.R. did less well in the first round of the election than might have been expected, scoring only 3.6 million votes, or under eighteen per cent of the poll – less than the four million votes of the 'classical' Right, with twenty per cent. However, under the *scrutin d'arrondissement* system, the U.N.R. gained many more votes in the second round, which turned out to be a major victory for it – and for the 'classical' Right. The U.N.R. registered 4.8 million votes and the 'classical' Right 4.2 million, which represented 189 plus 133 seats – a total of 322 seats or an almost abolute majority in the new National Assembly. The election, in short, was a sweeping victory for the Right and the 'Gaullists'; the Communist vote dropped from 5½ million in 1956 to 3.7 millions, to capture only ten seats; the Socialist vote fell from 3.1 to 2.4 millions, for forty seats; and there were even bigger drops in the Radical and M.R.P. vote. It was a top-heavy parliament – not at all what de Gaulle had hoped for – and included far more Algerian *ultras* than he had expected. This lopsidedness of the new Assembly was further aggravated by the results of the election in Algeria. Here de Gaulle's instructions to Salan had been blatantly ignored, and only Army and *ultra*-sponsored candidates were allowed to stand for election. In consequence, the already inflated U.N.R. representation in parliament was further reinforced by sixty-five or seventy deputies for Algeria. But this enormous 'Gaullist' Party was not going to hang together for long, since some of its members were violently to oppose de Gaulle's attempts to reach a settlement in Algeria.

*

De Gaulle had himself not yet finally made up his mind that Algerian independence was inevitable; the emphasis he now placed was on the Constantine Plan and on the development of the oil and gas deposits of the Sahara, which would bring the Algerian population a kind of prosperity that they had never known before. But by the end of 1958 Salan was removed from Algeria, and, during the following year, as many as 1,500 officers who had been more or less closely associated with the 13 May 'movement' were transferred to France. Salan was replaced as military chief by General Maurice Challe, and as civil chief by M. Paul Delouvrier. Challe was determined to intensify 'pacification', while Delouvrier, an outstanding economist, dwelt chiefly on the economic benefits that the Algerian population would derive from the Constantine Plan. Nominally, at any rate, Challe was under the authority of the civilian chief, Delouvrier, as were also the three military regional chiefs – Generals Massu (Algiers), Rethoré (Oran), and Ollié (Constantine).

For a considerable time there was no further talk of any negotiations with the Algerian 'government', despite the feverish activity displayed by its representatives in and around the U.N. When John Foster Dulles came to Paris in December 1958, de Gaulle went so far as sharply to upbraid him for the 'disloyalty' shown by the United States in not opposing a U.N. motion in favour of Franco–Algerian negotiations ...

*

The last weeks of de Gaulle's premiership in December 1958

were marked by an avalanche of economic ordinances issued without parliamentary approval; most of these concerned various economy measures (cuts in war veterans' pensions, social security benefits, etc.), which de Gaulle had been careful not to issue before the referendum and the election. They caused considerable discontent, which was to be reflected in the local elections the following March. For Common Market purposes, a 17 per cent devaluation of the franc was decreed. Another ordinance, which caused violent controversy, was one making any criticism of a Court decision a serious offence. Eminent jurists like M. Maurice Garçon argued that if such a law had been in force before, a revision of the Dreyfus Case would have been impossible. Many began to wonder what other laws the new régime would produce to cripple French justice.

The new National Assembly met on 9 December, with its hundreds of fresh faces – including dozens of prefabricated Algerian deputies, wearing Arab garb, and quite a few Algiers thugs, among them, as *L'Express* said, 'three notorious killers'. M. Chaban-Delmas was elected President of the Assembly against M. Paul Reynaud, the candidate of the 'classical' Right, and *Le Canard Enchaîné* produced a snappy sketch of this profiteer of the Fourth Republic, one-time Algiers plotter, and now an unctuous and self-righteous personage of the Fifth – a portrait reminiscent of some of Balzac's grand careerists.

5. *De Gaulle Elected President*

On 21 December, de Gaulle was, as was to be expected, elected President of the Republic by 62,000 votes (78.5 per cent) of the electoral college, with the remaining 17,000 votes going to two other candidates – a Communist and 'anti-Mollet' Socialist. Then, on 8 January 1959, a solemn ceremony took place at the Elysée in which de Gaulle took over from President Coty. Coty paid his successor glowing compliments, and declared that 'a necessary and constructive revolution' had taken place in France.

In his reply, de Gaulle said, among other things, that 'in the vast union of countries united under the tricolour flag' (he still seemed to think that the 'Community' had come to stay) 'a special place would be held by the Algeria of tomorrow'.

'Having been pacified and transformed, she will develop her own personality while being closely associated with France.'

This inaugural address by de Gaulle as President of the Republic did not fail to infuriate the Algerian *ultras.* as did, too, the traditional *mesures de grâce* which marked de Gaulle's accession to power. 181 Moslems under sentence of death were reprieved; 7,000 (out of some 30,000) Algerian 'administrative internees' were released; and the four Algerian 'ministers' who had been in the Santé Prison since 1956, among them Ben Bella, were moved to more comfortable quarters on an island off the Atlantic coast.

The leniency shown by de Gaulle to Ben Bella and his comrades was treated as a most sinister omen in Algiers: was it not a first step towards recognizing the 'Algerian government'?

CHAPTER 8

THE LIQUIDATION OF THE ALGERIAN WAR

DURING the same week de Gaulle appointed Michel Debré Prime Minister. Mollet having resigned a few days before, the new government included no Socialists, but it was still largely a 'parliamentary' one; a few important posts were held by non-parliamentary figures (Couve de Murville, Foreign Affairs; Malraux, Cultural Affairs; Guillaumat, Army), but most of the other posts were allocated to members of the U.N.R., M.R.P., the classical Right and the Radicals. Pinay was still Minister of Finance. Soustelle, the principal *ultra* in the Cabinet, who had hoped at least to become Minister of the Interior, and so control the police, was given the fancy job of 'Minister delegated to the Prime Minister', and was later made simply Minister for the Sahara. De Gaulle handled Soustelle with a touch of irony and humour – and this the highly ambitious Soustelle can scarcely have appreciated.

There was a short parliamentary session marked by a very long and woolly programme speech by the new Prime Minister, whose utterances on Algeria, however, seemed very much more '*Algérie française*' in character than de Gaulle's. In particular, he declared that, although the 'white flag' offer still stood, there would be 'no political negotiations with the rebels'. This produced a storm of applause from the greater part of the Assembly which revealed the kind of parliament that had been elected. At the time, public opinion polls invariably showed that at least seventy-five per cent were in favour of a negotiated peace.

Yet, even in 1959, there began a marked evolution in the

attitude of deputies towards Algeria. A large part of the 'classical' Right continued to stand for *'Algérie française'*, as, of course, did all the European–Algerian representatives, and a handful of Socialists, with Max Lejeune at their head; but, among the U.N.R., the tendency was growing to think more and more in terms of a 'modernized and renovated' France, freed, as far as possible, of its outmoded colonialist shibboleths. Though with some mental reservations, the majority were tending to identify themselves with de Gaulle and to see their best chance in an 'unconditional support' for the President.

1. The 'Self-Determination' Offer

This evolution within the U.N.R. during 1959 – which accompanied a growing impatience in the country on the Algerian issue – encouraged de Gaulle to put an end to the *immobilisme* that had persisted for nearly a year, and to come forward, on 16 September 1959, with his sensational 'self-determination' proposal. Some outside factors also counted. France was having a very bad press abroad, especially in Britain and the U.S.A., and there was now a danger of a U.N. vote 'condemning' France.

De Gaulle's broadcast was full of obscurities and ambiguities. He offered to enter into negotiations for a ceasefire with the rebel leaders but said, at the same time, that 'pacification' by the Army must continue. Once pacification had been achieved, and the number of dead 'in clashes and ambushes' did not exceed 200 a year, all Algerians (Moslems and Europeans) would, after a four-year transition period, be asked to choose between 'Francization', independence, and autonomy within the 'Community'. It was this third solution that de Gaulle himself seemed to favour; independence (i.e. secession) he identified with starvation, political chaos and communism. His proposal also implied a possible partition of the country. He stressed that the interests of the European community would, in any case, be defended, and that France would remain in possession of the mineral wealth of the Sahara. But whatever choice Algeria made, de Gaulle would ask France to endorse it.

Though, on the face of it, this was a very cautious and long-term programme, the 'self-determination' principle produced a storm of rage in Algiers, where the *ultras* screamed that it 'stank of treason'. Generals and officers, not only in Algeria but also in France, took it badly. An important rally of Reserve Officers in France passed a hostile resolution, and Marshal Juin made no secret of the alarm with which de Gaulle's new move filled him. Although the bulk of French metropolitan opinion[1] was favourable to de Gaulle, it was now more doubtful than ever that the Army would support him. It was this 'self-determination' proposal which was at the root of that Algiers rebellion in January 1960 known as the *semaine de barricades*. Would the Army support an *ultra* rebellion this time, as it had done in May 1958?

2. Algiers Rebellion Number Two

Although the Algerian nationalists failed to give any favourable response to de Gaulle's 'self-determination' offer – for this, in their view, implied a cease-fire without any political guarantees for the future – the European community in Algeria seethed with hostility. F.L.N. terrorism continued, particularly against the *colons* in the Mitidja, a rich rural area near Algiers; and when, in December, Georges Bidault, now

1. Curious was the attitude of the Communists. They at first dismissed the offer as so much eyewash; then, on 26 October, Maurice Thorez wrote an article suggesting a change of line; and, a week later, the Communist attitude changed completely after Khrushchev had spoken favourably of de Gaulle's self-determination offer in his Supreme Soviet speech on 31 October.

a leader of the *ultras* in Paris, held public meetings at Algiers and Oran, there were violent anti-de Gaulle demonstrations and cries of '*Bidault au pouvoir!*'

Oddly enough, the great January 1960 crisis started with something that, on the face of it, had nothing to do with Algeria – the conflict over financial and economic policy between M. Pinay (the Finance Minister and a leader of the 'classical' Right) and de Gaulle and Debré; yet there is every reason to suppose that Pinay was aware that the government was facing a major crisis in Algeria, and was anxious to disengage himself. M. Duchet, a close associate of Pinay's and a leader of the Right-wing 'Independents', had, only a few days before, violently attacked de Gaulle as a 'monarchist', and had sharply criticized his Algerian policy of 'self-determination' as contrary to the Constitution. Instead of simply resigning, Pinay forced de Gaulle to dismiss him, and replace him by M. Baumgartner, the Governor of the Bank of France. All this meant, in fact, that the government's parliamentary majority had been seriously weakened. Even more damaging was an interview with the notorious General Massu which a German news-paper published on 18 January. In it he strongly criticized de Gaulle's self-determination policy and expressed serious doubts over whether the Army would obey his instructions. He even said that, on 13 May, the Army had 'made a mis-take' in backing de Gaulle and he raised the question of a possible successor to the General. Massu was summoned to Paris where he denied (without much conviction) having made these statements, and on 22 January it was announced that the 'hero of the Battle of Algiers' would not return to Algeria; he had been replaced as head of the Algiers army corps by General Crépin.

To the *ultras* in Algiers this was the last straw. The 'Bloody Sunday' of 24 January started with a mass demon-stration against de Gaulle in the centre of Algiers. The original plan was to get many thousands of Moslems to take part in it, but this 'fraternization' stunt came to nothing. In the afternoon, after several radio appeals by M. Delouvrier ordering the crowds to disperse, several companies of gendarmes (loyal to the central government) were ordered, without using their firearms, to clear the streets between the Gouvernement-Général building and the Grande Poste facing the war memorial – the scene of this, as of so many other, European riots. As the gendarmes were coming down the great staircase from the G.G. building, they were fired on, apparently from the Compagnie Algérienne, a large corner building which Joseph Ortiz, a notorious *ultra* thug, had made his headquarters. Fourteen gendarmes were killed and 123 wounded; in the fusillade that followed, eight people were killed among the demonstrators, and fourteen wounded. General Challe, the Commander-in-Chief, then declared a state of siege in Algiers, and announced that troops were being rushed to the city from the interior to deal with the situation.

What then happened was something new. Ortiz and his gunmen barricaded themselves in the Compagnie Algérienne building, while the adjacent university buildings were occupied by several hundred men under the command of Pierre Lagaillarde, a bearded young deputy and one of the heroes of 13 May. Lagaillarde's and Ortiz's 'ultimatum' to the government amounted to no less than a demand that de Gaulle renounce 'self-determination' and proclaim his allegiance to 'French Algeria'. Despite the massacre of the gendarmes on the previous afternoon, the Algiers Europeans seemed full of sympathy for their 'heroes'. There was obvious fraternization between the defenders of the two 'fortresses' and the paratroopers who were supposed to isolate them, and arms and food supplies were freely delivered to the insurgents.

On the night of 25 January Prime Minister Debré arrived

in Algiers and, after conferring with the generals on the spot, returned to Paris with the strong conviction that the rising was not limited to the extremists entrenched in the two 'fortresses', but enjoyed the support of the entire European population, and might well lead to a new military *putsch* with the support of the Army leaders.

But even if Debré was in a state of near-panic, de Gaulle was not. Following his instructions, Delouvrier suddenly announced on 28 January that he and General Challe were leaving Algiers for a command post in the *bled*, whence they could more easily conduct military operations against the insurgents if these still persisted in their adventure. It seems obvious that even then Ortiz and Lagaillarde hoped that they would receive support from the Army. But, the next day, Massu's paratroopers were withdrawn from Algiers, and replaced by 'loyal' government troops brought from the interior. That night de Gaulle, pointedly wearing uniform, spoke on TV. He declared that he would not go back on his self-determination offer; treated the insurgents as 'liars' and 'conspirators' who had fired on French soldiers; and also condemned the 'complacent attitude of certain military elements'. Then, addressing the Army, he demanded from it the strictest discipline. No doubt, de Gaulle made a slight concession to the French Algerians by saying that he would 'seek the most French solution' to the Algerian problem; and by assuring the Army that it would control the self-determination vote. But that was all. *In France the new Algiers insurrection had aroused a mass movement in favour of de Gaulle* – one in which all the trade unions and even the Communists took part. There was, indeed, something strangely moving in the words de Gaulle used at the end of that famous TV speech:

'Finally, I want to say a few words to France. Well, my dear, old country, here we are, together again, facing a heavy ordeal. In virtue of the mandate given me by the people and in the name of that legitimacy I have incarnated for the last twenty years, I ask all my countrymen and countrywomen to support me, whatever happens.'

The sharp reaction of French opinion against the 'liars and conspirators' was not wasted on the European Algerians; the 'fortresses' were now surrounded by 'loyal' troops, and the open support given by the Algiers crowds to the insurgents became much more lukewarm. In the end, on 1 February, despite Lagaillarde's threats 'to blow up the whole of Algiers', the insurgents surrendered. Lagaillarde was flown to Paris and locked up in the Santé prison. Many of the other ringleaders were arrested, though Ortiz mysteriously escaped. Most of the rank-and-file followers of Lagaillarde and Ortiz were given the option of entering combat units of the Army; but some of those who made this choice, such as Demarquet, a Poujadist ex-deputy, were arrested all the same. Numerous other arrests were made, and a number of drastic administrative measures were taken in Algeria – such as the abolition of the Army's 'psychological services', the disbanding of the territorial troops (composed of French Algerians) who had openly fraternized with the insurgents; and the dissolution of five right-wing extremist societies. Several generals – Jacques Faure, Gribius, Mirambeau among them – notorious for their fascist activities, were simply cashiered. Many others were transferred to France. M. de Sérigny, editor of the *Echo d'Alger*, who had supported the insurrection, was placed under house arrest and later, along with several others who were to figure in the 'barricades trial', flown to Paris. There were also government changes, the most important of which was the elimination of M. Soustelle, who had made no secret of his sympathy for the insurgents.

French opinion was enormously impressed by the firm manner in which de Gaulle had handled the situation; this was very different from the complete helplessness Pflimlin

had shown – and different also from the signs of panic
Debré had betrayed during his visit to Algiers at the
beginning of the insurrection. Great admiration for de
Gaulle was also shown by some of the Moslems in Algeria;
at Mostaganem, in particular, thousands of them staged a
'Gaullist' demonstration. Ferhat Abbas and the other
members of the Algerian government, now established in
Tunis, did not care for this new development at all. It suggested some Moslem support for de Gaulle's 'paternalist'
policy, as exemplified by the Constantine Plan.

3. *Appeasing the Army*

Yet de Gaulle could not overlook the fact that it had been
touch-and-go. The conscript troops in Algeria were no
doubt wholly satisfied with de Gaulle, but the drastic purge
in the Army had created a great feeling of uneasiness among
the professional soldiers. Since de Gaulle's broadcast of 29
January had clearly implied that they were no longer to
fight for 'French Algeria', what were they to fight for now?

There followed, on the part of de Gaulle, a new 'appeasement' of the Army, which started at the beginning of March
with what came to be known as the '*tournée des popotes*'.
De Gaulle, accompanied by General Ely, the Chief of Staff,
and M. Messmer, the Minister of Defence, visited a large
number of Army headquarters, mostly in the operational
zones in Algeria, talking informally to officers and N.C.O.'s
in their *popotes* (i.e. messes). Far from saying that peace
was round the corner, he was now telling the soldiers that it
would be a long war; that the rebels would 'never throw
France out of Algeria'; that 'there must be a military victory
before there is peace '. At Batna, on 4 March, he declared:

'I don't think "Francization" can be a solution. The Moslems
can never become Provençaux or Bretons . . . The old colonialist
system – the *Algérie de papa* – will have to go; but independence is
not possible either. It will mean utter pauperization, a complete

monstrosity. What I think the Algerians will choose in the end will be an Algerian Algeria linked to France.'

This meant that de Gaulle believed in some kind of 'association' between France and Algeria, and he thought this was acceptable to the Army – all the more so as the 'association' would be preceded by a complete French military victory, which, he stressed, would take a very long time.

The press had not been allowed to accompany de Gaulle on this trip, and what he had said was reported by a single A.F.P. correspondent. How accurate were these reports? Many wondered. But the general reaction to de Gaulle's talks with the soldiers was what was to be expected. In metropolitan France de Gaulle's great popularity in January slumped heavily, though some observers suspected that here was a typical case of Gaullist 'finessing', not to say plain double-crossing. The official reaction of the Algerian provisional government was that, since de Gaulle wanted a fight to the finish, he would have it. Not that the Algerian rebels were doing well at this period; their military activity was being, more and more, reduced to bomb-throwing and minor guerrilla warfare.

At the same time M. Delouvrier and the other civilian authorities in Algeria were making the most of the paternalist Constantine Plan, aimed among other things, at creating 400,000 new jobs in the next five years.

During a visit to Algeria in April, Debré stressed the great economic benefits that 'the Algerian people' would derive from the Constantine Plan and from 'association with France'. He added, however, that if they still chose independence, then there would be a partition of the country – apparently meaning that at least Algiers, Oran and the coast between them would remain part of France.

4. The Abortive Melun Meeting with the 'Rebels'

Despite the defeat suffered by the *ultras* at the end of 'Barricades Week', the ferment among the Europeans, especially in Algiers, continued and the *ultra* organizations, such as the *Front de L'Algérie Française* were, more or less officially, reconstituted. In June, there was great agitation among them when de Gaulle suddenly made a public appeal to the 'leaders of the rebellion' to start talks in Paris. During the next few days there were rumours that a suite of rooms had been booked at the Hotel Crillon for Ferhat Abbas and several other Algerian Ministers; but this proved premature. The Algerian provisional government merely sent two emissaries on an 'exploratory mission' – MM. Boumendjel and Yahia. On landing at Orly, they were not taken to the Crillon, but whisked off in a helicopter to Melun, where conversations went on for three days between them and two relatively junior French representatives. The Algerian emissaries were told, in effect, that even if de Gaulle were to see Ferhat Abbas, this would in no way imply a recognition of the Algerian provisional government; moreover, before any such talks took place, the Algerian government would have to order a cease-fire. In a communiqué they published in Tunis after the talks were over, the Algerian leaders said that all de Gaulle was expecting from any negotiations was plain capitulation. One can only assume that the whole Melun stunt was another gesture calculated to reassure the Army.

5. De Gaulle's Next Step: 'Algerian Republic'

De Gaulle was biding his time. His press conference on 5 September sounded uncompromisingly opposed to any settlement that the Algerian nationalists would be likely to accept and it was not till 4 November that he suddenly produced new proposals, this time speaking of 'the Algerian

Republic with its own laws and institutions', in such a way as to suggest that it would even have an independent foreign policy. While he still refused to recognize the Algerian provisional government, and left the issue of further talks with them entirely obscure, he proposed the setting up of 'provisional new institutions' in Algeria, pending the self-determination vote. Soon afterwards it was announced that a referendum would take place in both France and Algeria on 8 January 1961, and although the wording of this was confusing to many, it meant, in effect, that de Gaulle was asking for approval of his Algerian policy.

What had helped to persuade de Gaulle that an 'Algerian Republic' had now become inevitable was the virtual dislocation of the 'Community' in Africa, with practically all the members demanding, and obtaining, independence, though on a basis of 'cooperation' with France. Since Tunisia and Morocco were also independent, the perpetuation of Algeria as a 'French province' seemed more and more anachronistic.

But, with a million Europeans living in Algeria, the final act of the Algerian drama was both long and horrible. A new explosion was to be expected after de Gaulle's 'Algerian Republic' announcement of 4 November. He himself spent four days in Algeria, and though he avoided both the Algiers and Oran 'madhouses', visiting instead a number of smaller towns, there were, here too, hostile demonstrations by the Europeans and favourable counter-demonstrations by Moslems. Shaking off his bodyguard, de Gaulle mixed, in a display of uncanny personal courage, with furious Europeans. His visit to Algeria was used as a pretext in Algiers itself for violent anti-de Gaulle and anti-Moslem demonstrations by Europeans, but for the first time in the city, there was now a mass counter-demonstration by Moslems, who poured out of the Casbah waving green F.L.N. flags. In the fusillade that followed seventy-five Moslems and five

Europeans were killed, and there were similar riots, though
on a smaller scale, at Oran and Bône.

6. *The Growing Nightmare of Algeria – the O.A.S.*

From the end of 1960 right up to the final exodus of the
Europeans from Algeria in the summer of 1962, the country
lived in an atmosphere of almost unbearable tension and
terror. At the beginning of 1961 I myself spent a fortnight
at Bône and Constantine; it was one of the most uncomfortable fortnights I can remember. The day before I arrived at
Bône and took a room in a small hotel near the central
market, an F.L.N. terrorist had thrown a bomb into the
New Year's eve shopping crowd at that very market, killing
three and wounding forty-nine people, mostly European
women and children. In shops, bars and cafés, though
protected by thick wire netting, one could never feel safe.
The French family keeping my little hotel, outside which
they had witnessed that blood-bath on New Year's eve,
were in a state of chronic fear. The European terrorists, for
their part, were also throwing bombs into Moslem cafés
and other gathering-places, and were, moreover, terrorizing
the few 'liberal' Frenchmen – like M. Barra, a former
socialist mayor of Bône – still in Algeria. Some months later
M. Barra and his wife fled to a small town in Central France
following repeated threats by the O.A.S. ('Secret Army') to
murder them, as well as their children and grandchildren.
These were also forced to flee, after their house had been
half-wrecked by an explosion.

The atmosphere was very similar at Constantine. Indeed,
the only people who still seemed to have their wits about
them were the French Army. The conscripts, believing in de
Gaulle, had no desire to get mixed up in the Algerian
cuisine, and had an equal dislike for the Moslems and the
Europeans. By this time, too, most of the officers also
appeared to be wholly on the side of the Paris government,

or were, at any rate, determined to carry out its instructions – an outstanding achievement for de Gaulle. Most of the *ultra* officers had been transferred from Algeria to somewhere else. Very different, however, was the attitude of some paratroopers and Foreign Legion soldiers – Germans – with whom I talked; and these – especially the Germans – openly boasted of how they tortured and murdered Algerian prisoners. But even these second-generation S.S.-men had no illusions that Algeria would be 'held', and some talked of soon becoming private citizens, and opening 'some nice little shop' – in Spain or Portugal . . . When asked why they had left Germany (many were only 25 or 26) and joined the Foreign Legion, they were very cagey indeed.

*

In the referendum of 8 January 1961, de Gaulle again received a substantial majority in France – fifteen million YES against five million NO votes – though there was a much larger number of abstentions than in 1958. In Algeria the F.L.N. had instructed the Moslems to boycott the referendum, and this they successfully did in the cities; but in the countryside, army trucks took thousands of Algerians to the polling stations, where they mostly voted 'for' de Gaulle – a total (officially at least) of 1.7 millions. Almost all the Europeans voted NO; there were over 700,000 such votes.

The exasperation of the Algerian Europeans mounted steadily throughout 1961 and O.A.S. terrorism rapidly extended itself to metropolitan France, where *plastiquages* now became a daily occurrence. Throughout 1961 Algeria continued to overshadow the French political scene, and even began to eat into everyday life.

7. April 1961: The Third Algiers Rebellion – the Generals' Revolt against de Gaulle

Although the Army in Algeria had undergone a drastic

purge, especially after the *semaine des barricades* in January
1960, the next great challenge to de Gaulle and the Fifth
Republic again came from there when, in April 1961, four
'former' generals – who had only recently resigned (or been
retired) from the Army – staged another *putsch* at Algiers.
Two of them – Salan and Challe – were former Commanders-
in-Chief, and the other two, Jouhaud and Zeller, had also
held high posts in Algeria until recently. Challe had been
Commander-in-Chief at the time of the 'Barricades Week'
the year before. Salan, openly disagreeing with de Gaulle's
policy, had gone on 'a visit' to Spain in December 1960 and
was known to be in contact with Lagaillarde who, after his
arrest in January 1960, had escaped there. Late at night, on
Friday, 21 April, it was learned that paratroopers of the
Foreign Legion had occupied all the main public buildings
in Algiers, and had arrested M. Delouvrier's successor, M.
Morin, the Government's Delegate-General, General
Gambiez, the Commander-in-Chief, and M. Buron, one of
de Gaulle's Ministers, who happened to be there on a visit.
On the following morning General Zeller broadcast from
Radio-Algiers that 'the High Command' had decreed a
state of siege and that there could be no peaceful solution
other than 'French Algeria'. The three generals – who were
joined by Salan the next day (he had flown in from Madrid) –
called on the generals, officers and troops in the rest of
Algeria to join them. Would the Army, not only in Algeria,
but also in France, follow these new insurgents?

The government seems to have been taken by surprise.
De Gaulle happened to be that night, with an official visitor,
President Senghor of Senegal, watching *Britannicus*, at the
Comédie Française (where, it was later learned, he had
narrowly escaped assassination). On the following day
drastic measures started to be taken in France; 'doubtful'
members of the Army were arrested, and the principle was
decided upon of a financial and economic blockade of

Algeria. This was certainly much more than Pflimlin had ever dared do. M. Joxe was sent on a flying visit to Algeria, where he narrowly escaped arrest by the insurgents, and his report on the situation persuaded de Gaulle to assume dictatorial emergency powers under Article 16 of the Constitution. The Algiers insurrection was making headway on the 22nd; a few generals and numerous colonels were joining, and it seemed to be spreading to Constantine and Oran. The great turning point came on the 23rd, when de Gaulle made his famous broadcast sharply condemning 'this foursome of retired generals who, supported by a group of ambitious and fanatical officers, are leading us straight into national disaster'.

'In the name of France I order that every means be used – and I repeat *every* means – to stop these men, pending their final elimination ... I order all soldiers to disregard the orders of these heads of the mutiny ... I forbid every Frenchman and, above all, every soldier, to carry out any of their orders.'

These usurpers, he added, would be crushed with all the rigour of the law. And he then announced that he was assuming the emergency powers given him under Article 16 of the Constitution. '*Françaises, Français, aidez-moi!*' he concluded.

It was later said that this broadcast produced in Algeria what was called 'a transistor victory' for de Gaulle. The hundreds of thousands of French conscript soldiers there had, through their transistor radios, listened to this broadcast, and the effect had been overwhelming; they were determined to resist the 'foursome'. Countless officers who had wavered, decided against embarking on an adventure which might end very badly for them. It was obvious to them that de Gaulle was a man who would stand no nonsense.

De Gaulle himself was calm and firm, and does not seem

to have lost his head for a moment. Not so some of his
Ministers. Debré was in a panic at the prospect of an army
revolt in France and, especially, of paratroopers descending
on Paris from Algiers. While the neighbourhood of the
Elysée was black with troops and police (there were even
some tanks in the Concorde), Debré made his incredible
broadcast – which he was never quite to live down – declaring
that planes full of paratroopers were about to land on
various airfields round the capital, and calling on the people
'to go there in cars, or on foot, to persuade these misguided
soldiers of the grave error they were making'. Meantime, at
the Ministry of the Interior, following a dramatic appeal by
M. Malraux, volunteers were pouring in and clamouring to
be given firearms.[1]

Even more than in January 1960, the whole of France –
except certain elements on the Right – was now behind de
Gaulle – or rather, against any military or fascist *putsch*. A
one-hour general strike was proclaimed. The trade unions
were demanding that arms be given to the workers. But, by
the 25th, it was quite clear that the Algiers insurrection had
collapsed. Neither the Navy nor the Air Force in Algeria
would support the four generals and, more effective still,
the conscripts were strictly carrying out de Gaulle's orders.
Zeller, Salan and Jouhaud went into hiding, while Challe
surrendered to the 'loyalist' troops and was flown to Paris,
where he was put in the Santé Prison. The third Algiers
insurrection had, like the second one, failed. There followed
hundreds of arrests among officers and officials in Algeria,
and the regiments guilty of rebellion were disbanded while
thousands of 'loyal' police and gendarmes were flown to
Algeria.

1. The first French atom bombs were exploded in the Sahara in
1960, but there was one more atom bomb at the Sahara base of
Reggane. De Gaulle ordered it to be exploded immediately – in case the
rebel Generals got hold of it!

8. The First Evian Conference

The trouble, however, was not yet over. Exasperated by the failure of the generals' *putsch*, the O.A.S. – 'Secret Army' – intensified its terrorism in Algeria, while the F.L.N. gunmen and bomb-throwers continued theirs. What characterized this phase of the Algerian tragedy was the growing hostility between the *colons* and the French Conscript troops.

De Gaulle was now determined to 'finish with the Algerian affair'. Without adversely affecting economic conditions in France, it was, by tying up the bulk of France's armed forces, largely paralysing her foreign policy. Nevertheless, the first Franco–Algerian conference at Evian, between 20 May and 13 June, failed, with no agreement having proved possible on numerous questions, particularly the status of the European minority and the territorial status of the Sahara. A further conference in Lugrin at the end of July also failed, largely because the French refused to include the Sahara in the new 'Algerian State'. On 5 September, however, de Gaulle gave way on the Sahara, allowing its inclusion in the Algerian state, provided that France's economic and strategic interests were respected.

9. 'Kill de Gaulle'

This further 'surrender' intensified the O.A.S. terrorism in both Algeria and France, and on 8 September an attempt was made to assassinate de Gaulle by blowing up his car on the road to Colombey. O.A.S. leaflets openly declared that 'the physical elimination of de Gaulle' was the last hope of saving 'French Algeria'.

It was not, however, till November that secret negotiations were resumed between France and the Algerian provisional government, where Ben Khedda had by now replaced the more moderate Ferhat Abbas as 'prime minister'. Meantime, the O.A.S. became more active than ever; on 30

October there were seventy explosions in Algiers alone. It continued like this, day after day, in the Algerian cities while, in the countryside, there were countless attacks on French farms by Algerian commandos. Algeria was rapidly moving to that state of complete chaos which was to mark the first six months of 1962.

10. The Terror Spreads to France – A Deal with the O.A.S.?

O.A.S. activities had, by now, grown very extensive in Metropolitan France. Numerous *plastic* explosions were a daily occurrence in Paris and other cities, while the assassination of 'liberals', which had long been a practice in Algeria, now became frequent in France. Bombs exploded outside the doors of leading liberals like M. Beuve-Méry, editor of *Le Monde*, in the *Le Monde* office itself, even in the offices of *Le Canard Enchaîné*. A large number of bombs were thrown at Communist premises also, and several Communists were assassinated – an aspect of O.A.S. activity which met with some favour here and there. It was discovered in January that there were now O.A.S. cells in a number of schools and student organizations.

A highly curious development was a lunch organized by the French director of an American bank and a close associate of M. Jean Monnet, a gathering attended by Mollet, Pinay, other leading anti-de Gaulle politicians and even some trade union leaders. Some newspapers saw in this 'luncheon' an attempt to form a kind of coalition which would be anti-Communist, pro-American, 'European', anti-de Gaulle, and willing to cooperate with the 'more reasonable' elements among the O.A.S. who could be won over with the help of men like Georges Bidault.

What had made such a lunatic scheme possible was that some of these 'moderate' republican leaders had become frightened not only of the O.A.S. but also of the Communist appeals for united action. It was thought that de Gaulle was losing his grip, and that the O.A.S. was creating an atmosphere in which a Popular Front might succeed. Had not the O.A.S. hinted that it would like de Gaulle to be replaced by 'a coalition from Mollet to Bidault'? No doubt it was now too late to 'save' Algeria, but at least the end of Algeria would also mean the end of de Gaulle.

11. The Evian Peace Conference

On 5 February, de Gaulle made it clear that the settlement of the Algerian problem was now a matter of weeks, and that practically the entire French Army would be brought back to metropolitan France by the end of 1962 and thoroughly reorganized. By the end of 1963, he said, France would have 'the first operational elements of an atomic force of her own; in this way, no State could take the risk of destroying France without risking its own death'.

De Gaulle was now clearly anxious to get rid of Algeria, and turn to more serious matters. But the O.A.S. was continuing to cause trouble; on 6 February an attempt was made to assassinate M. Malraux; but instead, a small child outside his house was blinded by the explosion. This produced an enormous anti-fascist demonstration in the east end of Paris. In order to underline its 'anti-communism', the government foolishly prohibited the demonstration, and there were violent clashes with the police; eight demonstrators were killed and 100 wounded while some were crushed to death in a stampede at the Charonne metro station. Several hundred thousand people attended the funeral of the victims, and this time the government did not interfere. Meantime the secret talks between the French government and the Algerians continued, and on 7 March the Evian Conference opened. The French delegation was headed by M. Louis Joxe, Minister for Algerian Affairs.

All the essential work had been done during the 'secret'

negotiations of the previous weeks, and on 18 March the eighty-page Evian Agreement was signed, with a cease-fire ordered on the following day. In their broadcasts, Ben Khedda and de Gaulle expressed their great satisfaction at the successful conclusion of the negotiations. Ben Khedda, in particular, stressed that the territorial integrity of Algeria, including the Sahara, had been recognized, as well as the unity of the Algerian people. The Europeans could stay in Algeria to become, after a few years, either Algerian citizens or 'privileged foreigners'. Although the naval base of Mers-el-Kebir had been leased to France, Algeria would not enter into any alliances and would remain neutral. He also declared that during the transition period, pending the self-determination vote, the greatest vigilance would have to be observed towards the O.A.S. and other trouble-makers. De Gaulle himself stressed the future 'association' between France and Algeria, and particularly the fruitful and constructive role that the European community would be able to play in the new Algerian State.

The Evian Agreement provided – amongst much else – for the closest economic and cultural cooperation between the two countries; for the preservation of French property rights both in Algeria and in the Sahara; and for the free circulation of persons between the two countries. In de Gaulle's view, there was no fundamental reason why such 'friendly co-existence' could not be possible; and the Evian Agreement was, in fact, largely based on the assumption that the greater part of the Europeans in Algeria *would* remain. As it turned out, however, the complete chaos caused by the O.A.S. during the next few months drove practically the entire European population out of Algeria, and ultimately led to that overall confiscation of European property (except in the Sahara) which the Evian Agreement had ostensibly set out to protect.

Perhaps de Gaulle, who knew quite enough about the

O.A.S., had foreseen all this. To him, as, indeed, to the greater part of French opinion Algeria was a good riddance.

Although several angry scenes were made in parliament by members of the Right, and some question was even raised on whether a referendum giving de Gaulle full freedom to draw up laws on the basis of the Evian Agreement was strictly in agreement with the Constitution (for this did not provide for a separation of Algeria from France), the referendum of 8 April was itself an overwhelming success: over ninety per cent voted YES, and only $9\frac{1}{2}$ per cent voted NO. The NOES were almost all those of the extreme Right. The vast majority of the French people were delighted to see the end of the Algerian war and, whatever the various parties said to the contrary, identified this achievement with the name of de Gaulle.

12. The Bloody End of French Algeria

It is impossible here to describe in detail all the tragic and horrible events that took place in Algeria after the announcement of the Evian Agreement and especially after the referendum of 8 April. The O.A.S. and, with it, a large part of the European population ran completely wild. On 15 March, even before the Evian Agreement was signed, an O.A.S. commando at El Biar had massacred the three Moslem and three European officials of a welfare centre, and on the 17th there had been about 100 casualties in forty-eight similar O.A.S. outrages. After the Evian Announcement was made, General Salan declared from a pirate radio station that he was taking command of the 'operations against the enemy forces'. He ordered the O.A.S. to take the offensive, and to attack the gendarmerie and other troops serving the Paris government. At Bab el Oued, the Algiers suburb, on 23 March, a French officer and five conscript soldiers were murdered, the area was surrounded by loyal troops, and a week's fighting followed between French regulars and the Europeans. On 26 March, provoked by the O.A.S., regular French troops fired on a vast European demonstration in the rue d'Isly, in the centre of Algiers, killing forty-one and wounding 130. This hideous massacre had also resulted from Salan's instructions.

Very many Europeans were, at that time, seized by a kind of blood-lust. Moslems were lynched day after day in the streets of Algiers, and some European women even killed Arab children by running their cars into them.

The bomb outrages against the Moslems became so numerous that in certain cities like Oran, where some parts were inhabited by a mixed population, a form of segregation took place, with the Moslems fleeing to predominantly Moslem areas of the city, and the Europeans to predominantly European ones.

Under the Evian Agreement a mixed Franco–Algerian Provisional Executive, pending the self-determination vote, was set up at Rocher Noir, outside Algiers, on 7 April. This, with the help of a French High Commissioner, M. Christian Fouchet, was to maintain law and order in Algeria; but what followed in fact was the worst chaos yet seen. On 25 March, it is true, General Jouhaud, Number Two chief of the O.A.S., was arrested, and so, on 20 April, was General Salan. Both were flown to Paris. But others took over the O.A.S. command. The arrest of Salan himself had a demoralizing effect on the Europeans, who now feared that the game was up, and who began a mass exodus to France – at least 'for the time being'. This did not suit the O.A.S. at all. Already in November 1961 they had forbidden any Europeans to leave for France, except with their special permission. Now they were afraid of losing their mass support, and did all they could to stop the exodus. At the same time, terrorist activity against the Moslems assumed horrible proportions: On 2 May, an enormous time bomb blew up in the port of Algiers, killing sixty-two Arab dockers and wounding 110. Despite strict orders from the nationalist leadership to the Moslem masses not to answer these O.A.S. provocations, it was becoming more and more difficult to restrain them. In May there were a few cases of the Moslems beginning to hit back, and here and there Europeans were murdered or kidnapped. This intensified the panic among the Europeans, and precipitated their exodus; by the middle of May, there were mile-long queues outside the airport and shipping offices, even though the O.A.S. threw hand-grenades into crowds of those queueing for tickets so as to discourage such desertion.

As some of the O.A.S. leaders later admitted, it was about the middle of May that this panic flight persuaded them that there was no more hope left for 'French Algeria', or for that 'partition' that Salan had had in mind.

*

What had persuaded the Europeans to leave? It had all started with the 'temporary' evacuation of women and children, because of the general state of insecurity. But gradually most of the men, though in sympathy with the O.A.S., felt that they were fighting a losing battle. They had antagonized not only the Moslem masses, who might well hit back on a terrifying scale before long, but also the French Army, particularly the conscript troops and the gendarmerie; and these troops would, in any case, soon be pulled out of Algeria. So, rather than 'die for French Algeria', most of the men simply decided, in the end, to join their families in France. The chances of the O.A.S. itself looked particularly bad after M. Fouchet's order to the troops to 'stamp out the O.A.S. plague', and the stern disciplinary measures taken against any French officials guilty of connivance with the O.A.S. This 'gutlessness' shown by the rank-and-file O.A.S. sympathizers 'at French Algeria's most crucial moment' helps to explain why, though embittered, so many of them later decided to adapt themselves to a new life in France. The horrors and mass-panic of those last weeks just before and after the Evian Agreement were hard to forget.

But in May 1962 there were still many thousands of O.A.S. diehards in Algeria and, faced with the mass exodus of the Europeans – who were leaving at the rate of 10,000 a day – they decided on a 'scorched earth' policy to destroy the economic superstructure of Algeria and 'give back to the Algerians the Algeria of 1830' – i.e. before the French had landed there. Between 26 and 30 May alone forty schools in Algiers were destroyed by fires and explosions; between 7 and 17 June, the Library of Algiers University and dozens of other public buildings were burned down.

Negotiations of a curious kind began between the O.A.S. and the Provisional Executive; i.e. by the head of this exe-cutive, M. Abderrahmane Farès, a moderate (not F.L.N.) Algerian, assisted by a number of other French and Algerian personalities on one side, and on the other, Jean-Jacques Susini, one of the most extreme *ultra* leaders of the O.A.S., notorious in the past for his kidnapping and ter-rorist activities and for the role he had played during the *semaine des barricades* in January 1960. Susini was the recog-nized O.A.S. chief of Algiers, and had sufficient authority to stop the 'scorched earth' policy there, though his jurisdic-tion did not extend to Oran and Eastern Algeria. The negotiations collapsed, however, for Susini, who thought of himself as the leader of the 'European revolutionaries' in Algeria, and still vaguely hoped that these could somehow fit into the 'new' Algeria, was anxious to deal direct with the 'Algerian revolutionaries', i.e. the F.L.N., thus ignoring the Metropolitan France that had 'betrayed' the Europeans. So finally, on 17 June, with the agreement of the Algerian provisional government and F.L.N. leadership in Tunis, Dr Mostefai, the chief F.L.N. representative on the

Provisional Executive (with a well-known Algiers liberal, M. Jacques Chevallier, former mayor of Algiers, acting as middleman) arrived at an agreement with Susini, in terms of which the European community would, together with the Moslem majority, take part in the future development of Algeria, and in the maintenance of law and order; the 'scorched earth' policy was to end that day.

But O.A.S. terrorism continued in other parts of Algeria, particularly at Oran, where it went on for several more weeks, even after ex-General Salan (now a prisoner in France following his famous trial) had given his blessing to the Susini–Mostefai agreement. 'Now, all of you,' he wrote, 'join hands. Too much blood has been shed by the two communities. The Europeans must find a place to which they are entitled in the fraternal Algeria of tomorrow. Let your fair country continue to cooperate with France.'

By the end of June about 300,000 Europeans – or one-third of the total – had left for France, many of them with the idea that they might yet return when the atmosphere had calmed again. But this was not to be. The referendum, in which over ninety-nine per cent of the votes polled were in favour of independence was held on 1 July, and two days later the independence of Algeria was proclaimed. On the 5th, there was an enormous Moslem demonstration at Oran celebrating independence; shots were fired from windows, and, in the clashes that followed, seventy-five Moslems and twenty Europeans were killed. This, and much else that happened in the next few weeks, enormously accelerated the European exodus from Algeria. In the Mitidja, where murders and kidnappings of European farmers now became a daily occurrence, three-quarters of the 45,000 Europeans had fled by the end of July. The summer of 1962, following the proclamation of Algerian independence, was truly chaotic. The Algerian provisional government officially came to power on 3 July, but the country was to remain under the administration of the Provisional Executive until the election and the formation of a regular Algerian government. But a part of the Algerian leadership, headed by Ben Bella, released by the French after six years' imprisonment, would not recognize the authority of the provisional government in Algiers, headed by Ben Khedda. For a time, Algeria was split in two with Ben Khedda's government, recognized by thirty-three foreign states, established in Algiers, and Ben Bella taking up his headquarters in Eastern Algeria, first at Tlemcen and then at Oran. After a period of the utmost confusion bordering on civil war between the two main Algerian factions, the Ben Bella group, helped by the Army under Colonel Boumedienne, finally gained the upper hand, and it was Ben Bella who, on 29 September, formed the first official Algerian government, – one composed entirely of his own supporters. The 'single lists' of candidates for the Constituent Assembly had been drawn up by Ben Bella, Ben Khedda and other members of the provisional government were excluded. Ben Bella openly declared that democracy was a luxury which Algeria could not yet afford. The 196 candidates comprised sixteen Europeans, but none of these was included in the government.

During that summer and early autumn, the political chaos in Algeria was at its height, with heavy fighting in numerous places between the local troops of willaya III and IV and those of Ben Bella. But the economic chaos was even worse. In the greater part of the country the harvest had not been brought in, and practically all industries had come to a standstill. With the Europeans fleeing to France in ever-growing numbers – by the end of the year only 150,000 were to be left – vast sums of money were being transferred to France. In August, with this economic paralysis at its worst, M. Farès flew to Paris, begging the French government to give emergency help to Algeria; but he met with a blunt refusal, the French government declaring that no help could be given so long as it was not even clear who, in Algeria, was in charge. How desperate Algeria's needs were may be seen from the fact that by the end of 1962 – according to the Algerian government itself – there were two million unemployed and over four million others 'without means of subsistence', out of a total population of nine millions.

On 8 October 1962 Algeria became the 109th member of U.N., her initial delegation led by Ben Bella in person. But, in view of the lukewarm attitude shown to the new Algeria not only by the United States but also by the Soviet bloc, the Algerian government had no serious alternative to remaining largely dependent on French economic and technical aid. For a time at least, Ben Bella had to steer an uneasy middle course between the F.L.N.'s Tripoli programme of 'integral socialism', proclaimed in June 1962, and an observance of the Evian Agreements – even though those parts of it relating to the coexistence of the two communities in Algeria had become largely meaningless.

*

One of the 'miracles' of the de Gaulle régime was the admittedly costly, but nevertheless relatively smooth way in which some 750,000 Europeans from Algeria were, within little more than a year, absorbed in Metropolitan France. Officials and manual workers were given houses and jobs, while a variety of credit facilities were given to the *colons* to settle on the land. After their fearful experiences in the spring and summer of 1962 – first from O.A.S. terrorism, then from the general Algerian anarchy – they no longer even felt as nostalgic for their 'native land' as they thought they would be.

There were still among them, of course, a few O.A.S. extremists who, together with a number of accomplices in metropolitan France, continued to bear de Gaulle an intense hatred for having abandoned Algeria. And it was these people who, on 22 August, failed by two inches to assassinate the President of the Republic.

CHAPTER 9

1962: THE CRISIS AND REINFORCEMENT OF THE DE GAULLE RÉGIME

1. After Algeria

DURING the first four years of the de Gaulle régime – up to the middle of 1962 – the political life of France was overshadowed, if not altogether dominated, by the Algerian problem. Yet in this period de Gaulle's foreign policy had already acquired certain specifically 'Gaullist' characteristics, and these were to become much more marked after the end of the Algerian war.

It is significant that the Evian Agreement was soon followed, in May 1962, by de Gaulle's sharpest outburst against a supra-national Europeanism – an outburst that was to drive the M.R.P. Ministers out of the government, and that a few months after the end of the Algerian war, de Gaulle announced his famous veto on Britain's entry into the Common Market.

If the end of the Algerian war gave de Gaulle much greater freedom of action in his 'reserved domain' of foreign policy, it also had some immediate repercussions – some of far-reaching importance – on French home affairs. It should be recalled here that de Gaulle himself, though brought to power by the Algiers revolt of May 1958, never believed for a moment in 'integration' and 'French Algeria'; 'Algerians are Algerians, and it's no use expecting them to become Frenchmen' he started saying openly as early as 1959. At most, he was willing to try out some kind of loose confederation between France and Algeria and, about the time of the Constantine Programme, he seemed to think that this was not altogether impossible. But, as his whole African policy showed between 1958 and 1962, he considered that Morocco and Tunisia had become independent for good and that it was becoming more and more inexpedient to deny independence even to the much more economically backward Black-African territories which had formed part of the French Empire, Union and Community. In the circumstances, a special status for Algeria – even a close 'association' with France – was becoming a curious anomaly. When the extreme aggressiveness of the European population finally condemned them to 'repatriation' to France, de Gaulle was not, at heart, displeased. The great European exodus from Algeria removed that one anomaly which stood in de Gaulle's way of figuring as the Great Decolonizer of Africa.

In August 1962 he could look back on his work with some satisfaction. The European population of Algeria, which had loathed him almost from the outset, had, as it were, cut its own throat; he himself had succeeded, despite two very serious challenges to his authority – first in January 1960, and then in April 1961 – in getting the Army to obey him. No doubt among the upper ranks of the Army, and among some of the 'special' troops – the Foreign Legion and the paratroopers – there was still much anger against him; but the *ultra* officers had been transferred to Germany or Metropolitan France between 1959 and 1961, and the most disloyal troops had been disbanded. No doubt many officers – men like Marshal Juin or General Massu – were, at heart, in sympathy with rebels like Salan, Challe, Jouhaud and Zeller; but, after all, not only they, but also their juniors had to think of their bread-and-butter, and their future careers; and most of them accepted in the end the accomplished fact of an independent Algeria. A psychologically important factor in this process were the mutual massacres that had taken place in April–June 1962 between regular French troops and the European Algerians, as represented by the O.A.S.

No less important as an achievement for de Gaulle was the gradual conversion of a largely colonialist French bourgeoisie to that different France which had been developing since 1958 – and which was to receive a sort of official consecration in the general election of November 1962.

2. Pompidou Replaces Debré – Growing Revolt of Parliament

After the referendum of 8 April 1962, with its ninety per cent vote approving the Evian Agreement, de Gaulle, surely displaying a conscious touch of humour, caused Prime Minister Debré to hand in the government's resignation. Debré had been a fanatical *Algérie Française* man in the past, and, even during his premiership since 1959, he was much more willing than de Gaulle to yield to the pressure and intimidation of the Army. On at least two occasions, indeed, he had lost his head; but de Gaulle had maintained him in office as Prime Minister, even though he knew how deeply Debré loathed the 'surrender' of Algeria. Now, after Evian, Debré was obviously a man with a grievance.

So, on 14 April, de Gaulle made the curious choice of appointing M. Georges Pompidou in his place. There were two reasons for this. First of all, Pompidou was a man with no regrets about Algeria, and one who was willing to think in terms of that 'new' France that de Gaulle was trying to build – a technically-efficient France, a France with an 'independent' foreign policy, a France with a nuclear deterrent of her own. Secondly, unlike Debré, Pompidou had never been a member of parliament, and his appointment to the premiership was generally interpreted as meaning an even greater subservience and 'fidelity' of the government to the President of the Republic. It marked a further step towards a presidential régime – a tendency which, for all his personal devotion to de Gaulle, Debré had tended to resist.

Who was this M. Pompidou, the comfortably round and amiable-looking man with bushy eyebrows? All the general public knew was that he was a personal friend of de Gaulle's and a big shot in the banking world. Actually, Pompidou was a man of many parts. Born in 1911 in a village in the Auvergne, he was of peasant stock, though his father was an intellectual – a lycée teacher and a follower of Jaurès, the Socialist leader. Pompidou himself was a socialist in his youth, and, after graduating in 1931 from the select École Normale Supérieure, became a teacher of Greek and Latin in various lycées. His tastes were literary and artistic, and he composed several anthologies of French poetry. After fighting for a few weeks in 1940, he was demobilized, and returned to his Lycée Henri IV in German-occupied Paris. While teaching there under the German occupation, he became converted to Gaullism, and, after the Liberation, joined de Gaulle's secretariat. Though by this time a high civil servant on the Conseil d'État, he was particularly active as de Gaulle's adviser during the R.P.F. period. In 1954, again through sheer luck and personal 'pull', he became a director of the Rothschild Bank and of many other companies. He continued to maintain close contacts with de Gaulle during the latter's retirement in 1955–8, and certainly played an important part behind the scenes in May 1958. During de Gaulle's premiership in 1958, he became his *directeur de cabinet*, but did not follow him to the Elysée when he was elected President. He returned to the Rothschild Bank, but was also a member of the newly-formed Constitutional Council, to which de Gaulle himself had appointed him. He continued his literary activities and to collect abstract paintings. The common reason given in 1962 for de Gaulle's surprising choice was, therefore, simply that the general regarded Pompidou as a wholly-trusted friend. Moreover, de Gaulle thought that, since there was no 'second de Gaulle' in existence, he might as well be succeeded by a distinguished, but still eminently 'typical' and 'ordinary' Frenchman.

This, however, can only be regarded as a partial explanation. Pompidou, besides being a literary dilettante and a *bon gaulliste*, was a highly typical representative of that 'neo-capitalism' which combined big business with state planning and important nationalized industries. In a sense, Pompidou was the exact opposite of M. Pinay, who represented small and medium business, and the opposite, too, of the men in the colonial and Algerian lobbies; in short, he was a representative of a modern and efficient France holding a central position in Europe and free at last of her colonial empire.

Further, Pompidou had never been a member of parliament, and although the general public remained rather indifferent to the appointment, the press drew some uncomfortable conclusions from it. Since the referendum, besides approving the Evian Agreement, had also been a kind of pro-de Gaulle plebiscite, it was scarcely surprising, as *Combat* noted, that the President's 'personal style should also be reflected in the choice of the new Premier'.

In parliamentary quarters, the Pompidou appointment was badly received, and the new Premier tried to appease them by persuading at least five M.R.P. Members to join his government. But, in view of Pompidou's (and de Gaulle's) hostility to European integration, the false position of the M.R.P. Ministers was stressed by many speakers in the National Assembly when the new government first appeared before it. This meeting (at which Pompidou received a very dubious confidence vote of 259 to 128, with 119 abstentions) was, indeed, to mark the beginning of that first great parliamentary offensive against de Gaulle following the end of the Algerian war. Both de Gaulle and parliament felt that a new chapter had opened in the history of France; they only differed on the nature of that chapter. The 'old' parties (the classical Right, the Radicals, M.R.P. and the Socialists), thinking that the Algerian problem had now been settled, hoped that the 'construction of Europe' could now go ahead and that, moreover, the régime would become not less, but more parliamentary than before.

De Gaulle, however, had his own views on the subject. As regards Algeria, the orgy of violence that marked April and May, especially in Algiers and Oran, was creating a new situation; the violence was not only failing to prevent the independence of Algeria but, worse, was rendering that 'cooperation' between the two communities, provided by the Evian Agreement, quite meaningless. The mass exodus of the panic-stricken Europeans was creating a new problem in France itself, a problem which seemed terrifying at the time – though, in the end, it was solved more easily than most people (except de Gaulle himself) had expected.

As for Europe, de Gaulle held a press conference on 15 May, in which he advocated a 'Europe of States', ridiculing the concept of an 'integrated' Europe 'composed of stateless persons talking some kind of esperanto or volapük'.

On N.A.T.O., de Gaulle now declared that times had changed:

'The defence of France, the battle of Europe and even a third world war all present themselves in a very different way compared with the days when N.A.T.O. was born. Much re-thinking will have to be done. A French nuclear deterrent has come into being, and will go on developing, and this will change the conditions of our national defence. Moreover, the return to France from Algeria of our armed forces will provide us with a modernized army, not, indeed, one that would play a separate or isolated part, but still, one proper to France.'

All of this, and, especially, his contemptuous remarks on European 'integration', made M. Pflimlin exclaim at the end of the press conference: 'It couldn't have been worse!' A few hours later he and the four other M.R.P. Ministers resigned from the Pompidou government. The 'traditional' parties were now preparing for a major showdown with de Gaulle. Pompidou reshuffled the government, adding only one new member, and, as a result, it had an even weaker parliamentary base than before. Its majority in parliament was now highly precarious.

It should be added here that, following closely on the trial of General Jouhaud in 11–13 April before the High Military Tribunal (set up by de Gaulle in April 1961, after the attempted *putsch* of the four generals) the trial of General Salan, head of the O.A.S. terrorists, came before the same Court on 15 May and lasted for a week. All that was fascist and *Algérie française* in France, came to give evidence in Salan's favour, and although Jouhaud, the O.A.S. Number Two had been sentenced to death, the Court, surprisingly, found 'extenuating circumstances' in Salan's conduct, and sentenced him to life imprisonment. In the circumstances, Jouhaud's execution was suspended.

Both trials were marked by the sharpest hostility to de Gaulle, who looked upon the strange verdict in the Salan trial as an act of defiance towards himself by the very Court that he had set up, and four days later an ordinance appeared in the *Journal Officiel* dissolving the Tribunal. A few days later a new Military Court of Justice, composed of five officers and five N.C.O.'s, was established, with its presiding judge the famous Free French general, de Larminat. The fearful *crise de conscience* this whole sorry business had created among part of the army élite may be judged from the fact that, soon after his appointment to the new Court, General de Larminat committed suicide.

So, strange as it may seem, the Evian Agreement putting an end to the Algerian war (though not to the chaos in Algeria) was followed by one of de Gaulle's most difficult periods. The extreme Right and part of the Army were more hostile to him than ever (hence the verdict in the Salan trial). And although the bulk of French opinion was shocked by the

lenient verdict on Salan, the Number One Killer of the
O.A.S., it also found something disquieting in the arbitrary
way in which de Gaulle had set up an emergency tribunal and
had then thought fit to replace it once it had failed to carry
out his wishes.

At the same time, the 'traditional' political parties,
whether they liked the Evian Agreement or not, thought
that now they would be freer to make their influence felt
than during the Algerian war. Hence their determination
to overthrow the Pompidou government at the first convenient opportunity.

The censure motion presented against the government on
1 June by the extreme Right and supported by practically all
the 'Algerian' deputies of the *Unité de la République* group
together with sixty (i.e. about half) of the Independents of
the classical Right, was not, however, a convenient opportunity; the peace settlement in Algeria was unsuitable
ground for attacking the government and the régime. In
the end, the motion was supported by only 113 votes, but
it showed, all the same, that an important part of the
Right was more hostile to de Gaulle than ever.

De Gaulle himself was very conscious of this hostility, and
in his broadcast of 8 June on the coming self-determination
referendum in Algeria, he not only expressed the hope that
the French would still find their place in the Algeria of
tomorrow, but referred to the O.A.S. as 'these blood-
drenched madmen'. He did not hesitate to denounce the
whole 13 May 1958 *putsch* as '*a usurpers' enterprise ready to
plunge the whole of France into civil war*'. This was one of de
Gaulle's most spectacular pronouncements – an extraordinary departure from his '*Je vous ai compris*' of June 1958. The
ultras of Algiers and their offspring, the O.A.S., were now de
Gaulle's (and France's) Enemy Number One. If they did not
mend their ways, he suggested, the France of the future
would be built without them. He, in turn, was charged with

black ingratitude towards those who had brought him to power, and with 'rewriting history'.

To mark his determination to fight the O.A.S. to the finish de Gaulle refused to reprieve two O.A.S. killers, who were shot on 7 June, and soon afterwards it was learned that de Gaulle was thinking of having Salan retried; but this intention was not followed up, and de Gaulle continued to show some hesitation in dealing with the military top brass in the O.A.S. The government did, however, unhesitatingly demand the raising of the parliamentary immunity of M. Georges Bidault, who had associated himself with the O.A.S. and had set up a clandestine 'National Resistance Council' in France. Paradoxically, both Bidault and Soustelle, now identified with fascist extremism, were, from their respective hiding places, accusing de Gaulle of dictatorial ambitions. The left-wing parties charged de Gaulle with a certain incoherence in dealing with the O.A.S., and spoke in particular, of the numerous accomplices that these had in the Army and administration, about whom nothing was being done.

After the 1 July referendum in Algeria, the functions of sixty-eight Algerian deputies and thirty-four Algerian senators in Paris automatically lapsed, and this slightly strengthened the government majority in the National Assembly. But the tension between parliament and the government continued; on 16 July another censure motion was defeated by a relatively narrow majority, the government's *force de frappe* policy being a pretext rather than the real reason for the Assembly's demonstration of hostility.

*

Already in his broadcast of 8 June de Gaulle had vaguely referred to an important constitutional change which he had in mind. It was not quite clear whether he had meant by this an amendment to the Constitution whereby the President of

the Republic would be elected by universal suffrage, but the
idea had been in the air for some months before, and had
even given rise to some lively exchanges, with many deputies
and senators suspecting him of unconstitutional intentions.
As early as February, M. Monnerville, the president of the
Senate, had expressed his anxiety over de Gaulle's plans for
'reinforcing' the Constitution by unconstitutional means,
and M. Paul Reynaud had also uttered a warning against
'violating' the Constitution. It was, indeed, becoming more
and more apparent that, in de Gaulle's view, the 1958
Constitution provided an insufficient basis for that strong
State which France needed above all else. And he felt particularly troubled over the question of his 'succession'; it was
wrong, he felt, to leave the election of the Head of the State
to the whims of an electoral college largely composed of rural
and rustic worthies, subject to wire-pulling and capable of
all kinds of unsavoury deals. To give the President the maximum authority, he had to be chosen by the majority of the
people themselves.

But here he came up against the strong and traditional
anti-plebiscite prejudice in both the National Assembly and
the Senate, while the 1958 Constitution itself did not provide
a simple procedure for making so far-reaching a constitutional change. In view of the numerous signs of parliamentary resistance, de Gaulle hesitated, during the first eight
months of 1962, to raise the question squarely. And then,
on 22 August came that 'psychological shock' which greatly
improved de Gaulle's chances of having it his own way.

It was nothing less than the very-nearly-successful attempt
to assassinate him. And, as so often in the past, de Gaulle
took the fullest advantage of this almost providential combination of the *planned* and the *unforeseen*.

3. One Hundred and Fifty Bullets Fired at De Gaulle

Usually de Gaulle travelled by car between Paris and his

country house at Colombey-les-Deux-Eglises 200 miles to the east; but sometimes, to save time, he flew there. This he did on the afternoon of 22 August. As the car carrying him, Mme de Gaulle and his son-in-law, the party only feebly escorted by a few motor-cyclists, was passing through Petit-Clamart, the Paris suburb, on its way to Villacoublay airfield, there was a sudden fusillade. It is reckoned that 150 bullets were fired. Several hit the President's car, one of them missing his head by two inches, and many more hitting the tyres. The driver, however, stepped on the accelerator and, a few minutes later, arrived safely at the airfield. Stepping out of the car, de Gaulle, looking remarkably cool and unperturbed, merely remarked: 'Well, this time it *was* a close shave!'

Near the spot where the firing had taken place, a yellow car was discovered containing a load of hand grenades. It took about a fortnight before the dozen would-be assassins were arrested or identified; they all belonged to an O.A.S. commando, and included ex-soldiers who had fought in Indo-China, Korea, and Algeria, together with other 'activists'. Among them, strangely enough, was a certain Bastien-Thiry, who had directed the whole operation, and was a high Ministry of Air official, while three Hungarian refugees had also taken part. When questioned, Bastien-Thiry himself claimed that he had acted on behalf of Bidault's 'Resistance Council', which had, he said, supplied the killers with funds. It was also revealed that the head of the O.A.S. terrorist organization still functioning in France and associated with the 'Resistance Council' was a certain Sergent, a former French army captain. One of the would-be assassins committed suicide in prison on 14 September. After a long and stormy trial early in 1963, Bastien-Thiry and two other members of the Petit-Clamart commando were sentenced to death; de Gaulle commuted the death sentences of these two, but Bastien-Thiry was shot on 11

March, despite the five-hour speech in his defence by the notorious *ultra* barrister, Tixier-Vignancour,[1] who argued that his client, like the others, had been acting from the highest motive – to avenge the French Algerian 'victims' of de Gaulle's 'policy of betrayal'.

4. De Gaulle's Double Victory

The Petit-Clamart shooting caused a tremendous sensation in France, and everybody asked the obvious question: What if it had succeeded? There was also, even among de Gaulle's opponents, much admiration for the courage and *sang-froid* that the General had shown on this occasion, as on so many previous ones.

De Gaulle, for his part, realized almost at once what political capital he could make out of the affair. First of all, the police action against O.A.S. terrorists was greatly intensified, and there followed a succession of trials showing that there were still several thousand people in France – embittered ex-soldiers, French Algerians, and all kinds of fascist sympathisers, among them some very young people – who were determined to 'avenge French Algeria'. A leading figure in this movement was ex-Colonel Argout, one of the leading Algiers 'activists' who was later to be kidnapped in Germany and brought to France for trial – an occasion for an embarrassing Franco–German diplomatic incident.

But, more to the point, de Gaulle decided that the anxiety caused by the Petit-Clamart shooting gave him an undreamed-of opportunity for obtaining a change in the Constitution concerning the 'succession'. After his triumphal

---

1. According to M. Jean Foyer, the Minister of Justice, speaking in May 1963, 2,360 sentences had been passed (some *in absentia*) on charges of conspiracy against the safety of the State, among them forty-one death sentences; but of these, at the time, only four had been carried out. Most of these cases concerned the O.A.S.

visit to Germany at the beginning of September (in which he went out of his way to flatter the Germans as never before), de Gaulle declared on 12 September that he would propose a referendum approving his plan for having the President of the Republic elected by universal suffrage.

It is perhaps not widely realized that this proposal brought on the biggest crisis in the career of the Fifth Republic – a showdown between the traditional parties, survivors, as it were, of the Fourth Republic, and the President. In the end, French public opinion supported de Gaulle, first in the October referendum and then in the November general election – and if this support was not overwhelming in the referendum, it was still significant.

The traditional parties, it should be remembered, had been lying low while the Algerian war continued, and although the bulk of public opinion in France (as the April referendum showed) was grateful to de Gaulle for having put an end to the war, many of the traditional leaders felt that he had, as it were, served his purpose – just as Mendès-France had 'served his purpose' in winding up the Indo-China war in 1954 and then in steering the Paris Agreements on German rearmament through parliament. Not that they expected de Gaulle to go; but they saw in the end of the Algerian war an opportunity for 'liberalizing' the régime. De Gaulle, on the other hand, saw in it an opportunity for strengthening his Fifth Republic, with diplomacy, military policy and much else concentrated, more and more, in the hands of the President.

The outcry against de Gaulle's proposed constitutional reform had two aspects to it. In the first place, his proposal was considered strictly unconstitutional. As a Radical resolution put it: 'There can be no referendum on the revision of the Constitution unless the terms of the referendum have been approved by Parliament.' Secondly, the whole proposal went against the grain of those who saw in the election of the President by popular vote a dangerous return to 'bonapartism', with all its inherent dangers of 'rushing the country into unpredictable adventures'. M. Monnerville, the President of the Senate, and de Gaulle's foremost enemy in parliament, was to be the most violent exponent of this view.

*

On 20 September de Gaulle gave his first broadcast on the subject, declaring universal suffrage to be the most democratic way of electing the President, and a referendum the most democratic way of amending the Constitution. He did not trouble on this occasion to argue with the constitutional purists.

More significant still were some of the new phrases he used. He no longer spoke of the President as the 'arbiter'; he said instead:

'The cornerstone of our régime is the President appointed by the people to be the Head of the State and the Guide of France. According to the Constitution, he is, indeed, the guardian (*le garant*) of the independence and integrity of the country and of the treaties he has entered into. He answers for France. On the other hand, it is for him to assure the continuity of the State ... In short, he answers for the Republic.'

He claimed to have personally conducted the Algerian affair to its peaceful conclusion, and argued that, for the President's authority to be as great as possible, it was important that he should be explicitly elected by the people themselves, and no longer by a small college of 80,000 electors; at a stretch, this procedure would do while he (de Gaulle) was still alive, but it would not do in the case of his successor. He also suggested that the Petit-Clamart shooting had made of the reform an urgent matter.

Apart from the Gaullist U.N.R. (and a few hesitant M.R.P. members), all the parties were hostile to de Gaulle. The Radicals, roused to Jacobin indignation by M. Monnerville, the President of the Senate, at their Vichy Congress, denounced the de Gaulle plan as 'illegal and unconstitutional', one that would 'throw the road wide open to the most dangerous adventures'.

Although the Conseil d'État and the Constitutional Committee both commented unfavourably on his project, de Gaulle took no notice. Instead, he sent a Message to Parliament defending his plan. Supported by most of the parties, therefore, a censure motion was tabled in the National Assembly on 2 October, proclaiming that a proposal for the revision of the Constitution must be (a) voted by the two Chambers, and (b) approved by referendum after the French people had been 'enlightened on the nature of the proposal by previous parliamentary debates'. The debate on the censure motion itself opened on 4 October and was followed a few hours later by another de Gaulle broadcast in which the President now openly threatened to resign if he were refused 'the people's confidence'. After a long and stormy debate the Pompidou government was overthrown by 280 votes to 200, with its antagonists a motley coalition stretching from the Communists to the 'classical' Right, and its supporters comprising nearly all the U.N.R. deputies and a handful of others. Although there had been frequent government changes and reshuffles since 1958, *this was the first time under the Fifth Republic that a government was overthrown by Parliament.*

Five days later de Gaulle dissolved the National Assembly. The traditional political parties seem to have misjudged the mood of the country, and de Gaulle to have assessed it much more correctly. It is true, however, that his battle against the parties was not fought by fair means. First of all, de Gaulle and the government enjoyed a virtual monopoly of radio and television, and the General had, by now, developed into France's leading TV star. Secondly, de Gaulle dwelt much less on the pros and cons of electing the

President by universal suffrage than on the 'apocalyptic misfortunes' that France might face if he went. Many of the
anti-de Gaulle leaders argued that it was high time people
realized de Gaulle's departure would not mean the end of the
world. But this argument, somehow, failed to convince; nor
did M. Monnerville achieve much by referring to 'an enlightened bonapartism' as the least of the disasters that would
befall France if she agreed to de Gaulle's proposal. He
stressed that there was no connexion at all between what
de Gaulle had in mind and the United States Constitution,
which did not give the President the right to dissolve the
legislature. Instead, he said, the most arbitrary and unlimited
powers would be concentrated in the hands of one man – and
who could tell what adventurer would succeed de Gaulle?
Referendum questions were always put in such a way as to
produce a YES answer; and what de Gaulle was trying to do,
in creating the 'direct communion' between the people and
the Great Man was practically to eliminate representative
popular assemblies at all levels, including the electoral
college that used to elect the President. The new parliament,
indeed, would be at the constant mercy of the dissolution
decree (Monnerville assumed at that time that the new
Assembly, to be elected in November, would be strongly
anti-Gaullist).

On 18 October de Gaulle gave his third broadcast in which
he now declared that a simple majority was insufficient:

'If your answer is No, which is what the old parties want, so as
to re-establish their régime of misfortune, and which is also what
the rebels want in order to launch themselves into subversive
activities, or even if the Yes majority is weak, mediocre and
half-hearted, then I can only consider my task as finally ended.
And there can be no return.'

Again he referred to himself as 'the Guide', and many
remarked that this was the French word for *Führer* and

Duce. The traditional parties were furious that de Gaulle should call on the people to choose between them and himself; a 'low form of demagogy', they said.

Although de Gaulle's opponents could make use of the 'peripheral' radio stations, such as Luxembourg, Europe I and Monte Carlo, the French government virtually monopolized for its own propaganda both the French radio and, more important, television. The five major opposition parties were allowed only five minutes each on radio and five minutes each on TV throughout the whole referendum campaign.[1]

*

This naturally helped de Gaulle enormously. And then a quite unforeseen factor played into his hands. Six days before the referendum, the Cuban crisis, with its threat of a nuclear cataclysm, reached its height.

It seems that many, at that stage, felt it the wrong time to get rid of de Gaulle. On the contrary, now was the time to rally round France's leader. The political capital made out of the Cuban crisis by the Gaullists prompted Mendès-France to urge de Gaulle to postpone the referendum.

The vote took place all the same on 28 October. Some 62 per cent of the voters, though only 47 per cent cf the electorate (since there were 23 per cent abstentions) voted YES. In fourteen (out of ninety) departments, most of them in the south, the NO vote had a majority.

Whether 'half-hearted' or not, de Gaulle decided that the mandate was good enough, and he did not carry out his threat to leave.

On the contrary, he seemed to welcome his 'mediocre' victory against a vast coalition of political forces in the country, and he set out to make the parliamentary election a truly brilliant victory for himself.

1. A Gaullist argument in defence of this system was that the greater part of the press was anti-de Gaulle in this campaign.

It would be tedious to describe the election campaign in great detail, but two points should be mentioned. The so-called *Cartel des Non* in the referendum campaign, which had comprised practically all the traditional parties and virtually included the Communists, was an artificial *ad hoc* creation and could not be expected to hang together in the much more intricate battles of the general election. Secondly, de Gaulle himself came out openly, on 7 November, with an appeal to the French electorate to vote for the 'Gaullist' candidates – i.e. the U.N.R., the U.D.T.,[1] and those others (some members of the 'classical' Right and of the M.R.P. in particular) who had 'associated' themselves with the Gaullists under the banner of M. André Malraux's newly-created 'Association for the Fifth Republic'. *It was almost unprecedented for the President of the Republic to take sides in a general election.* The last time it had happened was in 1924, when President Millerand had openly supported the right-wing candidates and after the election victory of the Left, he had been forced out of office as a result. But de Gaulle was not dealing with the Third Republic, and could afford such luxuries.

The election, in fact, proved another triumph for de Gaulle. Not even counting their various allies, the U.N.R. – U.D.T. Gaullists secured 32 per cent of the poll in the first round and *over 40 per cent in the second.* With the existing electoral system this gave them an almost absolute majority in the new National Assembly – 229 seats out of 465; even a handful of allies were enough to give them an absolute majority.[2] The Communist poll of 21 per cent increased the Communist seats from ten to forty-one; there was a slight increase in the number of Socialist seats (though not votes); but for the other 'traditional' parties – the non-Gaullist

1. The U.D.T. were the so-called Left-wing Gaullists.
2. Principal among these was a small right-wing group including M. Giscard d'Estaing, the Minister of Finance.

Right, the Radicals, and the M.R.P. – the Election was a disaster. The extreme Right (the wild men representing the Algiers *ultras*) was wiped out altogether.

Most of the *Cartel des Non* leaders were eliminated, notably Paul Reynaud and Mendès-France; and those who survived, like Guy Mollet, did so only thanks to Communist support in the second round. All the seats for Paris went, without exception, to the Gaullists.

Now at last de Gaulle had that *chambre introuvable* which would be an obedient tool in his hands. No doubt the electoral system had greatly helped, and under proportional representation the Gaullists would have had no majority. But the 40 per cent poll (or about 45 per cent including allies) in the second round was sufficiently indicative. It was another vote of confidence in de Gaulle and yet another reaction against the 'old fogeys' of the Fourth Republic. No doubt the leaders of the traditional parties tried to console themselves by saying that there was no majority in the country for 'personal rule', but that no longer mattered to de Gaulle. To de Gaulle, the old Assembly had been, if not a major obstacle, at least a major nuisance in its attempts to interfere with his foreign and military policy. The 'traditional' parties – Radicals, M.R.P., classical Right and Socialists – were, in the main, 'European' and 'Atlantic' in outlook, as well as highly critical of de Gaulle's *force de frappe*. So long as the Algerian war was on, they had kept reasonably quiet; but, since May 1962, there had been growing signs of revolt against the President's policies. The revolt of the M.R.P. leaders with their 'supra-national' Europe in May, and the Socialist agitation for a *rapprochement* with Britain were typical. One of the most significant reactions to the election victory of the Gaullists came from the United States, where it was observed that this had been a crushing defeat for the parties of the old 'system' and their staunch support of the Atlantic Alliance. De Gaulle would now be sole master of France's foreign policy, and might not prove an easy partner.

With the Algerian war out of the way, and with no serious opposition coming from parliament, Gaullist foreign policy was, indeed, to assume many novel features in the course of the next few years. To de Gaulle, the 'age of the big blocs' was coming to an end. He was to give France greater independence of manoeuvre towards Europe, the United States, Russia, Africa, the under-developed countries generally and, in the end, the Far East, than she had ever had in the past – 'at least not,' as de Gaulle said, 'since 1940, when France had been in the subservient position of somebody's satellite.'

*

At home, after his double victory, his attitude was curious to watch. There were times when he was extremely arrogant; but also times when he was surprisingly conciliatory. He made one of his most arrogant pronouncements on 27 November, soon after the election, at ex-President Coty's funeral in Le Havre. Recalling the role that Coty had played in bringing him back to power in 1958, de Gaulle paid a tribute to the ex-President for having realized that he (de Gaulle) represented a *deeper legitimacy* than the parliamentary system, which only confused and disunited the Nation; in short, de Gaulle was identifying himself in a new way with what was in effect Maurras's *pays réel*, as distinct from the *pays légal*.

At the same gathering, he pointedly refrained from shaking hands with M. Monnerville, the President of the Senate, and with ex-President Vincent Auriol, both of whom had sharply opposed him.

And yet, soon afterwards, he made it clear that, despite all the annoyance it had caused him, he was not proposing to abolish the Senate, or try to merge it with the Economic Council, as had been rumoured. Moreover, in the same

Message to Parliament, he explicitly stated that he was opposed to the 'single party' concept.

The 1962 election marks, as it were, the watershed between two distinct phases of de Gaulle's Fifth Republic. The end of the Algerian war had much to do with the great change. Underrating the great credit that de Gaulle had gained in the country by ending the war, the old Assembly had thought that it had, on the contrary, facilitated a revolt against de Gaulle. In this it proved wrong. The Petit-Clamart shooting – which precipitated the constitutional reform – was also, in a sense, the final flash of O.A.S. terrorism in France and so a by-product of the Algerian war. De Gaulle took the most skilful advantage of both the revolt of parliament and of the Petit-Clamart shooting to consolidate the Fifth Republic according to his own lights. Here was not only clever, if at times unscrupulous, political manoeuvring, but also an understanding of the country's mood – with its trust-daddy *apolitisme*. The opposition had underrated it. All things considered, *there were different kinds of opposition to de Gaulle, but none of them was truly active* – except that of the O.A.S. gunmen. Nobody had any very serious alternative to propose. And, deep-down, de Gaulle flattered that nationalism for which there is a little corner in every Frenchman's heart. This was to become even more apparent in the next period of 1964–5, when French foreign policy developed a much more individual and spectacular style of its own. But this nationalism was different from the *nationalisme de papa* of the Algerian settlers and of the *ultra* Right in France. The latter had been pulverized in the 1962 election, though they were, oddly enough, to re-emerge in the next two years, with the venomous Jean-Louis Tixier-Vignancour as their potential leader. It was these people, far more than anybody on the Left, or even on the extreme Left, who loathed de Gaulle with a pathological hatred. To these people he was 'a man of the Left', and, in the light of his great decolonization work, together with his increasingly subtle attitude to the 'Third World' and even the Communist states (including China) it was easy enough to demonstrate that there was a grain of truth in this.

CHAPTER 10

DE GAULLE, EUROPE AND THE WORLD

1. The Useful Heritage of the Fourth Republic

DURING the four years prior to 1962, Algeria and, to a lesser extent, the allied problems of Morocco, Tunisia and Black Africa formed the main preoccupations of de Gaulle's foreign policy. Algeria was not merely a 'colonial' affair; it affected the very future of France and, indeed, on two occasions attempted to impose its will on de Gaulle and on Metropolitan France. Even after de Gaulle, with the support of French public opinion, had foiled both these insurrections, the danger of the Fifth Republic being overthrown could not be ruled out altogether – either through some shabby deal between the O.A.S., part of the army and the 'traditional parties', or through the assassination of de Gaulle; the attempt on him on 22 August 1962 in fact very nearly succeeded.

Although the Algerian millstone impeded de Gaulle's freedom of movement in pursuing a distinctive foreign policy since the summer of 1958, it had been clear that once the Algerian problem had been solved, there were certain ideas which he intended to put into practice.

But there is a curious paradox. As some Soviet histories of Russia suggest that there was 'nothing' before 1917, so certain Gaullist statements and writings make believe that, before 1958, France, with her 'régime of parties', was simply a hopeless mess.

In reality, the Fourth Republic had some impressive achievements to its credit, even though it was constantly harassed and finally overthrown by 'Algiers' and by the Army. For one thing, France's expansion had been remarkable between 1952 and 1958. As André Siegfried wrote at the beginning of 1958:

If there was any economic crisis in 1957, it was only a crisis of growth or rather, adaptation, from which France could only emerge stronger and better-equipped than ever. For the last four years, France had shown *a more remarkable industrial progress than at any other time since the beginning of the century – a greater progress, indeed, than any other European country, not excluding Western Germany.* Certain industries had reached peaks of efficiency unsurpassed anywhere in the world. The electrification of our railways, the modernization of our mines are models that others come to France to study ... The Renault Works produce cars which even make a hit in the U.S.A.; our aircraft, electronic and other industries reach the highest level of research. Coexisting alongside an increasingly localized old traditionalism, there now exists an industrial society run by young people, sold on expansionism. A sharp rise in the birth-rate, an agriculture in a state of progress, the addition to coal of mighty new sources of energy (such as natural gas) – all these give France every opportunity of developing an ultra-modern economy.

And Siegfried concluded:

It was this spirit of optimism that made us embark on the adventure – for it is an adventure – of the Common Market.

At first sight, one would suppose that Siegfried was speaking of Gaullist France. But no; he was speaking of 1957 – the year before de Gaulle's return to power. And he even stressed:

In this respect 1957 marks perhaps, as far as France is concerned, the greatest turning-point since the Liberation.

The truth is that the 'dynamic, expanding, ultra-modern' economy of France, which is often made out to be a sort of 'Gaullist' invention, was already in existence when de Gaulle came to power. Indeed it was these 'young people, full of optimism and sold on expansionism' who very largely rallied to the Fifth Republic, to its technological élite, and to the U.N.R., leaving 'the increasingly-localized old traditionalism' either to the 'old' parties, and particularly to the 'classical' Right of a M. Pinay, or to the 'shopkeepers' of the extreme Right, as personified by Pierre Poujade. There is, indeed, nothing fortuitous in the fact that the 'shopkeepers' and the *Algérie Française* extremists should so often have been the same people. The 'ultra-modern, dynamic' France was essentially European and anti-colonialist, even though many of the bright young technologically-minded Gaullists had first to shake off their colonialist prejudices. Some older men, like Soustelle and Bidault, could not take it, and went into violent opposition. *It was one of de Gaulle's supreme qualities to have realized, in returning to power in 1958, which way the wind was blowing, and to what extent France had changed since the days when he himself could be ranked among the Indo-Chinese, and even Algerian diehards.*

*

And here we come to another paradoxical phenomenon. It would be tedious to give endless quotations from de Gaulle's speeches between 1950 and 1955 showering the greatest scorn and sarcasm on 'Europe', on the 'supranational' Schuman Plan of 1950 which developed into the Coal–Steel Community (C.E.C.A.), on any other sort of 'integration' – first the E.D.C., the 'European Army', and then the Common Market itself. Senator Debré had ridiculed and condemned the Rome Treaty of 1957, laying the foundations of the future Common Market. *And yet, when in 1958 de Gaulle returned to power, he found that an enormous amount of valuable work had been done under the Fourth Republic to lay the foundations for an economically integrated Europe.* On 25 March 1957 the Common Market and the Euratom treaties had been signed, to complete the older Coal–Steel Community.

For a time there were, in 1958, some wild rumours that de Gaulle would somehow wreck the Common Market. Yet, by 1 January 1959 it was already clear that he had no intention of resorting to the 'safeguard clauses' of the Rome Treaty, and that *he had decided to make the Common Market work to France's political, as well as economic, advantage*. At the end of 1958 he had indeed even decided on a 17 per cent devaluation of the franc which would enable France to hold her own in the Common Market. To de Gaulle, the Common Market no longer appeared as a mere trade agreement but as an instrument of French power and influence in Europe and the world at large. What worried him were the attempts to extend the European Economic Community to a Political Community, and here his concept of Europe differed from that of the all-out federalists, both inside France and abroad. But this great battle, which is not yet ended, did not begin in real earnest until after the end of the Algerian war in 1962.

*

In addition to inheriting from the Fourth Republic an expanding and modern French economy, as well as those Rome Treaties of 1957 which laid the foundations for the Common Market and Euratom, de Gaulle also inherited a whole machinery for producing not only nuclear energy but, quite specifically, the French atom bomb.

The C.E.A. (*Commissariat d'énergie atomique*) had been set up as early as 18 October 1945, when de Gaulle was still head of the post-Liberation government, but this organization was to be primarily concerned with scientific research, and it was, in fact, not until 1952–3 that the question of making a French bomb arose. During the following years, with the growth of France's atomic installations and the large capital investments sunk into them, it was clear in which direction the French atomic industry was moving. The second Five-Year Plan of 1957–61 endowed the C.E.A.

with 500 billion old francs and, early in 1958, Premier Félix Gaillard explicitly decided to make the first French plutonium bomb and to explode it not later than 1960. When de Gaulle came to power, the policy of the 'national' bomb had already in effect been decided upon, and the Pierrelatte isotope separation plant was already in process of construction. De Gaulle's return to power merely gave greater weight and continuity to France's military nuclear policy. As *Esprit* was to write:

> Very quickly the military objectives of the Commissariat for Atomic Energy were given top priority ... At the same time, the Ministry of Defence was instructed to build a centre for nuclear tests at Reggane in the southern Sahara.[1]

On 13 February 1960 the first French atom bomb was exploded at Reggane – a bomb of some sixty kilotons, three times the power of the Hiroshima bomb. De Gaulle was delighted. He cabled to Reggane: 'Hurray for France! Since this morning she is stronger and prouder.'

2. The New Style of Diplomacy – the Cult of Independence

It may well be argued, accordingly, that there was, in many respects, a greater continuity between the Fourth Republic and the Fifth than appears on the surface. The Fourth Republic had laid the foundations of 'Europe' and, in particular, of the Common Market; of 'Gaullist' economic prosperity; and even of de Gaulle's *force de frappe*, though the question of whether this was to be a purely 'national' deterrent was left for the future to decide.

For all that, de Gaulle began to develop his new style of diplomacy very soon after taking office in June 1958. When Mr Dulles came to Paris on 4–5 July, de Gaulle, alluding to the Eisenhower 'instructions' at the time of the Murphy

1. *Esprit*, December 1963, p. 760. Most of this issue of the journal is a monograph on the *Force de Frappe*.

Mission, remarked to the Secretary of State: 'Remember, I am no Monsieur Gaillard!' He then bluntly declared that he wished France to become a member of the 'atomic club'. He was not asking the United States to approve of France's nuclear policy. But France was ten years behind in the atomic armaments race; what he wanted to know was what France was entitled to receive, by way of scientific and industrial secrets, under the MacMahon Act. He was not asking for any favours, and was not offering the U.S.A. rocket sites, or anything like that, in exchange. He also criticized N.A.T.O. policy, saying that a 'global strategy' was needed, and that, in his view, American preponderance in N.A.T.O. was far too great. Dulles was rather non-committal, but remarked, none the less, before leaving Paris, that he considered de Gaulle 'one of the great men of our time'.

Only a few days later the Middle East crisis broke out following the Bagdad revolution of 14 July, in which King Feisal and Nouri Said were murdered, and in the next three days U.S. troops were landed in the Lebanon and British troops in Jordan at these countries' request. Britain and the U.S.A. acted without consulting the French, and de Gaulle took great exception to this. Since the Lebanese government had appealed for French help, too, a French warship, the De Grasse, was sent to Beirut, but only to be told by the American military that the French were not wanted there.

In the major international crisis that followed the British and American landings, de Gaulle adopted a line very different from that of London and Washington; then, in his letter to Eisenhower and Macmillan of 24 September, he sharply criticized the Atlantic alliance on numerous grounds. The Lebanon affair – and, since then, the Quemoy crisis – had shown that there was no proper coordination among the Allies, and that the U.S.A. could 'endanger peace' in taking independent action in areas not covered by the Atlantic alliance: there was an excessive atomic preponderance on the American side; and the U.S.A. was, in fact, free to decide on the use of the atom bomb without consulting its allies, particularly in 'non-Atlantic' areas. It was another call for a coordinated 'global strategy', and the letter suggested the creation of a super-directorate of the U.S.A., Britain, and France.

The letter met with no response, since the U.S.A., in particular, considered that France counted for little as a 'global' military power, so long as her hands were tied by the Algerian war.

In the circumstances, de Gaulle decided, early in 1959, to withdraw the French Mediterranean fleet from the Allied High Command; to take a similar step in respect of certain French fighter forces in France; to ban American nuclear warheads from French territory; and to deny the Americans French rocket sites. Later much of the U.S. Air Force in France was moved to Britain. These measures must not be regarded as a display of bad temper on the part of France, but rather as an example of de Gaulle's preference for the 'coalition' rather than the 'integration' concept.

*

France is a relatively small country of less than fifty million, and everybody knows de Gaulle's mot: 'Ah, *cher ami*, if only we had 180 million people!' Nevertheless, de Gaulle was determined, even since 1958, to make the most of France's strong strategic position in Europe and in the world, of her 'cultural radiance', and of the fact that the world of the 'two super-blocs' was no longer what it had been in 1950. De Gaulle himself denied on one occasion ever having used the phrase 'policy of greatness'; what he had in mind was not so much *grandeur* as greater independence, above all towards the two super-blocs, and particularly the United States. At the beginning of 1963

M. Edgar Faure described the 'grand Gaullist design' as consisting of six major points:

1. A strengthening of France's internal institutions;
2. A certain French military independence arising from France's entry into the 'atomic club';
3. Colonial disengagement;
4. Reconciliation between France and Germany, the cornerstone of the new Europe;
5. The build-up of a European confederation, but with only a minimum of supra-nationality, in which France, with Western Germany as a seemingly equal but in reality junior partner, would set the pace;
6. An attempt at general 'global' settlements together with the U.S.A. and the U.S.S.R., such settlements comprising the attainment of a *modus vivendi* with the East, and a world-wide organization for dealing with the under-developed countries.

If this was de Gaulle's 'grand design', some of its points were clear enough, but others were obscure and confused. The clearest were those relating to France's internal institutions and to decolonization; for France to play a leading role in any 'global' settlement, it was essential for her to cease to be a colonial power, and to exchange the moral liability of the 'Empire' for a more authentic and concentrated strength in Europe. Whether 'Europe' would share in France's responsibility for keeping the former 'empire' going was, however, a moot point. There was an obvious contradiction, for one thing, between de Gaulle's desire to see 'Europe' help the under-developed countries and the very special role he assigned to France's 'cooperation', 'presence', and 'cultural radiance' in these countries.

*

It was often said in the past that de Gaulle was a man with a single-track mind. 'He is not complicated,' Stalin had said about him at Yalta. Churchill, Roosevelt, and others have commented on his allegedly primitive nationalism. In reality, as his whole foreign policy since 1958 shows, the workings of de Gaulle's mind are often extremely tortuous. Greater prestige for France, greater influence for France doubtless have always been de Gaulle's permanent aim. But his means of achieving this have varied from year to year, sometimes even from month to month. Similarly, the old idea that de Gaulle is a megalomaniac imagining himself to be Joan of Arc is just as much an over-simplification as the assertion that he is 'pathologically' anti-American and anti-British. Certainly de Gaulle considers himself – and with some justice – as an altogether exceptional man who 'saved France' on two occasions – in 1940, when he 'saved her honour', and in 1958, when he 'saved her from civil war'. There is also little doubt that he bears the United States and, to a lesser extent, Britain, a grudge for the 'humiliations' he – and, therefore, France – suffered during the Second World War. Also, he considers it important to free both France and Western Europe from being satellites of the United States. To him the American Alliance is essential though not quite in the way it was essential in say, 1950. Europe today is an economically prosperous concern which can stand on its own feet. The question whether, in de Gaulle's view, Europe can become a 'Third Force', equal in many, though not all, respects to the U.S.S.R., is, however, a difficult one to answer: at times it seems that de Gaulle would like this Third Force to be, as it were, wholly independent of the United States, at other times he makes it clear that, for all its independence, this Third Force still belongs to the West, but as an 'equal partner' of the United States – not a 'Third Force', but a 'Second Western Force'; which is why de Gaulle, at the height of the Cuban Crisis in October 1962, hastened to assure Kennedy of France's wholehearted support.

But this was an extreme emergency; at other times de Gaulle's attitude to the United States is very different, and the 'de-satellization' of France and, if possible, of the whole of Western Europe is one of his principal aims.

It has been said that de Gaulle's most spectacular move in the foreign field – his exclusion of Britain from the Common Market, following his famous press conference of 14 January 1963 – was no more than an example of his anti-British and anti-American 'paranoia'. This is another gross oversimplification. The whole background of that dramatic decision is one of extreme complexity, and the responsibility for this 'disaster' – if it *was* a 'disaster' (the British Labour Party and half the Conservatives did not think so, though they resented the way it was brought about) – cannot be attributed to de Gaulle alone. In *Atlantic Crisis: American Diplomacy Confronts a Resurgent Europe*, Robert Kleiman, the distinguished *New York Times* correspondent[1] brilliantly explains in great detail to what extent the United States, and particularly Kennedy himself, and the British Government had played into de Gaulle's hand. Kennedy and de Gaulle clashed on a great number of issues. True, Kennedy visited de Gaulle in 1961 in an atmosphere of great cordiality (Mme de Gaulle later confided, it is true, that she had found Jackie *un peu vulgaire*): but, afterwards, unlike Eisenhower, Kennedy had gone out of his way to avoid any close contacts with de Gaulle, and the main points against Kennedy that Kleiman makes amount to this:

By 1961 Kennedy had come to the conclusion that the Common Market was, in Mr Dillon's phrase, a 'fantastic success'; already in 1960 it had become clear that it would take only eight, and not twelve or fifteen years for it to become a complete customs union.

Kennedy's answer to the Common Market was therefore

1. Published in England by Sidgwick and Jackson in 1965.

the Trade Expansion Act of October 1961. Already in 1957 the British had tried to wreck the Common Market by creating a vast Free Trade Zone. The Trade Expansion Act, pursuing a similar object, aroused intense suspicions in Europe as it threatened to demolish the external tariffs of the Common Market. Kennedy was interested both in protecting U.S. trade, and avoiding power-sharing even though it was clear by 1961 that power with Europe must be shared. The ambiguous offer made to France of Polaris missiles after Nassau was one that Kennedy did not expect de Gaulle to accept, especially since de Gaulle was anxious to manage without American help for his *force de frappe*.

But Kennedy urged Britain to join the Common Market for political as well as for economic reasons, so as to give it 'greater stability', especially as France and Germany were ruled by two old men – de Gaulle and Adenauer.

Kennedy greatly underrated the fact that the Common Market was not only an economic, but also a political union, especially in the economic field. For had not Hallstein said: 'We do not only business, but also politics'? Kennedy's Atlantic Free Trade Zone was wholly contrary to this concept. Moreover, these 'Atlantic' aims were combined with all kinds of contradictory American aims, such as the virtual atomic monopoly of the U.S.A. in the West and the U.S.A.'s unilateral talks with the Soviet Union – a point on which Adenauer felt particularly strongly, and which greatly helped in the spectacular Franco–German *rapprochement* of 1962.

There were to be further differences between Kennedy and de Gaulle on other issues, such as the M.L.F. (Multilateral Force) which, in de Gaulle's view, had the double disadvantage of being largely European-financed and American-controlled and of helping to turn Western Germany into an 'American Foreign Legion'.

Not only de Gaulle, but also many other Europeans, saw in Kennedy's Trade Expansion Act a threat to the Common Market. This, as well as Kennedy's desire to keep Europe in a state of great military inferiority *vis-à-vis* the United States, with the bulk of the U.S.A.'s nuclear arsenal under its own exclusive control, constitute part of the background of de Gaulle's famous 'No to Britain' in January 1963. Kennedy's Grand Design was giving nightmares not only to de Gaulle, but also to many other Europeans.

It may, of course, be argued that in 1962 the Common Market was only an economic union and not, in any real sense, a political one. But is this quite true? The French Government had already produced the so-called Fouchet Plan, in January 1962. This was based primarily on de Gaulle's concept of a union of States (i.e. sovereign states), with only a minimum of that supra-nationality that de Gaulle had always abhorred. Nevertheless, when it was submitted to Adenauer and Fanfani, they thought it went much further than they had expected. But the real opposition to the Fouchet Plan came from the Dutch who suspected that it was designed to exclude Britain from Europe, and who argued along these lines:

'If we had been given the supra-national political Europe of our dreams, we might have put up with a temporary exclusion of Britain. But since the French plan is only a caricature of such a Europe, we want Britain at least in this version of 'Europe'; if Britain still will not enter, then we are not prepared to accept anything short of a political supra-national Europe.'

The French had no doubt that the British had put the Dutch up to it.

The breakdown of the Fouchet Plan was a blow to de Gaulle, as he showed by his angry and sarcastic remarks at his press conference in April 1962 about *volapük* as the future language of Europe, and about the interference of the 'non-European federator', i.e. the United States. It was this press conference, which drove the all-out French 'Europeans' – the M.R.P. ministers – out of the Pompidou government.

Having failed with his Fouchet Plan, de Gaulle then attempted to safeguard the 'independence of Europe' by a direct understanding with Western Germany. Adenauer came on an official visit to France in July 1962; and the following September was marked by de Gaulle's genuinely spectacular and triumphant journey to Western Germany.

3. The German Card

Germany was always central to de Gaulle's scheme of things. In 1944 he still saw her as the 'permanent threat' to France. He wanted to see the Ruhr internationalized and the Rhineland placed virtually under French control, and the rest of Germany split into a mosaic of small states. By 1947 Russia had become the great menace, and, soon afterwards, he began to play with the idea of some sort of Franco–German Union, and even mentioned Charlemagne's Empire as the ancestor of the plan he had in mind.

The Great Friendship with Adenauer – who was in time to become the only real wholehearted 'Gaullist' outside France – began soon after de Gaulle had taken office in June 1958. That autumn Adenauer visited de Gaulle at Colombey-les-deux-Eglises, and soon afterwards, de Gaulle paid him a return visit at Kreuznach. It was these first two meetings which had upset the Russians so much. During the summer of 1958, they had treated de Gaulle with much consideration as an 'anti-American' influence in Europe and as a disruptive element inside N.A.T.O.; but now they found that he was consorting with a different kind of devil, and their attitude became much more critical.

De Gaulle and Adenauer continued to meet during 1959 and 1960 and although on the surface, Khrushchev's visit

to France in March 1960 passed off in a general atmosphere
of good humour, Khrushchev was disappointed to find that
de Gaulle would not budge an inch on the question of
Berlin. In his numerous speeches, the Soviet leader never
stopped harping on the failure of the French to appreciate
the 'German danger'. De Gaulle's unresponsive attitude to
these warnings may well have had something to do with the
failure of the famous Summit Conference a month later.

There were further de Gaulle–Adenauer meetings in 1961.
The most notable was de Gaulle's visit to Germany in May
on the eve of Kennedy's visit to Paris, when de Gaulle went
out of his way to assure Adenauer that he could rely on
France's absolute support, on the question of Berlin. At
that time Kennedy was planning an international conference
on Berlin, as well as bilateral talks with the Russians; de
Gaulle and Adenauer felt that both these might prove highly
dangerous and could only produce concessions from the
West.

The Kennedy visit to Paris went off better than might have
been expected. On his return to the U.S.A., Kennedy spoke
warmly of de Gaulle, declaring himself much impressed by
his 'exceptional personality' and his 'great charm' and by
the breadth of his views on 'the political and economic independence of the under-developed countries'. Curiously
enough, he dismissed his disagreements with de Gaulle as
'insignificant' – even though these concerned nothing less
than the French atom bomb, France's integration in
N.A.T.O., the Congo, and de Gaulle's critical attitude to
U.N. – *le machin*, 'that thingummy', as he called it. Whether
Kennedy was wholly satisfied with de Gaulle's uncompromising attitude to Berlin and with his hostility to bilateral
American–Soviet talks is another matter, but little was said
about that. In reality, that de Gaulle–Kennedy meeting
sharpened, if anything, the subsequent Franco–American
disagreements on Europe.

However, Adenauer had every reason to be pleased with de Gaulle.

It was not till July 1962, when the Algerian war was over, that Adenauer came to France as an official guest of the French State for the first time. There were some hostile demonstrations; but, even so, he visited several French cities; and the visit was crowned by a *Te Deum* at Rheims Cathedral as well as by the even more symbolic review of both French and German troops at Mourmelon – something that had never happened before.

More spectacular still was de Gaulle's visit to Germany in September, barely a fortnight after the Petit-Clamart *attentat*. He visited Cologne, Munich, Bonn, Hamburg, Stuttgart and other cities, and, in contrast to Adenauer, was everywhere given an enthusiastic reception. He addressed large crowds in German (a language he had learned at St Cyr): exclaimed '*Sie sind ein grosses Volk!*', and spoke to the workers of the Thyssen plant at Duisburg, addressing them as '*Meine Herren*', and to the officers of the War College at Hamburg. On one occasion he 'boasted' of having one German ancestor. He drew, however, the line at visiting Berlin. Couve de Murville explained that such a visit might be misinterpreted, and would go 'outside the immediate Franco–German framework'.

The purpose of the German tour was clear enough: it was intended to convert Germany to a 'European', as against an 'Atlantic' outlook or, as some of de Gaulle's German critics said, to 'lay the foundations for a new kind of Franco–German nationalism which would dominate the rest of Western Europe'.

'*Germany is and always will be a menace; I've been saying it for the last thousand years!*' de Gaulle used to say. But now all seemed to be forgotten. Now he told the German officers at Hamburg how happy he was that Germany had realized the absurdity of that 'duel' between the two nations, and that it had now come to an end. At the same time, the speech was a glorification of both French and German (!) military valour:

'The Atlantic Alliance can be valid only if, on both sides of the Rhine, the French and Germans are in agreement ... The way the world is going shows that the two countries complement each other; by joining together all that they are and have been and all that they are worth, they can create a base for *a Europe whose prosperity, power and prestige would be equal to anybody's.*

'Everything suggests to us that we must build up this Franco–German union. But what place will the solidarity of our military might hold in it? It is true of both France and Germany that they have never achieved anything great, either nationally or internationally, without the military element having played an eminent part in it.'

He then dwelt on the great 'scientific, technical, industrial and financial factors' on which military power was based nowadays.

De Gaulle was still speaking in riddles; even so, many in both France and Germany read into his Hamburg speech a proposal for a sort of Franco–German directorate in Western Europe, and a suggestion that France might even contemplate a future cooperation with Germany in the production of nuclear weapons. To reassure Western critics, the final communiqué on the visit, drawn up at Bonn on 7 September, stressed the importance of the 'progressive development of a united Europe' and, in Paris, an official statement said that Franco–German cooperation could in no way be prejudicial to the Atlantic Alliance or the Common Market.

The impression, nevertheless, prevailed that de Gaulle had Adenauer under his spell, and that the now eighty-six-year-old Chancellor was, at heart, a strong supporter of the 'Paris–Bonn Axis', and was less interested than most of his ministers in smoothing things out with Britain. As Nora Beloff put it:

> The degree of his indifference to Britain's entry into the Common Market was finally demonstrated when, disregarding all his critics, he insisted on signing the Franco–German Treaty one week after the General's No to Britain.[1]

The 'Atlantic', 'pro-British' and 'integrationist' preamble that the Bundestag thought fit to attach to the Franco–German Treaty before ratifying it on 16 May 1963, (a Preamble de Gaulle was to describe to Willy Brandt as 'insulting' (*outrageant*)) reduced this bilateral Treaty to much less than de Gaulle, Adenauer and the 'German Gaullists' had hoped for. With Adenauer gone, other people now set the tune – 'Erhard', as the *Monde* put it, 'who wants to be friends with everybody, and Foreign Minister Schröder who is more Anglo-Saxon than the Anglo-Saxons'.

Later, too, de Gaulle ruefully remarked one day that this was not the only treaty that had faded 'as quickly as a rose'. No doubt the periodic bilateral talks provided for under the Treaty continued, but they no longer meant as much as they would have done under Adenauer. The truth seems to be that, on this question of Franco–German union, Adenauer did not enjoy overwhelming support in Germany; de Gaulle's 'No' to Britain in January 1963 was received with very mixed feelings there, and there was, above all, great reluctance in Western Germany to weaken the country's bonds with the United States. Kennedy's visit to Germany - and Berlin - in June 1963 aroused at least as much enthusiasm as de Gaulle's visit a few months before, even though some of his remarks were pointed against de Gaulle.

There was to be a further deterioration in Franco–German relations, particularly in 1965, when de Gaulle embarked on his policy of *rapprochement* with the Russians at the height

1. *The General Says No*, Penguin Books, 1963, p. 101

of the American war in Vietnam. No one was more upset
about it than Adenauer who, with Erhard's approval, wrote
de Gaulle a half-plaintive, half-angry letter in April 1965.

4. 'No' to Britain

Criticizing British policy since the war, and Lord Avon in
particular, Lord Boothby wrote in *The Times* of 25 March
1965:

> If we are out of Europe to-day, it is because we never did any-
> thing to encourage what might have been the most hopeful
> international development since the war; we refused to take part
> in the discussions which led first to the Coal and Steel Community
> ... next to the abortive E.D.C., and finally to the highly successful
> European Economic Community (Common Market).

On the face of it, this policy was reversed by Mr Macmillan
in July 1961; in August Britain officially applied for admission to the Common Market and, a month later, the
negotiations began. These were slow, almost unbelievably
slow, and dragged on for nearly eighteen months till January
1964, when de Gaulle suddenly – or perhaps not so suddenly
– said No at his famous press conference of the 14th; a
fortnight later, the Brussels negotiations were broken off,
with the French simply vetoing any further discussion.

There was an uproar in England; not, as one commentator
put it, that she particularly wanted to enter the club, but
because she felt it an insult to be kept out of it. A few weeks
later, the British government, thoroughly piqued, forbade
Princess Margaret to go and lunch in Paris with General de
Gaulle.

Who was to blame for this breakdown – the French or the
British? The truth is that there had been a great deal of
disagreement and double-think over this issue on both sides.
Not only was the Labour Party hostile to Britain's entry into
the Common Market, but the Conservative government
itself was divided; Maudling, Butler, and Hailsham were

hostile, even if Heath was favourable. In fact, it was not till the autumn of 1962 that the majority of the Conservative leaders may be said to have been converted to the Common Market. By this time, de Gaulle had convinced himself that the negotiations would still drag on for a very long time. But much more important was his conviction that the next British government would be Labour. Labour's attitude may be gauged not only from Gaitskell's speeches, but also from Spaak's remark, after a conversation with Gordon Walker, the Labour Shadow Foreign Secretary: 'Good God, the fellow nearly turned me into a Gaullist!'

But there were other factors which were even more important in bringing about the General's sonorous No – some of them long-term, others almost last-minute.

It is often asked whether de Gaulle had been against Britain's entry into the Common Market ever since he had taken over in 1958. In fact, for a long time, the question did not even arise. During de Gaulle's visit to London in March 1960, Macmillan still told him that Britain's entry into the Common Market was 'unthinkable'. Nevertheless de Gaulle continued to think that, in the end, Britain might join. Before the Council of Europe meeting on 2 March 1961, Couve de Murville declared that the Common Market was open for other countries to join and expressed the hope that their negative attitude would change. And a few months later, in a speech at Metz, de Gaulle was even more explicit: 'It is *necessary* that Britain should join the Common Market, though without laying down any conditions.' After Britain had announced her decision to join, de Gaulle declared on 5 September 1961:

'The Six have always wanted other countries, *and particularly Britain* to join the Common Market, accept its obligations and reap its benefits. We are quite aware of the complexity of the problem, but now that everything is being done to solve it, I can only *express my satisfaction*, whether I look at it from the point of view of France, Europe, or the world at large.'

The problem proved indeed 'complex', and the negotiations dragged on for many months. In June 1962 Macmillan visited de Gaulle at the Château de Champs and both the British and French press declared that the meeting had been 'promising' – though the French government found it necessary to deny British reports that de Gaulle had made Anglo–French nuclear cooperation his condition for letting Britain enter the Common Market. This curious denial shows that at least at that stage de Gaulle was anxious not to exclude Britain from Europe; more than that, he had gained the impression that once Britain entered the Common Market, there would also be Anglo–French cooperation in the nuclear field. That Macmillan suggested this last is clearly indicated in the French minutes of the meeting.

Yet the evidence of de Gaulle's true thinking after the Champs meetings remains contradictory. According to some of his ministers, he declared himself convinced that Britain had 'chosen Europe'. In Brussels, soon afterwards, Couve de Murville said that there were four chances in five that Britain would enter the Common Market. On the other hand, it is curious that, during de Gaulle's visit to Germany in September, he should have made numerous speeches suggesting a sort of Franco–German directorate of Europe, and should scarcely have mentioned Britain at all.

Matters were complicated, from August 1962 onwards, by the bogging down of the Brussels negotiations on agricultural problems – which suggested to de Gaulle that the British were not in a hurry to make a deal with the Six and were, in fact, waiting for the Gaullists to suffer a severe defeat in the French general election. After his unexpected election victory, de Gaulle became increasingly self-assured and also more sceptical than ever about the British eagerness to enter the Common Market. Shortly before Macmillan's visit to

Rambouillet in December, Ambassador de Courcel reported that the Labour Party was making headway, that the Tories were hesitating to make the Common Market their election platform, and that they might like to postpone a decision till after the general election, dragging out the Brussels conversations meantime.[1] It seems that it was some time between the election victory of the Gaullists on 25 November and Macmillan's arrival at Rambouillet on 15 December that de Gaulle almost made up his mind to say No to Britain. His meeting with Macmillan at Rambouillet hardened his resolve, while the Macmillan–Kennedy meeting at Nassau was to prove the last straw.

At Rambouillet de Gaulle delivered himself of many of the unpleasant remarks to Macmillan that he was to repeat at the press conference a month later: that Britain was an insular power; that she would not observe the rules of the Common Market – rules, after all, which she had persistently tried to modify; and that Adenauer was right in proposing that Britain become not a full, but an associate member of the Common Market. More devastating, de Gaulle declared that Britain would act as a 'dividing factor' inside the Common Market, upset its present balance, and reduce 'France's weight'; moreover, the British had inconsiderately committed themselves to not entering the Common Market unless the other members of E.F.T.A. were admitted as well in one capacity or another. In short, once inside the Common Market, Britain would do all she could to isolate France, and to ruin the present cohesion of the Six.

There was something else, even more significant – Kennedy's Grand Design as outlined in his Philadelphia speech of the previous July. De Gaulle had reason to suspect that the United States was urging Britain to enter Europe as a first step towards that vast free-trade association that

1. Kleiman, pp. 117–18. They were, of course, worried about the farmers' rate.

Kennedy had in mind, complete with an increase in dollar investments in Europe and in American agricultural 'dumping'. The 'equal footing' of which Kennedy had spoken could not be taken seriously. Even René Massip, a French writer generally hostile to de Gaulle, admitted:

> Kennedy was in fact asking Europe, whose economic unity was still at an early stage and whose political unity was still a distant target, to associate herself with a solidly-established America. It looked like an alliance between the wolf and the sheep. Britain's entry looked like the first step in a huge American commercial operation. (R. Massip, *De Gaulle et l'Europe*, Paris, 1963, p. 110.)

The same writer claims that de Gaulle urged Macmillan at Rambouillet to 'break once and for all the "special links" between London and Washington'; warned him against playing the role of America's Trojan horse; and hinted at the possibility of a European atomic force based on the British and French national deterrents, and not under American command or control. He also argued that, as the recent Cuban crisis had shown, Europe was no longer the U.S.A.'s Number One defence problem, and that the whole question of European defence needed 're-thinking'.

*

And then came Nassau. Though complicated and, indeed, confused, the story of the Kennedy–Macmillan Polaris deal is too familiar in its general outline to need recalling here. The French took the Nassau deal, and above all, the Nassau communiqué very badly. Although, at his press conference, de Gaulle kept the questions of the Common Market and the Nassau negotiations distinct, his ministers did not hesitate to declare that it was Nassau which had finally sealed the fate of Britain's entry into the Common Market. Couve de Murville declared in Brussels that Britain had now become 'America's satellite', and de Gaulle himself, after it was all over, said disdainfully at an Elysée reception: 'Britain transferred to the United States all the meagre nuclear forces in her possession. She could have handed them over to Europe. Well, that's the choice she made. . . .' He sharply remarked on how very curious it was that she should have haggled for sixteen months over the Common Market, but had settled – with the U.S.A. – her whole problem of defence in forty-eight hours.

The real reason for France's anger at the Nassau agreement lay elsewhere. On the face of it, the offer made to France herself of Polaris missiles looked like a consecration of de Gaulle's long-cherished aim to enter the nuclear club and belong to a Western Three-Power directorate; but having got that far, Kennedy would go no further, and refused to communicate to France the technical data on the submarines and warheads, data which were to be made available to Britain. It was a clear case of discrimination; and de Gaulle disdainfully rejected the Polaris offer. In his sharp criticism of Kennedy, Robert Kleiman says that the late President missed a great opportunity. Had he offered the Polaris missiles not to Britain but to an integrated European nuclear force based on the British and French deterrents, 'Atlantic unity' would have been greatly strengthened, instead of reduced.

The indications are that it was the Nassau communiqué describing the Anglo–American deal – published at once on Macmillan's insistence – that finally provoked de Gaulle's No. Without this *fait accompli*, de Gaulle might have entered into long negotiations with the U.S.A., and while these were in progress, it would have been impossible to slam the Common Market door in Britain's face.[1] But Kennedy was not keen to associate France with the Anglo–American arrangements and *wanted* de Gaulle to refuse the Polaris missiles. What he apparently did not suspect was that the Nassau communiqué would persuade de Gaulle to exclude Britain from the Common Market. Despite all the

1. Kleiman, p. 98.

unpleasantness at Rambouillet only a few days before, Macmillan too had, surprisingly, no suspicion of what was coming. In fact he should have been pleased: what with the farmers' vote and the Commonwealth, de Gaulle had saved the Tories from a huge election defeat.

*

Nobody enjoyed that historical press conference more than de Gaulle himself. Here, once again, he was 'making history'. He loved his role as Champion of European Independence, even though France's five partners in the Common Market had not commissioned him to speak on their behalf; indeed far from it. He knew that the whole world was looking at him; and, once again, he and France were the same old Holy Duality as they had been in 1940, 1944 and 1958.

With the Algerian war out of the way, de Gaulle felt himself in a strong position on that January 1963 afternoon. France, he began by saying, was now 'well-placed to treat world problems no longer in a tentative and hesitant way, but in terms of long-term designs and decisions'. The conditions for this were all the more suitable, since France's economic development, like that of the Common Market as a whole, was proceeding favourably. And then came the attack on Britain:

'The Common Market of the Six [he said] formed a coherent whole; they had many points in common, while Britain was very different. She was scarcely an agricultural country at all; also, unlike the Six, she had "special political and military relations" with the outside. For a long time, far from wanting to enter the Common Market, she had tried to impede its progress. Her way of buying most of her food at low prices overseas and of subsidizing her farmers was incompatible with the Common Market system. Would she accept the Common Market tariff, abandon Commonwealth preference, stop claiming privileges for her agriculture, and cancel her commitments towards the E.F.T.A.? *This was the real question.*'

De Gaulle then showed what his even deeper objections were:

'Following Britain, the other members of the E.F.T.A. will want to join ... But Britain and these countries have peculiarities of their own and, in the end, we shall have to start building up quite a different Common Market – one with perhaps eleven, twelve or even eighteen members, which would have no connexion at all with the Common Market of the Six.'

And then came the parting shot, the Trojan Horse argument:

'The cohesion of all these numerous and very different states would not last long, and what would emerge in the end would be a colossal Atlantic Community *dependent on America and directed by America, which would not take long to absorb this European Community.*'

Some, he added, might like the idea, but France did not. France wanted a strictly European formation.

He then tore to shreds the Nassau agreements. Alliances, he said, no longer had an 'absolute virtue', and in the atomic age, when a country like France was exposed to the danger of destruction, a 'combination of alliance and independence was justifiable'. The Alliance by itself was all very well so long as the U.S.A. had her atomic monopoly: but now, with Russia capable of destroying America, the defence of Europe was no longer America's primary problem. The Cuban crisis had amply demonstrated this. Certain American circles were objecting to France's own nuclear deterrent; these people still felt that there was nothing better than a monopoly in these matters. But small though France's national deterrent was, it could still destroy millions of people, and would make any prospective aggressor think twice. As for the Nassau decisions –

'We have been asked to join this Anglo-American agreement. I wouldn't talk about this agreement if it hadn't already been published.[1] What is proposed is the formation of a so-called multilateral force, to which the British contribute what they have, while the Americans contribute some of their weapons. This force will be intended to defend Europe, and will be under American N.A.T.O. command ... But the bulk of America's nuclear weapons will remain outside the M.L.F., and be under the command of the President.

By way of compensation, as it were, Britain will be able to buy Polaris missiles ... In building the submarines and the missiles, Britain will enjoy the privileged help of the Americans. We – I mention this only incidentally – were never offered such help and, whatever some people may say, we never asked for it.'

In the absence of the submarines and the warheads, France was not interested, de Gaulle said, in buying Polaris missiles; by the time that the French could build submarines by their own devices, the Polarises would be out of date.

As for the idea of contributing France's nuclear deterrent to a foreign-commanded multilateral force, this was contrary to the whole of France's policy. In theory, France, like Britain, could use her own weapons in a great national emergency, but how, in practice, de Gaulle asked, would this be possible 'in the incredible moments of an atomic apocalypse'?

*

Turning then to Germany and to Adenauer's impending visit, de Gaulle came nearer than at any other time to suggesting that Western Germany was master in her own house and that it was for her to decide whether she wanted or needed nuclear weapons of her own. This was to raise something of a storm inside France, as well as abroad, and especially in the Soviet Union. In the Franco–German Treaty signed a few days later, there was a section on defence – dealing with coordination, joint research, etc. – though no specific mention was made of nuclear weapons.

1. Here was a hint that, but for the *fait accompli*, France might still have negotiated a Polaris deal with the U.S.A.

Soon afterwards Couve de Murville recalled that, under the 1954 Paris Agreements, Western Germany had undertaken not to make nuclear weapons, while de Gaulle tried to reassure Ambassador Vinogradov that the United States, with its M.L.F. project, and not France, was the more likely to give the Germans access to nuclear weapons. This was to remain a chronically sore question, and when Mr Gromyko came to Paris in April 1965, he proclaimed the Soviet Union's eagerness to discuss with France and all other countries concerned a German settlement, but only on two conditions – no nuclear weapons for Germany, and no revision of her frontiers.

But the great question was whether, by saying No to Britain, de Gaulle had not 'wrecked Europe'. It was certainly a calculated risk. As he said in private about his five partners in the Common Market: 'They'll scream and kick, and then – then they'll get used to it'. And he added, with apparent inconsistency: 'Anyway, after a disastrous Labour experiment, there'll be a Tory Government under Heath, and *that* one will join the Common Market.' Prophetic?

The other five were, indeed, angry and upset at Brussels on 29 January, when the final blow fell. But, as Kleiman says, in recalling all the British shilly-shallying that had consumed so many months, it was all like the death of a decrepit old uncle; everybody looked very sad, but heaved a sigh of relief.

In reality, however, it soon became apparent that de Gaulle had made one major miscalculation. America's 'Trojan horse' was not so much Britain as Western Germany. If, at his famous press conference, he took it upon himself to speak (at least by implication) in the name of Europe (i.e. the Europe of the Six), it was because he was wholly confident of Adenauer's support. But although, throughout 1963, de Gaulle continued to glory in the economic progress that Europe – and especially France –

was making,[1] he was becoming increasingly uneasy over the way that 'Little Europe' was going. At his press conference on 31 January 1964, he spoke with some bitterness about France's Common Market partners. No doubt, these had, at the end of 1963, more or less surrendered to France's 'ultimatum' on the thorny problem of agricultural prices, and for once de Gaulle refrained from poking fun at the Brussels 'technocrats', since it was they, after all, who had brought about this settlement. But on the kind of 'political union' that de Gaulle had in mind, the other five would not budge. He recalled, with a touch of nostalgia, his friend Adenauer who had not only been favourable to the Fouchet Plan, but had himself proposed the Franco–German treaty of January 1963. Now the others (including Erhard, Adenauer's successor), were being difficult. Some, said de Gaulle, were still determined to put Europe under American domination; others would hear of no Europe other than a 'supra-national' one; others still were against any European

1. Thus, on 19 April 1963, he declared that, under the current Plan, the French people's standard of living would increase by twenty per cent in the next four years – a total increase of thirty per cent since 1960. He foreshadowed a five per cent increase a year in the country's national income during the next four years – which was over-optimistic in the light of what happened in 1964–5.

Then, on 29 July, he declared that French industrial production had trebled since pre-war; agriculture was making spectacular progress; there were two million children in secondary schools, four times more than in 1938; with eight million cars, the number of these had also quadrupled. Speaking on New Year's eve, he said that nearly a million babies had been born in France in 1963; and many of these would live to see a France of 100 million inhabitants! On another occasion he referred (perhaps a little rashly) to the growing prosperity of the French working-class and to the now almost general four-weeks' holidays with pay. This important reform, doubling the two weeks of 1936, had, significantly, been first introduced by the state-owned Renault works. He also spoke of the 'greatly-reduced tensions' among the different categories of Frenchmen.

Union that would not include Britain, or did not form part of the Atlantic Community. De Gaulle, for his part, rejected a Europe that would be 'largely run by foreigners' (i.e. Americans); nor did he think Britain would like it. It is hard to say whether the compliments that he suddenly paid Britain, 'a great nation and a great state', had any immediate purpose, but they marked a retreat from his hard anti-British line of a year before. They also suggested that he was disappointed in the support given him, in the last year, by Western Germany and Italy.

Later, at the end of 1964, these disagreements with France's European partners, and particularly with the Western Germany of Erhard, Schröder, and von Hassel, grew even sharper, especially when the question was revived of creating an M.L.F. of atomic submarines and surface ships with nuclear missiles and mixed crews, all of them virtually under American control. One of de Gaulle's ministers again declared it 'intolerable' that Western Germany should behave as 'America's Foreign Legion' in Europe. Nor did this Atlantic M.L.F. meet with much support from the new British Premier, Harold Wilson, and the scheme was shelved for the time being.

5. *From China to Peru*

De Gaulle's disappointment with France's European partners in the Common Market was given, particularly by *Le Monde*, as a major reason for his entry into new fields of 'anti-American' activity during 1964. In the course of that year he recognized Communist China, without consulting the United States, or even Germany, despite the relevant clause in the Franco–German Treaty of 1963. He then publicly advocated the neutralization of South-East Asia and suggested that the Americans had no business to be in Vietnam. In April he went on a short visit to Mexico and, in

DE GAULLE

the autumn, on a much longer tour of all the ten South
American republics, visiting even remote places like Bolivia
and Paraguay.

The reception he was given was a somewhat mixed one;
the 'Latin family' allusions did not go down equally well
everywhere, and de Gaulle (though his speeches were
studiously free of anti-American attacks) seemed to appeal
most of all to certain 'anti-Yankee' factions, such as the
Peronist elements in the Argentine. His visit, without
producing any immediate and tangible results, was intended
as a sort of psychological operation, a reminder to the
South American countries that potentially, at any rate, they
had friends in Europe (though de Gaulle had, of course, not
been commissioned by 'Europe' to go on his journey) who
would like to give Latin America economic help – without
political strings. All this did not mean very much in practical
terms. De Gaulle himself realized, before very long, that he
was dealing with a vast continent ruled in the main by
more-or-less disreputable cliques, and with an immense
undernourished urban and rural sub-proletariat for whom
very little was being done. In a speech during his visit to
Chile he also made the melancholy reflection that what had
struck him most in South America was the extraordinary
lack of contact, let alone solidarity, among the ten states,
and he mentioned Western Europe as an example of the
kind of cooperation that South America should adopt. Many
observers – both French and South American – finally dismissed the whole de Gaulle venture as a 'series of banquets
and speeches and nothing else'. French businessmen, who
shortly afterwards visited South America to explore the
possibilities of investing capital and expanding trade, found
the prospects both risky and disappointing.[1] Politically, de
Gaulle himself remarked with a touch of sarcasm that it was
hard to make out what exactly each of these countries

1. *Le Monde*, 12 and 13 December 1964.

needed, and that the whole continent was a rather incoherent mosaic of amiable dictatorships and democratic police states. He added that he had the impression of having seen only the 'best people'; that, here and there, he had been allowed to see some students, but that no contact had been encouraged between him and the 'hungry masses' – a trick, by the way, which was to have a curious parallel during Prime Minister Pompidou's visit to India some months later. In the end, de Gaulle tried to console himself with the thought that, some day, South America would turn to Europe, and that he would then be remembered as the Pioneer of a new Latin American epoch.

*

More important as an 'anti-American' move was France's recognition of Communist China on 27 January 1964. De Gaulle devoted to this a large part of his press conference four days later.

Not so long before, he had spoken of 'the countless, wretched yellow multitudes of China' which would, before very long, represent a fearful problem for Russia. He attached little importance to the ideological quarrels between Moscow and Peking, but, characteristically, dwelt on the *national* interests of both nations. Communism – or any other ideology for that matter – he refused to take seriously. What was communism? he asked. There had been Lenin communism, and Trotsky communism, and Stalin, Beria, Malenkov, Khrushchev, Tito and Mao-Tse Tung communism. He suggested that all this was a lot of froth. Below all these ideologies there were the *nations*, and this applied to both China and Russia.[1] He took up this subject again on 31 January 1964. While Russia was anxious to 'conserve and maintain' what she had, he said, China needed to 'grow, expand and take'. Apart from this renewed reference to

1. Press conference, 29 July 1963.

China's potential aggressiveness, de Gaulle's tone in speaking of China was now, however, entirely different from what it had been during previous years. He paid the warmest tributes to the great Chinese people, with their 'deep and ancient civilization', their genius, patience and industriousness; he recalled all that China had suffered in the past at the hands of 'Europeans, Americans and Japanese'; and, a little surprisingly, suddenly revealed that 'deep down, there is great mutual respect and sympathy between China and France'.

Then came his main point. The recognition of China was essential if any peace settlement was to be reached in South-East Asia and particularly in Vietnam, where the Americans were continuing a senseless and cruel war.

'No war, no peace are conceivable in Asia without China having her say. In her absence it is inconceivable that an agreement can be reached on the neutralization of the states of South-East Asia, countries for which France feels a special and cordial solicitude.'

Considering the 'dirty war' that France had waged for eight years against Vietnam so recently, this could perhaps have been better put. But that did not worry de Gaulle. He had now made up his mind to be the world's Number One Peacemaker. Foreseeing that America's war in Vietnam might well take on very dangerous dimensions before long, he advocated a treaty under which the countries of South-East Asia would be neutralized under international guarantees, with the guarantors including China and the United States.[1] He recalled that China's presence had been absolutely

1. What he advocated was the establishment of neutralist régimes in all these countries; although he left this point vague, it was learned a few days later that while he advocated a neutralist régime in South Vietnam, he was not proposing either to unify South and North Vietnam, or to liquidate in any way Ho Chi Minh's 'Democratic Republic' in North Vietnam and replace it by a different régime.

essential in reaching the Geneva settlement on Vietnam in 1954; and China's role as a 'peace factor' could be even more effective if she established normal diplomatic relations with France (and, eventually, with other countries), so that 'France could listen to China and make herself heard by China'.

De Gaulle's statement was given a rather mixed reception in France. *Le Monde* remarked that China had an excellent case for demanding the withdrawal of foreign troops from Vietnam, the strict application of the 1954 agreement and so the unification of Vietnam. Why had de Gaulle been so vague on this point? Would this seem a solution *too* favourable to the Chinese and arouse excessive anger in the United States? *Figaro* commented that de Gaulle's grand design was all very well; but would not the neutralization of South-East Asia benefit China, since, as de Gaulle had admitted, she was going to 'grow, expand and take' anyway? Would the neutralization of South-East Asia automatically slow down this 'expansion' process? Others, however, thought there was much to be said for de Gaulle's plan; China's expansionist ambitions were, after all, only hypothetical, while American military activity in Vietnam constituted an immediate threat to world peace.

In the United States itself, the comments were mainly hostile. True, C. L. Sulzberger in the *New York Times* thought that, rather than go on with its absurd and hopeless war, the U.S. Government might do well to take de Gaulle's advice. But writers reflecting the White House view declared that America was fighting 'world communism' in Vietnam, that de Gaulle's realism was pure moonshine, and that, anyway, France 'counted in South-East Asia for just about as much as did Luxembourg'.[1]

When, by the end of 1964, the American war in South Vietnam began to spread to the North and threatened to

1. *Le Monde*, 2 February 1964.

extend to China, de Gaulle absolutely dissociated himself from it, urged that a peace conference be held 'without any preliminary conditions', and brought about something that was soon to be called the 'Paris–Moscow axis' – the Russians being at least as anxious as France to stop the rot in South-East Asia. Couve de Murville, who was sent to Washington to plead with the U.S. Government, was given an extremely frigid reception. The French argument that the Vietnamese were a strongly nationalist people, for whom independence mattered much more than communism, and that they certainly wanted to be independent of China, was rejected by Washington with disdain. And so the tragedy of Vietnam continued. Once the whole fury of the American and 'South Vietnamese' bombers had been unleashed over North Vietnam, a friend who saw de Gaulle found him in an extremely gloomy mood. 'The most difficult war in the world to wage,' he said, '*c'est la guerre contre la bêtise.*'

6. De Gaulle Likes Africans – The Under-developed Countries

De Gaulle makes a point of liking Africans. It is one of the trump cards of his foreign policy and he thinks it psychologically of the greatest importance; it suggests that if Germany and the United States are 'racialist', de Gaulle's France is not. He is very proud of the fact that a very large part of Africa is *francophone*, or French-speaking.[1] Ever since 1960, when practically all the former French colonies became independent (after the breakdown of the 1958 'Community' experiment), de Gaulle has taken a special pleasure in receiving at Paris with great pomp the presidents of the various new African states. Public buildings have been, on such occasions, decorated with the unfamiliar new flags of Dahomey, or Upper Volta, or Congo (Brazzaville). Some of

1. It may be argued that Britain's record in Africa and Asia is as good as, or better than, France's; but she still continues minor wars; and then there is South Africa!

these presidents have been on the disreputable side, like the Abbé Fulbert Youlou of Congo (Brazzaville), a clerical gentleman with a most unclerical way of life, or President Maga of Dahomey, equally famous for his riotous living. But both these were overthrown in the summer of 1963, one by a popular rising, the other by a military junta; and when they appealed to de Gaulle for French armed intervention, he did not respond.[1] Franco-African relations have remained generally good. When Sékou Touré's Guinea abandoned the Community under the 1958 referendum, de Gaulle cut off all French assistance in retaliation, and Guinea was forced to seek financial and technical aid from the Soviet Union. But the experiment proved disappointing and, in May 1963, de Gaulle agreed to resume technical and cultural aid to Guinea, complete with a grant of various credit facilities. On the other hand, he has kept strictly outside the mess in the Congo, except for one inconclusive visit that he received from Tshombe at the end of 1964.

De Gaulle has also done his best to maintain good relations with Morocco, Tunisia and the new State of Algeria. Hassan II of Morocco came on an official visit to Paris in June 1963 and had long talks with de Gaulle on Morocco's relations with the Common Market, the compensation payable to the owners of French lands 'recuperated' by the Moroccan state, French financial aid to Morocco, (amounting to $45 million that year), and much else. Agreements were later concluded concerning the respective contributions to the upkeep of the 5,000 French technicians and 8,000 French teachers in Morocco, and Hassan II stressed that there were now 155,000 Frenchmen in Morocco – more than were left in Algeria.

1. The only time when French paratroopers intervened was in Gabon in February 1964. Here they reinstated President Leon Mba who had been overthrown by a military junta the day before. De Gaulle's African admirers have tended to forget or minimize this episode.

During that first year following the end of the Algerian war, relations also improved with Tunisia; besides technical and financial aid and various agrarian measures, the running sore of the Bizerta naval base (where there had been heavy bloodshed only two years before) was finally healed. As part of his decolonization policy, de Gaulle agreed to evacuation.

Much more socialist than her two neighbours was the new Algeria, with its sweeping nationalization and expropriation measures; but even in its negotiations with Algeria, the French government showed striking patience and restraint – which produced from Fidel Castro the remark to Ben Bella: 'How lucky you are! If only *we* had a de Gaulle in the United States!'

A leading French authority, Alfred Grosser, argues that there are several reasons for helping Algeria: there is France's economic interest in the oil and gas of the Sahara, and her military interest in using the Sahara for nuclear tests; there is the need to maintain France's 'cultural presence' in Africa; and there is a more specific psychological reason.

I am convinced that, in the eyes of de Gaulle ... Algeria is invaluable as an example. Even if Ben Bella had not visited him in March 1964 ... and even if the expropriation of French property had gone much further, the aid would still have continued, if only to show the United States how to prevent a country from going over to the communist east ... It is no use trying to force a country *not* to go socialist. This was one way of showing the U.S.A. what they should have done about Cuba if they did not want Castro to go communist.[1]

De Gaulle's aid to under-developed countries, which goes under the euphemistic name of 'cooperation', has, of course, been severely criticized in France. The shortage of new houses and schools, the backward state of Brittany have

1. A. Grosser, *La politique extérieure de la V-e République*, Paris, 1965 p. 65.

all been blamed on this 'cooperation'. The most extreme exponent of this view is M. Raymond Cartier, of *Paris-Match*. French aid to the under-developed countries, chiefly to Africa, amounted in 1963 to 7 milliard francs (i.e. $1,400 million), or 2.5 per cent of France's national income, as against a contribution of 1 per cent by Britain, 1.2 per cent by Germany, 1 per cent by the United States, and 0.5 per cent by the U.S.S.R. Even a government committee set up in 1963 under M. J.-M. Jeanneney concluded that France was spending too much on Africa – or rather, that she was often spending the money in the wrong way; not enough went into long-term investments, and too much went into current expenditure. A high proportion of the Algerian budget expenditure, for instance, comes out of the French taxpayer's pocket. Other critics have compared the 'irresponsible' French aid with the more businesslike aid by Western Germany to under-developed countries – profitable loans and investments, etc. By 'irresponsible' investments they mean the thousands of French technicians and, above all, teachers whose 'presence' in these countries is meant to add to the 'radiance' of France.[1]

The Jeanneney Report claims that, in strictly economic terms, such investments are unsound; while a much sharper critic, M. Edouard Bonnefous[2] argues against the bilateral (not to say unilateral) nature of this aid, and argues in favour of a multilateral kind, in which the other members of the Common Market could contribute a fair share, and which would, moreover, be more 'economically viable'.

1. Apologists for this expenditure have also argued that a substantial part of the money spent on the underdeveloped countries ultimately comes back to France, since these teachers and technicians are well-paid, and usually hold higher posts than they would at home. Thus, I know a French secondary school teacher who earned in France about £1,000 a year, but who, as head of a technical college in independent Algeria, is now earning three times as much.

2. *Les milliards qui s'envolent*, Paris, 1963.

But to replace the bilateral agreements by multilateral ones is precisely what is incompatible with French 'radiance' in Africa and other countries. As one of de Gaulle's ministers, M. Foyer, put it:

'Our policy is, all the same, one of the means that France still has of maintaining her radiance in these countries. Secondly, we have, all the same, a certain responsibility before History.'

De Gaulle's critics have remarked that these two curious '*all the sames*' are as good as an admission that the aid given to Algeria and other African countries is economically unsound, but that, in de Gaulle's view, this is a secondary consideration. What is much more important in the long run is that France should be the best-loved Western country in the 'Third World'. It seems highly significant that, shortly before the abortive conference of Afro–Asian countries at Algiers in June 1965, the question should have arisen of inviting only three non-Afro–Asian guests of honour to the meeting: Castro, Tito and – de Gaulle.

De Gaulle's critics attribute, of course, his peculiar form of 'cooperation' (which has come to replace the former 'domination') to narrow nationalist motives. In a sense, this may be true; but de Gaulle's own answer, as given in his talks with Andrei Gromyko, the Soviet Foreign Minister, in April 1965, was simply this:

'Yes, we are helping these countries, and they like France as a result. In their view the contrast between us and the United States has become immense: while we are helping them, the Americans are using all their brilliant new technological inventions to exterminate in the most horrible ways thousands of these poor long-suffering Vietnamese, who merely want to be left alone. And look what they are doing at San Domingo ... And I'm afraid this isn't the end yet. *L'appetit vient en mangeant.*'

He thought that the early use of Cuba as another testing ground for all these new weapons was not to be ruled out . . . Despite the widespread impact of *cartiérisme* in France, the feeling that France is so much 'better' – in the highest moral sense – than America in the eyes of the world, and especially of the Third World, is, indeed, more widespread still. No doubt this 'cooperation' has its weaknesses: thus Algeria continues to be in a bad economic mess, with its over-population and its mass-unemployment, its administrative corruption and inefficiency; the idealization by French liberals of Algeria's 'freedom-fighters' while the war was on, has proved largely unjustified. It has been observed that Algeria's 'under-development' has been going from bad to worse since she acquired independence. Perhaps such a judgement is premature; the war ended only three years ago; owing to the O.A.S. terrorists practically all the French left. and the new Algeria had, in many ways, to start from scratch. The economic revival of Algeria will be a very long process, and may, in the end even fail; but, for the present, France's 'cooperation' there, as in other African countries, has been of great political value to France. Since the ruthless American intervention of April 1965 in the Dominican Republic, more and more Latin Americans, too, have been thinking of de Gaulle with particular warmth. Psychologically, this also counts.

7. The Bomb

One of the most controversial aspects of de Gaulle's 'policy of independence' has been the French national nuclear deterrent. In a rash moment de Gaulle once said that 'no country without an atom bomb could consider itself properly independent'. The phrase was particularly unfortunate, in view of the reactions it produced in Western Germany. He refrained from repeating it, and even got, on one occasion, his foreign minister to recall that Western Germany had undertaken, in 1954, not to make nuclear armaments.

The first French atom bomb was exploded in the Sahara in 1960, and there have been several more exploded in the same place since; later, plans were also drawn up for carrying out nuclear tests in the Pacific. This, by the way, was perhaps one reason for France's recognition of China; it was important not to arouse Chinese opposition. France and China were, indeed, about the only countries which did not sign the test-ban treaty of 1963, and the French argument was that the U.S.A., the Soviet Union and Britain had, for the time being, done all the testing they needed, while France's nuclear deterrent was still at a very early stage of development. If there was to be general disarmament, it would be a very different matter, de Gaulle said, but the test-ban treaty by itself did not greatly reduce the danger of an atomic war. In the circumstances, de Gaulle continued to look upon his *force de frappe* as absolutely essential to France's independence and her status as a great power. He never stopped repeating that American nuclear power would not necessarily come to the rescue of Europe if, at the same time, the United States was threatened with destruction.

The argument for and against the *force de frappe* has now gone on for years. Its critics have called it not only economically ruinous, but ineffective; de Gaulle's reply has always been that it was 'much better than nothing', for even with a relatively small nuclear force France could kill 'millions of people' if she were ever attacked, and this would make any potential aggressor think twice. The answer to this is that it is still uncertain whether, if it came to the point, France could ever 'deliver' her bombs, or even missiles; and even if she did, whether she would not be infinitely more vulnerable than any of the territorial 'giants'. Besides, who would launch an all-out nuclear attack on France – the U.S.A., the U.S.S.R.? And if France became involved in a nuclear war with one of these 'giants', she wouldn't stand a chance, anyway.

My private guess (though this has *never* been mentioned) is that, at the back of his mind, and with an eye on past history, de Gaulle has never entirely ruled out the possibility of a German military revival, complete with the development of a *German* nuclear force some day, and perhaps in the not very distant future. That being so, de Gaulle must have thought it essential for France to be several years ahead of Germany. Adenauer would not last long; there might, in certain circumstances, be a new deal between Russia and Germany, or a new flare-up of the *furor teutonicus*. All kinds of as yet scarcely imaginable situations might develop in Europe, and France must not be caught napping, as she had been in both 1914 and 1939. The revival of the 'Charlemagne Empire' (the Franco–German 'directorate') might work, and it was worth trying out – as de Gaulle, indeed, did in 1962; but even then he could not be absolutely certain of anything.

That de Gaulle was determined not to abandon his nuclear deterrent on any account and wanted to make it as difficult as possible for any successor to do so, may be seen from his firm resolution to get Parliament, in December 1964, to approve an enormous armaments programme covering the six years between 1965 and 1970. The cost of the nuclear programme proper was put at nearly 55 billion francs (over $10 billion), while – as M. Messmer, the Minister of the Army, announced – the total military expenditure during the period would amount to about 150 billion francs ($30 billion). Needless to say, all these figures were challenged by the government's critics, who claimed that these were merely minimum figures, and that the total military expenditure would be far greater with all the planned new missiles, launching sites, extension of the existing isotope-separation plants, the building of new nuclear planes, ships, submarines, etc.

The plan also provided that the land forces would be equipped in such a way that, as M. Messmer said, 'they would no longer be, as in 1914, an army of millions of men lacking heavy artillery, or, as in 1940, one without planes or tanks'. It would, in short, he said, be a relatively small, but admirably equipped army. Where had one heard this before? Of course, it was once again de Gaulle's old concept of the *armée de métier*, brought up to date in the nuclear age ...

The military programme was passed by the National Assembly, despite angry protests from the Opposition and much unfavourable comment from the press. And yet – it would perhaps be rash to claim that the bulk of French opinion was against the *force de frappe*. Both the desire for 'independence' and anti-Americanism are very deep-seated in France; and, by the end of 1964, it could not even reasonably be said that Germany would be a trustworthy friend for all time.

8. *De Gaulle Turns to Russia*

With France having, shortly before, converted several hundred million dollars into gold, in what was described as 'the biggest raid on Fort Knox in human memory', foreign observers waited eagerly for de Gaulle's press conference of 4 February 1965. It was a very strange performance. De Gaulle had never been keen on what he used to call *l'intendance*, or the 'commissariat' – social, financial and economic problems. But now, like a professor of economics, he suddenly produced a long lecture on a number of intricate financial matters, including a reasoned plea for the abolition of the Gold Exchange Standard and a return to the classical gold standard in international relations. This lecture had been prepared for him, it was rumoured, by M. Jacques Rueff, one of his chief financial experts, but he himself talked naturally for a whole hour, without looking at any notes, and with an ease that suggested that he had lectured on economics all his life. His memory was as stupendous as ever. His speech was a powerful assault on the U.S. dollar, which he castigated as an inflated currency, worth far more outside the United States than inside, so that there followed 'a growing propensity to invest abroad which, in many countries, amounts to no less than a sort of expropriation of such and such enterprises'. He declared the system – from which France, too, was suffering – unhealthy, and asked what would happen if the countries holding dollars suddenly all decided to convert them into gold. The implications of this were clear ; yet, soon afterwards, de Gaulle had doubts about these – and other – Rueff ideas. 'Isn't he a bit outmoded?' he asked.

In the second part of his press conference he proposed a return to the original U.N. Charter. The prerogatives of the Security Council, he argued, had been weakened by the General Assembly which, encouraged by the United States and two former Secretary-Generals, had taken upon itself 'illegal' decisions, such as the armed intervention in the Congo. He himself proposed that a conference be held at Geneva by the 'Big Five' – Washington, Moscow, Peking, London, and Paris – which would try to 'restore the legality' of the organization.

But this proposal, complete with the inclusion of 'Peking' among the 'Big Five', was only a minor pinprick, compared with what was to follow. Clearly implying that the United States had no business to meddle in the affairs of Europe, de Gaulle now declared that *the German problem was, in the highest degree, the European problem.*

How things had changed since that triumphal visit to Germany in October 1962! The bygones were no longer bygones. Germany, planted right there, in the centre of Europe, was, de Gaulle now said, a chronically disturbing factor in the life of Europe. And, as long as Germany remained uncertain of her future, she would continue to be in a state of anguish, sometimes 'in a state of fury'. He recalled Germany's guilt for the First World War, and then the Third Reich's 'immense enterprise of domination', which had caused the death of forty million people, including ten million who had been 'systematically exterminated'.[1] No doubt the smashing of the Third Reich had put an end to the ordeal, and Adenauer had greatly reassured many in the West. The present situation, which had lasted for twenty years, could continue for a long time to come, but it could not last for ever. There could be no real peace, still less a fruitful cooperation between East and West, so long as the present anomalies continued.

'It is for the European peoples themselves to settle the future of Germany. Let them agree to examine jointly, and then to settle in common and to guarantee together the solution of a problem which is essentially that of their continent. In this way only can the balance, peace and cooperation be restored from one end of the continent to the other.'

This, said de Gaulle, was a huge enterprise. It was important that Russia should evolve in such a way that she should not see her own future and that of other countries based on totalitarian coercion. Her present satellites should play their own role in the new Europe. It was essential that not only the other European countries of both East and West, but Germany herself should recognize a settlement which would necessarily also cover the questions of German armaments and Germany's frontiers.

'Europe, the mother of modern civilization, must establish herself all the way from the Atlantic to the Urals, and live in a state of harmony and cooperation with a view to developing her

1. There had been nothing like that in his 1962 speeches in Germany!

immense resources, and so as to play, together with her daughter, America, her worthy role in relation to the two billion people who so badly need her help.'

Germany, he added, could play a splendid role in this Europe, but only Europe herself, he repeated, could bring about such a settlement.

In conclusion, he made a friendly, but inconclusive reference to Britain and to Harold Wilson, whom he had met while in London for the funeral of 'the great Churchill'. Only a channel separated Britain from Europe, he remarked, and the Channel Tunnel might bring her even nearer.

What did this cry of 'Europe for the Europeans' mean?

A French *rapprochement* with Russia was already clearly implied in what he said. He had used the phrase 'from the Atlantic to the Urals' on many occasions before: but at the time of the R.P.F. he had used it in a threatening, 'roll-back' tone; and when he used it later, in 1959 or 1960, I remember Ambassador Vinogradov remarking to me: 'I don't know to this day what the phrase means.'

It was now beginning to mean something more precise, it seemed. There had, in 1964, been a distinct *rapprochement* between France and Eastern Europe. Not only had an important trade agreement been signed between France and the Soviet Union, but the Soviet satellites (or former satellites) had been positively queueing up in Paris to sign cultural and trade agreements – Poland, Hungary, Czechoslovakia, Yugoslavia, Bulgaria, Rumania. The Rumanians, in particular, had stressed their economic and even political independence from the Soviet Union. De Gaulle had gained the impression that the old Stalinist 'monolithic' bloc was becoming a very loose-knit affair, but that the common fear of Germany was still holding it together. Threatened by China – at least in the long run – Russia was, in de Gaulle's view, inevitably drifting towards Europe, and becoming more and more 'European' in her outlook. Disappointed in

Germany, hostile to the United States, de Gaulle now revived, in a different form, and in a new context, the old
concept, so dear to him in his youth, and so dear to him
even in 1944, of France and Russia cooperating as *the* two
continental powers which stood staunchly for peace.

What also created a new bond between France and Russia
was their uncompromising opposition to American policy
in the Far East, and particularly America's war against
Vietnam. Russia and France were the two great neutrals in
this war, who dreaded the fighting and its extension, and
would do what they could to stop it.

As for the proposal for a 'purely European' settlement of
the German problem, how realistic was it? Only time would
show. For the time being it was, above all, an appeal to the
world – and to Germany – not to be impatient. The 'European' settlement of the German problem would take a long
time, and it was no use forcing the issue. After all, the
abnormal situation had already lasted for twenty years,
without producing a war; it might continue for some time
yet. Compromises could perhaps be reached through long
and patient work – compromises on the unification of Germany, on her frontiers and armaments. At the back of de
Gaulle's mind was the idea that America was perhaps withdrawing from Europe, was more interested in the Far East
and in enforcing her hegemony over Latin America. Both
these tendencies were highly regrettable, but if America lost
interest in Europe, a purely 'European settlement of Europe'
might prove feasible, especially with Russia, scared of
China, willing to pay a price for greater security in the West.
Would Russia abandon Eastern Germany in certain conditions? Would Poland agree to a minor frontier revision?
De Gaulle had accepted the Oder–Neisse frontier; but could
not this and much else be reconsidered in a general 'European' settlement?

It all seemed very remote, and de Gaulle admitted it. But

he made this speech for the 'historical record', as it were. He felt that some day, perhaps after his death, Russians and Germans and other European powers might take these de Gaulle proposals as a basis for discussion.

The immediate reactions were, however, unfavourable – sceptical in France, hostile in America, highly distrustful in Germany. Despite the unwelcome remarks he had made about her 'totalitarianism', Russia alone reacted favourably. For the numerous reasons already mentioned, the stage was now clearly set for a Franco–Soviet *rapprochement*. De Gaulle's attitude to the Third World, and his role as Number One Decolonizer had made him look, in Russian eyes, very different from the other leaders of the capitalist world. Above all, he had declared himself an all-out opponent of 'American imperialism'. Even if the U.S.A. was 'Europe's daughter', she had fallen from virtue, and was unworthy to sit in the council of the European family! And Britain? De Gaulle made a minor unsolicited overture to Britain, suggesting that she might become part of Europe yet. But meantime,

> Where has Harold Wilson gone?
> Creeping to the Pentagon!

When somebody told de Gaulle about this ditty, he shook his head and said: '*C'est malheureux*. But that's also how it was during the War. At least they had an excuse then. ...'

*

In April Andrei Gromyko, the Soviet Foreign Minister, came to Paris, soon after the appointment of a very big shot in Moscow, Mr V. Zorin, as Ambassador to Paris – perhaps the most important diplomatic appointment since that of Litvinov to Washington during the War. The French and Russians at least implicitly joined in condemning America's war in Vietnam, spoke of Franco–Soviet relations, and cautiously approached a variety of German problems; the French, without being prepared to recognize the G.D.R., nevertheless regarded it (in Gromyko's words) as 'a State that existed'. Moreover, the talks were no more than a preliminary to more important conversations that were expected to take place later in the year. There were rumours of a visit by de Gaulle to Moscow, and even of a possible revival of the Franco–Soviet Mutual Assistance Pact of 1944 that the Russians had denounced in 1954 after France had agreed to the rearmament of Western Germany. At least the Russians seemed to hope that this might be de Gaulle's next step. But would it be?

*

In his broadcast, only a few days before the Gromyko visit, de Gaulle put all the stress on the independence of France. He no longer spoke of 'greatness'; the days had gone when France was a 'colossus' in terms of population and military and economic power. But she had to remain independent. Within the Atlantic alliance, she must still remain independent of the United States; she must be European, but not as part of an integrated Europe dominated by the United States. Independence, he said, meant that there must be no hegemony, no foreign intervention by any state in the affairs of another state, no (American) veto prohibiting the establishment of peaceful relations with other countries. France, therefore, strongly disapproved of the war in Asia, a war that was spreading further every day; she also sympathized with the movements of national and human liberation in Latin America. He then spoke of Africa, China, and of those East European countries with which old friendships were being restored. There was now a French policy, and this policy was made in Paris – (i.e. not in Washington).

In economic matters, too, international cooperation was essential, but it was important to avoid such cooperation with countries whose sheer weight would crush France; in the main, France's economy must remain under French direction and administration.

The Yalta epoch, which had set up the two rival hegemonies, was nearing its end; a new balance of power in the world was necessary, and France, with her hands now untied, was in the best position to bring it about.

The speech, which was described as de Gaulle's 'first election broadcast' for the coming presidential contest, met with a good deal of press criticism. Some newspapers deplored his undisguised hostility to the U.S.A.; others thought that de Gaulle, obsessed with his grandiose plan of a Europe 'between the Atlantic and the Urals', was flattering the Russians and annoying many of France's European partners, above all Germany. Still others thought that, with its echoes of Maurras's *La France seule*, the speech was intended to flatter the most primitive French nationalism and anti-Americanism. But above all, perhaps, the speech suggested that de Gaulle was now proclaiming France to be the real leader of the Third World, with himself the patron saint of the oppressed and underdeveloped countries. Hence his 'strong disapproval' of the war in Vietnam. Yet even many of de Gaulle's critics (like Claude Bourdet) admitted that President Johnson and the Pentagon were making de Gaulle's task 'appallingly easy'. He could never have spoken like this while the 'co-existence telephone' was still working between Moscow and Washington ... It was only now that the whole magnitude of the Dallas tragedy in November 1963 was becoming apparent. De Gaulle was making what political capital he could out of the infernal mess into which a Goldwaterized American administration now seemed prepared to plunge the world ...

At the same time, one could not help wondering whether the *La France seule* theme running through this strange broadcast, with its message of '*mon verre n'est pas grand mais je bois dans mon verre'*, did not point to a certain feeling of frustration on de Gaulle's part. What, apart from the friendship of the underdeveloped countries and a (still only tentative) *rapprochement* with Russia, had he achieved in his foreign policy since 1962? The German 'card' had not won; the Common Market partners were disgruntled at times; the new friendship with Wilson's Britain did not mean much.

Was he waiting (as he had already indicated in 1963) for a European-minded Tory Government under Edward Heath, the British leader most likely to lead Britain into the Common Market, and, moreover, on a non-supranational basis, which was particularly acceptable to France?

CHAPTER 11

THAT MAN DE GAULLE

READERS will, I hope, have acquired a clear idea of de Gaulle during the earlier stages of his career. He was proud; he believed in his star; but he was, more often than not, exasperated. One can well imagine how exasperated he was with the Pétains and Weygands and Léon Blums when they refused to listen to reason. When I first met him at London in July 1940, he was already fully conscious of what he was doing; but I also found him exasperated, not only with all those politicians of the Third Republic and the French proconsuls in North Africa who would have nothing to do with him, but also with the British who were not yet, in his view, taking him nearly seriously enough. The whole Free French epic was a continuous battle that he had to wage against opposing forces – against Vichy; against 'British intrigue'; above all, against the Americans and their French 'stooges' – the Darlans, Peyroutons and Girauds.

No doubt he had his happy moments; he wept with joy when he heard of Bir Hakeim, the first major battle fought by the Free French against Germans; he was elated at the defeat of that ludicrous Giraud; he gloried at his Paris apotheosis on 26 August 1944. But these rare moments of pure happiness were followed by long periods of anger and exasperation – over the Allies' reluctance to equip a large French army; over Stalin's remark, 'The Yugoslavs have more troops than the French'; over more British intrigues against France in the Middle East; and then, in 1946, over those detested parliamentary parties which would not accept his terms. If he loved France with a kind of mystical love, he did not love the French, or at least not very many among them. Or it may perhaps be truer to say that he loved the French *people* as a whole, but not as individuals. He believed in a kind of communion between the people and himself; he loved large and friendly crowds, and gloried in mixing with them and shaking hands with all the Duponts and Durands – even at the risk of being assassinated. He was overwhelmingly happy when eighty or ninety per cent voted in the referendums 'for de Gaulle'. And yet, here too, there was a kind of love-contempt (rather than love-hate) attitude to the 'crowds'; at times he referred to them as *cette canaille*, that rabble. They were fickle and unreliable: they had taken de Gaulle to their heart in August 1944; but, a few months before, they had been almost as enthusiastic about Pétain.

So he had much contempt for his fellow-humans and especially for his fellow-Frenchmen; indeed, during the unfortunate R.P.F. experiment, his contempt developed into actual hatred – hatred, above all, for the communists. His manner became harsher than ever before and he came closer to becoming a would-be totalitarian dictator than either before or later. His technique in building up, during those R.P.F. years, a Gaullist élite was something strangely familiar to anyone who remembered the rise of Hitler. It took him a few years to realize that France was not prepared to accept this kind of Gaullist state, with all its totalitarian trimmings.

He has not yet told us when exactly he realized that the R.P.F. experiment was built on a great psychological mis-understanding of the French people. But he certainly realized it, and drew many correct conclusions from his failure during those years he spent in the wilderness before returning to power in 1958. For by then he was a changed man – with none of the old harshness, and with none of that perhaps artificial hatred he had developed, especially for the communists, during the R.P.F. days.

What Frenchmen did he like then, and does he like now?

De Gaulle is least of all the back-slapping type; the back-slappers were only too numerous under both the Third and the Fourth Republic. Besides, as he said long ago, in *Le fil de l'épée*, a leader of men 'has to keep his distances'. And this applies even to his closest collaborators. He dominates them all with his own authority and personality. Even his communist ministers, back in 1945–6, admitted that they were overawed by him and found it difficult to argue with him. Small wonder, certainly, that the cartoonists should, more recently, have drawn pictures of Prime Minister Debré dressed up as a valet with a striped vest and a feather duster.

But who and what are 'Gaullists'? De Gaulle himself once said that 'everybody in France had been, was, or would be, a Gaullist'. There are – or were – the 'unconditional' Gaullists of the R.P.F. days; these were mostly the first-generation Gaullists, those associated with the Free French Forces or the Free French intelligence services, and some – much fewer – from the Home Resistance. Many of these – men like Soustelle, Bénouville, Philippe Barrès – have since become enemies of de Gaulle for having 'betrayed' French Algeria; but the bulk of the R.P.F. *cadres* are still prominent in de Gaulle's government machine today. Now, however, there is a second generation of Gaullists who fall, as it were, into two categories: young people, mostly of the technical élite, who believe in the peculiar virtues of the Fifth Republic, as well as seeing great opportunities for themselves in the Gaullist U.N.R.; and a galaxy of *grands commis*, who were high officials under the Fourth (and even the Third) Republic, and who are happy to place their administrative and diplomatic gifts at the disposal of General de Gaulle. Perhaps the most typical representative of this last class is M. Louis Joxe, who was Secretary-General of the French Foreign Office and Ambassador to Moscow under the Fourth Republic, and has become even more famous and

even more valuable to the State under the Fifth, first as
Minister of Education and then as the Minister of State
who negotiated the Evian agreements on Algeria. For a man
like Joxe – a great servant of the state in the real sense – de
Gaulle has the greatest regard and respect, and Joxe is one
to whose opinions he will listen very carefully. Joxe, indeed,
is one of the few men to whom de Gaulle seldom, if ever,
talks in that ironically-patronizing tone which he uses with
most of his ministers, even Prime Minister Pompidou.

There are also a few people for whom de Gaulle has a
genuine personal affection; one of them is André Malraux.
Malraux strikes many as eccentric almost to the point of
absurdity; and yet de Gaulle remembers his war and
resistance record, admires him as a writer (though Malraux
stopped writing long ago), enjoys (surprisingly) his almost
mystical harangues on de Gaulle's republicanism, and likes
the enthusiasm with which his Minister of Culture insists on
scrubbing Paris clean and with which he sends the Mona Lisa
to the U.S.A. – if only to remind those savages that even all
the oil of Texas couldn't buy *this* one.

And yet, is there a Gaullist Party? There is, of course, the
U.N.R., a party calling itself unconditionally Gaullist. But
it is not a 'structuralized' party. One of the strangest passages in François Mauriac's recent book on de Gaulle is a
lament on de Gaulle's fundamental failure to *change* France.
He has changed her institutions; he has changed her foreign
policy; but he has *not* changed the French people. By this he
means, in fact, that de Gaulle has been too tolerant, too
liberal, too *laissez-faire* since his return to power in 1958;
and Mauriac, curiously, seems to regret that the kind of
national discipline and regimentation implied in the R.P.F.
experiment should never have been taken up again. Without
defending Vichy, he still says that the *chantiers de la jeunesse*
– a sort of glorified religious boy scout movement – was a
very good thing; under that system, young people were

taught the highest form of Christian morality. De Gaulle might well be (and probably is) a devout Catholic, but he has never given a religious tone to his régime; and Mauriac wrings his hands at the thought that, under the seemingly austere Fifth Republic, sexual immorality among the young is just as bad as it has ever been! What Mauriac's argument really means is that if only de Gaulle had revived the R.P.F. in 1958, he could have brought about a 'moral revolution' in France; but he was reluctant (or afraid) to do so, in view of the deep prejudices in France against both clericalization and totalitarianism. As a result, with de Gaulle himself gone, and the 'moral revolution' unbegun, what will be left of 'Gaullism' in France?

*

The de Gaulle of today is a different person from the de Gaulle of earlier periods. Today he is 'the King'. A delightful book by P. Viansson-Ponté, the political editor of *Le Monde*, called *The King and his Court*[1] gives us numerous close-ups of de Gaulle as President of the Fifth Republic. It deals, for instance, with the 'ritual' at the Elysée. In welcoming guests at a great reception, de Gaulle is always gracious. To a diplomat, whether a Finn or a Paraguayan, he always says: 'I very much like your country, as you well know.' Any journalist or author is left with the pleasant impression that de Gaulle is one of his faithful readers – even though he may write only books on gardening. To an old man he says – 'Your experience is of great value to us'; to a young man – 'You are the future of France, *Monsieur*, be worthy of it'; to a priest – 'Help us with your prayers, *Monseigneur*, we need them.'

Sometimes, it is true, de Gaulle gets tired or absent-minded; thus, he welcomed one brilliant representative of the French press with a sonorous 'Bonjour, Madame' – even

1. Published in the U.S.A. by Houghton Mifflin. The French title is *Les Gaullistes*.

though there was nothing about his name, appearance or morals that could possibly have justified such a mistake.

Viansson-Ponté is also very funny about the big banquets (for about 200 guests) preceding gala receptions at the Elysée. Here the army of waiters will snatch away the plates still three-quarters full; no cheese is served because it 'smells bad', and no fruit, because it takes too long to peel. The whole banquet is over in an hour; the guests can always go and have supper at Lipp's or at the Halles afterwards.

De Gaulle is moody. When in a good mood, he can be witty, relaxed and charming. On other occasions, even visitors who were granted the special honour of being invited to lunch at Colombey, have found him an ordeal; the host says a few words about the weather, then dismisses them with a curt 'Thank you for having come', and they have to drive all the 200 miles back to Paris.

On the whole, however, de Gaulle's gestures are carefully calculated. Thus, when he goes on trips either in France or abroad, everything is worked out in advance – the 'few words' he will utter in a village; the three-to-six minutes' talk in a medium-sized town; the twenty-minute speech in a city. The last might contain a few sentences of international importance, and these are handed in advance to the press. But even in the small village, de Gaulle always tries to say something pleasing – with the suggestion that there is something rather special about *this* village.

De Gaulle, as the virtual head of French diplomacy, has two sets of diplomatic discussions – those that matter (for instance with Erhard, Wilson, or the Soviet Ambassador), and those that don't – for instance, with some minor African president or a Scandinavian king. But these last would be offended if de Gaulle did not devote at least an hour to the *tête-à-tête*. Since there is really very little to say (the details of 'cultural cooperation' and the like are left to the officials), de Gaulle usually fills in time by first exchanging a few

banalities, and then by treating his guest to a dazzling
monologue on the state of the world – with his favourite
observations on say, the European future of Russia, the
Asiatic future of China, and France's place in the world.
Completely enchanted, the guest leaves with the impression
that he has learned something terribly important straight
from the horse's mouth.

But de Gaulle's greatest political weapon – and he knows
it – is television; and he has spared no pains to attain the
position of France's foremost video star.

He takes all the trouble to write out his text, to learn it off
by heart (his memory is stupendous), to make the most of
his mannerisms which, in the end, move rather than irritate
people. He rehearses his TV speeches in front of a mirror
and with the help of a tape-recorder. He even took lessons in
diction from an eminent actor of the Comédie Française,
and knows all the right cadences, and is aware of the gestures
and intonations to avoid.

The same technique is applied to his famous press conferences; the questions are virtually pre-fabricated, and de
Gaulle knows in advance exactly what he is going to say.
When he wants to 'answer' a question that has not been
asked, he simply says: 'Oh yes, somebody also asked me
about so-and-so'.

Cabinet meetings can be interesting if de Gaulle is in good
form and treats his ministers to a brilliant monologue, or
deadly dull if he is in a bad mood. He then tends to snap at
his ministers. Thus, in the middle of a soporific report from
Couve de Murville, de Gaulle suddenly remarked: '*Monsieur le ministre des affaires étrangères*, may I just ask you,
without becoming stentorian, to raise your voice just a little
bit?' Often the communiqués after a cabinet meeting have
no relation at all to what happened at them and are simply
drawn up by de Gaulle and the Minister of Information in a
few minutes after the meeting. The important decisions are

usually taken not at the Cabinet meeting, but before – by de Gaulle and the ministers directly concerned or by those special committees set up in the days of Debré (whom de Gaulle often distrusted) and over which the Elysée rules as a sort of super-ministry. The other ministers are simply informed, and they rarely venture to raise objections. There are seldom any general discussions, except in some exceptionally serious situation, such as the Algiers *putsch*, or on the eve of a dissolution of the National Assembly.

De Gaulle reads a lot. He looks through not only most French newspapers, but also the principal English, American and German ones. The only paper he reads almost from cover to cover, however, is *Le Monde*. Of the weeklies, he reads *Le Canard Enchaîné* with the greatest interest – if not always with the greatest pleasure.

He has a great family feeling, and likes to get the whole group – grandchildren and all – together for Christmas at Colombey. To his brother-in-law Jacques Vendroux, he is 'discreetly grateful' for the financial help he received from him during the difficult years of his career. But, as Viansson-Ponté says, 'there is no nepotism in the de Gaulle family, and he has never dreamed of founding a dynasty'. But there is one person who matters, and that is Madame de Gaulle, the 'Madame de Maintenant'[1] of *Le Canard*. She plays no *direct* political part, yet her influence has been enormous in surrounding the 'Court' with an aura of Christian, almost Victorian respectability. Thus she has succeeded in vetoing the appointment to the government of any man who has been divorced or is known to be unfaithful to his wife; couples not married in Church are frowned upon; a few divorced people appear at great receptions, but are rigorously excluded from any more select gatherings at the Elysée.

De Gaulle is commonly believed to be not only arrogant,

1. After Mme de Maintenon, the *dévote* and straitlaced friend of Louis XIV in his old age.

but also extremely self-satisfied. Neither statement is strictly true. In his personal relations he can be gracious, considerate and warm-hearted. C. L. Sulzberger, of the *New York Times*, who has had several talks with de Gaulle in recent years, found him not only 'a great gentleman, but also a gentle man'.[1] He is, in a sense, self-satisfied – satisfied, that is, with the extraordinary role he has played in the history of France. And yet I am probably not the only one to have noticed a curiously pathetic, helpless, hang-dog look suddenly coming over de Gaulle even in the middle of an 'arrogant' speech on international affairs.

As one of his ministers remarked: 'He is seldom optimistic. He thinks this atomic age is horrible. Moreover, he is not sure that, in France, he is not building on sand. He likes to think that, before very long, France will have 100 million people; but then he adds: "By that time China may have fifteen times as many and, worse still, America will have four or five times as many." And he thinks America potentially very aggressive and power-drunk. He *hopes* his memory will have a lasting effect on France, but he isn't at all sure that it will.'

*

Is de Gaulle popular? This also is no easy question to answer. In a sense, he is a figure of fun. The cartoonists love him, and every other Frenchman tries to mimic his voice and his mannerisms. Tisot made a fortune with his gramophone records lampooning the general. (De Gaulle himself likes them.)

There have been times when de Gaulle has made France feel very proud of herself. He has flattered her vanity. His nationalism, his basic anti-Americanism, his peculiar form of 'neutralism' have all struck a chord in most French hearts; perhaps he has succeeded in curing France of the inferiority complex she acquired as a result of 1940. Perhaps,

1. C. L. Sulzberger, *The Test: de Gaulle and Algeria*, London, 1962.

thanks to him, France has today a less marked feeling of
international inferiority than Britain has. Since he made
peace in Algeria, nearly everybody in France has had a soft
spot for him – even the communists!

But, except for the revivalist type of meetings organized
in the days of the R.P.F., there has never been any mass
hysteria about de Gaulle, and his superior manner has often
had a chilling effect on people. Furthermore, although
between 1958 and 1962 he was generally considered indispensable, his popularity seems since then to have declined.
'In a major national crisis,' one of his ministers remarked,
'he is sublime.' And so he is. But in the confused situation of
1965, there were two factors, one favourable, the other
unfavourable, to de Gaulle. The unfavourable one was the
economic discontent in the country, as reflected in the
municipal elections of February, when the U.N.R. did surprisingly badly, and the 'traditional' old parties showed
that they were much more alive than they had seemed to be
in 1962.[1] Favourable to de Gaulle, on the other hand, was
his foreign policy, under which France, more than any other
Western Power, passionately defended the cause of peace

1. What greatly harmed de Gaulle on the home front was his
handling of the great miners' strike in March–April 1963. Overesti-
mating his authority after his referendum and election victories a few
months before, he issued an almost unprecedented and ill-considered
requisition order, ordering the miners to return to work unconditionally.
The miners defied the order and, with great moral and financial
support from numerous quarters, went on with the strike for over a
month, until the government had to give in. It was a striking example
of de Gaulle's lack of understanding of popular sentiment on trade
union rights. Some of his ministers, particularly M. Misoffe, went even
further and virtually proposed to outlaw the labour unions. De Gaulle
at least had the good sense not to follow this advice – an obvious
hangover from the R.P.F. days. The failure of his requisition order was
nevertheless to remain an important landmark in the history of the
5th Republic. Since then, during journeys through provincial France,
he has often had very lukewarm receptions.

throughout the world, regardless of any ideologies, and scarcely hesitated to treat the United States as a menace of the first magnitude – 'the greatest', de Gaulle privately confided, 'since Hitler'.

Whatever may happen in the next few years, I still believe that the day de Gaulle dies, France will feel smaller and very unhappy. Nearly everybody in France will mourn him – often for very different reasons – and so will many people in other parts of the world.

CHAPTER 12

1965: A RESTLESS YEAR

1. De Gaulle's Hard Fight for the Second Term

AS DE GAULLE entered 1965, the last year of his first
septennat, he remarked: '*Vous verrez, on ne s'ennuiera
pas* – you'll see, it's not going to be a boring year.' Nor was
it. One of the most troublesome for de Gaulle, it started,
paradoxically enough, with a curious kind of international
apotheosis for him. On 24 January Winston Churchill
died, and de Gaulle headed the French delegation at his
funeral on the 30th. As the London *Sunday Times* was to
write on the following day:

After the service, the nations spilled out on to the steps of
St. Paul's. In the few minutes informal court that ensued, it was,
inevitably, the one figure who matches Churchill that stood
out – de Gaulle again. He stood out among the medals by the
very plainness of his dress: the plain fawn service coat of the
French Army. He bent his head, graciously, to give audience
first to King Constantine of the Hellenes, then to the slim figure
of Baudouin, then to Juliana of the Netherlands.

'The one figure that matches Churchill.' What rich
memories must have rushed through de Gaulle's mind as
he remembered 1940 and the man to whom he owed so
much. There had been a strange love-hate relationship between them; there were times when the two had found each
other worse than exasperating; towards the end of the war,
de Gaulle once even referred to Churchill as 'that old
bandit'. Yet after Churchill had died, de Gaulle was to
speak, not without a touch of emotion, of that day in
London when he had gone to the funeral of '*le grand*
Churchill,' not an adjective de Gaulle would use lightly.

In 1965, he was no longer the lone Brigadier-General arrogantly demanding favours from the hard-pressed British Government. He was now the uncrowned King of France who was 'graciously giving audience' to the minor crowned heads of Europe.

De Gaulle's powers at the head of the State, as he saw them, had an almost divine and mystical quality. At a press conference only a year before – on 31 January 1964 – he had defined these as 'deriving straight from the nation'; the head of the State, he then said, was the source and holder of this power, the Constitution was 'a spirit', and the institutions 'a matter of practise' – the whole of it, as Jean Lacouture remarked, like a dream of Joseph de Maistre come true. This mystical concept was to be rudely shaken at the end of 1965, when the presidential election developed into a plainly 'democratic', if not downright mudslinging, dogfight in which de Gaulle himself had to join reluctantly during the later phases, when he found his re-election seriously threatened. His concept received an even ruder shock when the Ben Barka scandal blew up.

Yet even long before that, it was clear that the 'spirit' inevitably tended to be arbitrary (de Gaulle's violations of the 1958 Constitution in 1962 had shown this), while the 'practice' remained uncertain. For whereas the Republican Monarch had his own domain – foreign policy, military policy and the former Empire – he had no strong feelings about most of the home affairs of France, and left these largely to his ministers and top government officials. As an *étatiste*, an all-out state-builder, he had his weaknesses. In the words of Jean Lacouture, he was a Richelieu in world affairs, but only a Mazarin in dealing with conflicting interests at home. In his financial policy he was cautiously conservative; surrounded by liberal economists and classical financiers, he had made a fetish of monetary stability.

Although no man is less bourgeois than de Gaulle, who longs, moreover, to be a symbol of national unity, he still pursues a class policy at home. Is it not largely because there can be no national independence without a stable currency? It was not the parties of the Left, but the conservative M. Poincaré who stabilized the franc.[1]

The franc was a strong currency once again – which it had not been for a very long time – and this stability was essential to de Gaulle's policy of national independence ('See how Wilson has to crawl to the Americans,' he remarked in 1965, 'just because the pound is weak'). But at home this stability had been reinforced, especially since 1963, by Giscard d'Estaing's 'Stabilization Plan' of more or less frozen prices and wages, which had led to underinvestment, financial austerity, and something of a business and stock-exchange slump. Since 1963 wages in France had risen more slowly than in the other Common Market countries, and a widespread discontent was to be reflected at the end of 1965 in the large anti–de Gaulle vote in the presidential election. It should be emphasized that the fifty-six per cent anti–de Gaulle vote in the first round and the forty-five per cent anti–de Gaulle vote in the second round were indeed a reflection of discontent over economic conditions inside France, and not at all a protest (as some American commentators suggested) against de Gaulle's foreign policy. His foreign policy was explicitly condemned only by the fifteen per cent of the electorate who voted for the all-out 'Atlantic' and 'European' Jean Lecanuet, and the five per cent who voted for the extreme-Right-wing J. L. Tixier-Vignancour.

But internally there were plenty of reasons for discontent. The national income continued to rise, but unevenly; in 1964, the incomes of the privileged classes had risen by twelve per cent, and those of the underprivileged by only three per cent. Relations with the working-class continued

1. Jean Lacouture, *De Gaulle*, Paris, 1965, p. 165.

to be strained, especially since de Gaulle's abortive challenge to the miners in 1963. There was a lamentable shortage of schools; and then there was the housing shortage. Scrubbing Paris white at the cost of many millions, was all very well as a matter of prestige (apart from being artistically debatable), but the money would have been better spent on building new houses. In 1964–5 the housing shortage was worse than ever. Over one-third of the French nation were badly (often shockingly badly) housed; in 1964 only 370,000 new houses had been built, of which 70,000 were in the Paris area, where the Fourth Republic had planned over 100,000 a year. The cost of living had, at least nominally, gone up thirty per cent during the first seven years of the Fifth Republic. Discontent at these conditions was strikingly reflected in the municipal elections of February 1965. But the astonishing thing is that de Gaulle took no notice at all of these very recent municipal election results when he embarked with so much self-confidence on his presidential election in November 1965; he might have known that millions of those who had voted against the U.N.R. Gaullists in February would also vote in December against de Gaulle himself.

*

With America's war in Vietnam becoming increasingly murderous, the first few months of 1965 in France were marked by a worsening in Franco-American relations and, on the other hand, by the beginnings of a marked *rapprochement* with the Soviet Union. Two reasons for this seem obvious. First, de Gaulle dreaded the United States in the role of World Policeman and hoped that an aggressive American policy in South-East Asia and elsewhere would be at least partly discouraged if France, one of America's major allies, blatantly dissociated itself from U.S.

policy in Vietnam. If, for financial reasons, Mr Wilson's Britain could not do so, at least France would.[1]

Secondly, there was a certain balance-of-power element in de Gaulle's *rapprochement* with the Russians. As the phrase went, there was now 'only one super-power in the world, the U.S.A.' (the Russians lagged far behind the U.S.A. in the last few years not only economically, but also militarily) and the prospect of this 'one and only super-power' giving more and more support to an increasingly arrogant Western Germany created a common ground for both French and Russian misgivings.

The misgivings on the French side were well reflected in an interview M. Raymond Schmittlein, the Gaullist Vice-President of the National Assembly, gave to *Izvestia* on 22 May, soon after Soviet Foreign Minister Gromyko visited Paris. Schmittlein argued in favour of the closest bonds between France and the Soviet Union and suggested that the two of them should help keep Western Germany in order. As for France, she must strive to include Germany in a European system, 'and not leave her as an American satellite wholly depending on N.A.T.O.'

Any Western Power making use of the chauvinist sentiments existing in Germany may create a war situation. We do not want this. But our aim will not be easy to achieve, because French policy has many enemies in both Western Germany and the

1. Such non-conformism *vis-à-vis* a militant United States was not new in French post-war history; at the height of the Cold War in the late 1940s the Fourth Republic had already put up a great deal of passive resistance to the American exponents of an aggressive roll-back policy towards Russia. As I wrote in *France 1940-1955:* 'In the last analysis, the most important thing that France did during the Cold War years was (a) to put up a certain passive resistance to the pursuit of any dangerous foreign policy which might lead to war; (b) to reassure the Russians that Europe was not seriously contemplating a "crusade", and that it was therefore unnecessary for them to take preventive action; and (c) to render "dynamic" generals and senators in the U.S.A. sufficiently distrustful of France and of Europe generally to make them think twice before confidently embarking on World War III' (p. 391).

U.S.A. . . . . Since France and the Soviet Union are both determined to save peace, we can follow the same road, despite differences in other matters.

Schmittlein stressed that, although France was a member of N.A.T.O., she was not enthusiastic about it. She had banned American launching sites from French territory; she had withdrawn the French navy from N.A.T.O. command; she had an attitude of her own towards S.E.A.T.O.

These are not idle gestures. Nor are they anti-American. But we are determined on no account to be drawn into a war against the Soviet Union or any other country . . . We no longer believe in a war with Russia. Not that we are going to leave N.A.T.O., but we should like N.A.T.O. to become unnecessary. And we are dead against a nuclear monopoly of the U.S.A. under which that country might, at least theoretically, act in the name of France. Hence our *force de frappe*.

He added that he was against the M.L.F. or any other way of providing Western Germany with nuclear armaments.

All this was, of course, a reflection of the great uneasiness which America's war in Vietnam had produced in France – and in Russia. Where would this war end, and would it not have repercussions in Germany, where President Johnson's 'dynamic' policy was already beginning to produce some unhealthy reactions? Soon afterwards in Saigon, General Ky, one of the puppet rulers the Americans had set up, was saying that what Vietnam needed was a Hitler!

De Gaulle did not disavow Schmittlein; at heart he felt that France and Russia were the two most determined *status quo* – if not downright 'neutralist' – countries and were, paradoxically, less befuddled by 'ideology' than most.[1] He was to adhere to this 'pro-Russian' policy right

1. That the Russians, much to China's disgust, were much less interested in revolutionary ideology than in peace was nicely illustrated in January 1966 by their acting as the peacemakers between two 'capitalist' countries, India and Pakistan.

up to the presidential election and beyond.

But in the middle of 1965 de Gaulle had other worries. France's Common Market partners were becoming troublesome. At the Elysée garden party he gave on 10 June for members of Parliament, he sounded generally fed-up and *désabusé*. He was more devastating than ever about a supra-national Europe and 'a supra-national assembly sitting at Strasbourg and not caring a hang about the national interests of Paris, Rome or Brussels'. 'It's easy enough to be a *jean-foutre* making speeches about a supranational Europe,' he said.[1]

When somebody suggested that the United States was the product of a 'supra-national amalgamation', de Gaulle snapped back:

Absolutely no connexion. They started from nothing. It was virgin soil with nothing but the bones of the Redskins they had done in [*zigouillés*]! And soon afterwards they started a civil war, and this is still going on.

Which, presumably, was one way of saying: 'And what about the Negro Problem?'

As for the Common Market, he now sounded more doubtful than ever. There was nothing essentially supranational about it, he said; it was based on international competition, agreements and compromises; but the norms of international competition were not being observed.

If there are no amicable settlements, then there will just be no Common Market. . . . The Dutch are as nationally-minded as any; they've been like that ever since Louis XIV.

And then de Gaulle at his bitterest: '*A priori*, one mustn't trust anybody.'

Three weeks later came the great crisis of the Common Market. Not only did France's five partners fail to honour

1. *Jean-foutre* is a somewhat archaic term of abuse, which the world press found no end of difficulty in translating.

the 1962 agreement to settle the agricultural subsidy question by 30 June 1965, but France was now pressed to grant increased authority to the Common Market Commission in Brussels and increased control over the agricultural purse to the European Parliament. De Gaulle saw in these attempts a form of blackmail, with certain 'supra-nationalists' such as Hallstein, the German president of the Commission, and Mansholt, the Dutch vice-president, believing that the French Government would not dare break with the Common Market a few months before the presidential election. Behind the Common Market crisis there were, in fact, three problems:

Firstly, the financing of the agricultural policy of the Common Market. This was of the greatest importance to France, since she owned nearly one-half of the arable land of "Little Europe" and had large surpluses to sell to the West-European countries. It had been agreed in 1962 that the financial arrangements would be completed by 30 June 1965, but, as Couve de Murville was to say later – in the National Assembly debate of 20 October 1965 – 'For the first time a formal and ever-repeated commitment by the six governments had not been observed'. As the French Government had repeated time and again, since France's industrial potential was lower than Germany's, a purely industrial Common Market was of no interest to her unless it was supplemented by an agricultural Common Market, in which, with the help of subsidies and other financial devices, French agricultural exports would not be placed at a disadvantage *vis-à-vis* the cheaper produce from North America.

Secondly, in the French view, the Brussels Commission, before giving France satisfaction on the agricultural problem, was trying to give itself excessive, 'supra-national' powers; it was with reference to these attempts that the French used the word 'blackmail'. The French view of the

Brussels Commission was defined by Couve de Murville as follows:

It is the business of the Brussels Commission to make proposals to the six governments . . . We have never denied the utility of such 'objective' statements reflecting the European point of view, as against the national points of view, being put forward by an allegedly independent body. But what is then necessary is to arrive at a solution and a conclusion; in other words, to work out compromises. In this the Commission can help. When it has done so, it has been of great value. But it is not the Commission's business to try to impose its views on the governments, especially when these views are of a political nature. Yet that is precisely what the Brussels Commission tried to do ever since 30 March 1965, and persisted in doing (right up to 30 June) after our rejection of its proposals.[1]

Thirdly, there was the question of the Council of the E.E.C.:

Up till now [said Couve de Murville] decisions . . . were taken unanimously. This particularly applies to the acceptance or amendment of the Commission's proposals. But (in terms of the Rome Treaty), as from 1 January 1966, these proposals must still be amended unanimously, but can be accepted by a majority vote.

In view of what had happened, said Couve de Murville, this procedure now seemed to him 'inconceivable'. Already in the past, he said, he had commented on the anomaly of the Council's ever outvoting one of the member nations on an essential economic question, such as the price of cereals. The German Government had, soon afterwards, agreed with this French point of view. Now, however, France was expected by some to submit to such a majority rule; in the agricultural field, in particular, this was out of the question, especially in view of the atmosphere now existing among the Six.

1. National Assembly debate, 20 October, 1965.

Speaking for the Opposition in the same debate, M. Maurice Faure remarked that three weeks after the crisis of 30 June the Brussels Commission had virtually accepted all of France's demands, but the French Government had still gone on boycotting the Common Market. It was quite clear, said Faure, that the majority vote after 1 January 1966 was the real explanation for this disastrous attitude; but surely the French Government had read the Rome Treaty, and knew all along that at the third stage the majority rule would come into force.[1]

There followed a rather confused discussion on whether the Rome Treaty properly 'covered' agricultural problems at all, and even M. Faure admitted that, as regards agriculture, it dealt only with 'general principles'. In conclusion, Couve de Murville said that France was not seeking a way out of the Common Market.

But there can be no Common Market without a common agriculture. It is not we who refused the financial settlement . . . if we had wanted to get out of the Common Market, would we, in the last three years, have made the great effort of setting up a common agricultural policy? We threw in all our weight and authority with this end in view. . . . Only let me repeat that it is impossible to defend the interests of French agriculture by submitting to the majority rule.

All this was rather awkward, for what Couve de Murville clearly implied was that the French Government would be satisfied with nothing less than a revision of the Rome Treaty or, at any rate, a clear agreement among the Six not to apply the famous majority rule when a country's 'vital' interests were affected. For this was at the heart of the at first latent and now open conflict between certain supranational concepts included in the Rome Treaty and the principle of national sovereignty so dear to de Gaulle. As

1. *Ibid.*

de Gaulle himself said in the course of the presidential election campaign: 'I was not in power when the Rome Treaty was drawn up; had I been, there are certain things to which I would not have subscribed.'

From the crisis of 30 June right up to the presidential election and beyond, France boycotted the Common Market, and the question of her resuming negotiations with the other five was left open. This, as we shall see, played into the hands of certain anti–de Gaulle candidates, above all M. Jean Lecanuet, who assumed the part of the great champion of Europe and the Atlantic Alliance; he did not fail to make an impression among certain rural voters who were scared of the prospect of 'losing the European market'. A full-dress meeting of the Common Market, with France attending, did not take place in Luxembourg until after de Gaulle had entered his second *septennat* in January 1966. A compromise of sorts was made on the unanimity rule, but the agricultural problem still remained to be settled.

2. *The Fantastic Election*

It will be remembered that, under the 1962 amendment of the Constitution, the President of the Republic was to be elected by universal suffrage for the first time in 1965. De Gaulle's chief argument against all criticism of this change had been that the system he proposed was 'by far the most democratic'; the amendment provided that only the candidate who secured an absolute majority could be elected in the first round. If no one got over fifty per cent of the votes, then the two candidates topping the poll in the first round competed in the second round; if either of them stepped down, then the two 'best-placed' of the remaining competitors fought it out.

The 1965 presidential election campaign was extremely slow in getting into its stride. Apart from a Right-wing senator, M. Marcilhacy, who declared (nobody quite knew why) that he would run for President, the only candidate to make a lot of noise long before the election campaign had officially opened in November was the Rightist J. L. Tixier-Vignancour. This loud-mouthed lawyer, who had been an all-out fascist and Vichyite in the past, and had conducted a vicious smear campaign against men like Mitterrand and Mendès-France in the 1950s, and who, more recently, had openly associated himself with Algerian extremism and the O.A.S. terrorists (he had been counsel for the defence in the trials of General Salan, head of the O.A.S., Bastien-Thiry, the chief organizer of the Petit-Clamart *attentat*, and many others) now had the effrontery to declare himself not only the 'national' but also the 'liberal' candidate in the presidential election.

The Left-wing parties in France were in a state of great confusion. Although M. Gaston Defferre, the Socialist mayor of Marseilles, had been grooming himself for the presidential election for nearly two years (he had first been launched by *L'Express* as 'Monsieur X'), no agreement could be reached among the Left-wing parties and the M.R.P. Catholics about adopting Defferre as their common candidate. For one thing, Defferre was reluctant to seek the support of the Communists, who potentially controlled four to five million votes. As Pietro Nenni, the veteran Italian Socialist leader, bitterly remarked about that time:

France, the country without which Europe cannot be built, is facing a presidential election. *Yet the socialist and democratic forces in the country seem totally incapable of proposing an alternative*, not so much to the President-General as to Gaullism – which seems to be the latest French expression of the traditional French Right, with its usual blindness and its Bonapartist and Caesarian tendencies.[1]

1. *Le Monde*, 6 July 1965.

Nenni's definition of Gaullism may be highly debatable;
but his lament over the impotence of the 'socialist and
democratic forces' was significant. For it was, after all,
these 'socialist forces', with men like Guy Mollet at their
head, who only ten years before had been responsible for
Suez, and, unlike de Gaulle, had failed to stand up to the
Algiers *colons* and the War Lords. So the whole question
of 'Right' and 'Left' was not so simple as Nenni was making out; in his foreign and decolonization policy de Gaulle
was infinitely further to the Left than Mollet or Lacoste.
(As for Nenni's charge that de Gaulle was a Caesar or a
Bonaparte, this whole narrative surely shows that he had
little in common with either. 'Peace is a bore,' de Gaulle
remarked about that time, 'but war has become impossible.' No man is more conscious of belonging to the Nuclear
Age than this 'Caesar', and none more determined to make
war 'impossible' – at least as far as France is concerned.
Hence de Gaulle's boast during the election campaign that
France alone had good relations with 'everybody', and his
promise not to allow France to be dragged into the war in
Vietnam, or any other war.)

Until the autumn of 1965 it was generally assumed that
the re-election of de Gaulle was no problem. Although the
Gaullists had not done at all well in the municipal elections
during the previous spring, and the 'old parties' still
seemed to be very much alive, it was still thought that
de Gaulle would be easily returned by a sixty or sixty-five
per cent majority in the first round. Until the autumn of
1965 the real problem seemed to be not de Gaulle's re-election, but the succession. De Gaulle was going to be 75 in
November and was showing signs of physical fatigue. How
could his régime be perpetuated should he fall ill, die or
retire during the second term? During the summer a serious
attempt was made to build up M. Pompidou as the dauphin. He frequently appeared on television, and M. Merry

Bromberger, a star reporter of *Le Figaro*, published a long, gushing and sentimental biography of Pompidou, which was serialized in *France-Soir*. It was widely believed that after his triumphant election de Gaulle would propose a referendum on a new constitutional amendment whereby the Prime Minister, like the U.S. Vice-President, would automatically step into the President's shoes in the event of the latter's death or incapacity. But it somehow did not work. Pompidou failed to make a hit with his 'fireside chats' on television, and de Gaulle soon became aware of it. The idea of a referendum was dropped, at least for the time being, and the results of the election were to prove discouraging to any such project.

It was not till the beginning of November that de Gaulle officially announced that he was going to run for President. The announcement itself, made on television, was very strange. The common interpretation of it was that de Gaulle had called on the French voters to 'choose between de Gaulle and chaos'; this was not exactly what he said, but it was certainly the impression he left on many. After making the most of the immense services he had rendered France in the last twenty-five years, he declared:

May the wholehearted and massive support of our citizens make me stay in power: only in that case will the future of the new Republic be safeguarded. Otherwise, there can be no doubt that the Republic will immediately collapse, and that France – this time without my coming to the rescue – will sink back into an even worse state of confusion than she knew before. . . . Abandoned to the parties, the State will fall back into a condition of impotence.

Only if he were re-elected, de Gaulle then said, could France hold her place in the world in the midst of immeasurable dangers; only under him would she remain independent, the union of Western Europe be pursued 'in equitable and reasonable conditions', and fruitful cooperation with the former colonial peoples continue. On 5 December, he concluded, France would reassert or repudiate herself. 'French women, French men, I hope, I believe, I know that, thanks to you, France will triumph.'

One curious reaction to this broadcast was that in identifying himself – and only himself – with the destiny of France, de Gaulle had not been particularly complimentary to Pompidou and the other leaders of the 'new Republic', and it is certainly true that his ministers were not very pleased with this statement. (In fact, de Gaulle knew that day that a big scandal not very creditable to some of his ministers was brewing – the Ben Barka Affair.)

Who, then, were de Gaulle's competitors? Apart from the venomous Tixier-Vignancour (the 'Algérie française' candidate), the pointless M. Marcilhacy, who had been in the running for a long time, and a M. Antier, who dropped out at an early stage, there were a freak candidate – a M. Barbu, a worthy man and former résistant who, however, represented nothing – and two much more serious competitors. One was M. François Mitterrand, who was supported by the 'entire Left', including the Communists, the Socialists, part of the Radicals, and other, smaller groups. The other was M. Jean Lecanuet, president of the Catholic M.R.P., who joined in the fray at a late stage. Mitterrand, 49 and a handsome man, had been a minister in numerous governments under the Fourth Republic, and had, at one time, been closely associated with M. Mendès-France, whose mildly anti-colonialist (or, rather, neo-colonialist) policy he had supported. Like Mendès-France, he was hated by the Algerian colons. Mitterrand's government career, though creditable, was not outstanding, but under the Fifth Republic he came to be regarded as one of the most effective speakers of the parliamentary Opposition. He belonged to the small U.D.S.R. group, half-way between the Radicals and the Socialists, and his adoption as the candidate of the 'entire Left' was something in the nature of an improvisation. His programme, which had to be acceptable to Radicals, Socialists and Communists, was inevitably vague: vaguely pro-Atlantic, vaguely 'European', vaguely pro-Russian – in short, all things to all men. It was critical of de Gaulle's 'indiscriminate' aid to the underdeveloped countries, and perhaps its most striking feature was a pledge to abandon the *force de frappe*. For the rest, Mitterrand was, above all, opposed to the 'personal régime' the General had set up, but he strongly denied that his election victory would mean a return to the instability of the Fourth Republic. He also tried to catch women's votes by advocating the abolition of the 1920 anti–birth-control legislation.

It suited the Communist Party to support Mitterrand, rather than run a candidate of their own who might collect only an embarrassingly small number of votes; and although Mitterrand avoided any suggestion that he represented anything in the nature of a Popular Front, the Communist leadership regarded their support of him as a means of escaping at last from the political 'ghetto' to which they had been confined since 1947. Whether, at heart, they trusted Mitterrand or not, they could see themselves (were he elected) as possible members of a Left-wing government coalition. This was, in reality, very far from certain – indeed, it was more likely that Mitterrand would join forces with the Centre when it came to that point – but the Communists had really no alternative to supporting him. It was, of course, well-known that Moscow was praying for a de Gaulle victory; nevertheless it would have been awkward for the French Communist leadership to come out in favour of de Gaulle. Without sounding overwhelmingly enthusiastic about Mitterrand, *L'Humanité* carefully refrained from making a big song and dance over Couve de Murville's visit to Moscow shortly before the election (clearly an election move on de Gaulle's part) and from quoting Soviet ex-Ambassador Vinogradov's farewell words to the French Foreign Minister: 'I hope de Gaulle is re-elected.' To the Communist leadership, the advantages of de Gaulle's foreign policy were obvious, but they could not ignore the widespread economic discontent among their rank-and-file. The fact that Mitterrand was promising a housing programme of 600,000 houses a year could not be ignored.

It was not till 19 October that the Centre parties – in fact, the Catholic M.R.P. and the 'classical' Right, always more or less hostile to de Gaulle – found a candidate of their own. Ignoring the well-meaning but ineffectual M. Marcilhacy, who represented nobody but himself, they settled on Senator Jean Lecanuet, the 45-year-old president of the M.R.P. and deputy-mayor of Rouen. Having taken part in the Resistance towards the end of the war, Lecanuet was closely associated with the M.R.P., and his patrons included first M. P.H. Teitgen and then M. Pflimlin. He was the head of M. Pflimlin's secretariat in 1958, both during the last days of the Fourth Republic and later, when Pflimlin became one of de Gaulle's ministers of state. As a senator he became increasingly hostile to the de Gaulle régime, took part in organizing the 'Cartel des Nons' during the 1962 referendum, and later in forming the 'Comité des Démocrates', composed of anti-Gaullist M.R.P.s, Radicals and Right-wing 'Independents'. In the presidential election he came forward as the 'candidat démocrate-social et européen', and he was to make the most of his 'Europeanism', his attachment to the Atlantic Alliance, and his good looks, youth (he was only 44) and effective television manner. More harshly than Mitterrand, Lecanuet persisted in stressing the senility of de Gaulle, saying time and again that it was entirely pointless giving the old man 'merely a short respite': he (Lecanuet) was ready to take over right now.

One must distinguish between two stages of the election campaign – the fortnight before the first vote of 5 December, and the fortnight between the first vote and the second round on 19 December. The biggest mistake de Gaulle himself made during the first phase was to stay almost till the very end on his Olympian heights, assuming that his re-election on 5 December was absolutely certain. It is only fair to say that the election was thoroughly 'democratic' – in the sense that all the candidates were given an equal chance on radio and television. De Gaulle alone thought it beneath his dignity to take part in that dogfight – until the very last stages of the first round, when he became acutely aware of what had happened. *He had, in fact, abandoned television, his most powerful weapon, to his enemies, little realizing that they, too, could work wonders on that mighty propaganda machine.* What is more, the French people, who had for years associated television with de Gaulle and had come to regard it as a government monopoly, suddenly became acutely interested in the sharp anti–de Gaulle polemics with which television (as well as radio) was now providing them day after day and night after night. As distinct from the 1962 election, de Gaulle's rivals were now given plenty of time on both radio and television – roughly an hour a day on each.

Significantly, none of the five anti–de Gaulle candidates (Mitterrand, Lecanuet, Tixier-Vignancour, Marcilhacy and Barbu) attacked each other: all their attacks were reserved for de Gaulle, which justified the General's acid remark before the first round: 'Their desire to see me go is all they have in common.'

Another factor highly unfavourable to de Gaulle was the press. With the exception of *France-Soir* and one or two minor papers, the entire Paris press was anti–de Gaulle, *Le Monde* being particularly critical and hostile. The provincial press was mostly anti–de Gaulle, too. The campaign

was being conducted in circumstances very different from
those surrounding earlier elections and referendums under
the Fifth Republic. Things had settled down; there seemed
no longer any danger coming from Algiers, the Army, or
the O.A.S. terrorists. Even the best of governments gets
slightly eroded after seven years in office, and there was no
longer the same feeling of de Gaulle's 'indispensability' as
there had been in 1958 or 1962. Moreover, to the younger
generation the de Gaulle legend meant much less than it
did to older people. An ever-recurring theme in Mitterrand's and Lecanuet's propaganda was: 'He keeps talking
about the past; we are interested in the future.' They also
made the most of the economic shortcomings under de
Gaulle, and promised more new schools and more houses.
De Gaulle's foreign policy was attacked chiefly by Tixier-
Vignancour, the hero of the Algerian repatriates, and by
Lecanuet, who made the most of France's 'isolation' and
the 'disastrous' consequences of de Gaulle's having turned
his back on 'Europe'. Lecanuet promised to resume the
Common Market negotiations immediately if elected. The
United States Government, which had openly attacked
de Gaulle at the opening of the election campaign, showed
a warm interest in Lecanuet, the ideal 'Atlantic' and
'European' leader. Both Mitterrand and Lecanuet liked to
play the 'Kennedy' of France. As a television personality,
Lecanuet was the more successful of the two.

Lecanuet was given the open support of not only a
respectable 'European' like M. Jean Monnet, but also that
of certain more disreputable elements – the old Vichyites,
as represented by M. Isorni, and Poujade and his followers.
In short, much of the anti-Gaullist extreme Right was
divided between Lecanuet and Tixier-Vignancour. But
Tixier was perhaps too obvious a thug, and the anti–
de Gaulle *bonne bourgeoisie* – people of the Sixteenth
Arrondissement and readers of *Le Figaro* – somehow found

Lecanuet more respectable. He was clearly winning over many people who had voted for de Gaulle in the past. After about ten days of campaigning this was becoming extremely obvious, and among de Gaulle's ministers there were a few days of real panic. They begged de Gaulle to re-appear on television, and went round the country themselves organizing big Gaullist meetings. But it was too late. A worse disaster – under forty per cent for de Gaulle – was avoided, but it was clear by 1 December that there would be *ballotage*, a second round in the absence of an absolute majority for de Gaulle in the first. Would de Gaulle swallow his pride and run in the second round? The alternative was clear: not to run would mean handing France over to a young man with a Colgate smile – and the benediction of Washington; for in a straight fight between Mitterrand and Lecanuet the latter was sure to win.

At last the great day came: 5 December 1965. The poll was exceptionally heavy; only fifteen per cent abstained. The results for Metropolitan France were as follows.

	Number of votes	Percentage of votes cast
De Gaulle	10,504,000	43.97
Mitterrand	7,655,000	32.0
Lecanuet	3,771,000	15.8
Tixier-Vignancour	1,269,000	5.3
Marcilhacy	414,000	1.7
Barbu	278,000	1.1

Including the overseas territories, the Gaullist vote totalled 44.6 per cent. De Gaulle's vote was highest in Alsace and the East and in the North and the West, and lowest in the South; in Paris he had the national average of 44 per cent. In eighteen of the ninety departments, mostly in the South, Mitterrand headed the poll. Lecanuet had over twenty per cent in some parts of Brittany, Normandy and Alsace with its strong M.R.P. tradition. His 'Europeanism' had made some impact on the anxious rural population in the West. De Gaulle realized that he had made a serious mistake in not taking part in the election campaign except at the very end. 'We realised too late,' he said to Pompidou, 'that it was an election, and not a referendum.'

But were the results so disastrous? After all, even in the 'triumphal' election of 1962 the Gaullists had secured only thirty-two per cent of the votes in the first round and forty per cent in the second round (or forty-five per cent including their allies). With six candidates running – including four serious ones – an absolute majority would not have been easy to achieve, especially with every candidate having the same opportunities on radio and television. The fact could not be overlooked that there were certain political traditions in France which had never been permanently absorbed by Gaullism: a traditional Left, represented by Mitterrand; a traditional Right and Right-Centre, represented by Lecanuet; and a traditional extreme Right, represented by Tixier-Vignancour. Who had voted for de Gaulle, then? All those, on Left and Right, to whom either he or his régime appealed for one reason or another. It is reckoned that the female vote for de Gaulle was higher than the male vote, and that the older age groups voted for him more readily than the young people. A proportion of habitual Communist votes went to de Gaulle, though a smaller one than in 1958. But it was still, above all, the personality, record, and legend of de Gaulle that carried weight; no one was enormously impressed by his ministers, and a few of them – notably the Minister of the Interior, M. Frey – looked unpleasantly shifty. Not only had Frey done some very dirty work in Algiers in 1958, but he was the boss of some *very* dirty people inside the various police services. (It should be added, however, that at the time of the election the Ben Barka scandal had not yet burst into flower, as it did shortly afterwards.) After the first round de Gaulle had at least two consolations: Lecanuet did much less well than some Gaullists had feared, and Tixier's five per cent could only be regarded as a fiasco, especially in the light of his extravagant boasts before the poll. The all-out fascists, including the embittered Algerian repatriates, were only a very small minority in France.

*

After the first round of the presidential election it was said – in a reference to de Gaulle's famous 1940 remark – that the General had 'lost a battle, but not lost the war'. The 'war' was to be won in the second round, and two days after the first round de Gaulle announced that he would 'naturally' stand. Not only were his ministers sent all over the country to hold Gaullist meetings, but he himself completely changed his tactics. He now appeared several times on television, sometimes for as long as half-an-hour. What is more, besides delivering several prepared speeches, he took the almost unprecedented step of allowing himself to be interviewed, during several nights, by M. Michel Droit, editor of *Le Figaro Littéraire*. Without being hostile, M. Droit asked de Gaulle many pointed and even awkward questions. It may be said that in dealing with economic questions de Gaulle was slightly on the defensive. He said, in effect, that his régime's economic and social record was good, but that it would do much better still in the next few years, and that the French people's income would be doubled in ten years' time. He also defended his régime by going out of his way to stress that it was not a 'personal' régime, but one in which the President, the ministers and Parliament formed a coherent whole. He further insisted that the régime was democratic and that no freedoms had been destroyed: trade union freedom had been fully respected, this election showed how free everybody was to vote, and the full freedom of the press could be seen from the fact that nearly all the newspapers were hostile to him but were not being interfered with. A return to the 'régime of the parties', which Mitterrand represented, would merely land France in a worse mess than before. De Gaulle then declared that he firmly believed in the future of the 'new Republic' even after his death.

But what mattered even more than what he was saying was the manner in which he was saying it. If before the second round he looked not only like a tired oracle, but also like a very old man (especially on one occasion), he now suddenly seemed twenty years younger; he was witty, ironic, sarcastic – the old de Gaulle at his best. The interview he gave M. Droit on international affairs on 14 December was particularly lively. He started with a discussion of the Common Market, criticizing certain clauses of the Rome Treaty which had been signed before he came into power.

However, we took it as it was and tried to make the best of it. . . . But a country like ours cannot enter into economic competition so long as this is confined to industry. For if we had to carry, all alone, the heavy weight of our agriculture, we should be handicapped in our industrial competition, and the Common Market would be, for us, a mug's game. We must remember that the Rome Treaty dealt with agriculture in only the vaguest terms. . . . We have done our best to make French agriculture enter the Common Market, but . . . we met with much obstruction.

Conscious of the capital that Lecanuet had made of the Common Market crisis of 30 June, de Gaulle now stressed that France was anxious to resume the negotiations:

We are disposed, and indeed determined, to do so, but on condition that the entry of French agriculture into the Common Market is not adorned by unacceptable political conditions.

There followed a brilliant harangue on the nations: each had its own individuality, its own way of life and its own problems; there was every reason that they should cooperate. But – and here de Gaulle, jumping up and down in his chair, became really funny – 'One can, of course, jump about like a young goat bleating "Europe! Europe! Europe!" But it means nothing and gets you nowhere.'

We have to take things as they are. Every country, I repeat, has its own language, its own way of life. . . . I am the first to recognize the value of the Common Market, for a real economic solidarity among the nations of Western Europe – and I include among them countries like Britain and Spain – would be something of the greatest value and benefit.

But political problems, he said, were different. Germany was economically powerful and now had political ambitions, but there was no reason why France should share in these ambitions. And, with a typical Gaullist touch of irony, he added:

The British have a great number of embarrassments: in Africa, they've got Rhodesia on their hands; in the Arab world, they've got Aden; in the Far East, Malaysia. Must all these worries be ours, too?

He then referred to the Franco-German treaty of 1963.

Yes, it didn't produce much. Why? Well, just because each state has its own policy, and you can't prevent that. But some people talk about a supra-national Europe. It seems convenient and tempting to lump all the countries of Europe together. But it's a delusion and a myth. . . . Once, as I hope, we get over the Common Market ordeal, we should like to propose once again what we proposed in 1961 – the beginnings of a political cooperation among the states of Western Europe. . . . And I am sure that, sooner or later, England will join. But this would not be a supra-national Europe. . . . Europe is what it is. But it could become a cooperative body and, after a time, a confederation.

De Gaulle then denied that he was 'anti-American', but recalled that both in World War I and in World War II the Americans were always 'late' and that he wholly disapproved of their war in Vietnam. 'If you'd like to call me anti-American because of that, I can't help it.'

He briefly defended the *force de frappe* and France's aid to the 'Third World'; the 2 billion francs a year she spent on them were not wasted, for politically, culturally, economically, and from the standpoint of France's international standing and popularity, it was money well-spent.

In conclusion, he was glad to say that France was almost the only country in the world 'on good terms with everybody.' The world was changing: there was the new factor of China; Russia was now mostly concerned with her own affairs and was rapidly evolving; and America, on the contrary, was becoming increasingly interventionist – to put it mildly.

As for Germany, she is changing rapidly, and we are absolutely unable to tell which way her ambitions are going. In the right direction, we hope; but we can't be absolutely sure.

France, on the other hand, had no desire to dominate anybody any more; she was on good terms with everybody; and that was why she had a peace mission in the world.

Mitterrand in his television appearances dwelt chiefly on the anomalies of the de Gaulle régime and on the economic discontent in the country. But he also made some telling points in criticizing de Gaulle's foreign policy:

If the agricultural Common Market does not materialize, Germany will inevitably yield to the temptation of joining the Free-Trade Zone. If there is no political organization of Europe, Germany will seek salvation either by joining up with the U.S.A. or, worse still, by acquiring an atomic arsenal of her own – something no French Government could tolerate. Only how can you prevent Germany indefinitely from having nuclear weapons if we claim that right for ourselves?

In short, Mitterrand blamed de Gaulle's *force de frappe* and its 'narrow nationalism' for the ominous revival of German chauvinism.

This was to remain a moot point. De Gaulle's argument was that irrespective of the pros and cons of the *force de frappe*, Germany had placed herself in the special position where atomic weapons in her hands would automatically represent a threat to world peace. As for 'nationalism', there were, as M. Duverger wrote, two kinds of nationalism: the nationalism of a Big Power like the U.S.A., which meant a desire to dominate, and the nationalism of a small power like France, which merely meant 'resistance to satellization'. As for Germany's nationalism, this was a very special case, in view of her past record and her dangerous territorial appetites.

De Gaulle won the second round of the election: he got 12.6 million votes, or 54½ per cent – or, including the overseas territories, over 55 per cent. Mitterrand got 10.5 million votes, or 45½ per cent – or, including the overseas territories, 45 per cent.

Mitterrand's poll was very odd. Far from representing the Left vote in the country, it included most of the 1.3 million fascist votes that had gone to Tixier-Vignancour. The latter had, with extraordinary cynicism, asked his supporters to vote for Mitterrand, since 'getting rid of de Gaulle' was 'the most important thing of all'. The fact that Mitterrand was supported by the Communists and that Tixier himself had treated Mitterrand as a 'traitor' back in 1955 no longer worried him; what mattered to Tixier was to 'avenge French Algeria'. Lacanuet also advised his supporters not to vote for de Gaulle, but either to abstain or to vote for Mitterrand; nevertheless, most of the 2.3 million extra votes de Gaulle got must have come from former Lecanuet supporters who regarded de Gaulle as a lesser evil than the 'Popular Front' candidate. In thirty-four departments, all of them south of the Loire, Mitterrand had more votes than de Gaulle. This geographical division of France had deep historic roots. In Paris the de Gaulle vote was nearly fifty-seven per cent.

Compared with the constitutional referendum of 1958, which was at least implicitly a nearly eighty per cent plebiscite for de Gaulle, or even compared with the referendum of 1962 with its sixty-two per cent YES votes, the fifty-five per cent de Gaulle got in the presidential election could scarcely be regarded as an overwhelming victory. But after all, as the Gaullists hastened to point out, Harold Wilson had been supported in the general election of 1964 by only forty-four per cent of the electorate and Kennedy had been elected President only thanks to a handful of votes above the fifty per cent.

De Gaulle was, nevertheless, conscious of the fact that his charm was wearing off. Many had not voted for him because, unlike 1958 and 1962, there was no longer any sense of imminent danger which he alone could avert. Secondly, he was getting old; in seven years' time he would be 82. Though impressed by the personality of de Gaulle, a large number of voters were not impressed by his prospective dauphin or by most of the ministers who might continue the 'new Republic'. And then there was the widespread economic discontent, which was not confined to the lower income groups but was also shared by a large part of Big Business and the Bourse, who were complaining of the paralyzing effects of the government's 'stabilization' policy. As for de Gaulle's foreign policy, it had implicitly been approved by a large majority. Tixier and Lecanuet (who together got twenty per cent of the votes) had sharply attacked it. Nevertheless, there was some uneasiness, especially in the rural areas, about de Gaulle's 'boycott' of the Common Market.

*

After the election, de Gaulle hastened to resume negotiations with the Common Market nations, and at least a temporary *modus vivendi* was agreed upon. Then, after 8 January – when his second term of office officially began – he reorganized his Cabinet. The elimination of M. Giscard d'Estaing, the Finance Minister, and his replacement by M. Michel Debré was the most striking feature of this Cabinet reshuffle. It was as if Giscard, the author of the Stabilization Plan of 1963, were being made the scapegoat for the economic grumbles. Whether or not the dismissal of Giscard would in the long run mean any fundamental changes in financial and economic policy, there was a sharp rise in shares on the Bourse.

Debré was considered the 'strong man' of the U. N. R. – unlike Pompidou, who was not even officially a member – and his appointment to the biggest job in the government, the super-ministry of both financial and economic affairs, was obviously made with an eye on the general election of 1967. Debré, a man with a strong emotionally-nationalist temperament, was expected, among other things, to lend 'dynamic vigour' to the U.N.R. in the decisive showdown some eighteen months ahead. Whether de Gaulle's 'new Republic' would continue after 1967 or would be replaced by something not entirely unlike the Fourth Republic (except that the 1958 Constitution would, in the main, be preserved) depended on how well, or how badly, the Gaullists did in the 1967 election. That they would secure an absolute majority in Parliament was unlikely; the question was whether they would be strong enough to form the bulk of a government coalition, including at least part of the Right-wing Independents and part of the M.R.P. A common remark heard shortly after the second round was that if only the Gaullists could win over an M.R.P. leader like Pflimlin, they would have nothing further to fear from Lecanuet. A story widely current at the same time was that de Gaulle himself had no intention of going on as President for seven more years, but intended to resign after the 1967 election, leaving the succession (with luck) to Pompidou. Or would it be Debré, despite his unfortunate television manner? But, after all, with only two candidates running in the second round of any presidential election, de Gaulle's nominee would have a good chance of being elected.

At that time, no major developments in de Gaulle's foreign policy were in sight except some possible new proposals concerning NATO (these were to come before long) and his visit to Moscow, scheduled for the summer. How important this visit would be depended on what was going to happen in the meantime in other parts of the world, such as Vietnam and Germany.

3. The Ben Barka Bombshell

We could end here the story of de Gaulle's first *septennat* as President of France and his first few days in his second term of office. But less than a week after he had officially started on his second term, France was shaken by a big political scandal which at once suggested that the 'new Republic', to which de Gaulle (and Madame) had given such air of majesty, purity, integrity and respectability, had, in reality, a very grubby side to it – every bit as grubby as anything seen under the Third or Fourth Republic.

It would probably require a book at least three times as long as this to describe the Ben Barka Affair in all its lurid detail, and therefore only a brief summary of its main elements is possible here. On 29 October 1965 Mehdi Ben Barka, an influential Moroccan Left-wing leader who for several years had lived in exile, partly in France, partly in Egypt and Switzerland, was kidnapped in Paris on the initiative of the Moroccan secret services and, more particularly, of General Mohammed Oufkir, Morocco's Minister of the Interior – the 'strong man of Morocco', who was said to have both the police and the Army completely under his thumb and was notorious for his utter ruthlessness. King Hassan of Morocco, apparently anxious to widen the base of his régime, had established contact with Ben Barka in the course of 1965 and had reportedly urged him to return to Morocco. Oufkir was determined to prevent this at any price. As early as 10 May 1965 he mentioned his kidnapping project to Antoine Lopez, an unofficial but in fact important member of the S.D.E.C.E., the French counter-espionage service (roughly, the French C.I.A.) who was also allegedly an agent of the Moroccan Government. Significantly, Oufkir, who in 1953 had been the right-hand man of the French Resident-General in Morocco, General Guillaume, had himself been a member of the S.D.E.C.E. and a French Army officer.

After learning of Oufkir's plan, Lopez sent a number of reports to his superiors in which, without implicating Oufkir, he referred to a project to kidnap Ben Barka. These reports were, it seems, duly transmitted to Prime Minister Pompidou, under whose authority the S.D.E.C.E. was placed, and to M. Jacques Foccart, the secretary-general at the Elysée officially dealing with African problems, but in reality the man in de Gaulle's immediate entourage most directly concerned with police and intelligence matters. Lopez had not suggested that there was any question of murdering Ben Barka. That may be why Pompidou and Foccart took little or no notice of his reports – even though, as early as 29 September, Lopez gave the names of several of the people who were to take part in the kidnapping. Among those he named were Dlimi, head of the Moroccan secret services; a Moroccan agent called Chtouki; a *truand* (jailbird) named Georges Figon; a number of other shady Frenchmen, and a Gaullist deputy, Pierre Lemarchand. Lopez's denunciation of Lemarchand was typical of the rivalries existing among the various French police services – in this case between the S.D.E.C.E.

and the so-called 'parallel police', to which Lemarchand belonged and which Lopez was trying to compromise. The double agent 'serving' both France and Morocco may also have been aiming a blow at the Gaullists, for Lemarchand was a prominent member of the U.N.R. Party; he was also a lawyer, a member of the Paris Bar, and had amongst his clients the *truand* Figon, who, after spending many years in prison for shooting a policeman,[1] was now an agent of the 'parallel police'.

These 'parallel police' – or *barbouzes*, as they had come to be known since the latter stages of the Algerian war – were the descendants, as it were, of a variety of police services that had served de Gaulle ever since 1940. Although de Gaulle himself appeared to take no direct interest in either the official or the unofficial secret services working 'for' him, he looked upon them as an evil, but an inevitable and, indeed, indispensable evil which could, on occasion, be used as an instrument of policy. As we know, some very shady police business had already gone on in London among the Free French. Dewavrin, alias Colonel Passy, had been the moving spirit of de Gaulle's intelligence and police services, and many others, among them Jacques Soustelle, later took a very active part in this work. Admiral Muselier, it will be remembered, had referred to the '*basse police* and Gestapo atmosphere' surrounding de Gaulle in London, and later, in 1943, the same services had been highly active in Algiers. While there appears to have been no separate, specifically 'Gaullist' secret army or police service during the first years of the Liberation, a shadow army of some potential importance began to be formed when de Gaulle embarked on his R.P.F. move-

1. A member of a respectable bourgeois family, Figon had started his career of violence in the Resistance. He fought the Germans during the Liberation of Paris, but later became a member of a criminal gang. It was in the course of one of their smash-and-grab robberies that Figon shot the policeman.

ment. This R.P.F. 'army', euphemistically called *service d'ordre*, included not only many *bona fide* Gaullists, mostly drawn from the ranks of the Free French forces and Free French intelligence services, but also a great deal of riff-raff – former members of the Vichy *milice*, German collaborators, former members of the Doriot gangs, and other criminal and near-criminal elements. We have referred in an earlier chapter to the thugs and gunmen who formed part of the paramilitary organization of the R.P.F. During the later stages of the R.P.F., when it was already in decline as a political force, the shadow army was still maintained in a small way, and in 1954 its chief was one of de Gaulle's most trusted 'Companions', M. Jacques Foccart.

Between 1954 and 1957, when de Gaulle had seemingly retired for good, the shadow army was of no importance, but good use was to be made of it by Soustelle when, in anticipation of the Algiers *putsch* of May 1958, he founded his U.S.R.A.F. (*Union pour le Renouveau et le Salut de l'Algérie Française*), which was to give a 'Gaullist' twist to the otherwise fascist rebellion of May 13. During the next few years the shadow army grew considerably in numbers, but as the conflict matured between the 'Gaullists' and the Algerian *ultras*, this 'army' split, part of it following Soustelle and Delbecque and joining the O.A.S. 'French Algeria' commandos, and part of it forming anti-O.A.S. commandos and an intelligence network of its own. It was these people who constituted the 'parallel police', without an official existence but more or less under the direction of Foccart. M. Frey, the Minister of the Interior, and M. Maurice Papon, the Paris prefect of police, also appear to have resorted to the services of the 'parallel police'. Those who organized it were not squeamish about the moral character of the people they enlisted: on the O.A.S. side, as on the 'Gaullist' side, there were the so-called *truands*, people with extremely shady records who belonged to the criminal fringe of society. Many of them were plain gangsters.

When the O.A.S. terrorists were virtually liquidated, there seemed no reason why the 'Gaullist parallel police' should continue to exist, but it did; what is more, its ranks were augmented by all kinds of people who had previously been members of the O.A.S. commandos. The *barbouzes*, never very reliable, and on occasion capable of going over to the 'enemy' for a consideration, were even less reliable now. Several *barbouzes* of the gangster type were to be employed in the kidnapping of Ben Barka and to be paid by the Moroccan Secret Service.

While Lopez kept his superiors half-informed of what was going on, he was, it seems, working for the Moroccan Government, for Oufkir had promised him a very highly-paid job in Air-Maroc if he helped in the kidnapping of Ben Barka. Lopez, though unofficially, an important agent of the S.D.E.C.E., officially held a big administrative post at Orly airport. It was he who persuaded two regular police inspectors, Souchon and Voitot, to carry out the actual arrest of Ben Barka outside the 'Drugstore' at St. Germain-des-Prés on 29 October,[1] after which the Moroccan leader was taken by car to the villa of a certain Boucheseiche at Fontenay-le-Vicomte, outside Paris. Lopez also telephoned Rabat to inform Oufkir that 'the parcel' had arrived, and he made all the necessary arrangements for the Moroccan Minister's discreet arrival at Orly and his departure a day later, after his 'interview' with Ben Barka. The *truands* played a mysterious part in the kidnapping of Ben Barka. Several of them, including Figon, drove to the Fontenay villa where Ben Barka was held prisoner. Figon was apparently the only one who was a freelance only vaguely connected with the 'parallel police'. If he later produced a

1. It is not quite clear whether these two policemen were told the real purpose of the arrest.

sensational 'eyewitness' story, published in *L'Express*, of
how Oufkir personally stabbed Ben Barka to death and
how the body was then taken to Lopez's villa at Ormoy,
some distance away, it was allegedly only because the
Moroccans had failed to give him a promised share of the
large sum they had agreed to pay for the kidnapping.

For a long time it was impossible to say why regular
police inspector Souchon had agreed to arrest Ben Barka.
Then, on January 14, he declared to the examining magistrate, M. Zollinger, that Lopez had assured him that he
was fully covered because not only certain important police
officials but also M. Foccart, whom he knew as one of
de Gaulle's closest associates, and M. Frey, Minister of the
Interior, were *au parfum*, fully informed of the proposed
kidnapping operation. There is nothing to show that Foccart or Frey actually was *au parfum*, but the fact remains
that all three police services took part in the kidnapping –
the S.D.E.C.E., in the person of Lopez, who was also acting
for the Moroccans; the 'civil' police, represented by
Souchon and Voitot; and the 'parallel' police, represented
by Figon and various other gangsters, among them the
proprietor of the Fontenay villa.

Now, according to *L'Express*, three things went seriously
wrong. First, Ben Barka, at the moment of his arrest, was
accompanied by a Moroccan student whom the police did
not notice, but who promptly raised the alarm by informing Ben Barka's brother of what had happened. Secondly,
it had been agreed between the French police and the
Moroccans that Ben Barka would be delivered to them
alive and taken to Morocco – there had never been any
question of murdering him in France – but, according to
L'Express, the impetuous Oufkir could not resist his blood-
lust once he had his political arch-enemy at his mercy.
Thirdly, it was a fatal mistake on the part of the police to
allow the 'irresponsible' Figon to go to the villa at Fon-

tenay, for it was he who was the first to tell the 'real story' – or, rather, part of the story.

As I write this, late in February 1966, many details still remain obscure. Despite the *Express* story, which apparently came originally from Figon, it has not been definitely proved that Oufkir personally murdered Ben Barka, and there have been highly improbable rumours that Ben Barka is still alive, hidden away in a prison in southern Morocco.

One of the things that greatly interested French opinion were the motives behind Ben Barka's 'disappearance'. Obviously, Oufkir regarded him as a dangerous political rival and wanted him out of the way. But there was believed to be much more to it than that. Ben Barka was closely associated with Fidel Castro and was one of the organizers of the Three Continents Conference in Havana. The C.I.A. had an eye on him. His reappearance as a major political leader in Morocco would have given that country a 'Gaullist' and 'neutralist' twist. Papers like the *New York Herald Tribune* denounced Ben Barka, time and again, as a 'Communist' agent and treated Oufkir as the best protection against Communism in Morocco. De Gaulle, on the other hand, was believed to be very anxious to rid the whole of North Africa of American influence as far as possible. So, after the Ben Barka scandal blew up, there were more and more French papers which argued that the C.I.A. had killed two birds with one stone: it had helped Oufkir (especially financially) to organize the 'disappearance' of Ben Barka, and, more important still, it had pulled off a gigantic *coup* to discredit de Gaulle and his whole régime. As François Mauriac put it:

Yes, here is a trap, and who can doubt it? Either just before or just after the murder of Ben Barka (I don't remember the exact date), a Moroccan friend who knows all about these things told me of the closest bonds between Oufkir and the American secret services. However true this may be, one thing is certain: these services have pulled off a tremendous double operation – first, against the Third World by eliminating Ben Barka, and secondly against de Gaulle. If the American services are innocent, then the Devil himself must have played their game for them.[1]

There is another point. Whatever may have been the exact role played by the C.I.A. in this affair, there was a general conviction that some of the French police who took part in the kidnapping of Ben Barka were doing so not only in order to render Oufkir a service (and be paid by him), but also in order to create a régime-shaking scandal against de Gaulle. It may be argued, of course, that but for the three above mishaps (the Moroccan student, Ben Barka's death and the presence of Figon) Ben Barka might have disappeared without a trace. But was that intended by those who *wanted* a scandal?

*

It will take a very long time before we know exactly what went on inside the French Government after it was learned that Ben Barka had been kidnapped and that Oufkir had personally organized the operation and taken part in it. One thing, however, seems certain: on 4 November, when de Gaulle announced that he was running for President, he already knew some of the main facts. Among the most astonishing episodes of the affair were Oufkir's visit to Paris on 3 November – less than a week after the kidnapping – and the dinner he organized at the Moroccan Embassy, to which M. Frey was invited. Frey did not go, but sent an official to 'represent' him. At that moment de Gaulle did not have the slightest doubt about Oufkir's guilt; why, then, was he not arrested in Paris on 3 November? The answer is: *raison d'Etat*; it was no use stirring up that hornet's nest just then. It might lead to great international

1. *Figaro Littéraire*, 27 January 1966.

complications and, above all, might very seriously affect the outcome of the presidential election; all the dirt about the French police could not fail to play straight into the hands of the anti–de Gaulle candidates. It was, no doubt, for the same reason that M. Frey got the A.F.P., the French official news agency, to publish a semi-official statement on 12 November saying that 'no French policemen were implicated in the kidnapping of Ben Barka'. Later Frey tried to argue that he had made this statement simply in order to 'facilitate the inquiry'. In any case, it seems that at the beginning of November both Pompidou and Frey tried to suggest to de Gaulle that only some small fry among the French police were mixed up in the affair. Whether they convinced him or not, de Gaulle was sure of Oufkir's guilt; through his Ambassador at Rabat he informed Hassan II on 6 November of the role Oufkir had played in the kidnapping, and asked whether the King was 'disposed to put the accused on trial; otherwise, France would have to draw her own conclusions.' De Gaulle, to show his displeasure, also canceled the visit to Morocco of M. Pisani, the Minister of Agriculture. Continuing to assume that the role of the French police in the affair was limited to Lopez, a Moroccan agent who had merely 'misled' Voitot and Souchon, and not worrying, for the time being, about the wider ramifications of the whole sinister business, de Gaulle decided to concentrate on the presidential election. Although Ben Barka's brother urged the examining magistrate on 1 December to issue an international warrant for the arrest of Oufkir, nothing happened (or, rather, was allowed to happen). It is remarkable, when one comes to think of it, that the anti–de Gaulle candidates seem not to have known anything about the affair, or, if they did, that they did not know enough to make it an election issue.

Having been safely re-elected on 19 December, de Gaulle began to study the affair more closely. He became acutely conscious of the fact that it was going to be exploited against him and his régime in France and might cause France incalculable damage in the eyes of the Third World and the outside world generally. In reshuffling his Cabinet, he wanted first of all to get rid of Frey (whose name was beginning to stink throughout France), as Debré was urging him to do, but Pompidou defended Frey as best he could. Not that it can have been easy, for it is obvious that Frey had done everything *to slow down the inquiry* both during and after the election campaign by withholding from the examining magistrate much vital information in the hands of the police. The question inevitably arises whether de Gaulle had not, at some stage at least, encouraged such reticence.

Curiously enough, if one looks at the French newspapers of the first ten days of January, one finds in them very little about the Ben Barka Affair. But after the 10th, and the publication, in *L'Express, Minute* and other journals, of sensational revelations about the kidnapping on the basis of information allegedly supplied by Figon, things began to warm up. On the 17th, there came the bombshell: the news that Figon, the only important witness of the kidnapping available in France (all the others had escaped to Germany or otherwise vanished, or else were officials who would say no more than what they were allowed by their superiors to say) had shot himself just as he was about to be arrested. The circumstances of his death were too reminiscent of the death in 1934 of Stavisky, who had been 'suicided' by the police, not to arouse suspicions. The almost general reaction was that the police had done Figon in because he knew too much.[1] First of all, he belonged to that gang which had been contacted by the Moroccans as long ago as May 1965 with a view to

[1]. It should be noted that many of those who knew Figon thought his suicide not improbable, since the fear of going back to prison was a constant obsession with him.

liquidating Ben Barka. Secondly, he might have thrown some light on the previous activities of the gang; was it not the same gang which had helped to kidnap the O.A.S. leader Colonel Argout in Munich? Further, he might have provided more information on the death(?) of Ben Barka. Above all, he might have revealed which French police service was protecting him: for he could have been arrested long before the 17th, when the examining magistrate firmly demanded it be done; until then he was all over Paris, talking to newspapermen and even getting himself photographed outside the police headquarters in the Quai des Orfèvres!

By all accounts, the Cabinet meeting that took place after Figon's death was a very stormy one. De Gaulle is said to have fumed and raged and declared that he 'would bust the police, just as he had the Army'. Many of the ministers did not believe in Figon's suicide. De Gaulle made some caustic remarks about Frey: 'The Minister of the Interior suggests that everything has proceeded normally; that is not the prevailing impression in the Cabinet, it seems.'

And yet the measures de Gaulle himself took then (as well as a few days before) were not exactly spectacular. He showed his displeasure to Premier Pompidou by removing the S.D.E.C.E. from the direct authority of the Prime Minister and putting it under the Minister of Defence; he called on M. Léon Noël, a 77-year-old ex-ambassador (with R.P.F. associations, it is true), to draw up plans for an all-out reform of all the police services – a slap in the face for M. Frey; he expressed his displeasure to M. Foccart. But how much did all this mean in practice? And what was the meaning of this semi-censure of Pompidou and Frey? Either they were to blame and should be fired or they were innocent; why, then, these half-measures?

The Gaullist U.N.R. were deeply perturbed by what had happened, and many were begging de Gaulle to show far greater energy. Others were suggesting that he was the prisoner of his own system – for were not the police services and, above all, the shady 'parallel' police with its *barbouzes* part of the system he had set up?

The opposition parties were, needless to say, making the greatest political capital out of the *affaire*. An enormous mass meeting took place at which Mitterrand, Communists, Radicals and Socialists all displayed their righteous indignation and demanded 'the whole truth'. Some were demanding that Parliament be called and that a parliamentary committee of inquiry, including all the parties, be set up after the model of the parliamentary committees that were formed after the Stavisky scandal in 1934 and after the much smaller *affaire des généraux* and the *affaire des piastres* in 1950. These demands met with no response.

An international warrant was issued for the arrest of Oufkir. The French Ambassador was withdrawn from Rabat and the Moroccan Ambassador from Paris, but diplomatic relations were not broken off; there were too many interests at stake on both sides, and de Gaulle was anxious, anyway, not to 'hand Morocco over to the Americans'.

In any case, both internally and internationally de Gaulle and his régime had, at least for a time, been badly shaken. Would the Ben Barka Affair, it was asked, mark the beginning of the end of de Gaulle's Fifth Republic? In a sense, it was only an unfortunate accident brought about, allegedly, by the Moroccans, with the complicity of a few French gangsters and corrupt policemen; but was not much that the Affair was revealing inherent in the Gaullist régime?

There was a bitter irony in the fact that Ben Barka, the Third World revolutionary, should have been liquidated with the help of the fascist-tainted police services of General de Gaulle, himself, the best friend of the Third World. No wonder de Gaulle felt intensely bitter and, at moments perhaps, mortally discouraged. He had never, in his mind, identified 'France' with 'the French'; nor was it necessary for him to identify the French nation with the Lopezes and the Figons. But these people had splashed blood and mud over de Gaulle's 'certain image of France' and, more important still, had distorted the image of Gaullist France in the eyes of the world. But, significantly, if there was much malicious hee-hawing over de Gaulle's discomfiture in Germany, the United States and Britain, the reaction was not quite the same in some other countries. In Algeria, for instance, thousands of students demonstrated in the streets of Algiers, shouting for hours, *'Oufkir assassin, Oufkir assassin!'* – which was almost like a pro–de Gaulle demonstration.

How important will the Ben Barka Affair prove in the end? And will de Gaulle limit the damage with that 'immense upsurge' which is expected from him by his more idealistic followers and by those Gaullists who are anxiously thinking of the 1967 general election, now ominously threatening the very life of the Fifth Republic?

Or will not the Affair ultimately be more or less forgotten, with so many other things for the ordinary voter to worry about? May it not also prove very small stuff, compared with, say, the war in Vietnam, or a revival of Germany's militarist and territorial ambitions? On both of these – and many other – questions there remains much common ground between de Gaulle and his people. But will that in itself be enough for his régime to survive, especially after he is gone?

At his press conference on 21 February, de Gaulle did his utmost to minimize the importance of the Affair, suggesting that, as far as France was concerned, only some 'vulgar and subordinate' persons had been mixed up in it. He refused to disavow any of his ministers. His statement was sharply criticised in the press; but the fact remains that the French public was by this time already beginning to get bored with the whole Ben Barka business.

Much more important, at the same press conference de Gaulle launched his most violent attack on NATO, which was soon followed by his famous letter to President Johnson and other heads of Allied governments declaring France's desire to quit NATO for the usual typically Gaullist reasons. This did not mean that France was quitting the Atlantic Alliance, which would continue to provide that American 'atomic umbrella' in the unlikely event of a war with Russia. But de Gaulle clearly related his decision to the dangerous possibility that the Vietnam war might spread and France somehow become involved in it as a NATO member.

But there was also a more personal aspect to de Gaulle's decision. In making his announcement to his ministers, he said that he was getting old, that he might not last long, and that there was, therefore, no time to lose. All the more so he doubted whether any successor would have either his authority or his courage to take this 'necessary step.' In some of the more malicious anti-de Gaulle papers the suggestion was put forward that de Gaulle was, in reality, a very sick man, and that the end of his reign was now very clearly in sight.

De Gaulle's decision on NATO aroused much anger in the United States, produced loud applause in Moscow (possibly foreshadowing the liquidation of the Warsaw Pact as a result of de Gaulle's 'peace move'), and a remarkable degree of indifference in France, despite some highly critical articles in the press. A few of these charged de Gaulle with black ingratitude to the United States, 'which had twice helped to save France.' The Gaullist reply to this was, of course, that in both cases America had come into the war 'very late' and had done so, in any case, not out of kindness to France but simply because it was in America's own interests to prevent a German victory. And so the Franco-American argument continued . . . as it will no doubt continue long after de Gaulle.

BIBLIOGRAPHICAL NOTE

THE name of Charles de Gaulle has been so closely linked with France since 1940 that there is scarcely any book on the history of that country during and since the Second World War which does not discuss or at least mention de Gaulle. On the other hand, no books were written *on* de Gaulle before 1940, and what we know of his early career comes either from his own writings or from a large number of books written during or after the war.

A book indispensable to an understanding of his personality and philosophy is his *Le fil de l'épée*, published in French as early as 1932, and in English (*The Edge of the Sword*) in 1960 (Faber and Faber). Very important among his pre-war writings are also *Vers l'armée de métier*, published in 1934 (*The Army of the Future*, London, 1943), outlining his military doctrine, and his *La France et son Armée* (Paris, 1938, and London, Hutchinson, 1948), with its autobiographical undertones. Most of his war-time and immediate post-war speeches and 'messages' are to be found in *Discours et Messages*, published in Paris in 1946. De Gaulle's most monumental work is, of course, his *War Memoirs* in three volumes (Collins (Vol. 2, Weidenfeld & Nicolson), 1955–60). Though not entirely reliable as history, they are extremely revealing as a self-portrait.

Some very interesting episodes from the life of de Gaulle before he became famous are to be found in J. R. Tournoux, *Pétain et de Gaulle* (Paris, 1964). His childhood and adolescence are described in a number of popular biographies, including one in English, Edward Ashcroft's *De Gaulle* (Odhams Press, 1962). There are numerous references to de Gaulle in memoirs written by French politicians on the last years of the Third Republic; the most important of these are ex-Prime Minister Paul Reynaud's books, especially *La France a sauvé l'Europe* (2 vols., Paris, 1946).

There are many references to de Gaulle in practically all books on the defeat of France in 1940. Most important among English books are W. S. Churchill's *The Second World War* (6 vols., Cassell, 1947–51) and General Sir E. Spears's *The Fall of France* (Heinemann, 1954). Churchill also has much to say on de Gaulle from his arrival in London in June 1940 to the end of the war. On the relations between the United States and the Free French see Admiral W. Leahy's *I Was There* (Gollancz, 1950) and especially R. E. Sherwood's *The White House Papers of Harry Hopkins* (2 vols., Eyre & Spottiswoode, 1948, 1949). Apart from de Gaulle's own writings, one of the most important 'inside' accounts of the Free French is to be found in the two volumes of one of the general's closest war-time associates, Jacques Soustelle, *Envers et contre tout* (Paris, 1947–50). For an interesting 'close-up' of de Gaulle during the war, see Emmanuel d'Astier's *Sept fois sept jours* (Paris, 1947). Extremely hostile to de Gaulle are Admiral Muselier's *De Gaulle contre le gaullisme* (Paris, 1946), Henri de Kerillis's *De Gaulle dictateur* (Montreal, 1944), and General Giraud's *Un seul but, la victoire* (Paris, 1949). There are countless books on the French Resistance, but the best short survey is Henri Michel's *Histoire de la Résistance* (Paris, 1952). The best summary of the Free French movement is by the same author: Henri Michel, *Histoire de la France Libre* (Paris, 1964). One of the most important books on the Liberation is A. Dansette's *Histoire de la Libération de Paris* (Paris, 1945) explaining de Gaulle's role in the liberation of the French capital in August 1944. See also Dwight D. Eisenhower's *Crusade in Europe* (Heinemann, 1948).

For a general history of France during the war and during the first ten years of the Fourth Republic, with special reference to de Gaulle as leader of the Free French, as head of the Provisional Government and, later, as leader of the R.P.F., see Alexander Werth, *France 1940–1955* (Robert Hale, 1956). An excellent portrait of de Gaulle is to be found in David Thomson's *Two Frenchmen: Pierre Laval and Charles de Gaulle* (Cresset Press, 1951). On the political structure, institutions and parties under the Fourth Republic, see Philip M. Williams's *Politics in Post-War France* (Longmans & Green, 1954), and Jacques Fauvet's *Les forces politiques en France* (Paris, 1951). For de Gaulle's

R.P.F. period, see, in particular, Jacques Debû-Bridel's *Les partis contre de Gaulle* (Paris, 1948) and *La France sera la France*, a selection of passages from de Gaulle's speeches made mostly during his leadership of the R.P.F. movement, and published by the R.P.F. itself in 1951.

There is already a considerable literature on the change of régime in France in 1958, on the Fifth Republic and its institutions, and on the personality of its President. The most dramatic (if not wholly reliable) account of the Algiers putsch of 1958 and the parallel developments in France is S. and M. Bromberger's *Les 13 complots du 13 mai* (Paris, 1959). Detailed English accounts of the events of May 1958 and their aftermath are to be found in P. Williams's and M. Harrison's *De Gaulle's Republic* (Longmans & Green, 1960) and in Alexander Werth's *The de Gaulle Revolution* (Robert Hale, 1960). For the 'anatomy' of the Fifth Republic, see M. Duverger's *La Ve République* (Paris, 1960) and his *La VIe République et le régime presidential* (Paris, 1961), N. Wahl's *The Fifth Republic* (New York, Random House, 1959) and D. Pickles's *The Fifth French Republic* (Methuen, 1960).

For the anti-de Gaulle activities of the *colons* of Algeria and the Army since 1958, see *Barricades et colonels* by S. and M. Bromberger and others, (Paris, 1961), and the verbatim record of the two most famous rebel generals' trials: *Le procès de Raoul Salan* and *Le procès d'Edmond Jouhaud* (both Paris, 1962). A good general biography of de Gaulle up to 1963 is P. M. de La Gorce's *De Gaulle entre deux mondes* (Paris, 1964).

For de Gaulle's foreign policy in recent years see R. Massip's *De Gaulle et l'Europe* (Paris, 1963), Nora Beloff's *The General Says No* (Penguin Books, 1963), and A. Grosser's *La politique extérieure de la Ve République* (Paris, 1965).

The most rapturous recent book on de Gaulle is F. Mauriac's *De Gaulle*; rather more critical and ironical, though not hostile, are E. Mannoni's *Moi, Général de Gaulle* (Paris, 1964), P. Viansson-Ponté's *Les Gaullistes* (Paris, 1964; published in New York, Houghton-Mifflin, 1964, under the title *The King and his Court*), and J. Lacouture's *De Gaulle* (Paris, 1965). Violently hostile to de Gaulle are the writings of the former Vichyite,

A. Fabre-Luce, notably his *The Trial of Charles de Gaulle* (New York, Praeger, 1963). On de Gaulle's prime minister and possible successor, see *Le destin secret de Georges Pompidou* by M. Bromberger (Paris, 1965).

INDEX